S0-FMM-752

ORPHEUS

ORPHEUS

A HISTORY OF RELIGIONS

FROM THE FRENCH OF

SALOMON REINACH

BY

FLORENCE SIMMONDS

REVISED AND PARTLY REWRITTEN BY THE AUTHOR

NEW YORK
LIVERIGHT, INC.

PRINTED IN THE UNITED STATES OF AMERICA

PREFACE

WHY does the name of Orpheus, "the first of the world's singers," as Lefranc de Pompignan called him, appear on the title-page of this volume? Because he was not merely "the first singer," though the Greeks knew of poems by him which they held to be much earlier than those of Homer. Orpheus was also, to the ancients, the theologian *par excellence*, founder of those mysteries which ensured the salvation of mankind, and no less essential to it as the interpreter of the gods. Horace designates him thus: *Sacer interpresque deorum.* He it was who revealed first to the Thracians and afterwards to the other Greeks the necessary knowledge of things divine. True, he never existed; but this is of little moment. Orphism existed and, as Jules Girard has justly said, it was the most interesting fact in the religious history of the Greeks. It was something more, something still better.

Not only did Orphism enter deeply into the literature, philosophy and art of the ancient world; it survived them. The figure of Orpheus charming the beasts with his lyre is the only mythological motive which appears and recurs in the Christian paintings of the catacombs. The fathers of the church were persuaded that Orpheus was the disciple of Moses. They saw in him a type—or rather a prototype—of Jesus, since he too had come to teach mankind, and had been at once its benefactor and its victim. An emperor placed a statue of Orpheus in his lararium, besides that of the Christian Messiah. Between Orphism and Christianity there were, indeed, analogies so evident and so striking that it was impossible to accept them as accidental. A common source of inspiration was assumed.

Modern criticism seeks the explanation of these analogies in a hypothesis less daring than that of a supposed relation between Moses and Orpheus. It recognises that Orphism has traits in common not only with Judaism and Christianity, but with other more remote creeds such as Buddhism, and even with the very primitive beliefs of existing savages. If on examination we find something of Orphism in every religion, it is because Orphism made use of elements common to them all, drawn from the depths of human nature, and nourished by its most cherished illusions.

A little book destined to summarise religions and their histories could not invoke a better patron than Orpheus, son of Apollo and a Muse, poet, musician, theologian, mystagogue and authorised interpreter of the gods.

Having explained my title, I may add a few words in justification of the method I have adopted.

We have two learned manuals of the history of religions, by Conrad von Orelli and Chantepie de la Saussaye respectively. Both of these great works omit the history of Christianity. To study this, we must turn to other works, most of them very voluminous and full of details concerning sects and controversies which are of interest only to the erudite.

I see no reason for isolating Christianity in this manner. It has fewer adherents than Buddhism; it is less ancient. To set it apart in this fashion is becoming in the apologist, but not in the historian. Now it is as an historian that I propose to deal with religions. I see in them the infinitely curious products of man's imagination and of man's reason in its infancy; it is as such that they claim our attention. They are not all equally interesting, for those which have filled the greatest place in history are naturally those which deserve most study. In this modest volume I have accordingly given greater importance to Judaism and Christianity than to the religions of Assyria, Egypt and China. It is not my fault if, during the last two thousand years, the history of Christianity has intermingled to some extent with universal history, and if, in sketching the one, I have been obliged to make a brief abstract of the other.

The most readable, the most brilliant, the least pedantic of general histories—I do not say the most exact or the most complete—is to be found in Voltaire's *Essai sur les Mœurs*, supplemented by his *Siècle de Louis XIV*. and his *Siècle de Louis XV*. I do not share Voltaire's ideas of religions; but

I have a due admiration for his incomparable gifts as a narrator. Dealing with the same facts after him, I could only do worse what he has done so well. I have therefore borrowed freely from him—always with due acknowledgment, of course. Those who accuse me of having cut my book out of Voltaire will only prove that they have read neither Voltaire nor me.

I am deeply conscious of the moral responsibility I assume in giving for the first time a picture of religions in general considered as natural phenomena and nothing more. I believe that the times are ripe for such an essay, and that in this, as in all other domains, secular reason must exercise its rights. I have tried not to wound any conscience; but I have said what I believe to be the truth with the emphasis proper to truth. I do not think that the persecution of the Bacchanals by the Roman Senate, and of dawning Christianity by the Emperors, the furies of the Inquisition, of St. Bartholomew's Eve and of the Dragonnades ought to be coldly chronicled as insignificant episodes in history. I execrate these judicial murders, the accursed fruits of a spirit of oppression and fanaticism, and I have shown this plainly. There are zealots still among us who glorify these crimes, and would wish to see them continued.[1] If they attack my book, they will do both me and it a great honour.

Salomon Reinach.

[1] In the *Théologie de Clermont,* by the Rev. Father Vincent, re-published with episcopal approbation in 1904, I find the following passage: "The Church has received from God the power to reprove those who wander from the truth, not only by spiritual but corporeal penalties, such as imprisonment, flagellation, mutilation, and death." At various lectures given in Paris after 1900 there were cries of "Vive la Saint-Barthelémy!" and on February 9, 1906, M. V. . . . declared that "St. Bartholomew's Eve was a splendid night for our church and our country." Modern civilisation need not be alarmed by these survivals, but it must not ignore them.

FOREWORD TO THE NEW ENGLISH EDITION (1930)

Not one of the 38 French editions of *Orpheus* has appeared without slight alterations, especially in the bibliography, which has always been carefully revised. In 1924 a chapter was added on the period beginning with the Great War. This new English-American edition not only embodies an enlargement of that last chapter, up to the recent restoration of the temporal Power, but an almost complete rewriting of Chapter VIII, concerning Christian origins. Two great discoveries, that of Emperor Claude's letter to the Alexandrians and Jews, and that of the Slavonic text of Josephus about Jesus, as purged by Rob. Eisler of obvious interpolations, have opened, I believe, a new era in the scientific treatment of nascent Christianity. To ignore or to belittle, as many have done and still do, such invaluable pieces of information, and not to correct, according to them, what seemed most probable ten years ago, would have been, I may be allowed to say, unworthy of an historian who has no axe to grind and whose one aim in writing this little book on the greatest of subjects has been and remains, to work for truth.

S. R.

Musée de Saint Germain-en-Laye,
May 20, 1929.

CONTENTS

ILLUSTRATIONS

THE WORSHIP OF NATURE

INTRODUCTION

THE ORIGIN OF RELIGIONS

DEFINITIONS AND GENERAL PHENOMENA

Religion and mythology. Etymology of the word religion. Religion is a sum of scruples, *i.e.,* of taboos. Examples of taboos. Animism. Poetic survivals of animism. The theory of primitive revelation. The theory of imposture. False ideas of the eighteenth century. Fetichism. Fontenelle's true ideas. Totemism a hypertrophy of the social instinct. The worship of plants and animals: metamorphoses. The bears of Berne. Totemism and fables. Domestication of animals. The sacrifice of the totem. Alimentary prohibitions. The Sabbath. Abstinence. The codification and restriction of taboos by the priesthood. The progressive secularisation of humanity. Magic and science. Religions the life of primitive societies. Explanation of apparent retrogressions. The future of religions: the necessity of studying their history.

I

1. The terms religion and mythology are often confounded in common parlance. When, for instance, I speak of the religion of the Greeks, I know that I evoke the idea of fables, sometimes crude, sometimes exquisite, told by Greek poets of their gods, their goddesses, and their heroes. This confusion is natural and excusable, for religion is the basis of all mythology; but it must be avoided when we enter the domain of scientific inquiry.

2. Mythology is a collection of stories, not exactly invented, but combined and embellished at will, the actors in which cannot be subjected to the tests of real history. Religion is primarily a sentiment, and the expression of this sentiment by acts of a particular nature, which are rites.

3. A definition of religion is very difficult, not only because the word is very ancient, and has been widely used, but because the etymology of the Latin *religio* gives but a faint idea of the primitive meaning of the term. It is a mistake to

derive *religio* from *religare*, to bind, as if religion were essentially the bond of union between God and Man. Linguistic science counsels us to abandon this etymology and rather to admit that already recommended by Cicero: *religio* comes from *religere*, the antithesis of *negligere*, in short, a vigilant care (or, as we say, *religious* care), as opposed to indifference and negligence. Religion is then a faithful observance of rites; this is useful to know, but it leaves us in total ignorance of the nature of religious sentiment.

4. I might fill a whole volume with enumeration and discussion of the various definitions of religion propounded by modern philosophers.

"Religion," says Schleiermacher, "consists of an absolute sense of our dependence." "It is," says Feuerbach, "a desire which manifests itself in prayer, sacrifice, and faith." Kant saw in it "a sense of our duties as based on divine law." "Religion," said Max Müller, "is a faculty of the mind which enables a man to grasp the infinite independently of sense and reason." The great English ethnographer, Tylor, is more modest, and accepts as the minimum definition of religion "a belief in spiritual beings." Marie-Jean Guyau was the first, in 1887, to introduce into the definition of religion an element essential to all religions, a social character. "Religion," he said, "is a universal sociomorphism. The religious sense is the sense of dependence in relation to wills which primitive man places in the universe." Of all the definitions I have quoted this is indisputably the best.

5. But I would suggest another one. The word religion being what custom has made it, it is necessary that a minimum definition, as Tylor calls it, should be applicable to the term in all its acceptations. Now the Romans already spoke of the religion of the oath, *religio juris jurandi*, and we too use this term, as also those of the religion of the fatherland, of the family, of honour, &c.

Used in this sense, the word religion does not convey either the idea of infinity, or of the desire spoken of by Feuerbach, or even the dependence in relation to other wills advanced by Guyau. On the other hand, it implies a limitation, without any material constraint, of individual volition, or rather of human activity as far as this depends on volition. As there are a great many religions, so there are a great many limitations, and I propose to define religion as: *A sum of scruples which impede the free exercise of our faculties.*

6. This minimum definition is big with consequences, for it eliminates from the fundamental concept of religion, God, spiritual beings, the infinite, in a word, all we are accustomed to consider the true objects of religious sentiment. I have shown that it is applicable to the religion of the family, and that of honour; I shall try to show that it is no less applicable to that which constitutes the irreducible basis of all religions.

7. The term *scruple* is defective, in so far as it is a little vague, and if I may be allowed to say so, somewhat over-secular. Our scruples prevent us from talking loudly in a death-chamber; but they also forbid us to take an umbrella into a drawing-room. The scruples we shall have to deal with in the definition I propose are of a special kind; following the example of many contemporary anthropologists, I will call them *taboos*, a Polynesian word which has been naturalised in the language of ethnography and even in that of philosophy.

8. *Taboo*, in Polynesian, really means withdrawn from current use: a tree which may not be touched or felled is a *taboo* tree, and we should speak of the *taboo* of a tree if we meant the scruple which arrests a man who is tempted to touch it or to cut it down. This scruple is never inspired by any practical reason, as the fear of wounding or pricking oneself would be in the case of the tree. The distinctive mark of a taboo is that the interdict is quite arbitrary, and that the confirmation presaged, in the event of a violation of the taboo, is not a penalty decreed by the civil law, but a calamity such as death or blindness, falling upon the guilty individual.

9. The word is Polynesian, but the idea it expresses is very familiar to us; it is more especially so in countries where the Bible is widely read. At the beginning of this book, Adam is warned by the Eternal that he is not to eat the fruit of a certain tree under pain of death. This is a

characteristic *taboo*, for the Lord does not say *why* Adam must not eat the fruit of the tree.

10. Further on, in the religious legislation of the Hebrews, it is forbidden to pronounce the name of the Eternal under pain of death. Here we have a name tabooed. Another example of a taboo occurs in the Second Book of Samuel (vi, 4-7). The ark of the covenant was not to be touched, save by the members of a privileged family. When David wanted to transport it to Jerusalem, he had it placed on a cart drawn by oxen; the beasts stumbled during the progress, and a certain Uzzah sprang forward and upheld the ark of the Lord. In an instant he was struck dead. The ark was *taboo*, and death is the penalty for violation of a taboo. In the form this episode has received in our version of the Bible, it is peculiarly shocking, for we are told that the anger of the Lord was kindled against Uzzah, and that he smote him for this sin; now in the light of our modern morality, it was not a sin at all. But eliminate the notion of the Lord, and consider the ark as a reservoir full to overflowing of an invisible and redoubtable force; Uzzah, laying hands upon it, expiated his imprudence, like a man killed by touching an electric battery. One evidence of the antiquity of this story is that the author of the Book of Samuel, as it has come down to us, did not quite understand it, and garbled it slightly in the telling.

11. The idea of the *taboo* is one of the most prolific taught us by the ethnography of the nineteenth century. The transition from the *taboo* to the reasoned and reasonable interdict is almost a history of the intellectual progress of man. Not only are *taboos* common to all men and prevalent in every nation on earth, but something analogous may be observed among animals. The superior animals, to speak only of these, obey at least one scruple, since, with very rare exceptions, they do not devour each other nor their young. A mammiferous species unfettered by such scruples is not only impossible to discover but inconceivable. If there ever were animals destitute of scruples touching the blood of their own kind, they must have exterminated each other and

so have formed no species. Selection can only have been made to the advantage of those groups of animals which, threatened as they all are by foreign war, were at least safe from civil strife.

12. In primitive or savage humanity, which we are beginning to know well, the blood-scruple seems less general than among certain animals. Hobbes was able to say without paradox that man is a wolf to man: *homo homini lupus.* However, the facts revealed to us by the observation of contemporary savages are not, *a priori*, revelations of primitive humanity. Besides, certain peoples exist, such as the Esquimaux, who do not even know what war is, and have no word for this scourge. It is therefore possible that primitive men neither killed nor ate one another. In France at least, exploration of the most ancient caves, where vast accumulations of animal bones have been found, has yielded no indications of anthropophagy. But indeed, whatever the fact may be as regards this remote phase of humanity, it is certain that throughout historic times the scruple of affinity has manifested itself with peculiar intensity in certain groups united by the ties of a common ancestry, real or supposed, families, septs, clans, and tribes. The murder of a member of the clan or family, even if involuntary, was a crime difficult to expiate. It is thus we must interpret the precept of the Decalogue: *Thou shalt not kill;* one of thy tribe or clan, must be understood. This is the more obvious inasmuch as in the Scriptures many horrible massacres are ordered by the Almighty.[1] Moderns, reading the Bible with civilised eyes, have interpreted the passage as an absolute condemnation of war, an idea which never occurred to the authors of the Pentateuch.

Thus the scruple or *taboo*, this barrier opposed to the

[1] As, for instance, the slaughter of the Midianites, Numbers xxxi, 7: "And they warred against the Midianites, as the Lord commanded Moses, and they slew all the males. . . ." v. 15: "And Moses said unto them, Have ye saved all the women alive? . . ." v. 17: "Now therefore kill every male among the little ones, and kill every woman that hath known man."—See Voltaire's fine notes to his tragedy: *Les Lois de Minos.*

destructive and sanguinary appetites, is a heritage transmitted to man by beast.

It is not the only one.

13. Animals, as far as we can tell, do not distinguish between exterior objects possessed or not possessed of volition. Dog-lovers are unanimous on this point. M. Bergeret's *Riquet* is an animist.[1] But animals do not confide in us; their psychology is obscure to us. This is not the case with children and savages. It is not possible for every one to go and study savages; but we have almost an equivalent at hand in children. We may declare the savage and the child to be animists; *i.e.*, they project their own volition outwards, and invest the world, more especially the beings and objects that surround them, with a life and sentiments similar to their own. I might give innumerable instances of this tendency; to find conclusive examples we have but to carry our minds back to our earliest recollections of childhood.

14. This fact was recognised and demonstrated even in the eighteenth century. In his *Natural History of Religion*, Hume wrote: "There is an universal tendency among mankind to conceive all beings like themselves. . . . The unknown causes which continually employ their thought, appearing always in the same aspect, are all apprehended to be of the same kind or species. Nor is it long before we ascribe to them thought and reason and passion, and sometimes even the limbs and figures of men."

15. Animism is so natural to man and so difficult to uproot, that it has left traces in the language of every people, even in that of persons apparently of the highest culture. I have just said that animism *has left traces*. Is not this an animistic fashion of expressing myself, as if animism, that abstraction of my mind, were a little genius, a sprite whose footsteps make an imprint on the dust or the wet earth? The personifications of poetry are in fact nothing but an animistic survival; they delight the civilised man the more because they recall to him the dearest and the most ancient

[1] In M. Anatole France's *L'Anneau d'Améthyste, &c.*

of his illusions. Listen to Lamartine speaking to Lac du Bourget:

O Lac, l'année à peine a fini sa carrière . . .
Regarde, je viens seul m'asseoir sur cette pierre
Où tu la vis s'asseoir! [1]

The year is a chariot rolling in its course round the sky, or rather the driver of this chariot; the lake *saw* Lamartine's love sitting on the stone; the poet addresses it, and enjoins it to *look*. Is there any great gulf between the state of mind indicated in these verses and that of the Redskin, who, when asked: "Why does the water of the river flow?" answers: "It is the spirit of the water taking flight." When we read a modern work of any sort, even one without any literary pretensions, we see that the great difficulty our languages, which are far from scientific instruments of analysis, have to encounter, is not that of personifying objects to make them more vivid, but that of stripping them of their personality to prevent them from speaking to the imagination—and so rousing, to the detriment of logic, that faculty which has so aptly been called by Montaigne "the madwoman of the house."

16. Animism on the one hand, and *taboos* on the other, such are the essential factors of religion. To the natural, I might almost say the physiological, action of animism are due the conceptions of those invisible genii with which nature teems, spirits of the sun and of the moon, of the trees and the waters, of thunder and lightning, of mountains and rocks, not to speak of the spirits of the dead, which are souls, and the spirit of spirits, who is God. To the influence of *taboos*, which create the ideas of sacred and profane, of things or actions forbidden or permitted, religious laws and piety are due. The Jehovah of the rocks and clouds of Sinai is a product of animism; the Decalogue is a revision of an old code of *taboos*.

.·.

[1] "O lake, the year has hardly finished its course . . .
Lo! I come alone to sit on this stone
Where you saw her sitting!"

17. The doctrine I have now briefly propounded is absolutely opposed to two explanations which were long received and still find partisans. The first is the theory of *revelation*, the second that of *imposture*. The first obtained throughout the Middle Ages, and finds its present champions among those who seek their instruction in the past; the second was, broadly speaking, the theory of the philosophers of the eighteenth century. Before going any further, it will be well to say a few words about each.

18. The theory of revelation is based on the Bible. That I may not be suspected of presenting a parody of this doctrine, I will quote, as far as possible, the actual expressions of a liberal theologian, the Abbé Bergier, who wrote the majority of the theological articles for Panckoucke's *Encyclopédie Méthodique*. God, when he called our first parents into being, himself taught them what it was necessary for them to know; he revealed to them that he is the sole Creator of the world, and of man in particular, and that therefore he is their sole benefactor and their supreme law-giver. He taught them that he had created them in his image and likeness, and that they were, accordingly, of a nature far superior to that of the brutes, which he put in subjection to them. He granted them fecundity by means of a special blessing, and they understood clearly that they were to transmit to their offspring the lessons which God had deigned to give them. Unhappily, men, with the exception of a few families, were unfaithful to the divine precepts, and forsaking the worship of the one God, fell into the errors of polytheism. Nevertheless, the memory of their sublime instruction did not perish altogether. This explains the fact that the idea of a tutelary divinity is found in different forms among all races. Not to the natural light of reason, but to revelation alone does man owe his knowledge of God and of religion.

19. Strange as this doctrine seems, it rests on the authority of all the great theologians of the Church, and in the nineteenth century a learned layman and distinguished Hellenist, Creuzer, professor at Heidelberg University, actually undertook the task of reviving it under a somewhat different

form. Creuzer taught that in very remote ages there existed, in Asia or in Egypt, a sacerdotal caste imbued with lofty religious and moral ideas (divine unity, the immortality of the soul, supernatural sanctions, &c.), but that, to make these more accessible to the multitude, they thought it necessary to disguise them under symbols. These symbols were speedily taken literally, and erroneously accepted as an adequate expression of human knowledge of the invisible world. Hence the extravagances of Greek polytheism, and hence also the secret teaching of mysteries, which admitted the initiated to the benefits of a purer religion, that of the golden age of humanity.

20. Creuzer, who wrote about 1810, in the middle of the religious renaissance of which Chateaubriand was the prophet, hoped by such means to refute the dry and prosaic doctrines of the eighteenth century. As a fact, his fate was the common lot of men who, brought up in a certain intellectual atmosphere, find it impossible, do what they will, to throw off the prejudices they have received from it. In his theory of the origin of myths and creeds, Creuzer attributes a very important part to the priesthood. The priest, possessing sublime truths, dressed them up skilfully to ensure their diffusion. Now the error of the eighteenth century was precisely the exaggeration of primitive sacerdotalism, the failure to perceive that religion is anterior to any priesthood, and the classification of priests as clever charlatans—beneficent charlatans, according to some—who invented religions and mythologies as instruments of domination. Hence the logical conclusion that religion, far from being contemporary with the dawn of humanity, was offered to or imposed upon it at an advanced period of its evolution. This was the doctrine taught even in our own days at the Ecole d'Anthropologie in Paris, by one of the founders of prehistoric science, Gabriel de Mortillet.

21. The basis of this doctrine is an absurd anachronism, into which the eighteenth century fell the more readily, because the state of Christianity in Western Europe seemed to justify it to some extent. Because men saw atheistic cardinals like Dubois, Tencin and many others, and licentious

priests, who, according to a common formula, "dined at the altar, and supped at the theatre," they imagined that this state of things existed from the beginning. Voltaire, while still a young man, had evoked applause with the following verses in his *Œdipe* (1718):

> Les prêtres ne sont pas ce qu'un vain peuple pense;
> Notre crédulité fait toute leur science.[1]

In 1742, he put these words into the mouth of Mahomet, who, to his mind, was a charlatan rather than a fanatic:

> Je viens mettre à profit les erreurs de la terre . . .
> Il faut un nouveau culte, il faut de nouveaux fers,
> Il faut un nouveau Dieu pour l'aveugle univers.[2]

22. Later in life, he continued, even in his most serious works, to consider priests as impostors, and religion as a sort of accident in the life of nations.

"Who was it who invented the art of divination? It was the first rogue who met a fool" (*Essai sur les Mœurs*, vol. i, p. 133). And in another place (vol. i, p. 14): "Blacksmiths, carpenters, masons, and ploughmen were all necessary before there was a man of sufficient leisure to meditate. All manual arts undoubtedly preceded metaphysics by several centuries." What Voltaire means here by metaphysics is the idea of the soul as distinct from the body, or, in other words, a direct consequence of that animism which is the universal belief of primitive races. "When, after many centuries," continues Voltaire, "some societies were established, we may presume that there was something in the nature of religion, some rude form of worship." Thus he postulates first, material civilisation, a more than rudimentary civilisation, comprising a knowledge of agriculture, of the working of wood, of stone and even of metals; religion, he takes it, came afterwards. Voltaire may have thought this theory a sensible one; to-day, it strikes us as almost childish, so true is it that we have

[1] "Priests are not what silly people believe; our credulity makes all their science."

[2] "I come to profit by the errors of mankind. We want a new cult, new fetters, a new God for the blind world."

made considerable progress since the *Essai sur les Mœurs* was written.

23. Rousseau was hostile to Voltaire, and many persons who have never read him imagine that he upheld the rights of religious sentiment against Voltaire. This is not the case; Rousseau and Voltaire are in agreement on the essential point, the priority of material civilisation to religion, and the artificial and adventitious nature of the latter, just as Creuzer and Voltaire agree in exaggerating the part played by priests in the creation and diffusion of dogmas. In 1753 Rousseau wrote his *Discours sur l'origine et les fondements de l'inégalité parmi les hommes,* in which he attempts to reconstrue the primitive history of all human societies solely by logic. He shows us first the lonely savage discovering the rudiments of industry and agriculture; then the savage building a hut and thus founding a family; afterwards comes an ambitious being who marks out a boundary round a field and claims the field as his own. Others follow his example; soon there are rich and poor; finally the rich, fearing for their own safety, combine to deceive the poor by promulgating constitutions and laws.

In all this romance there is no question of religion; but we feel that Jean Jacques abstains from discussing it for prudential reasons. These rich impostors who cheat the people, forcing them to sanction their usurpations, were, no doubt, in his mind, priests, or at least they were upheld by priests. Thus Rousseau and Voltaire shared the strange idea that man, the religious animal *par excellence,* lived for centuries without any religion, and that human societies were purely lay societies before the spirit of domination and fraud introduced the worship of the gods.

24. Voltaire and Rousseau do not sum up the entire thought of the eighteenth century; if it were my purpose to set forth the ideas of this period on religion, I should speak in detail of the remarkable work of President De Brosses[1] published in 1760, which introduced the idea and the term of *fetichism* into the science of religions.

The Portuguese navigators who first traded with Western

[1] *Du Culte des dieux fétiches.*

Africa had noticed that the negroes of this region bestowed a kind of worship on material gods, such as stones or shells, which the Portuguese called *fetiches*, from a word in their own language derived from the Latin *factitius* (fabricated), used to denote small devotional objects. De Brosses thought that the worship of fetiches was the origin of all religions, and compared the sacred stones of Egypt and Greece to these negro fetiches; he supposed fetichism to have been the first step towards the worship of idols. Therein he went too far; however, he was not unaware that the negro fetich is of no intrinsic account, but is reverenced as the abode of the spirit who is supposed to inhabit it. Fetichism, to us, is nothing but an individual case, a development of animism. We now know that the negroes of West Africa, far from being exclusively fetichists, recognise general or local spirits which are actual gods and are worshipped as such.

Serious as was the exaggeration into which he fell, De Brosses deserves full credit for having sought the origin of religions in the study of the savage tribes of our own days. Voltaire and Rousseau are also fond of discoursing on the savage, but they know very little about him.

25. Eighty years or so before De Brosses, Fontenelle, a gifted if somewhat superficial thinker, wrote a little study on the origin of fables which passed unnoticed; yet it was certainly the most remarkable contribution of the seventeenth century to this question, though it deals rather with mythology than with religion (1694?). It was not until quite recently that Andrew Lang, enlightened by a chance reading, set forth the merit and the importance of these pages. Fontenelle admits that there was "philosophy," that is to say, a desire to study the causes of phenomena, even in the most barbarous ages:

"This philosophy turned on a principle so natural that even now our philosophy has no other; that is to say, we explain the unknown things of Nature by those we see before us, and we give a physical form to the ideas suggested to us by experience. . . . We make all Nature act by levers, weights and springs. . . . From this rude philosophy, which necessarily obtained during the early centuries of humanity, the gods and goddesses were born. Men saw many activities they could not emulate, they beheld the fall of the thunderbolt, the violence of the winds, the agitation of the waves. . . . They imagined beings more powerful than themselves, capable of producing these great effects.

"Those beings, they argued, must be made like man; what other form could they have? One of the results of this has not perhaps received the attention it deserves: in all the divinities imagined by the heathen, they made the idea of power predominate, and insisted hardly at all on other attributes of the divine nature, such as wisdom and justice. There is no more striking proof that these divinities are very ancient. . . . It is not surprising then that men should have imagined several gods, often hostile one to another, cruel, capricious, unjust and ignorant. . . . These gods naturally bear the impress of the age in which they were created. . . . The heathen have always made their gods after their own image; thus, as man became more perfect, the gods also improved. . . . Primitive man gave birth to fables, by no fault of his own, so to say."

Here we are far enough from Voltaire's rascally priests! The whole of the essay is not of equal value, but how greatly Fontenelle was in advance of his age—and indeed, of the majority of nineteenth-century men of science—when he recognised the spontaneity of mythic creations, and explained the analogies they show among the most remote and various races by the very nature of the human intelligence:

"The origin of fables is usually ascribed to the vivid imagination of the Orientals; I, for my part, attribute them to the ignorance of primitive man. . . . I could show, if necessary, an amazing conformity between the fables of the Americans and those of the Greeks. . . . Since the Greeks, with all their intellect, were not more enlightened in their early stages than the barbarians of America, we may reasonably suppose that the Americans would have come in time to think as intelligently as the Greeks, if leisure had been given them."

In these lines we have the germ of the whole theory of modern anthropologists, who see in fables, just as in flint and bone implements, comparable products of the civilisations of various peoples at comparable periods of their evolution.

26. Fontenelle concludes with a few remarks on the borrowings of the Greeks from the Phœnicians and Egyptians, on the misunderstandings that must have arisen among the Greeks from their ignorance of foreign languages, and on the influence of literature, which sometimes preserves, sometimes develops fables, and even creates new ones. "In fables," he concludes, "we need seek nothing more than the history of the errors of the human mind. It is not science to fill one's head with all the extravagances of the Phœnicians and the Greeks, but it is science to know what led the Phœnicians and the Greeks into these extravagances. All men are so much alike that there is no race whose follies should not make us tremble."

This last phrase is pregnant with things Fontenelle did not dare to say; he also, like d'Alembert (in a letter to Voltaire), thought "the fear of the stake is cooling to the blood." But the quotations I have given will suffice, I hope, to convince all readers that Fontenelle, the light and lively Fontenelle, must be reckoned among the founders of that anthropological method of which I am endeavouring to give a summary.

II

27. I have tried in the preceding pages to show that animism on the one hand, and *taboos* on the other, may be considered the principal factors of religions and mythologies. But they are not the only factors. There are two others, which, though less primitive, have not been less general in their action. I mean totemism and magic.

28. It is difficult to define totemism. We may say, leaving a more precise definition to be given later, that it is a kind of worship rendered to animals and vegetables, considered as allied and related to man. What is the origin of this conception, and how was it developed?

29. The ancients already noted that man is a social animal. It was in vain that in the eighteenth-century Jean

Jacques Rousseau refused to recognise this characteristic, and tried to see in human society the result of a convention, a contract. Voltaire confuted him, and in our days every one agrees with Voltaire. In the most primitive state of which we have any knowledge, we find men living not only in hordes or flocks, like many of the superior mammals, but constituting social groups and obeying various scruples which were the embryo of morality and of law.

30. The social instinct of primitive man, like that of the child, readily transcends the limits of species and even those of the organic world to which he belongs. The illusion of animism makes him recognise everywhere spirits similar to his own; he enters into communication with them, and makes them his friends and allies. This universal tendency of the human mind is reflected in fetichism, which is not, as is sometimes supposed, the worship of material objects, but the friendly intercourse of man with the spirits who are supposed to inhabit these objects. As a child, when I had never heard of fetichism, I had a bright blue shell which was a veritable fetich to me, for in my mind it was the abode of a protecting spirit.

31. If at the present moment some one were to turn out all our pockets, and examine our watch-chains and our jewellery, what a fine harvest of fetiches they would furnish! We should, perhaps, protest that these objects are not fetiches, but trinkets and souvenirs. It is nevertheless certain that the sentiment we feel for them is, in a more or less literary and secular form, a survival of old prehistoric fetichism, the animism of our most remote ancestors.

32. When once primitive man has yielded to the tendency to enlarge the circle of his real or supposed relations almost indefinitely, it is natural that he should include within it certain animals and certain vegetables to which he assigns a place in the offensive and defensive group formed by the members of his clan. Very soon, a like scruple protects men and totems against his caprice or violence, and seems, to those who observe it, to attest their common origin, since the members of the clan, who respect one another's lives, claim a common mother or a common father.

33. This respect for the life of an animal or a vegetable, a primitive form of the worship of animals and plants, which we find mingled more or less with anthropomorphism in Egypt, Greece, and many other countries, is nothing but an exaggeration, a hypertrophy of the social instinct. Animals lend themselves thereto more readily than plants, and plants more readily than lifeless objects. We need only take a young child to a Zoological Garden to convince ourselves that this hypertrophy is very natural to man. Civilisation curbs but does not destroy it.

34. The worship of animals and plants is found as a survival in all ancient societies. It is the origin of the belief in *metempsychosis* (transmigration of souls) and of the fables called *metamorphoses*. When the Greeks tell us that Jupiter—Zeus—transformed himself into an eagle or a swan, we must recognise an inverted myth. The divine eagle and the divine swan made way for Jupiter when the gods of Greece began to be worshipped in human form; but the sacred animals remained the attributes or companions of the gods, who occasionally disguised themselves in the form of animals. Their metamorphoses are merely a return to their primitive state. Thus the fable tells us that Jupiter became a swan to charm Leda. To us this means that at a very remote period a Greek tribe had a sacred swan for their divinity, and that they thought this swan had intercourse with mortals. Later on the swan was replaced by a god in human form, Jupiter; but the fable was not forgotten, and it was supposed that Jupiter had changed himself into a swan to beget Helen, Castor and Pollux, the children of the divine swan and of Leda.

35. From the beginning of the eighteenth century, missionaries observed among the Indians of North America a more general and intense form of the worship of trees and animals. The word *totem* is derived from these Indians, or, to be exact, the word *otam* (mark or sign). It designates the animal, the plant, or (more rarely) the mineral or celestial body in which the clan recognises a protector, an ancestor and a rallying sign. Totemism seems to have been as widespread as the animism from which it is derived; we find

it to some extent everywhere, if not in the pure form and unmixed with more recent religious conceptions, at least as a survival more or less clearly defined. The religions of Egypt, of Syria, of Greece, of Italy and of Gaul are all impregnated with totemism.

36. I will cite an example of the survival of totemism in our own countries. The town of Berne has from time immemorial kept bears. To explain this custom, we have a story of a great bear which was killed near Berne in the ninth century by a hunter whose very name is given. This story, like many antique fables, was invented from beginning to end to explain the name of Berne and the traditional respect of its inhabitants for bears. As a fact, the cause of this kind of alliance is much more ancient. A bronze group was discovered near Berne dating from the first or second century of the Christian era, representing an enormous bear approaching a seated goddess, as if to offer homage; an inscription on the base of the bronze tells us that it was a pious offering, an *ex voto* to the goddess Artio. *Artio* is a Celtic word very closely allied to the Greek name of the bear, *arktos*. The goddess Artio was therefore an ursine divinity, a divinity who had a bear as her attribute or companion. Thus, before the period of divinities in human form, Artio was a bear-goddess, a sacred bear; the memory of the worship of the bear has persisted in the city of the bear (Berne) [1] throughout the ages, and it was not until our own times that a fortunate discovery enabled us to recognise in it a survival of prehistoric totemism.

37. Primitive totemism has left traces no less marked in literature. The ubiquitous animal-fable is the most ancient form of popular literature, and the modern child prefers it to all others. We begin his education with it. Now fables are simply the residuum of the narratives which human imagination constructed and human credulity accepted in the distant ages when the beasts could talk. Our children love these tales, because they are unconscious totemists. In our version of the Bible, animals only speak on rare occa-

[1] Popular etymology, of course; *Berne* is the same Celtic name as *Verona*.

sions; but we may recall the serpent in Genesis and Balaam's ass. The primitive stories which were combined and revised to form the Bible must have bristled with tales of animals. In the Gospels, we find the dove, a sacred bird in Syria, playing a characteristic part in the scene of the river Jordan; and the apocryphal Gospels, which are products of popular literature, give several instances of talking beasts and talking trees. When there are no traces of totemism in a monument of popular literature, it is because they have been erased by revisers.

38. The animal *totem*, considered as the protector of the clan, is in principle inviolate; even in these days there are hunting tribes who have the bear for their *totem*, and who ask pardon of a bear before killing him. In the most remote periods to which pure totemism carries us back, it is probable that every clan had at least one *totem* which might no more be killed or eaten than the human individuals of the clan. The *totem* was, in fact, protected by a *taboo*. The consequences were immense, and are still recognisable. The first was the domestication of animals and plants, that is to say, agricultural life. Let us suppose that there was a tribe composed of two clans, the *totem* of one being the wild boar, of the other a variety of wild cereal. It would be to the interest of each clan and of the individuals composing it to keep near their encampment at least a couple of wild boars, which would reproduce themselves under the protection of man, and a little plantation of cereals which cultivation would renew. Even if pressed by hunger, the hunters would not eat their *totem*, which would be preserved by a religious *taboo*, and they would only in very exceptional cases eat or destroy their neighbour's *totem*. In the course of a few generations, the sacred boars would become domesticated boars, that is to say, pigs, and the wild corn, cultivated grain.

39. How and why did this state of things come to an end? Here again religion intervenes, and gives the only satisfactory explanation. The *totem* is sacred; in this capacity it is looked upon as a source of strength and holiness. To live beside it and under its protection is a salutary thing;

but could not greater strength be gained—in the case, for instance, of an epidemic or some natural disaster—by assimilating the actual substance of the *totem?* Thus, at first on exceptional occasions, and for purposes of sanctification, the men of a clan agreed to kill and eat their *totem* ceremonially. By degrees, as they multiplied, these religious feasts became banquets; then, with the progress of rationalism, the sanctity of plants and animals was forgotten in their utility. It is possible that the communion rites, as understood and practised throughout the Middle Ages, were a survival of this very ancient superstition, which consists in fortifying and sanctifying oneself by assimilation of a divine being. If primitive Christianity, with its theophagistic practices, conquered Europe so rapidly, it was because this idea of the manducation of the god was not new, but simply the presentation of one of the most profound religious instincts of humanity in a more spiritual form.

40. On the other hand, in certain conservative centres, the idea that it is necessary to abstain from eating certain *totems* survived the progress of material civilisation. The forbidden animal or vegetable is sometimes regarded as sacred, sometimes as unclean. As a fact, it is neither; it is *taboo*. The cow is *taboo* to the Hindus, the pig is *taboo* to the Musulmans and the Jews, the dog is *taboo* practically throughout Europe, the bean was *taboo* in Greece in the Pythagorean and Orphic sects. In the eighteenth century, philosophers propagated the erroneous notion that if certain religious legislators had forbidden various aliments, it was for hygienic motives. Even Renan believed that dread of trichinosis and leprosy had caused the Hebrews to forbid the use of pork. To show the irrational nature of this explanation, it will be enough to point out that in the whole of the Bible there is not a single instance of an epidemic or a malady attributed to the eating of unclean meats; the idea of hygiene awoke very late in the Greek world. To the Biblical writers, as to contemporary savages, illness is supernatural; it is *an effect of the wrath of spirits.* The pious Jew abstains from pork because his remote ancestors, five or six thousand years before our era, had the wild boar as

their *totem*. The hygienic explanation of an alimentary prohibition must now be considered a mark of ignorance; that delusion was definitely discarded in 1889 by an illustrious English Orientalist, William Robertson Smith.

41. Nothing can be more absurd, generally speaking, than to explain the religious laws and practices of the remote past by considerations based on modern science. It is often said, for instance, that the Jews observed the Sabbath because their lawgiver, Moses, knew that man requires a day of rest. Moses knew nothing of the sort; he merely codified an ancient *taboo*, according to which one day in the week was considered unpropitious, and unfit for useful and productive work. If the Hebrew of the twentieth century before Christ did not work on a Saturday, it was because Saturday was an "unlucky day," just as we now see people, even among those who pride themselves on being freethinkers, who will not start on a journey on the 13th of the month or on a Friday, because the 13th and Friday are "unlucky days." We may explain very ancient customs by seeking points of comparison in modern times, but only if we look for these among the survivals of superstition, and not in science.

42. I hasten to add that in our intensive civilisation, the hygiene of body and mind enjoins us to devote one day of the week to rest; this is why the sabbatical custom has persisted and has even been confirmed by secular legislation. I might give many other instances of superstitious *taboos*, which, accidentally conforming to the exigencies of reason or hygiene, have survived in our modern civilisation, and thus secularised, deserve to survive.

43. Why did the medieval Christians, and why do members of the Romish and Greek churches, fast on Friday? They do not know themselves, nor do the Jews know why they should eat fish on Friday night. This latter custom is so deep-rooted among pious Jews that in Galicia Jewish families, reduced to the utmost penury, will get a single gudgeon on Friday in order to eat it in tiny morsels at nightfall. The fasting of the Christians, alleviated by the

permission of eating fish, has no doubt some connection with the old religious custom of eating fish on a Friday.

44. As this custom is common to Jews and Christians, it is evident that the circumstance of the Saviour's death on a Friday has nothing to do with it. The fish is an ancient Syrian *totem*. Among the Syrian tribes, some, the Jews among them, abstained from certain fish; others kept sacred fish in ponds, and ate sacred fish to sanctify themselves. This latter practice was adopted by the early Christians, who went so far as to identify Christ with a very large fish [1] and to call themselves little fishes. "We are little fishes," says Tertullian, "born in the waters of baptism," and a Christian inscription of 180 A.D. speaks of Jesus as "the great fish." The eating of the sacred fish was a primitive form of the Eucharistic meal, for this usage was very much earlier than the birth of Christ. It persists under various forms among the Jews, who observe it without understanding it, and among the Christians, who have invented innumerable contradictory reasons to explain it, into the details of which I need not enter here.

45. If the system of *taboos* and *totems* explains many things in religions and mythologies, ancient as well as modern, we must not conclude that it explains everything. In spite of the flagrant abuse of solar myths, and the myths of storm and thunder, it is undeniable that a naïve interpretation of the great phenomena of Nature gave rise to a certain number of fables. But these fables assumed and retained a character rather literary than religious; all that is deep and essential in religion came from animism, of which the worship of the dead is a consequence, and from totemism, which preceded anthropomorphic religions and imbued them with its elements.

Let us return for a moment to our *taboos*.

46. The origin of these religious scruples is certainly not

[1] This has nothing to do with the famous acrostic *Ichthus* (fish), the letters of which are the initials of the phrase: *Jesous Christos Theou uios sôter* (Jesus Christ, Son of God, Saviour). The acrostic was a subsequent invention to explain and justify the Christian cult of the fish.

rational, in the modern sense of the word. The offspring of fear, the fruits of hasty generalisations and of arbitrary comparisons such as children and ignorant persons are constantly making—consider all our contemporary superstitions about spilt salt, crossed knives, words and deeds of evil omen—taboos are peculiarly numerous and rigorous in the most backward civilisations, such as that of the Australians of the present day, where they are transmitted by oral tradition, and constitute almost the entire science of these savages. The idea evolved in the eighteenth century, of the free savage, emancipated from all constraints, is irreconcilable with the most elementary facts of ethnography. Rousseau's free savage is no real savage, but a philosopher who has stripped himself naked.

47. If the white race had remained imprisoned in a network of *taboos*, of interdicts bearing upon food, working days, the liberty to come and go, marriage, the education of children, we should not now be enjoying the freedom it has given us. Happily, among the more energetic and gifted nations, selection takes place in the domain of *taboos*. Those of which experience has shown the social utility have persisted, sometimes in the form of rules of etiquette, sometimes in the guise of moral precepts and civil laws; the rest have disappeared, or survive only as low superstitions. This work of progressive emancipation was seconded by the religious lawgivers, the priests, who, by codifying the *taboos*, prevented their excessive multiplication and suppressed many, inasmuch as they did not sanction all. Here again, in a question of capital importance, eighteenth-century Rationalism went astray; whereas it looked upon the first priests as oppressors and knaves, we must recognise in them the artisans of a relative emancipation, which held its course later *in spite of* sacerdotalism, and opened the way for more complete emancipation. But the beneficent part played by the priesthood in the repression of irksome superstitions and puerile *taboos* is not only one of the great achievements of the past. Even in these days it is often the duty of Catholic priests to reassure their penitents in the confessional with reference to idle scruples, a heritage from prehistoric

taboos, with which ignorance is always ready to burden itself.

48. The history of humanity is that of a progressive secularisation which is by no means complete as yet. In the beginning the whole atmosphere in which it moves is saturated, so to speak, with animism; spirits, dangerous if not essentially maleficent, hover on all sides, modifying and paralysing man's activity. The selection of *taboos* was the first step in advance, but not the only one. Humanity did not remain passive in presence of the thousand spiritual forces by which it believed itself surrounded. To react against these, to tame them and subdue them to its ends, it sought an auxiliary in a false science, magic, which is the mother of all true sciences. I have proposed to define magic as the *strategy of animism*, and I think this definition is better than Voltaire's, *the secret of doing what Nature cannot do*, for primitive man had no idea what Nature can do, and magic aspires to control it. By the aid of magic, man takes the initiative against things, or rather he becomes the conductor in the great concert of spirits which murmur in his ears. To make the rain fall, he pours out water; he gives the example, he commands, and fancies he is obeyed. Of course in the instance I have given the magician wastes time and trouble; but remember Bacon's profound saying: *Natura non vincitur nisi parendo*—it is only by obeying Nature that we can conquer her. This notion of the solidarity of phenomena, of a reciprocal action of man's will on the wills of the spirits around him, is already a scientific principle, in spite of the illusions by which it is misled.

49. When once magic had become a profession, a necessary institution of the social body, the magician had perforce to produce some happy effects, calculated to command recognition and respect; so the charlatan became a physician, an astrologer, a metallurgist, and as the astrologer and alchemist of the Middle Ages, he increased the human capital of useful discoveries which ultimately made him useless. I might show that all the great inventions of primitive humanity, including that of fire, were made under the auspices of religion, and by the indefatigable ministry of magic. It

is true that magic did not produce the same results everywhere. It needed a propitious soil, but though in civilised countries it exists now only as a survival, after the manner of totemism, it is to magic and to totemism that the modern world owes the elements of its civilisation.

Thus—and this seems to me an essential result of our inquiry—we find that the origin of religion is merged in the origin of human thought and intellectual activity; its decadence and its limitation is the history of the progress it alone has made possible.

50. Religions are not, as Voltaire and more modern thinkers such as Carl Vogt and Mortillet have supposed, cancers engrafted on the social organism by cupidity and fraud, but the very life of nascent societies. In the course of time, religion gave birth to special branches of human knowledge, to the exact sciences, to morality, and to law, which naturally developed at its expense.

Even in our own age, *taboos* tend to codify into reasonable laws. Animism yields the ground to physics, chemistry, and astronomy, and takes refuge, on the confines of science, in spiritualism. Finally, magic, which plays so important a part in certain rites, loses its character, and these rites tend to become symbols, like the Communion in the Reformed Churches of Christendom.

. . .

51. The retrogressions towards animism and magic which historians record, and describe as "religious revivals," are, as a fact, merely apparent; they arise from the admixture of minds emancipated, but few in number, with the ignorant and superstitious multitude. Such a condition of things existed at the end of the eighteenth century, when the Revolution, initiated by liberal and liberated spirits, broke down the barriers which separated these from what Voltaire called *la canaille*, and increased French citizenship immeasurably. The result, after the lapse of a few years, was the Catholic reaction which triumphed from 1815 to 1830; its effects are still evident among us.

In the same manner, the premature establishment of universal suffrage after 1848, in a country where primary education hardly existed as yet, resulted in the apparent retrogression of French society, not only under the Second Empire, which was a product of this retrogression, but during the first twenty years of the Third Republic, the golden age of clericalism.

52. We have witnessed a recrudescence of thaumaturgy, of miraculous medicine, of the worship of gaudy idols, of the vogue of spiritualism, demonism and occultism. Similar phenomena are now conspicuous in Eastern Europe, where politic revolutions have taken place before the vast masses of the nation were educated and enlightened.

53. Those who talked and still talk of doing away with religions by police regulations, Voltaires, Holbachs or Edgar Quinets though they be, have ignored the conditions of intellectual progress, and the force of the survivals which obstruct it. Not only have the religions which are at present distributed throughout Europe an indefinite future before them, but we may rest assured that something of them will always remain, because the mysterious and the unknown will always persist in the world, because science will never have accomplished all its task, and because no doubt man will always retain something of his ancestral animism, perpetually fostered by grief seeking consolation, by the conscience of human weakness, by admiration or terror in presence of nature's phenomena. But religions themselves tend to become secularised, like the sciences to which they gave birth, and from which they in their turn are drawing inspiration. Within the span of three centuries, alchemy has become chemistry, astrology has become astronomy, Bossuet's *Discours sur l'Histoire universelle* has been re-written in a secular vein by Voltaire, Michelet and others. An irresistible current is driving all human thought in the direction of secularism. The same thing happened in Greece in the fifth century, in the time of Hippocrates and Anaxagoras, and will happen again long after our day.

54. Among the multiple tasks incumbent on science, one of the most important is to construct the history of religions, to retrace their origins and explain their vicissitudes.

These are very fruitful studies, which date but from yesterday, so to speak. The true founders of the science of religions, Mannhardt, William Robertson Smith, and Max Müller, have only been dead a few years; the teaching of the history of religions in the various universities is still in its infancy. But the need of it begins to make itself felt in every direction, the public is approaching it with marked interest, and there is every reason to suppose that our times will not fail to encourage studies which tend not only to elevate and instruct, but to liberate the human mind.

BIBLIOGRAPHY [1]

The best general manual of the history of religions is the work of Chantepie de la Saussaye (new German ed. 1925; French translation, 1904), but Christianity is omitted. G. Foot Moore's good *History of Religions* (1913, 1919) excludes the uncivilised races. For the history of Christianity, the student is referred to Funck, *Kirchengeschichte* (5th German ed. 1907; French translation, 1895), a lucid and accurate work, but partial in its attitude to the Roman Church. Hastings has published a general encyclopædia of religions (1908-1926), an admirable work; so is *Die Religion in Geschichte und Gegenwart,* by several authors, 1909-1913 (new ed. in progress).

It is impossible to keep abreast of the subject without studying special periodicals: in France, the *Revue de l'Histoire des Religions* and the *Année Sociologique;* in Germany the *Archiv für Religionswissenschaft;* in England, the *Hibbert Journal, Folklore, Man,* &c.

General Works.—R. Dussaud, *Introd. à l'histoire des religions,* 1914 (up to date); M. Guyau, *L'Irreligion de l'avenir,* 1887; M. Jastrow, *The Study of Religion,* 1902; Jevons, *Introd. to the Hist. of Religion,* 1896; Lang, *Myth, Ritual and Religion,* 1899; MacLennan, *Studies in Ancient History,* new ed., 1886; W. Mannhardt, *Wald- und Feldculte,* 3 vols. 1875-1877; *Mythologische Forschungen,* 1884; Max Müller, *Introduction to the Science of Religion,* 1875; F. Ratzel, *Völkerkunde,* 2nd ed., 1894; S. Reinach, *Cultes, mythes et religions,* 5 vols., 1904-1923; A. Réville, *Prolégom. à l'hist. des religions,* 1881; A. Sabatier, *Esquisse d'une philosophie de la religion,* 1897; M. Hébert, *Le Divin,* 1907; H. Schurtz, *Urgeschichte der Kultur,* 1900; Tylor, *Primitive Culture,* 2 vols., 4th ed., 1903. This last work is a masterpiece.

3. M. Jastrow, *Study of Religion,* p. 131.

8. S. Reinach, *Cultes,* vol. i, p. 1; vol. ii, p. 18; L. Marillier, *Tabou mélanésien* (in *Etudes de critique,* 1896, p. 35); Frazer, *Golden Bough,* 3 vols., 2nd ed., 1900; 3rd ed. in 12 vols., 1911-1915 (very important).

13. E. Clodd, *Animism,* 1905.

17. O. Gruppe, *Griechische Culte und Mythen,* vol. i, 1887 (a history of mythological exegesis).

[1] This bibliography is for the use of readers of the present volume; it refers them mainly to good popular works and articles, and rarely to collections or translations of texts, save when these are preceded by introductions comprehensible to the educated general public.

18. N. Berger, *Dictionnaire théologique,* in the *Encyclopédie méthodique* (it has been reprinted separately several times), article *Révélation.*

20. On Sacerdotalism, S. Reinach, *Cultes,* vol. ii, pp. 3, 22.

24. Haddon, *Magic and Fetichism,* 1906; C. W. Oliver, *Magic and Witchcraft,* 1928.

34. M. W. de Visser, *Die nichtmenschengestaltigen Götter der Griechen,* 1903 (important). On Metamorphoses, S. Reinach, *Cultes,* vol. iii, pp. 32, 76.

35. Frazer, *Totemism,* 1898 (reprinted in *Totemism and Exogamy,* 4 vols., 1910); W. Robertson Smith, *The Religion of the Semites,* new ed., 1906; Durkheim, *Formes élémentaires de la vie religieuse,* 1912 (Engl. transl., 1916); S. Reinach, *Cultes,* vol. i, pp. 9, 79 (exogamy).

36. The Berne bears: S. Reinach, *Cultes,* vol. i, p. 55.

38. Alimentary prohibitions: S. Reinach, *Cultes,* vol. ii, p. 12—Domestication of animals, *ibid.,* vol. i, p. 85.

39. G. d'Alviella, *La théorie du sacrifice et Robertson Smith,* in the *Rev. Université de Bruxelles,* 1897, p. 499; Hubert and Mauss, *Le sacrifice,* in the *Année sociologique,* 1899, p. 29; Loisy, *Essai sur le sacrifice,* 1920; S. Reinach, *Cultes,* vol. i, p. 97.

41. The Sabbath: S. Reinach, *Cultes,* vol. i, pp. 16, 429.

43. Fish: *ibid.,* vol. iii, pp. 43, 103; Dölzer, *Röm. Quartalschrift,* 1909, p. 3.

47. Beneficent taboos: Frazer, *Psyche's Task,* 1909.

48. Hubert and Mauss, *Théorie générale de la Magie,* in the *Année sociologique,* 1904, p. 1 *et seq.;* Van Gennep, *Les rites de passage,* 1909.

50. The Origin of Morality: S. Reinach, *Cultes,* vol. ii, p. 7.

53. See Peyrat, *La Révolution,* 1866, on Quinet's paradox: that the Revolution ought to have dechristianised France by force.

∴

Under the title *Religionsgeschichtliches Lesebuch,* M. Bertholet published, in 1908, a collection of translations of the most important texts relating to the religions of China, India, Persia and Islam; these texts are preceded by introductions and followed by bibliographies. A similar work on Semitic religions was issued by Gressmann, *Altorientalische Texte,* 1909.

CHAPTER I

EGYPTIANS, BABYLONIANS AND SYRIANS

I. The complexity of religious phenomena in Egypt. Essential traits of the religious evolution. Expansion of the Egyptian cults. Animism. Belief in a future life. Magic. Totemism. The religious function of the Pharaohs, priests and ritual. The myth of Osiris. The Egyptian cosmogony.

II. Babylonia and Assyria. The code of Hammurabi. The Babylonian gods. Animism. Cosmogony: the Deluge. The god Thamuz. The legends of Ishtar and Gilgamesh. Ritual, psalms and incantations. Divination. The calendar. Belief in a future life. Astrology and Astronomy. The lasting influence of Babylonian ideas.

III. The antiquity of the Phœnician civilisation. Gods and goddesses. The worship of animals, trees and stones. Baal, Melkart, Eshmun. Adonis and the Boar. Sacrifices. Ideas of a future life and of the creation. Syrian forms of worship. Atergatis, the fish and the dove. Syrian forms of worship at Rome. The Stone of Mesa.

I. The Egyptians

1. The texts and monuments which reveal the Egyptian religion to us extend over a period of forty centuries. In the early stages of its development, it was not a single religion, codified like Catholicism, but a multitude of local forms of worship, which were gradually amalgamated; many, no doubt, disappeared, eliminated by religious selection, many others were supplemented by foreign elements—Libyan, Arabian, Syrian and Greek—or increased in importance under the Pharaohs who professed them.

2. As the Egyptians were by nature extremely conservative, they were concerned rather to preserve the conceptions of the different forms of worship than to make a selection among them, and constitute a logical sum of beliefs. Their theologians increased the confusion by giving themselves up, from the earliest times, to all sorts of speculations—identifications, admixtures, marriages of the gods, creations of di-

THE PHARAOHS

vine groups (triads and enneads), and of genealogies, the introduction of philosophical ideas or historical theories into myths which seemed to them too absurd or too unmeaning. Accepting the tradition of an infinite plurality of gods, they tended to constitute a divine hierarchy on the model of that of Egypt itself, and to see in it, as it were, the emanation of a more mighty god; hence their imperfect aspiration towards monotheism, which is a kind of reflection of Egyptian policy in the world of the gods.

3. The result of all this was an almost inextricable confusion; we may speak, not of the Egyptian religion, but of the evolution of the religions of Egypt, and we are still very far from a definite idea of the subject.

4. The essential features of this evolution are the following: At an early stage, three divine personages, destined to the highest fortunes, Horus, Râ and Osiris, stand out from the swarm of local deities, the products of animism and totemism. Horus, often identified with Râ, the solar divinity of Heliopolis, is a falcon or hawk; Osiris, the god of Abydos, seems to have been simultaneously and successively a tree and a bull. Towards 1550 B.C., the Theban Pharaohs established throughout Egypt the worship of the ram-god of Thebes, Ammon, also called Ammon-Râ, by identification with the god of the sun; then the worship of the solar disc triumphed over the worship of Ammon and tended to absorb all the rest. In the time of Amenophis IV. (1370), this developed into a remarkable advance towards monotheism. Later, the worship of Ammon again prevailed but did not oust that of Râ. Osiris became and remained the god *par excellence* of the dead. During the Saïte period (seventh to sixth centuries B.C.) the most ancient conceptions came into favour again; animism and totemism flourished afresh in that decadent Egypt which the Greek historians have described to us. Finally, at the beginning of the Hellenic domination, a Greco-Asiatic deity, Serapis, analogous to Pluto and identified with Osiris, was introduced by the Ptolemies at Alexandria and remained the supreme divinity until the triumph of Christianity. At the time of the Antonines, there were forty-two temples of Serapis in Egypt.

5. Whereas, under the Pharaohs, Egyptian forms of worship were confined to the countries subject to their rule, from the outset of the Greek domination, and more especially under the Roman Empire, they showed an extraordinary force of expansion. From Asia Minor to Gaul and Britain, Egyptian statuettes, or local imitations of the images of Egyptian gods, are to be met with; itinerant priests diffused the consolatory worship of Isis, Serapis, Anubis and Harpocrates (the Infant Horus). In spite of the opposition of the Senate, and the hostility of Augustus and Tiberius, these forms of worship enjoyed a growing popularity in Italy and in Rome. The priests of Isis were healers, wizards and exorcists; associations sprang up around them which practised ecstatic rites, weeping for the death of Osiris to the sounds of the sistrum, or noisily celebrating his resurrection, the prototype of that of his adherents. It is probable that there was a temple of Isis even in Paris, towards the third century. This religion received a mortal blow at the close of the fourth century, when the Christian Patriarch Theophilus burnt down the Serapeum of Alexandria; but paganism did not disappear from Egypt till the time of Justinian.

6. Animism was as strongly developed in Egypt as among the most primitive savages. All natural objects, from the heavenly bodies and the Nile to the humble sycamores, took the form of gods; popular imagination peopled the deserts that fringe the valley of the Nile with fantastic demons. A belief in the after-life of the soul was naturally associated with this quasi-universal animism; but according to the Egyptians, the body was necessary to the support of the soul, even after death, and to ensure the felicity of the soul it was essential to safeguard its tenement. Hence the customs of embalming and mummification, the use of sarcophagi, often encasing one another, the care with which tombs were constructed, the enormous royal pyramids and the hypogea hollowed in the rocks.

7. The ideas of the Egyptians on the condition and abode of spirits varied greatly, and were confounded at a very early period; contradictory yet contemporary conceptions

are recorded, which theology had to harmonise as best it might. The soul is a bird which mounts to heaven; it is a man resembling the dead man, who goes to cultivate the fields of Ialou, somewhere towards the west, with the servants who people his tomb in the form of statuettes or *respondents;* the soul had a long journey to accomplish to the land of the dead. This journey was full of dangers and snares which it escaped by following the very complicated instructions of a guide, the Book of the Dead, which was placed in the tombs, and passages of which were inscribed on their walls, on the mummy-cases, and on the statuettes. Many different versions of this book have survived; it is a collection of incantations and magic formulæ. Finally, beside the soul of the man, there is what was called his double, the *ka*, a kind of tutelary genius or guardian angel of the individual. The *ka* is incarnated in one or more material objects (statuettes), which must remain in the tomb, and represent the lasting support of the soul, even when the mummy has disappeared by the action of time or a violation of the sepulchre.

Belief in the survival of the soul was for a long time complicated by no moral ideas; but these at last asserted their claims. The soul of the dead man had to appear before Osiris to be weighed, and to affirm before forty-two judges that it was guiltless of a whole series of specified faults. Guilty souls were hurled into some unknown region, a hell as to which we have no details. The souls of the good became Osirises, identifying themselves with the royal deity of the infernal kingdom.

8. The principle of the worship of the dead is magic, the virtue of images and formulæ. It was this which ensured for the dead enjoyment of realities corresponding to those deposited or figured in his tomb: numerous servants, rich pastures, fertile fields, food, raiment and furniture of every kind. The scenes represented on the walls of the great tombs were not only portrayals of the dead man's occupations, but their material support, their magic condition. Diodorus justly observes, about the time of Augustus, that the Egyptians considered their houses as temporary habitations, and

their tombs as their eternal abodes. It was not that they did not love life; far from it; they loved it so passionately that they wished to preserve it after death, in a condition as closely akin as possible to that of the most fortunate of living persons.

9. Totemism appears in Egypt in three forms. First, there were a considerable number of sacred animals and trees, some honoured throughout Egypt, like the cat, others only in certain districts. These trees and sacred animals were gods, represented originally by animal or vegetable forms, then, in the progress of anthropomorphism, as divinities lodged in trees, and divinities with the heads of animals, or wearing the attributes of animals. Osiris, who was probably a bull originally, is always represented as a man, but his wife and sister Isis retains the heifer's horns as a symbol of her primitive nature. Finally, together with those sacred species which characterise totemist forms of worship, Egypt worshipped individual animals, chosen specimens with certain natural but rare distinctions, such as the bull Apis of Memphis, and the goat of Mendes. When the sacred animals grew old, they were sacrificed ritually. They were embalmed like human beings; there are in existence enormous cemeteries of Apis-bulls, cats, rams, ibises and crocodiles.

10. In Egypt, as elsewhere, alimentary prohibitions resulted from totemism; these were often restricted to certain portions of an animal, or imposed only on priests, who, for instance, were not allowed to eat pork in the time of Herodotus. Decrees forbidding the slaughter of sacred animals were absolute; under one of the Ptolemies, a Roman nearly brought about an insurrection by accidentally killing a cat. The Egyptians valued their cats so highly that the exportation of these animals was forbidden and missions were periodically despatched to ransom those which had been carried off surreptitiously; it was not until after the triumph of Christianity that the Egyptian cats were distributed throughout Europe. They were the more in request inasmuch as the invasion of the Asiatic Huns had introduced rats in its train.

11. The Egyptian Pharaoh, approximating to a god, is

a great priest and a great magician; his prayers and invocations ensure the due progress of natural phenomena; he is the sole intercessor for the dead to Osiris. The priests of the different temples did not form castes, as has been supposed; but the priesthood, which was held in great veneration, was often hereditary. Ceremonies, sacrifices and prayers were all imbued with magic; just as Egyptian religions were the outcome of animism, their worship was the outcome of magic, which is the strategy of animism. Talismans of all kinds, extravagant remedies, maledictions, incantations, frauds of every sort belonged to the province of the priests. But, as invariably happens, science was born of religion, science, an impatient daughter, who claims her heritage while her mother is still living; Egyptian science emerged from the temples, tended to become secularised, and exercised a beneficent influence on early Greek science.

12. Hieroglyphic inscriptions and papyri reveal the details of the ritual, more especially that of the dead; but the myths of the gods elude us for the most part, and the only one familiar to us, that of Osiris, was preserved by a Greek author. Osiris was a civilising hero of great antiquity; he reigned over Egypt, ensured her wealth and peace, and suppressed anthropophagy. His wicked brother Set or Typhon put him to death out of jealousy, and tore his body into fourteen pieces. His wife and sister, Isis, went in search of the fragments of this beloved body, found them one by one, and erected over each a magnificent tomb. His son Horus, when he grew up, avenged his father, and restored him to life by magic formulæ. Thenceforth Osiris reigned over the empire of the dead. Thus Osiris, like Adonis, Actæon, Hippolytus, Dionysos Zagreus and Orpheus, was a suffering hero, a hero who is lamented and finally resuscitated; his myth implies a very ancient sacrificial ritual, probably the sacrifice of a sacred bull, cut up into fourteen parts, eaten in communion by the faithful, and then replaced by another sacred bull; in other words, resuscitated. The Greeks were struck by the similarity of the legend of Osiris and that of Dionysos Zagreus, the young bull devoured by the Titans, to which Zeus granted a new and glorious life. These legends,

both based upon sacrificial rites, coincide without having necessarily borrowed one from another.

13. In the most ancient Egyptian tombs, dating from three or four thousand years before our era, before the custom of embalming had been adopted, bodies have been found cut up, as was that of Osiris according to the legend. The dead man was, in fact, an Osiris, a subject of the god with whom he was identified; his scattered limbs had to be collected to ensure his resuscitation. It was not till a later period that the cutting up of the body was abandoned, and that it was swathed in bandages, perhaps at first for fear of ghosts; but the survival of the soul could only be assured by the piety of descendants, by their formulæ; just as the resurrection of Osiris was due to the magic arts of his son Horus. The great antiquity of the Osirian myth is thus attested by the permanent influence it seems to have exercised on the funereal customs of Egypt.

14. The ideas of the Egyptians as to the creation of the world seem to have been no less confused and contradictory than their ideas of death. One of the most widely held explained the origin of things by the union of the god of earth with the goddess of heaven, a conception common to many nations. An obscure legend made Râ the creator of the world and of man; irritated by their wickedness, he was supposed to have destroyed humanity in order to reorganise heaven and earth. Another doctrine attributed creation to the magic power of the god Thot at Hermopolis, whose voice, "with its true intonations," had called forth the world from nothingness. This recalls the creative Word, the fecund speech of the God of Scripture. Râ the Sun, emerging from an egg, sails in a boat on the Ocean; he is sometimes a swift falcon, sometimes a glittering beetle. This humble insect, perpetually reproduced by art, was one of the most popular talismans. Thus contradictory conceptions were juxtaposed without amalgamating, and the Egyptian religion, in spite of the progress of Pharaonic royalty, preserved the image of primitive anarchy.

II. The Babylonians and the Assyrians

1. In religion as in art, Assyria was merely a continuation of Babylon, save that she gave the highest honour to her eagle god, Ashur. The Babylonian religion itself was an adaptation of the earlier Sumerian creeds.

2. From a very remote period, the Babylonians had a cosmogony, a mythology and a ritual; but as political unity was only achieved some 2000 years before Christ, it was natural that many local forms of worship should have contributed to the formation of their pantheon.

3. Marduk, the god of Hammurabi, the first king of united Babylon, was placed by the latter at the head of the Pantheon. It was in the temple of Marduk at Babylon that Hammurabi set up his code of laws, engraved on a large *stela,* now in the Louvre. It was discovered in 1901 at Susa, whither it had been carried off as spoil. The king is represented at the top of the *stela,* standing devoutly before the seated Sun-god, Shamash. Not only does Shamash here play the same part as the Biblical god on Sinai, but the code of Hammurabi presents analogies with the so-called Mosaic code which cannot be explained as accidental. The Babylonian code is anterior by *six centuries* to the date assigned by tradition to the Mosaic code; if then this latter was dictated by God to Moses, God must have plagiarised from Hammurabi. Such a conclusion seemed, with very good reason, inadmissible to the most universal of German *savants,* the Emperor William II.; in a famous letter addressed to an admiral, he decided that God had successively inspired various eminent men, such as Hammurabi, Moses, Charlemagne, Luther, and his grandfather William I. This opinion found general acceptance in court circles.

4. The idea of a divine trinity is much earlier than Christianity, for we find that several of the Babylonian deities were grouped in triads. Thus we have at a very early date, Anu, the god of heaven, Bel, the God of earth, and Ea, the god of the abyss, or of the waters. Goddesses play a less important part than gods, with the exception of the powerful Ishtar, who presided over war and over love.

5. At a very early period, Babylonian animism lent life to the sun (*Shamash*), the moon (*Sin*), the morning and evening star (*Ishtar*), the earth (*Bêl*), fire (*Gibil*), and the waters (*Ea*). But it is also certain that the Babylonians had animal gods, a lion (*Nergal*), a bull (*Ninib*), a fish (*Ea* or *Oannes*), a dove (*Ishtar*). The gods who were the products of terrestrial totems had a tendency to choose a domicile in the heavens; now the Greek mythology sufficiently shows that these two conceptions, evolved at different periods, were somehow readily harmonised by faith.

6. Thanks to the fragments which have come down to us of the Babylonian priest Berosus' writings (third century before Christ), and more especially to the thousands of cuneiform records excavated in Babylonia and Assyria, we are fairly well informed as to the Babylonian gods. We have accounts of the creation, the deluge, and the descent of Ishtar to hell. The general theme of these narratives is the subordination of man to the gods, who demand not only piety, but purity and justice. The authors of the Jewish Bible, who had at least an indirect knowledge of the Babylonian traditions, only took a farther step in the same direction, by giving a moral character to all their legends.

7. The first gods came out of chaos, which was conceived of as an illimitable sea, the dragon Tiamat. To introduce order into the world, they had to fight and overcome Tiamat. Marduk led the attack, and after his victory, became the chief of the gods; then he set impassable limits to the power of the sea. Men were not created until later, probably out of clay. But they responded ill to the goodness of the gods, who decided to destroy them by water. Ea revealed this purpose in a dream to the Babylonian Noah Utnapishtim, who built an ark and took refuge in it with his family. A terrible cataclysm began, which alarmed even the gods. After seven days, the ark rested on a mountain, and Utnapishtim sent forth a dove and then a swallow, who returned, finding no resting-place. A raven sent out shortly afterwards did not return. Then Utnapishtim came forth from the ark, and offered a sacrifice, the savour of which attracted the gods "like flies." This version, an

earlier one than that of the Bible, is marked by more primitive characteristics, notably the incident of the disagreement among the gods: Bel, who let loose the deluge, reproaches Ea with having saved one family. In the monotheistic Scriptures, God addresses a reproach of an opposite character to himself; he promises never again to let loose the deluge, an inconsequent confession of an excessive rigour, useless for the moral reform of humanity, as the sequel sufficiently proved.

8. The god Thamuz, the Adonis of the Syrians, was the husband of Ishtar. He died in the spring and descended into hell. Ishtar also descends in her turn to find him, and to discover the fountain of living water which will restore him to life. At every gate through which she has to pass, the custodian demands a piece of her robe, till at last she arrives naked in the empire of the dead. The earth, deprived of Ishtar, becomes barren; everything dries up and dies. The gods take counsel, and agree to satisfy the goddess. In spite of the wrath of the goddess of the dead, Allatu, they send a messenger who seizes the living water. Thamuz is restored and comes back to earth with Ishtar.

When we read this myth, which resembles that of Demeter and Proserpine, we naturally think of the vegetation, scorched by the sun of Babylonia, which revives with the first rains. But the analogy with the history of Isis and Osiris is no less striking, and suggests that we have here a sacrificial myth. We shall meet with it again when we speak of the Phœnicians.

9. Gilgamesh, the *protégé* of Shamash, is the hero who saves Uruk, the town of Ishtar, besieged by the Elamites. He has a hairy creature for a companion, Engidu (formerly misread *Eabani*), the victor over a lion—probably a lion himself. On the mount of the Cedar, Ishtar offers her love to Gilgamesh, but the hero repulses her, for he knows that Ishtar slays her friends. Then she complains to her father, the god Anu, who incites a divine bull against Gilgamesh; Gilgamesh and Engidu kill it. But the malediction of the incensed Ishtar pursues them; Engidu dies; Gilgamesh is stricken with leprosy, and departs to the Island of the

Blessed, to consult his ancestor Utnapishtim. On the way he has to overcome lions, and scorpions; he arrives at last at the sea, where a marine goddess shows him the way; at the end there is a ferryman who takes passengers to the island. Gilgamesh lands and Utnapishtim tells him the story of the deluge; and then cures his leprosy by means of a magic drug. The hero purifies himself at the spring of purification, and tries to obtain the plant of life, but a serpent snatches it from him. Full of grief at not having found Engidu, he returns to Uruk. Finally he obtains an interview with his friend in a dream. The end of the story has not yet come to light.

10. We have certain other fragments of legends relating to gods and heroes, where talking animals—eagles, serpents and foxes—play an important part as in our fairy tales. A semi-historical, semi-legendary myth describes the birth of Sargon I., son of an unknown father, whom his mother exposes in a basket made of reeds on the Euphrates; he is saved by a peasant and beloved of Ishtar; thanks to the goddess, he becomes king. The main features of the story resemble those of the legends of Moses and of Romulus.

11. Babylonia and Assyria had a multiplicity of gods. About 860, an Assyrian king counted more than seven thousand gods and genii. They were represented in human form, the gods appearing much more frequently than the goddesses; the king was the first of their devotees. The ritual was extremely complicated, and comprised long formulæ which had to be recited without a mistake; the sacrifices were supposed to serve as food for the gods. In Babylonia there was a powerful priesthood, masters of the secrets of magic. Attached to the various temples enriched by the devout, they formed a hereditary clergy; the young priests were brought up in schools adjoining the temples, which also possessed libraries. The military state of Assyria, on the other hand, reduced the priest to a subordinate position, or rather, made the king the chief priest, at once the temporal and the spiritual sovereign.

12. A large number of hymns have come down to us, series of incantations and of magic formulæ. Many are pen-

itential psalms; a sick or afflicted person addresses himself to the great god whom he does not name, through the intermediary of a god whom he names, confesses his sins and begs for mercy. These hymns have an incontestably moral tendency; they insist that the gods are not only angry when man treats them with disrespect, but also when he behaves ill to his fellow-man.

The incantations and exorcisms, the object of which was to cure diseases, that is to say, to put demons to flight, entailed the use of medicinal plants, of fumigations and ablutions, in which a faint glimmer of science may be distinguished amidst a mass of absurdities.

13. To Babylonian divination we also owe the first notions of anatomy. The object studied was a sheep's liver, because life seemed to dwell in the liver rather than in the brain or the heart. It was not the liver of any ordinary sheep, but that of a sheep consecrated by a long ritual; this liver, becoming sacred, offered a kind of foreshortening of the universe. A kindred sentiment led the Babylonians to ask the secrets of the future from the starry heavens; we shall see that their false science was the mother of astronomy.

14. In their calendar, the Babylonians distinguished between propitious and unpropitious, working and non-working days. Among the latter, it is believed, were the first days of every septet, to the number of four per lunar month; this constituted the Babylonian *Shabbatum*, analogous to the Biblical Sabbath, which has preserved some of the characteristics of the tabooed day, unfavourable to any enterprise, in addition to its more recent character of a day of rest.

15. The world of the dead was somewhere to the west, in a place whence no one could return; it was an immense prison surrounded by walls, shrouded in perpetual darkness, which resounded with lamentations. Allatu, the mistress of this empire, received the dead, who were completely naked. To bring them back to life, it was necessary to reach the source of life and the plant of life, which are hidden in the infernal regions. Only a few privileged mortals such as Ut-

napishtim and his wife were able to pass over the waters of death and land in the Island of the Blessed.

16. Burial seems to have been the customary rite; libations were made on the tombs, and lack of sepulture was looked upon as a dire calamity. The excavations made at Ur have recently shown that, in very old days (about 3200 B.C.), human victims accompanied kings and queens to their last resting-place.

17. In Babylonia, where the sky is very clear, the study of the stars dates from remote antiquity. Its inhabitants were persuaded that this divine society was in harmony with human society, and that the secrets of the one might be learnt from the other. Hence the false science of astrology, which, introduced into Egypt, Greece and Rome, preserved the name of Chaldæan science to the end of antiquity. Though frequently persecuted, the Chaldæans or astrologers always reappeared and even made dupes in high places. About the seventh century before Christ, astrology had acquired an accurate knowledge of the movement and occultation of the heavenly bodies: these elements of a serious science began to fructify among the Greeks from the beginning of the third century. Aristarchus of Samos and Seleucus of Babylon had more than an inkling of the system of Copernicus; they recognized that the sun is the centre of the planetary world and that the earth is a planet which travels round the sun.

18. The Babylonians distinguished seven planets as divine, and gave their names to the days of the week. As the Greeks and Romans adopted their designations, Babylonian astronomy survives in the names still in use for the days of the week in Latin countries. Again, the astrologers declared that the character of each planetary divinity sets its impress upon individuals born on the various days; thus we still speak of *lunatic*, *martial* and *jovial* temperaments, and so talk astrology without knowing it. Finally, our celestial maps show the names of animals or other objects, the Lion, the Bull, the Fishes, the Scales, under which the Babylonians grouped the constellations: "fossil remains," says Franz Cumont, "of a luxuriant mythological vegetation."

19. This installation of the celestial powers in the heavens had two consequences. First, they became the abode of deified heroes who were transformed into stars, and of the souls of the dead. The Christian conception of heaven is derived from this, for even in the Gospels, all the dead are supposed to dwell under the earth (St. Luke xvi, 22), as in the ancient Biblical doctrine. Secondly, the sun, the chief of the planetary choir, became the manifestation of the supreme God, and the result was a kind of monotheism to which the Emperor Aurelian gave his adhesion when he built the magnificent temple of the Invincible Sun at Rome; it was also the religion of the Emperor Julian.

20. By the intermediary of the Bible and Greek science, we are the heirs of the Babylonian religion; it is not wholly dead, and its most tenacious illusions have borne the fruits of truth.

III. The Phœnicians and the Syrians

1. The Phœnicians were the inhabitants of the Canaanite coast to the north of Palestine. They spoke a tongue almost identical with Hebrew. Their ports, Tyre, Sidon and Byblos, were flourishing centres as early as 1500 B.C., according to the cuneiform tablets discovered at Tell-el-Amarna in Central Egypt. Long before this remote period the coast region of Syria had felt the influence of Babylonia and Egypt. From about 1450, Phœnicia was the vassal of the Pharaohs; she regained her independence about 1000 B.C. The supremacy of the Phœnician navy, of which the foundation of Carthage (*circa* 800 B.C.) was an episode, dates from this period.

2. Phœnicia had a host of minor gods, called *el* (chief?), *baal* (in the plural *baalim*), *melek* (king), *adon* (lord). The gods of the neighbouring nations, Canaanites, Philistines, &c., bore the same Semitic titles, sometimes slightly modified. From Melek was derived the Moloch of the Bible, a term still popular, though the god was never worshipped under this name. The goddesses were called *baalat*, *milkat*, *ilât*, *ashtoreth* (the Ishtar of Babylonia, the Astarte of the Greeks).

These divinities showed themselves in high places, such as rocks and trees, in the form of hewn posts (*ashera*), animals and stones. *Bait-el*, "the abode of the god," became in Greek *bætylos*, a word which signifies upright stones analogous to our menhirs; they were generally conical in shape, as we see on the coins of Byblos.

3. A *baal* and a *baalat* formed a couple who reigned at once over heaven and earth, and fertilised the earth with the waters of heaven. Fecundity and life depended on the association of these two principles, male and female.

4. At the period on which texts begin to throw some light, the worship of animals, as of trees and stones, was a mere survival. Nevertheless, we may measure its importance by that of the sacred animals, the attributes of the gods, such as the bull, the lion, the wild boar, the eagle and the dove. A fly-god of Ekron in Philistia, Baal-zebub, has penetrated through the Bible into modern language as the famous devil Beelzebub. The *Baalim*, after having been animals, became solar deities; the goddesses were identified with the morning star and the moon.

5. The Aphrodite Urania (celestial) of the Greeks was no other than the Phœnician celestial goddess, or Astarte, held in special reverence at Carthage, where the Romans called her the Virgo Cœlestis. The lunar Tanit of Carthage, whose real name was perhaps Taint, was assimilated to the Greek Artemis, or the Diana of the Romans. The *Baalim*, among the Greeks and Romans, were generally considered local forms of Zeus or Jupiter, and, more rarely, of Poseidon or Herakles.

6. As Phœnicia never formed a political unit, there was no supreme Baal. The god of Sidon was Baal-Sidon, that of Lebanon, Baal-Lebanon, &c. Personal names of divinities are very rare: Melkart, the Baal of Tyre, assimilated by the Greeks to Herakles, was simply Melek-Kart (the king of the city); as to Eshmun, assimilated to the Greek Asklepios, his name has not yet been expounded. When a Phœnician spoke of Baal, he thought of his local deity; this is apparent in the numerous names known as *theophori* (god-bearers), in which some protecting deity is invoked, as Hannibal, "the

favour of Baal," Adonibal, "Baal is the lord." The Greeks wrongly imagined that Baal was a generic name, and adopted a god Belos, whom they identified with Zeus. The god Bel of Babylon was a Baal who had become a great god; on the other hand, in spite of assertions to the contrary, the Celtic divinity Belenus (Apollo) had nothing in common with a Baal.

7. Adonis (the lord) was a god of Byblos. The legend describes him as a young hunter beloved of Aphrodite (Astarte); he was killed in the chase by a wild boar, and bemoaned by his mistress. Every year, on the anniversary of his death, the river of Byblos was tinted red, and women bewailed the youthful hero. His body was exhibited on a bed of flowers which faded quickly, as the festival was celebrated in summer, and these flowery couches were called "the gardens of Adonis." This form of worship, which was also practised in Babylonia, passed from Phœnicia to Cyprus and thence to Greece and Rome. Although the pig was considered a sacred or unclean animal (which was originally the same thing), boars were sacrificed to Aphrodite of Cyprus in memory of Adonis. This, it was said, was to avenge the goddess; but the true explanation is a very different one. The Lord Adonis was himself originally a sacred boar, the object of worship of a clan of women, who, in order to assimilate to their god, said and believed that they were sows. Once a year, the boar was killed, torn in pieces and eaten at a communion feast; the women then bewailed Adonis, and, after a few days, celebrated his resurrection, in other words, the capture or purchase of a new sacred boar, which was their tutelary deity till the following summer. The true or sacred name of Adonis was Thamuz, the husband of the Babylonian Ishtar. This sacred name was never uttered save in the lamentations for the death of Adonis. In the reign of Tiberius, the Greek passengers of an Egyptian vessel, whose pilot happened to be called Thamus, heard voices crying in the night on the coast of Epirus: "*Thamuz, Thamuz, Thamuz, panmegas tethnéké,*" which means: "Thamuz the great is dead!" The pilot thought the voices were calling him, and announcing in this mysterious fashion the

death of the great Pan (*Pan megas*). A report of the matter was sent to Tiberius, who ordered an inquiry to be made as to the death of the god. Down to our own times it was supposed that the cries of these Syrians, lamenting the death of Adonis, were an announcement to man of the approaching end of paganism at the moment of the death of Jesus. I put forward the explanation here given in 1906.

8. The Phœnician gods, who in principle were the masters of everything, demanded the first-fruits of all produce; this is equivalent to saying that their worshippers ransomed (*desecrated*) the harvest or the spoils of war by sacrificing a part for the whole. Did the Phœnicians really preserve to historic times the dreadful custom attributed to them by the Hebrews and the Greeks of offering up their first-born to the gods? It is difficult to believe it. It may be that these sacrifices were for the most part simulacra, ritual comedies, like that described as making their children pass through the fire. When Diodorus (xx, 14) tells us that in 310 the Carthaginians placed two hundred noble children in the arms of a bronze idol, whence they were hurled into a brazier, how can we be sure that he was following a trustworthy author, or that this author understood what he had heard? Nine times out of ten, nay, I may say invariably, the ritual cruelties of a people are only attested by its enemies. It has often been said that circumcision, a rite common to the Phœnicians, the Hebrews, the Arabs and many other people (even in Oceania), proves the anterior existence of infant sacrifice, the victims being ransomed by this offering of a part of their person; but this partial sacrifice may very well have been the simulacrum of a total sacrifice which was never practised. Baptism is the simulacrum of drowning, after which the baptized person is born to a new life; but did submersion ever result in the death of the participant?

9. The dead dwelt under the earth, among the shades; we know nothing definite of the Phœnicians' ideas of a future life. Their cosmogony is equally obscure. They may perhaps have accepted a primitive being who combined the sexes, like the "bearded Venus" whose image a Roman writer noted at Cyprus; we may compare the Scriptural text, which

describes how God, creating the first woman, took a rib (or a *side*) of the first man. The Phœnician accounts of the creation transmitted to us by the Greeks imply traditions closely akin to those of Babylon. Chaos, fertilised by a divine breath, produced two principles, male and female, from which came an egg; this broke, and so constituted earth and heaven. The details are confused and contradictory.

10. In addition to the temples there were many sanctuaries, open to the sky, the "high places" of Scripture, with an altar, often of uncarved stone, surrounded by sacred stones and posts. Phœnicia had priests and priestesses; certain sacerdotal dignities were hereditary in the royal family.

∴

11. What I have said of Phœnicia makes it unnecessary for me to dwell upon Aramaic Syria, its Hinterland. It is of no particular use to know that it boasted a god *Hadad* (the bull), and a goddess *Gad*, who was assimilated by the Greeks to their goddess of Fortune, or that the worship of *Malakbel*, *Jarhibol* and *Aglibol* obtained at Palmyra. The Syrian goddess of Hierapolis, called *Atergatis* or *Derceto*, deserves greater attention, because of the detailed description which the Greek author Lucian, writing in the second century, has left of her worship. Sacred fish, only to be eaten ritually by the priests, were kept in a pond adjoining the temple; the statue of the goddess was surmounted by a dove, a sacred creature in Syria, like the pig and the fish. Atergatis was thus both fish and dove. The rites were celebrated by men dressed as women, who endeavoured thus to assimilate themselves to the goddess. This assimilation, as I have already pointed out, is the essential object of primitive worship; if its legends humanised the gods, its rites tended to deify men.

12. The worship of the Syrian goddess spread into Greece and Italy, where it was propagated by itinerant priests and beggars, by soldiers, merchants and artisans, who founded confraternities as far as Gaul. Together with the Syrian goddess, other gods of her country found devotees, especially the Baalim or Jupiters of Heliopolis and

Doliche (in Commagene). In the third century these forms of worship were favoured at Rome by the Syrian empresses, and the Emperor Heliogabalus, priest of the black stone of Emesa, introduced the worship of this fetich even in the palace of the Cæsars.

13. At Ascalon, in Philistia, Atergatis was worshipped under the form of a woman with a fish's tail; her husband Dagon was represented in a similar form. These fish-gods recall the Babylonian Oannes and the legend of Jonah. Gaza, also in Philistia, had a temple of *Marna* ("our Lord"), a god to whom supplications for rain were especially addressed, and who was traditionally identified with Zeus, "born in Crete"; this is one of the arguments adduced to establish the Cretan origin of the Philistines.

14. In the famous inscription of Mesa, king of Moab, discovered near Dhiban in 1868 and now in the Louvre, this prince (*circa* 860 B.C.) who is mentioned in the Bible, boasts of having vanquished the Israelites by the help of his god Kemosch, of whom he speaks in the same manner as the Hebrews speak of their Jahvé (Jehovah); his god is an only god, on whom his happiness or his misery depends. Thus we see that the war-god of a robber tribe may prepare the way for *monotheism*, of which *monolatry*, or the adoration of a single god, is an inferior form. A companion or consort of this Kemosch is mentioned in the same text; she is called Ashtar, a variant of the name Astarte.

BIBLIOGRAPHY

I. 1. Budge, *Gods of the Egyptians*, 2 vols., 1902; Erman, *Die ägyptische Religion*, 1905; Maspero, *Hist. anc. des peuples de l'Orient*, 3 vols., 1895-1899 (Engl. transl.); E. Naville, *La religion des Egyptiens*, 1906; Fl. Petrie, *Religion of Ancient Egypt*, 1906; A. E. Knight, *Amentet*, 1915 (an illustrated dictionary of the gods); A. Moret, *Au temps des Pharaons*, 1908; *Le Nil et la civil. égyptienne*, 1926.

4. Serapis: S. Reinach, *Cultes*, vol. ii, p. 338, and art. in Roscher's *Lexicon*.

5. Lafaye, *Culte des divinités d'Alexandrie*, 1884; Roscher, *Lexicon der Mythol.*, articles *Isis, Osiris*, &c.

7. Budge, *The Book of the Dead*, 1895 (*cf.* Maspero, *Etudes*, vol. i, p. 325).

9. Loret, *L'Egypte au temps du totémisme* (in *Conf. Guimet*, 1906, p. 151).

10. Cats: S. Reinach, *Cultes*, vol. i, p. 95.

11. Moret, *Caractère religieux de la royauté pharaonique*, 1902; *Le rituel du culte divin journalier*, 1902; *Mystères égyptiens*, 1913.

12. Frazer, *Adonis, Attis, Osiris*, 3rd ed., 1914.

13. A. J. Reinach, *L'Egypte préhistorique*, 1908; Capart, *Primitive Art in Egypt*, 1905.

II. All questions relating to the Babylonian religion are treated of in the great Biblical and theological dictionaries of Cheyne, Hastings, Hauck, Vigouroux, and also in Roscher's *Lexicon der Mythologie*.—M. Jastrow, *The Civilization of Babyl. and Assyria*, 1915; *Hebrew and Babyl. Traditions*, 1914; P. Dhorme, *Relig. assyro-babylonienne*, 1910; L. Delaporte, *La Mésopotamie*, 1905; *Cambridge Ancient History*, 1921 (in progress); Contenau, *Manuel d'archéologie orientale*, 1927.

3. Jeremias, art. *Marduk, Nebo*, &c., in Roscher's *Lexicon;* also *Rev. archéol.*, 1923, I, p. 178 (Passion of Marduk, compared with that of Osiris).—S. A. Cook, *The Laws of Moses and the Code of Hammurabi*, 1903; art. *Hammurabi* in Hastings' *Dict.*, vol. v.; Dareste, *Le Code d'Hammourabi*, in *Journal des Sav.*, 1902, pp. 517, 586; Dhorme, *Hammourabi et Amraphel*, in *Rev. bibl.*, 1908, p. 205.—For the controversy known as *Bibel und Babel*, see *Rev. archéol.*, 1903, I, p. 419.

6. P. Dhorme, *Choix de textes religieux assyro-babyloniens*, 1907.—On myths: Delitzsch, *Das babyl. Weltschöpfungsepos*, 1896; Gunkel, *Schöpfung und Chaos*, 1895; Jeremias, *Izdubar*, 1891; *Höllenfahrt der Istar*, 1886; Loisy, *Les mythes babyl. et la Genèse*, 1901; Langdon, *Le poème sumérien du Paradis, du Déluge et de la Chute*, revised French transl., 1919.

11. Fossey, *Magie assyrienne*, 1902; King, *Babylonian Magic and Sorcery*, 1895; W. Schrank, *Babyl. Sühnriten*, 1908.

13. Divination: *Rev. arch.*, 1906, ii, p. 446; 1908, ii, p. 139.

14. Sabbath: H. Webster, *Rest Days*, 1916; *Rev. Hist. Relig.*, 1928, p. 112.

16. Excavations at Ur: *Museum Journal*. 1927, p. 121 *et seq.*

17. Astrology: See article *Astrology* in Hastings' *Encycl. of Religion*, vol. ii; Cumont, *Relig. orientales dans l'Empire romain*, 1907.

III. 1.—See the articles *Phœnicia, Syria*, in Cheyne, Hastings, Hauck, as well as the articles concerning the different gods.—Lagrange, *Etudes sur les religions sémitiques*, 2nd ed., 1905 (Phœnician myths, p. 396 *et seq.*); P. Vincent, *Chanaan*, 1907; Dhorme, *Les pays bibliques au temps d'El-Amarna*, in *Rev. bibl.*, 1908, p. 500; Contenau, *La civil. phénicienne*, 1926.

2. Articles *Astarte, Baal, Moloch*, &c., in Hauck.—F. Lenormant, article *Baetylia*, in Saglio's *Dict. des antiq.*

5. On the goddess TNT (Latin inscr. at Carthage, *Taintida*): *Bull. archéol. du Comité*, 1886, p. 13.

7. The great Pan: S. Reinach, *Cultes*, t. iii, p. 1.

9. Phœnician ideas of a future life: J. Halévy, *Révue sémitique*, 1894, p. 31 *et seq.*

11. A. Dussaud, *Notes de mythol. syrienne*, 1903; article *Atergatis* in Hauck.

12. Cumont, *Les religions orientales*, 1907.

14. Article *Mesa* in the *Jewish Encyclopedia* (with facsimiles, text and translation of the inscription).

CHAPTER II

ARYANS, HINDUS AND PERSIANS

I. The Aryans and the Aryan tongues. The diffusion of the European physical type. Hindu and Persian Gods. The history of India. Animism and totemism. The migration of souls and asceticism. The worship of the dead. Cosmogonies. The Deluge. The Vedas. Vedic Sacrifice. The Vedic Gods. Ritual. Brahmans and Brahmanas. Upanishads. The laws of Manu. Philosophical systems. Jaïnism and Buddhism. The life of Buddha. The Buddhic books. Nirvâna. Buddhism and Christianity. King Asoka. Buddhist conquests in Asia. Lamaism. Hinduism. Siva and Vishnu. Reformers in India. The Sikhs. The future of Indian religions.

II. Indo-Iranian unity. Medes and Persians. The Zendavesta: Zoroaster. The Magi. Animism. The worship of animals and plants. The conflict of good and evil. Insistence on ritual purity. Belief in a future life. The weighing of souls. Fire-worship. The main features of Mazdeism. Mithra and the spread of Mithraism in the Roman Empire. Analogies with Christianity. Manicheeism. The Mandæans.

I. The Aryans and the Hindus

1. Arya, which means "noble," is the name by which the Iranians and Hindus distinguished themselves from the indigenous races they subdued. The languages of Iranians and Hindus, old Persian and Sanscrit, are akin to those of the Slavs, the Germans, the Greeks, the Italians, the Celts, just as Italian, French and Spanish are akin. As the inter-relation of these three tongues is explained by their common derivation from Latin, it has been supposed that the affinities of the first named are due to the existence of a lost language called Indo-European, and (incorrectly) Aryan. This is a legitimate conclusion; but that which postulates an Aryan race is the less so, inasmuch as there was no Latin or Roman race, but merely a political aggregation of nations who spoke and diffused the Latin language.

2. Scholars used formerly to seek the source of the Indo-European tongues in Central Asia; it now seems probable that it must be located in Europe, somewhere in the vicinity of the Baltic. In Northern Europe, the men who speak the

THE RITUAL OF THE VEDIC GODS

Indo-European languages are still for the most part tall and fair; now this type is also to be found, at least in the martial aristocracy, in those regions where the Indo-European languages were originally spoken. The Indian Arya, in the most ancient texts, boasts of being fair and of having handsome features; the natives, whom he calls Dasyus (enemies), had sun-burnt skins and flat faces. Thus, in India as in Persia, we may assume the invasion of a North-European type, which found its way into these countries together with the Indo-European languages, and gradually mingled with the pre-existent indigenous element, without becoming completely merged.

3. The name of heaven, and by expansion that of the lord of heaven, *Dyaus pitar* (Sanscrit), *Zeus pater* (Greek), *Jupiter* (Latin), is found in several Indo-European languages; but only the Iranians and the Hindus, who were still united about 1400 B.C.,[1] give a common name to several gods: Indra, Mithra, the Asuras, the Devas, and also to a sacred plant, *somâ* (Sanscrit), *haoma* (Iranian). We must accordingly admit that the Hindus and Iranians had common rudiments of mythology, but we lack elements sufficient to enable us to speak of an Indo-European mythology or religion.

4. Our knowledge of the religions of India is founded on a large number of books in prose and verse written in Sanscrit, Pâli, Prâcrit, Thibetan, Chinese, &c. The chronology of these texts is very uncertain, and the most ancient in date are far from revealing a corresponding antiquity of ideas; this applies more especially to the Vedic and Brahmanic books, the works of the priests who, like the Hebrew prophets, borrowed from popular conceptions only those elements which agreed with their doctrines and their designs. It may even be said that the religious literature of India shows a progressive accretion of the most ancient popular ideas in the philosophic and religious systems. These ideas are revealed to us more especially by the Hindu literature of a late period, and also by the accounts of modern travellers, who have studied Hindu customs and superstitions.

5. The most important religious texts are the hymns

[1] See below, The Persians, §1.

known as *Vedas*, with the commentaries known as *Brahmanas*, the so-called Laws of the Manu, the theological manuals known as *Sûtras* and *Upanishads*, the Buddhist books, the great epics, and the *Pûranas* or collections of legends. In this brief summary, I shall use Hindu words as little as possible, and I shall only speak of the original texts when strictly necessary.

6. The only dates that can be accepted as more or less incontestable in the history of India are furnished by the alien races which have been in contact with her. The Hindus possess hardly any historical literature. They incline to live in an atmosphere of dreams. Their art, like their poetry and their philosophy, works in a domain of exuberant fancy, comparable to the vegetation of their tropical land. Thought is smothered, as it were, by the world, and is indistinguishable from it; hence the pantheistic tendency of all their systems. India has been inhabited by races of widely different origin, but all have rapidly acquired kindred characteristics, as a result, it would seem, of climate and surroundings.

7. It will be useful to remember the following dates:

B.C. 1500–1000.	The Aryas in the Punjaub.
520– 440.	Buddha.
327– 325.	Alexander the Great in India.
300.	Megasthenes at the Court of Palibothra (Patna).
264– 227.	Asoka, the Constantine of Buddhism.
120.	Scythian and Tartar hordes establish themselves in Bactriana.
A.D. First cent.	Kanishka, a Scythian king, embraces Buddhism, which also spreads to China.
535.	The Huns in Northern India.
629– 645.	The Chinese pilgrim Hiuen-Tsang visits India.
711.	Beginning of the Arab conquest.
1398.	Tamerlane's invasion.
1527.	Baber founds the Mogul Empire, which lasted till 1857.
1672.	The French at Pondicherry.
1757.	Beginning of the English conquest.
1857.	The Indian Mutiny.
1858.	India attached to the British Crown.
1877.	Queen Victoria proclaimed Empress of India.

8. Every superstition reigns or has reigned in India. Animism manifests itself in ancestor-worship, in the adoration of the heavenly bodies, mountains, rivers—the Ganges in particular—trees, plants, shells, stones, implements, &c. Totemism has left its traces not only in certain alimentary restrictions—the cow—but in the widespread worship of a host of deities in animal form—such as the elephant-headed Ganesha—in the myths of creation and the deluge. Even in the present day certain tribes, whose languages are non-Aryan, are divided into clans distinguished by the names of animals, within the limits of which inter-marriage is forbidden. There were formerly in the Brahmanical caste, certain classes where union was forbidden, which may indicate a totemistic survival. Magic, the basis of all ritual, has not ceased to flourish in India. These are characteristics common to all primitive civilisations. But there are in India two popular conceptions, related by a logical bond, which are nowhere else to be found in such a highly developed form. They are the belief in the *transmigration of souls* and a *redeeming asceticism*.

9. The idea of the transmigration of souls corresponds to the metempsychosis of the Greek Pythagoreans. Like totemism, it is the product of an exaggeration of the social instinct; the Hindu feels himself at one with all about him; he thinks that his soul, before animating his body, may have existed in beings of every kind, organic and even inorganic, and believes that, after his death, it will pass into a great variety of bodies. This incessant transmigration of souls (*samsâra*) is what the Greek Orphics called "the circle of birth" (*kyklos tês généséôs*). The Hindu, very susceptible to the miseries of life, and enervated by a climate which is either damp or scorching, yearns for immunity from this fatal law which condemns him to ceaseless activity; hence the second widespread belief in the efficacy of asceticism, of silent contemplation and of ecstasy. By reducing as far as possible his material life, his pleasures, his very thoughts, the Hindu hopes to destroy the principle of action which manifests itself in the infinite series of reincarnations (*karman*). Asceticism (*tapas*) appears even in the Vedas; and if the

doctrine of metempsychosis is not to be found in them, this is perhaps because it was originally that of the natives rather than of their European conquerors.

10. Together with the widely diffused beliefs in the transmigration of souls, ideas very closely resembling those of the Greeks and Romans are to be found in India; the souls of ancestors (*pitris*) inhabit heaven, with the first man (*Yama*); they remain in communion with mortals, and come to take part in sacrifices, and in the meals offered to them; oblations (*srâddhas*) are a sacred obligation which no son may neglect. This belief was held by the invaders, and no doubt also by some of the natives, who built great stone tombs analogous to our dolmens in honour of their dead. The rite of inhumation soon made way for that of cremation, the apparent object of which was to facilitate the ascent of souls to heaven; the primary cause, however, was rather the desire to annihilate the body, which was considered dangerous, or, in other words, the dread of ghosts. The funeral rites were prolonged for a year, in order to appease the soul of the dead, who is supposed to hover round the living till the end of this period, when he takes up his abode in heaven. The idea of a hell for delinquents only appears in a very definite form in the religions known as Hinduistic; but traces of the belief are to be found in the Vedas.

11. The custom of Suttee, which obliged a widow to burn herself on her husband's tomb, and was only abolished by the English in 1829, seems to be of great antiquity, though there is no mention of it in the Vedas.

12. Hindu legends concerning the origin of the world and of man are numerous and confused. Some are mystical, such as that which represents things as produced by primitive Unity, divided by the force of Desire; many are puerile and extravagant. A giant was supposed to have been sacrificed by the gods, and all living creatures issued from his severed limbs; the same idea is found among the Scandinavians and the Iroquois; some Redskins substitute a dog for the giant of this legend. The primitive soul of the world became dual in the forms of a man and a woman, then in a bull and a

cow, then in a horse and a mare, and so on, to produce the various species, "down to the ant." The god Brahma fished the world up out of the waters, by the help of a boar, a fish, and a tortoise; he created the other gods one by one, then man, and finally the remaining creatures. All nature came out of a golden egg, which produced the first man, who created the gods by his word. The simplest version, which is common to many nations, speaks of the primitive marriage of heaven and earth, *Dyaus* and *Prithivi.*

13. India has her story of the Deluge: Manu, the Hindu Noah, was saved by the god Vishnu, who, in the form of a fish, dragged Manu's vessel to the top of the rock. This legend is perhaps of Babylonian origin. The fish-Vishnu recalls the Babylonian god Oannês.

14. The texts called Vedas (from *vid*, to know) are collections of hymns and prayers constituting a sacrificial ritual, which were attributed to ancient poets divinely inspired (the *Rishis*). The earliest is the *Rig-Vedâ* (Veda of praise); the most recent the *Atharvaveda* (from the name of a mythic family of priests, the Atharvans). In this collection, magic plays an important part, but the main substance was already familiar to the poets of the Rig. The first collection of the Vedas dates approximately from between 1500 and 1000 B.C. They were composed for the Aryan invaders, who were still in the north-west of India, but who were already moving towards the valley of the Ganges, in spite of the opposition of the natives with whom they were warring. The civilisation to which the poems bear witness is fairly advanced; it embraced domesticated animals, chariots, and bronze weapons, but there were no temples at this period. The occupations were more especially martial and agricultural; wealth was already very unequally distributed. The priests, who were exclusively entrusted with the rites of sacrifice, were recompensed by the faithful; the princes had priests attached to their service, who often treated their masters with some arrogance. Below the priests and warriors were the workers or agriculturists, who were naturally of more consideration than the natives. Thus we have the rudiments of the four castes, the Brahmans, the

Kshatriyas, the Vaisyas and the Sudras, who have subsisted in India to our own times.

15. One of the characteristics of the Vedic sacrifice is the vast magical efficacy attributed to it. By virtue of its own powers, and of the words which accompanied it, it claimed to exercise control over the good genii of nature, and over the gods. These were supposed not only to participate in it but to draw from it forces indispensable to their beneficent action; thus the yellow juice of the *sôma*, a medicinal plant, poured out in libation was looked upon as a terrestrial fire which revived the fire of heaven. All that passes on earth was held to have its echo in heaven; and the visible and the invisible world alike were deemed subject to the magic of sacrifice and incantation.

16. The natural forces which were to be conciliated or controlled by these means were personified under divine names. The Vedic gods are somewhat vaguely outlined; they were not a hierarchy, like those of the Greek Pantheon, but rather a divine confraternity. They were thirty-three in number, and divided into three groups of eleven; they dominated the heavens, the earth, and the intermediate regions respectively. The god most frequently invoked was Fire, *Agni*, assimilated of course to the sun; then *Indra*, the martial god of heaven, who killed the serpent *Ahi* or *Vritra*, and liberated the waters which Ahi kept imprisoned in mountains or clouds. *Dyaus pater*, the old god of heaven, *Prithivi*, the earth, *Brahma* and *Vishnu*, the great gods of Hinduism, play but a secondary part here. *Varuna*, a celestial and perhaps lunar god, was the guardian of cosmic and of moral order. *Rudra*, whose arrows let loose pestilence, was the father of the *Maruts* or genii of the wind. *Ushas* was the Dawn. The two *Asvins* are heroes analogous to the Greek Dioscuri, who have been identified with the morning and evening star.

17. The sacrifice *par excellence* was that of the horse, which was probably considered an auxiliary of celestial fire. The traces of human sacrifice supposed to have been discovered are very dubious. In general, the Vedic ritual is mild in character; moral ideas, ideas of sin and repentance, begin to

find expression. Nevertheless, the essential object of prayer was to obtain terrestrial benefits: rain, sunshine, health. The grosser magical or naturalistic elements have been left in the shade by the Rishis, or rather by the priests to whom we owe the existing text of the Vedas. The primitive religious basis is everywhere veiled by a ritualism on its way to evolution towards a mystic pantheism. Philosophic speculation is not lacking: Whence came the world? Was it created or uncreated? He alone knows who sees all things, and perhaps even he does not know. There were already sceptics, men who denied Indra because he was invisible.[1]

18. Scholars, especially since the time of Bergaigne, have ceased to hold up the Vedas to admiration as the first hymns of humanity, or of "the Aryan race," in the presence of the splendours and terrors of nature. They are, in fact, learned sacerdotal poems, deliberately complex and obscure, because the priests who lived by the altar were determined to preserve their monopoly; to speak frankly, a good deal of the Vedas is pure nonsense. Indian specialists know this, and privately admit it.

19. The *Brahmanas*, a prose explanation of the ritual, are the work of Brahmans grouped into a caste, the successors of the Vedic priests. They are commentaries on the Vedas considered as sublime and infallible scriptures, but the Brahmans actually understood them much more imperfectly than we do. We find in them certain legends which are absent in the Vedas, such, for instance, as the story of the Deluge. The importance of sacrifice is more strongly insisted upon; it is represented not only as fortifying but as creating gods. The Brahmans are supposed to possess *brahma*, the magic principle which gives them power over spirits; the honours they claim for themselves are quasi-divine: "There are two kinds of gods; first, the gods, and then the Brahmans who have learnt the Vedas and can repeat them." The four social classes are constituted, though the division is not as yet marked by that intolerant rigour which it assumes in the law of Manu. Between the Brahmans

[1] Bergaigne, *Religion Védique*, vol. ii, p. 167.

and the warriors a rivalry is indicated, from which great heresies were to spring at a later period.

20. The *Upanishads* ("sessions"), which originally formed a part of the *Brahmanas*, are the oldest theosophical speculations based upon the Vedas, which were accepted as divine from beginning to end. The *Upanishads*, over 200 in number, have remained the source of all the intellectual movements in India, even in the present day.

21. The same faith in the infallibility of the Vedas "the root of the law, the imperishable eye, the support of all created things," manifests itself in the so-called code of Manu, a compendium of the common law of Northern India, formulated in verse after the Christian era. These laws insist upon duties to the dead, and upon future sanctions to result from the transmigration of souls; the good are to rise in the scale of being, while the wicked are to be abased. A virtuous man, for instance, will be born again into the Brahman caste; a stealer of corn will become a rat.

22. Two other philosophic systems which have exercised great influence on Indian thought are related to Brahmanism. The *Vedânta* (the completion of the Veda), systematised in the eighth century after Christ by Sankara, affirms the identity of the individual soul with the universal soul; the external world is but an illusion (*mâyâ*); the aim of life is not virtue but knowledge, for only knowledge can raise man to the divine spirit. The antithesis of this pantheism is found in the realism of the school known as Sânkhya, founded, it is said, by Kapila, which recognises the plurality of individuals and the existence of matter as well as of spirit. When this latter understands its essence, it can disengage itself from matter and fulfil its destiny. There is no longer any question of gods; but as the Sânkhya accepted the infallible authority of the Vedas, its atheism was considered inoffensive by the Brahmans.

23. Two reformers of unequal celebrity rose from the warrior class in the sixth century before Christ: Mahâvîra, the founder of Jainism (*jina* = "conqueror") and Gautama, the founder of Buddhism (*buddha* = "the awakened"). Mahâvîra was the earlier of the two, but he seems to have been

living still at the time of the preaching of Buddha. The two doctrines are very much alike, because both are hostile to Brahmanical ritualism and both are inspired by the popular theory of transmigration. The most important difference is that Jainism gives great prominence to asceticism and severity towards oneself, whereas the religion of Buddha is all gentleness. There are still Jains in the west of India; but Buddhism is now confined to Ceylon. I propose only to examine Buddhism here, but I may make one important observation upon the art of Jainism. The Jains are the only Hindus who represent absolutely nude men in sculpture. These were the Jain saints. Now there is not the slightest doubt that the model which suggested all these images was a Greek statue of the type known as the archaic Apollo, dating from about 520 B.C. One of these statues must have come from Ionia into India and have been indefinitely imitated there. Other indications seem to point to somewhat close relations between Ionia and India, and the Greeks were always known in India as *Yavanas* (*Ionians*); now it is just at this period that a legend, which may not be altogether negligible, declares Pythagoras to have travelled to India.

24. Although the very existence of Gautama, called Buddha Sakyamuni, has been questioned by Indian scholars of authority, there would seem to be some foundation for the traditions of his life that have survived. But it must be noted, before going further, that the sacred writings of Buddhism, which are far more voluminous than our Bible, do not contain a line which can be safely attributed to Buddha himself or even to one of his immediate disciples. The Buddhists indeed assert that immediately after his death a council of five hundred devotees was assembled, at which the teachings of Buddha were sung in chorus; but this council was a myth, as was also another, supposed to have been held a hundred years later. On the other hand, history records the council of 244 B.C., convened by King Asoka, the Constantine of India, who became a convert to Buddhism, and peaceably pursued its diffusion; we possess numerous inscriptions of this period, lapidary sermons, which afford a very solid foothold. Taking into account the

tenacious memories of the Hindus, and their habit of assimilating very long texts (there are still Brahmans who can recite the whole of the Vedas without understanding them), it seems highly probable that the Buddhist books have preserved some authentic aspects of the life and teachings of the founder.

25. The son of a king or rather of a warrior, Gautama was born about 520 B.C., at Kapilavastu, a hundred miles to the north of Benares. He belonged perhaps to one of those Scythian tribes which were perpetually descending into India from the north-west. An inscription by Asoka has been found in our own days in Nepaul, at the foot of the Himalayas, in which he records his pilgrimage to Lumbini, the birthplace of Buddha.

26. Gautama, who was addicted to the pleasures of his rank and age until his twenty-ninth year, suddenly abandoned them after contemplating three manifestations of human misery: an impotent old man, a forsaken sufferer, and a corpse. In vain the Tempter appeared and offered him the sovereignty of the world if he would renounce his vocation; abandoning all, even his wife and his young son, he became a mendicant monk, and for half a century wandered in Northern India, preaching and recruiting disciples.[1] The partial authenticity at least of a fine sermon he preached at Benares is generally admitted. He died at the age of 80 of an indigestion caused by a meal of rice and pork; his body was burnt, and his relics, divided among his disciples, were dispersed in all quarters by their means. The date of his death may be approximately fixed at 440 B.C. by various testimonies combined with the known chronology of Asoka: this reduces uncertainty to a term of some twenty or thirty years, more or less.

27. At the time of Gautama's appearance, Northern India was subjected to the dual tyranny of Brahmanical formalism and of the caste system. The country was under the rule of petty princes whose rivalries were of advantage to the priests. Certain warriors, unable to enter the caste

[1] The analogy of this with the legend of St. Francis cannot be denied; see below, p. 307.

of the Brahmans, became monks or ascetics, and sought thus to gain the veneration of the people. Gautama was one of these. The schism he created was essentially anti-clerical and anti-ritualist; he repudiated a priesthood, because each man must work out his own salvation, and sacrifices, because there are no gods to whom to offer them. The Brahmans, whose interests were thus attacked, persecuted and even tried to assassinate him. If Buddha did not expressly condemn the caste system, he implicitly abolished it by opening the ranks of his confraternity to all men without distinction of birth. His religion, like the Christianity of St. Paul, was universalist.

28. The idea which dominates it was not a new one; it was that of the old Hindu asceticism. Life is suffering, divided into existences past and future which were and will be full of sadness. Suicide cannot deliver us, for it does not prevent reincarnation. What is necessary is to kill the desire to live by renunciation; those who kill it completely will not live again; those who only partially suppress it will be born again under a less material form in which they may make fresh efforts to escape another birth. The self-inflicted tortures of the ascetics are unnecessary; it is enough to reduce all that binds us to life to a minimum. Virtue and charity towards men and animals are not in themselves excellent, but are forms of self-renunciation; they must therefore be practised unceasingly, for liberation is one of the fruits of love. When all desire to live is exhausted, man enters into *nirvâna;* he may, like Buddha himself, do so in his lifetime; so *nirvâna* is not physical death; it is absolute detachment, death in life, non-existence.

29. The calling of mendicant monk is best calculated to achieve this ideal; but a layman full of faith and charity (especially towards monks) is in the "way of salvation." He may, unlike the monks, take a wife, and possess goods, which is forbidden in their case; he must not kill (either man or animal), he must not steal, he must not lie, he must not commit any impurity, he must not drink wine. Thus self-control and charity are the keystones of the Buddhistic edifice.

30. Gautama, like Pythagoras, claimed to remember his former incarnations, and he recounted them to his disciples under the form of edifying stories and fables. These are the *Jâtakas* (stories of birth) which have been called "the epic of transmigration." They contain many charming and touching things, an exposition by images of that human fraternity, that solidarity of the universe which Hindu genius felt by instinct, greatly to its honour.[1]

31. The analogy between Buddhism and Christianity has given rise to overbold speculation. It is twofold, bearing on certain legends and on the doctrine: the miraculous birth of Buddha, the saintly old man and the pilgrims who came from afar to salute him in his cradle, the story of the Saint's temptation (§ 26) suggest comparisons which, after all, can be explained as folklore, the Indian stories being no doubt the older. On the other hand, Christianity appropriated the legend of Buddha in the devotional tale of the Christian monk Barlaam, who converted the son of King Josaphat in India (6th century?). As to the affinity of doctrine, more striking than that of the legends, there is just a possibility of some Buddhistic influence on Hellenistic and Essenian circles, King Asoka claiming, about 250 B.C., to have sent missionaries to the Greek kings his neighbours, in Egypt and Syria. Truly, we hear nothing further about him; but it may be accidental that the first mention of Buddha in a Greek text (Clement of Alexandria) occurs two centuries after the Christian era.

32. The communities of men and women founded by Gautama multiplied rapidly and received great domains which they owned in common. The afflux of new-comers, often persons of doubtful character, necessitated the creation of a hierarchy, and the formulation of a severe rule, which was observed more or less; at the same time the veneration for the relics of Buddha and later for his images, for which innumerable monuments (*stûpas*) were erected, opened the door to idolatry and to a new ritualism.

33. The most important event in the history of this religion was the conversion of the wise king Asoka (264-227

[1] S. Lévi, *Conférences du Musée Guimet,* 1906, p. 13 *et seq.*

B.C.), whose son and daughter introduced Buddhism into Ceylon, where it has been preserved in relative purity. In India proper, it degenerated very quickly; a school known as that of "the Great Vehicle" introduced a sterile asceticism and a charlatan magic (*yogi* and *tantra*). Sectarian disputes and the tenacious hostility of the Brahmans aggravated the evil. It was in vain that Buddhism found a new protector in the first century after Christ in the Scythian king Kanishka, whose coins, which reveal Greek influences, are the first to bear the image of Buddha. About A.D. 630, when the Chinese pilgrim Hiuen-Tsang visited India, he found Buddhism in absolute decadence. Inscriptions attest that it survived till the thirteenth century; but for causes as yet obscure, it died out at the fountain-head.

34. Beyond India, its success had been extraordinary. At about the dawn of the Christian era, it passed into Kashmir, then into Nepaul, Thibet and China, Burmah and Siam (650), and now reckons some 500 millions of adherents. Ceylon, Siam and Burmah constitute the southern group; Nepaul, Thibet, China and Japan the northern.

35. Everywhere, as it has acquired power, Buddhism has been corrupted by the inevitable assimilation of indigenous belief, first consummated in India, and by the cupidity and charlatanry of its monks. Relatively faithful to its precepts in China, where the civil law wisely limited the multiplication of convents, and where Confucianism gave a predominating influence to ancestor-worship, Buddhism has imposed on Thibet a monstrous theocracy, which resists all progress and opposes the penetration of any European ideas. This form of Buddhism is known as Lamaism (*lama*, the superior), so called from the popes or *Lamas* who control innumerable convents, and indeed the whole country. The primitive religion of Thibet was extremely gross, and was characterised by totemist conceptions such as that of the Heaven-god astride a dog, the ape venerated as an ancestor, the sacred dogs kept in the monasteries to devour the dead, with an amazing development of the lowest kind of sorcery. The form of Buddhism introduced in 650 was already infected with magic and with ascetic practices.

Lamaism differs from Buddhism more particularly by a belief in the permanent incarnation of celestial Buddhas in the two Lamas; when one of these popes is about to die, a child, to be born nine months afterwards, is designated by lot to succeed to his dignity. In the nineteenth century, the Chinese government substituted its selection for the choice by lot; but neither the suzerainty of China, nor the English expedition to Lhassa in 1904, has affected the extravagances of Lamaism. It has often been said that Lamaism, with its shaven priests, its bells, its rosaries, its prayer-mills, its idols, its holy water, its popes and bishops, its abbots and monks, its processions and festivals, its confessionals, its Purgatory, its Hell, is a caricature of Romanism.

36. The Buddhist literature of Thibet comprises two immense collections, the *Kandjour* and the *Tándjour*, one consisting of 108, the other of 225 folio volumes. Some great libraries possess copies, and long extracts from these have been translated; they are mostly ancient versions of Sanscrit books.

37. If in the religious history of India, Buddhism marks the introduction of the popular belief in the transmigration of souls, the confused group of sects known as Hinduism connotes that of polytheism and popular magic, the imperfectly developed beliefs of the native population, superficially converted to Brahmanism. It is probable that the Brahmans entered into an alliance with these degraded forms of worship, out of hatred to the Buddhists, on the sole condition that their authority should be recognised.

38. It is generally but superficially believed that Hinduism is essentially the worship of the *Trimourti* or Trinity, consisting of Brahma, the creative spirit, Vishnu and Siva, the former rather of a creator, the latter a destructive god. As a fact, this trinity is held in small esteem in India, where Brahma, an abstract deity, has never been popular. Siva and Vishnu, however, are mighty divinities, celebrated in the Hindu epics of the middle ages, the *Mahâbhârata* and the *Râmâyana*, as well as in the chaotic literature of the *Purânas* ("antiquities"), which describe the various transformations or *avatars*) of Vishnu into animals, and thousands of other

things. Siva, "the merciful," is an epithet euphemistically applied to the redoubtable Rudra of the Vedas. In spite of his name, he appears as a terrible god, entwined with serpents, his neck adorned with a necklace of skulls, and having a third eye in his forehead like the Greek Cyclops. His wives are *Kâli* (the black), *Durgâ* (the inaccessible), *Parvati* (the daughter of the mountain), who are in turns amorous and bloodthirsty. He himself is at once creator and destroyer, now carried away by sensual passion, now plunged in the practices of asceticism. Bulls are sacred to him, and these peripatetic idols wander freely through the streets of cities. The Greek Megasthenes, ambassador from Seleucus Nicanor to Palibothra, about 300 B.C. stated that the Hindus worshipped Dionysos and Herakles. Dionysos was Siva, whose worship was orgiastic. The Herakles of Megasthenes was Krishna, the slayer of monsters, the incarnation or *avatar* of Vishnu. The latter, who is sometimes mentioned in the Vedas, is not only incarnated in Krishna, but also in Râma, the hero of the *Râmâyana.* Sîtâ, the wife of Krishna, was carried off by Râvana, the prince of the demons, and taken to Ceylon. Râma rescued her, thanks to his alliance with the ape Hanuman and the army of monkeys commanded by him. Hanuman is a very popular deity in the India of the present day; Râma is even more so.

39. Vishnuism, in its very inception, was more austere than Sivaism; but Love (*bhakti*) was incorporated in Lakhsmî, the wife of Vishnu, and the result was a development of sensual mysticism which has enervated and degraded Vishnuism.

40. Hinduism has divided itself into innumerable sects, and peopled its structure with such a horde of gods, goddesses and demons that it resembles a tropical forest. The worship consists in a veneration, too often extravagant, of fetiches and idols, accompanied by the ringing of bells, illuminations, and the strewing of flowers; the music howls or sighs, the bayadères dance, heads are turned, and not even the horrible tortures of the Hindu hell suffice to inspire the faithful with any respect for ordinary morality.

41. A favourite place of pilgrimage is Benares, "the lotus

of the world," with its two thousand temples; another is the sanctuary of Vishnu at Jagannath (Orissa), where a hundred thousand devotees assemble to witness the progress of the idol on his car, and where many were believed to hurl themselves under the wheels. The custom of bathing in multitudes in the sacred waters of the Ganges, which are often infected with cholera germs, is a superstition which tends to propagate this scourge in India; this, and the Musulman pilgrimages to Mecca, are a perpetual menace of contagion for civilised countries.

42. There has, happily, been no lack of reformers to combat these degrading and belated creeds. As early as the fifteenth century, a simple weaver, Kabir, taught belief in one god, who demanded, not sacrifices, but truth and purity. The Great Mogul, Akbar (1556-1605), who was a Musulman, attempted to fuse the religions of India, Christianity and Judaism among them, into a monotheism more philosophical than religious. The most interesting of these attempts was made by a Lahore merchant called Nânak, born in 1465, who founded the sect of Sikhs (disciples), on the basis of a monotheism inspired by the Koran, although he rejected the authority both of the Koran and of the Vedas. His successors gave the sect a military organisation, a novelty in India, and one in which the imitation of Islam is apparent. Long conflicts with the Musulmans taught martial ardour to the Sikhs, who had a king at Lahore from 1800 to 1839. In 1849, after a disastrous war, they submitted to the English, who admitted them into the ranks of the British army; but they remain sectaries, and make pilgrimages to the temple of Amritsar, where their sacred book is preserved.

43. If Nânak's reform was due to contact with the Musulmans, that of Rammohun Roy, the scion of a family of Bengali Brahmans, betrays the influence of Protestantism. Establishing himself at Calcutta, Rammohun learned foreign tongues, even Greek and Hebrew, and made an attempt to reconcile Hinduism and Christianity in a broad monotheistic synthesis. Dying prematurely at Bristol, in the course of an almost triumphal progress in the British Isles, he had

various successors, one of whom, Keshab Chander Sen, was the friend of the learned Indian scholar of Oxford, Max Müller, and preached with some success in London. Rabindranath Tagore (born 1861), the founder of the "Abode of Peace" at Bolpur, is a poet belonging to the same school. But these unitarian tendencies have only resulted in the rise of new sects; the attitude to be adopted towards the Vedas, and above all the question of caste, continue to be stones of stumbling.

What has the future in store for India? "The religion of the Hindus," wrote Max Müller in 1858, "is a decrepit creed which has but a few more years to live." That was a mistake. India will not become Christian; nor will she accept Mahometanism, though Islam reckons sixty million adherents there as against two hundred and ten millions of Hindus and two and a half millions of Christians. The moral and intellectual regeneration of this great country depends on the elementary schools, which, while inspiring respect for a venerable past, will teach to all the idea of evolution, a more scientific one than that of metempsychosis, and will gradually raise them to the level of cultured Europeans, to whom the religion of social duty is all-sufficient.

II. The Persians and Iranians

1. A cuneiform text, discovered in the centre of Asia Minor, at Pterium, tells us that about fourteen hundred years before Christ, certain tribes, which were in relation with the Hittite Empire, had for their gods Mithra, Indra, Varuna and the Nasâtyâs. The first two names are found both in India and Persia, the last two are peculiar to India. This seems to indicate that at this period the ancestors of the Hindus and Iranians were not yet separated. Why did they separate? It may perhaps have been, as used to be supposed long ago, in consequence of a religious schism, for the word *deva*, applied to the gods in India, is the designation of the demons in Iran, whereas *asura*, the title of the beneficent gods in Persia, is that of the demons in India.

2. Iran—modern Persia—was inhabited, about 800 B.C.,

in the north by the Medes, near relations of the Scythians, in the south by the Persians. About 600 B.C. the Medes made considerable conquests, but they were subjugated in 560 B.C. by the Persian king Cyrus, who founded a vast Asiatic Empire. When Cambyses, the son of Cyrus, was engaged in the conquest of Egypt, the Median priests, called *Magi*, attempted to regain the supreme power; but the Persian Darius, the son of Hystaspes, dethroned their creature, the false Smerdis, and re-established the kingdom of Cyrus on behalf of the Persians (523 B.C.). The Persian Empire was in its turn destroyed by Alexander, and passed under the domination of the Seleucidæ, the descendants of a Macedonian general; it was conquered in 256 B.C. by the Arsacidian Parthians; then, in the year 226 of our era, the Persian element once more got the upper hand and founded the Sassanide Empire, which the Arabs destroyed in A.D. 652.

3. The most ancient collection of the sacred books of Persia is called the *Zendavesta* (commentary of the revelation), only a portion of which has been preserved. There are more recent ones, such as the *Bundehesh* (first creation), written after the Arab conquest, and others still more recent, such as the epic of Firdaûzi, the *Shah Nameh* (Book of Kings), a vast collection of all the Iranian legends.

4. The *Zendavesta* is a compilation of documents dating from various periods, transcribed at the time of the Sassanide Renaissance (about A.D. 230). It is admitted that the sacrificial hymns called *Gâthâs* (songs) are by far the most ancient, and the sacerdotal code called *Vendidad* (given against the demons), the most recent.

5. The name of Zarathustra (Zoroaster), the religious law-giver of Iran, is attached to the *Avesta*. We know nothing definite about his life; his very existence has been called in question, like that of Moses and of Buddha. According to the sacred legend, he was brought by angels before Ahura Mazda (the great Lord of Wisdom), who conversed with him at length and revealed his laws to him. Hence the name of Zoroastrianism given to the religion of the *Avesta*. Those who consider Zoroaster a historical personage describe him as a Mede or a Bactrian, who, about

700 B.C., founded a religion which was adopted by the Persians. It is certain that Cyrus conformed to a prescription of the *Avesta* relative to the purity of water, when he turned aside the course of the Gyndanês to find the corpse of a horse which had been drowned, also that Darius I. in his inscriptions invoked Ormazd (Ahura Mazda), who is the great god of the *Avesta*.

6. If we accept this hypothesis, we cannot but feel some surprise to find that the *Avesta* never mentions the Magi; it calls the priests by a more ancient name, Athravans (priests of fire). This may be a deliberate archaism; or it may be that the name Magi was avoided because of the unpleasant memories left by their rebellion under Cambyses (*cf.* § 2).

7. These priests of the *Avesta* formed a hereditary caste, the members of which were alone competent to offer sacrifices or perform the rites of purification; the priest was born, not made. They lived on the proceeds of their ritual, which were strictly defined by law, and also on the numerous fines they exacted in return for indulgences. They were, in short, a regular clergy.

8. A study of the *Avesta* shows that the volume contains elements of widely divergent dates, some very primitive, others relatively modern. Animism is very strongly developed; the whole world is represented as peopled by demons, some good, others bad; the elements, animals, plants, even the utensils used in worship are personified. The souls of the dead are looked upon as the protectors of the living, their guardian angels (*Fravashis*). Totemism has left obvious traces in the sacred character attributed to certain plants, the bull, the cow, the horse, the dog, the serpent. The taboos are innumerable and the purifications by which they are removed hold a preponderant place in the ritual. The form of worship is impregnated with magic; the sacred plant gathered upon Mount Elbrouz furnished the divine drink, the sacrificial liquid *par excellence* (*haoma*, in Sanscrit *sôma*). The priests operated with bundles of magic wands called *baresmân*, which were gathered with certain rites, as was the mistletoe by the Celts; a magic power was attributed to the eye of the dog, and the urine of the ox.

On the other hand, many of the divinities have an abstract character which seems to indicate a long religious evolution; evidences of morality, of a desire for progress, even of hygiene, are to be traced in the taboos; in certain prescriptions, the magic germs of impurity have become the principles of contagion. Science secularises everything, even microbes; there is a germ of this tendency in the *Avesta.*

9. The dominant idea is the conflict of good and evil. The god of goodness, Ahura Mazda, or Ormazd, created the world; but each of his benefits was counterbalanced by a maleficent deed on the part of Ahriman, or Angra Mainyu, "the spirit who destroys." This state of things has existed and will exist for many centuries. Ahura Mazda is mighty, but his power is not infinite; in his struggle against Ahriman and the myriads of evil genii (*Devas, Drujs*), he is supported by good genii, and by archangels (*Ameshas spentas*, beneficent immortals); one of them, Sraosha, is the judge of souls in the journey beyond the tomb. Just as all evil actions, all impurity are an assistance to Ahriman provided by humanity; so every virtuous life furthers the cause of Ahura Mazda, whose powers are also increased by the prayers and sacrifices of men. The consequence of this dualism is not only, in practice, ritual exactitude and purity—the greatest good of man, after his birth, says the *Vendidad*—but active virtue, veracity, courage, charity (even towards animals), humility. To plough a field, to make a canal, to build a bridge, to destroy noxious creatures such as ants and frogs, is to serve the cause of the good god; a well-filled life is a perpetual exorcism. At the end of the centuries, Ahura Mazda will engage in a decisive struggle with Ahriman, and will conquer, by the help of the archangel *Sraosha* (the obedient), victor over the demon *Aêshma* (perhaps the demon Asmodeus of the Book of Tobit). A virgin will then conceive by Zoroaster a Messiah, the Victorious, a second Zoroaster, who will bring the dead to life, and first of all the first man, *Gayomart*. The good will be separated from the evil, but the sufferings of the latter will not be eternal; after a general conflagration, which will purify the world, all humanity will unite in adoration of Ormazd.

10. The grossest form of impurity is that which defiles the sacred elements, fire, earth or water. It is an abomination to burn, to bury, or to immerse corpses; they must be exposed to the air, as is still done by the Parsees or Guebers of Bombay, the last adherents of Mazdeism, on their Towers of Silence. Under the Roman empire, a Magus refused to travel by water, for fear of defiling the sea by his excrements.[1] But the number of impurities man can commit is infinite, and the Avestic ritual of purification is so complicated that we cannot but ask if any active society could ever have practised it. Many of the purifications consist of penances; two thousand strokes with a rod for an involuntary offence against purity, and ten thousand for the "murder" of a loach. These flagellations might be compounded for by fines paid into the treasury, according to a tariff. Other penances imposed the performance of good works, or the destruction of unclean creatures. "He shall bind 1000 bundles of *baresmân*, he shall kill 1000 serpents, he shall kill 1000 land-frogs, 2000 water-frogs; he shall kill 1000 corn-stealing ants and 2000 of the other sort."[2] There are besides inexpiable offences, and many others which can only be purged by repentance and confession, without prejudice to the temporal punishment, which repentance does not commute.

11. The conflict between Ahura and Ahriman fills the stage to such an extent that the other gods of Mazdeism play very secondary parts. *Mithra*, who was to have such a brilliant destiny, only takes on importance as a luminous god, the guarantor of contracts and vows, in the more recent parts of the *Avesta*. The goddess *Anâhita* (the Lydian *Anaïtis*) was of foreign origin. The Iranian Pantheon is, as a rule, deficient in goddesses; woman was always suspect, and the religious law aggravated the miseries of their sex by the cruel and complicated purifications it imposed on them.

12. Death is a state of impurity, requiring minute precautions to drive away the spirits of evil, more especially "the corpse fly," the "carrion *druj*." When the end ap-

[1] Pliny the Elder, xxx, 6.
[2] Darmesteter, *L'Avesta*, ii, 254.

proached, the priest made the dying person repeat a penitential confession, and poured *hâoma* into his mouth and ears; it was a veritable extreme unction, and perhaps the origin of this Christian rite. After exposing the corpse in a solitary place on a kind of tower where it was devoured by birds of prey, funeral rites were celebrated for three days to facilitate the journey of the soul. These ceremonies included an offering of holy bread, which was divided among those present. During this period Sraosha conducts the soul, and protects it against demons, if it is pure enough to escape them; the weighing of souls takes place subsequently on a high mountain; those which are light pass over the bridge that leads to Paradise; the others are cast into hell. All these conceptions are so akin to those of Judæo-Christianity that the hypothesis of a Persian influence in Palestine seems inevitable; but when we take into account the late period at which the *Avesta* was compiled, we may occasionally ask which creed borrowed from the other.

13. There were no images in the temples; the ancient religion forbids them. Artaxerxes Mnemon was the first who put up statues of Anâhita about the year 398 B.C. Fire was the principal object of worship. Each temple contained a fire-chamber, protected from the light of day, in which burnt an eternal flame which no one might touch or even sully with his breath. The fire-priest wore gloves on his hands and a veil over his mouth. The maintenance of the fire and the choice of the elements it consumed were minutely regulated.

14. Of all the ancient religions, Mazdeism is the one that most resembles Judaism in its aversion from asceticism and barren contemplation, as well as in the elevation of its social and personal morality. Though some of its gods bear names in common with those of India, the spirit which animates it is a very different one. Its influence on Judaism, and by this means or even directly on Christianity, has been the stronger, because from the beginning there was a kind of sympathy and affinity between these three creeds.[1] But the Avestic lit-

[1] Iranian influences have also been traced by Reitzenstein in classical Greece (*Journ. of Hell. Stud.,* 1929, p. 111.)

erature is greatly inferior to the Bible. It is full of the most absurd puerilities. Here is a specimen of a conversation between the prophet and his god:[1] "Zarathustra asks Ahura Mazda: Beneficent Spirit, creator of the world of bodies, holy one! What is the most energetically mortal act by which mortals sacrifice to demons? Ahura Mazda replies: It is when men, combing and cutting their hair, or cutting their nails, let them fall into holes or crevices. By means of this negligence, the earth brings forth *Daëvas* and *Khrafstas*, which are called lice and which devour the corn in the granaries, and the garments in the wardrobes. Thou, therefore, O Zarathustra, when thou combest thy hair or cuttest thy nails, carry them ten paces from the faithful, twenty paces from the fire and fifty paces from the sacred fasces of the *baresmân*. And dig a deep hole and place the hair in it, saying in a loud voice these words. . . . Then at the entrance make with a metal knife three furrows, six furrows or nine furrows, and pronounce these words," &c. It is a widely spread idea, even outside of Persia, that the cuttings of hair and nails should be buried, lest a sorcerer should make a maleficent use of them. But what prolixity and pedantry obscure this simple prohibition! I may quote hundreds of passages no less absurd. Thus, though the doctrine enounced by the Avesta is a lesson of activity, of progress and even of justice, the work in which we have to seek it nevertheless deserves the severe judgment of Voltaire, who knew the Avesta through Anquetil's translation: "One cannot read two pages of the abominable balderdash attributed to this Zoroaster without pitying the human race. Nostradamus was a reasonable person compared with this energumen."

15. Mithra was a divinity of the Hindus and the Iranians even before their separation (§ 1). In the religion of the *Avesta* he plays an important but not a preponderant part; he is the luminous god, good to man, the guarantor of fidelity, with some of the amiable traits of the Greek Apollo. But Mithra seems to have been the principal god of another Persian sect, differing from that whose beliefs became the

[1] Darmesteter, *L'Avesta,* ii, 237.

official religion of the Sassanids. It was this popular creed which the Roman soldiers and their Oriental auxiliaries carried into the west from the beginning of the first century, and which seemed for a time to have caused the fate of Christianity to tremble in the balance.

16. Mithraism is known to us primarily by the statues, reliefs and inscriptions which reveal its myths and mysteries. At the head of the divine hierarchy was infinite Time, identified with the Greek Kronos, who is represented by winged figures with lion-heads holding the two keys of heaven and encircled by the folds of a serpent. The son of Time is Ormazd (Ahura Mazda), assimilated to Zeus and called by the Romans *Cœlus*. The maleficent genius, Ahriman, becomes *Arimanius* in the Latin inscriptions; he is identified with Pluto. The lion is the symbol of the sacred fire; the serpent, that of earth: the crater or vase, that of water. Mithra sprang from a rock; he causes a spring to gush from it by striking it with an arrow, concludes an alliance with the Sun and engages in combat with a bull, which he overcomes and sacrifices. This final scene is often represented at the back of the subterranean temples or caverns of Mithra; a dog and a serpent lap the blood which flows from the wound of the bull. According to a Persian tradition, all living creatures were born of the blood of the sacred bull immolated by Mithra. Mithra is not only the creator, but the mediator between the supreme God and man, the conqueror of evil, the saviour of souls. Initiation into the Mithraic mysteries ensured happiness upon earth and posthumous salvation. The initiated (*sacrati*) were called, according to their hierarchic rank, crows, lions, &c.; the highest grade was that of *fathers*, and these gave each other the name of *brothers*. Tertullian (*c.* 200) applies the term *sacraments* to the Mithraic ceremonies of initiation, which comprised baptism, purification by honey, the use of consecrated water, bread and wine; they were regulated by the priests called "fathers," of whom the "father of fathers" was the chief.

17. Mithraism, adopted by the Emperor Commodus, was the more strenuously combated by the Christians for its very

resemblance to Christianity. But in spite of the support of Julian, who introduced the mysteries of Mithra at Constantinople, the second capital of the Empire, it could not withstand the assaults of the new religion. By A.D. 400, the *Mithræa* were destroyed, and the worship proscribed; it may perhaps have dragged out an obscure existence for a lengthy period, to reappear later in the guise of Manicheeism.

18. The sacrifice of the bull seems to indicate that the worship of Mithra under the most ancient form was that of a sacred bull, assimilated to the sun, which was immolated as a god, its flesh and blood being consumed in a communion meal. Mithra, the slayer of the bull, was the result of a duplication common to all the religions which have passed from totemism to anthropomorphism.

19. The analogies with Christianity may be summed up as follows: Mithra is the mediator between God and man, he ensures the happiness of mankind by a sacrifice; his worship comprises baptism, communion and fasts, his adherents are called *brethren;* among the Mithraic clergy there were men and women vowed to celibacy; its moral code was severe, and akin to that of Christianity. The Fathers of the Church were as much impressed by this as the pagans. St. Augustine relates that an Asiatic priest[1] told him one day that they worshipped the same god. About 200, Tertullian explained the analogies between Mithraism and Christianity by alleged artifices of the Evil One. It is obvious that he could not bring the charge of plagiarism, in view of the acknowledged priority of some of the Mithraic rites. Nor, on the other hand, did the pagans accuse the Christians of having borrowed from Mithraism. We are bound to conclude that Christianity and Mithraism had a common origin in some of those old Asiatic religions, of which only the relatively modern forms are known to us, and that one of the essential features was the sacrifice of a god and communion. As to the identity of morality in the two religions, it has never been better or more simply explained than by Anatole France: "Each period has its dominant morality, which is the result neither of religion nor of philosophy. . . . As

[1] A priest of Attis or Mithra (*pileatus*).

morality is the sum of the prejudices of a community, two rival moralities cannot exist in the same time and place." This applies, be it understood, to the morality men exact from others. At the time of the triumph of Christianity, Christians and pagans were in agreement as to this, and also, with rare exceptions, agreed not to practise it.

*
* *

20. From the confines of Babylonia and Persia sprang a new universalist religion, *i.e.*, a religion which, like Christianity and Mithraism, offered itself to men of all conditions and all races as the way of salvation. This was Manicheeism, which, from the fourth century onwards, spread from Turkestan and China to North Africa and Spain, and only succumbed to cruel persecution after a long and heroic resistance.

21. Mani or Manichee, born in Babylon, but of a mother of Arsacid race, was educated by the Magi, and presented himself to Sapor I., King of Persia, as a reformer of Zoroastrianism (March, A.D. 242). Being unfavourably received, he started on his travels to recruit disciples; he proclaimed himself the envoy of God, after the manner of Zoroaster, Buddha and Jesus. Returning to Persia, he converted the king's brother; but the Zoroastrian clergy pursued him relentlessly, and at the age of sixty, he was flayed and crucified (A.D. 276).

22. The doctrine of Mani, preached by enthusiastic disciples, drew its essential dogmas from the religions of Babylonia and Persia; but Buddhism and Christianity also contributed to it.

23. The dominant idea is the opposition of light and darkness, in other words, of good and evil. The visible world is a result of the mixture of these two eternally hostile elements. In man, the soul is luminous, the body opaque; in fire, flame and smoke represent the two warring principles. This conception is the basis of all Manichæan morality, the object of which is the liberation of the luminous elements, of the souls which suffer in the prison of matter. When all the captive light and all the souls of the just shall have mounted

to heaven, the end of the world will come after a general conflagration. In practice, men are divided into the *perfect* or *elect*, and the simply faithful or *auditors*. The former constitute a kind of priesthood; they must abstain from marriage, from the flesh of animals (with the exception of fish occasionally), from wine, from all cupidity and all lying. The faithful are subject to the same moral law, but they may marry and work like other men; they must not, however, accumulate riches, or sin against purity. The Christians, it is true, accused the Manichæans of gross immorality. But that this was a calumny inspired by theological animus is shown by the fact that St. Augustine, who was a Manichæen for nine years, does not make confession of any turpitude due to his association with the sect.

24. The Manichæan religion is very simple. It enjoined no sacrifices, no images, but frequent fasts, four prayers a day to the sun and the moon, which were not worshipped as gods, but revered as manifestations of light; these prayers, some of which have survived, are closely akin to certain Babylonian hymns. The Manichæans practised baptism, communion, and a sort of initiation, often bestowed *in articulo mortis*, which implied the remission of sins and was called, in the Latin West, "consolation."

25. According to the Manichæans, the true Jesus had been an emissary of light, whose body, birth and death upon the cross were illusory phenomena. They rejected large portions of the Gospels as erroneous, but accepted and admired the discourses and parables of Jesus. The Old Testament they condemned unreservedly. Moses and the Prophets were devils. The God of the Jews was a Prince of Darkness. As early as the year A.D. 150 we find a similar opinion formulated by the Christian schismatic, Marcion, founder of the sect of Marcionists, from whom the Manichæans may have borrowed.

26. Like the Persians, they further admitted the existence of a whole army of good and evil genii, of gods and devils; the chief of these latter, Satan, had a lion's head and a dragon's body. Touching the origin of humanity, and the conflict of the luminous powers with darkness, they recounted

a series of complicated stories, derived from the Babylonian cosmogony, which are too absurd to deserve record.

27. The Manichæans were gentle and peaceable persons; this was the opinion of the Greek philosopher Libanius. But as they rejected the rites of existing Churches, and claimed to confine themselves to the ministrations of their own priests, those of other religions persecuted them furiously, and excited the mob against them by calumnies. When it was first attacked in Persia, Manicheeism spread towards Turkestan, India and China, and at the same time towards Africa by way of Syria and Egypt. Diocletian prohibited it in A.D. 290, and the Christian Emperors from A.D. 377 onwards legislated against it; the Vandals burnt or exiled the Manichæans. African Manicheeism is known to us chiefly through the works of St. Augustine, who wrote long treatises against its doctors, after having been their pupil. In the east, the sect was almost exterminated by the severity of Justinian, but it formed again in Asia Minor. We read of the *Paulicians* in Armenia (seventh to twelfth centuries), the *Bogomiles* in Thrace (tenth to eleventh century). The Byzantine Emperors, Alexis Comnenus in particular, pursued these inoffensive sectaries with fire and sword. In the eleventh century Manicheeism, brought by the commerce of the Levant, penetrated into Southern France, and gave rise to the powerful sect of the *Cathari*, who were exterminated by the Inquisition. I shall give this painful story later on, in connection with medieval Christianity.

28. An extravagant mixture of Babylonian, Persian, Jewish and Christian ideas characterises the sect of the Mandæans. Their name is derived from *Manda* (science), a word which corresponds to the Greek *gnosis*. The Mandæans are therefore Gnostics. In his youth, Mani had belonged to the sect; Mahomet mentions it, together with Judaism and Christianity; and adepts still exist to the south of Bagdad. The Mandæans have a collection of sacred books, the *Ginza*, the earliest of which date from the Sassanid period. Their essential rite is baptism, which they administer very freely. Hence their name of "Baptist Sabians" and even "Christians of St. John," in spite of their hostility to Christianity. In

the *Ginza*, they generally call themselves *Nâsôrâje*, a name which cannot be that of the Christians (*Nazarenes*), but may be related to the root *ns'r* "to help." According to the Mandæans, St. John was the real prophet, and Jesus nothing but an impostor. Their moral code condemns celibacy, and every kind of asceticism; they practise a sort of communion with unleavened bread and water, to which wine is sometimes added. Their temples are entered only by their priests, and are always near running water, which they call "Jordan." It is not impossible that John the Baptist may have belonged to a primitive sect of Mandæans; if at this early period they already called themselves *Nâsôrâje*, we should have an explanation of the tradition which made Nazareth the birthplace of the Messiah, who was himself called a Nazarene.

29. The most interesting feature of Mandæism is the fact that it has preserved, at least partially, its ancient books. In these, if we discount the borrowed passages, we may find some remnants of those semi-scientific conceptions which prevailed before the Christian era in Persia, Babylonia and perhaps Syria. It was here and elsewhere that spiritual sustenance was found by those so-called Gnostics against whom the church waged a perpetual war, sects which, with the exception of the Mandæans, are known to us only by the writings of their theological adversaries; in other words, by abuse and calumny.

BIBLIOGRAPHY

I. The richest source of information is still Bühler, *Grundriss der indo-arischen Philologie*, 1896 *et seq.*

1. Hirt, *Die Indogermanen*, 1905; A. Carnoy, *Les Indo-Européens*, 1921; S. Reinach, *L'origine des Aryens*, 1892; art. *Indo-European* in *Encycl. Brit.*, 11th ed.

4. Barth, *Les religions de l'Inde*, 1879 (numerous editions and translations); *Œuvres d'A. Barth*, 1914 *et seq.;* E. Hardy, *Indische Religionsgeschichte*, 1904; Max Müller, *Collected Works*, 1898; E. W. Hopkins, *Religions of India*, 1895.

7. S. Lévi, *Histoire ancienne de l'Inde*, in the *Journal des Savants*, 1905, p. 534.

8. V. Henry, *La magie dans l'Inde antique*, 1904.

9. L. de Milloué, *Métempsychose et ascétisme* (in *Conférences du Musée Guimet*, 1901, p. 135); cf. S. Reinach, *Cultes*, vol. i, p. 47 (*Metempsychosis* and *Totemism*).

14. Bergaigne, *La religion védique,* 3 vols., 1878-1883; *Dieux souverains de la relig. védique,* 1877; Oldenberg, *Die Relig. des Veda,* 1894 (*cf.* Barth, *Journ. des Sav.,* 1896, p. 133); L. v. Schroeder, *Mysterium und Mythus im R. V.,* 1908; M. Bloomfield, *Religion of the Vedas,* 1908; *The Atharvaveda,* 1899 (*cf. Journ. des Sav.,* 1906, p. 657).

20. Gough, *The Philosophy of the Upanishads,* 1882.

21. Bühier, *The Laws of Manu,* 1886 (*cf.* Dareste, *Journ. des Sav.,* 1884, p. 45).

22. Deussen, *Gesch. der Philosophie,* vol. i, 1894; Max Müller, *Six Systems of Indian Philosophy,* 1900.

23. G. Bühler, *Die Jainas,* 1881; M. Stevenson, *The Heart of Jainism,* 1915; A. Guérinot, *La relig. djaîna,* 1926.

24. Eug. Burnouf, *Introd. à l'hist. du bouddhisme,* 1844 (1876); Rhys Davids, *Early Buddhism,* 1908; E. Hardy, *Buddha,* 1903; H. Oldenberg, *Buddha,* 15th ed., 1906 (Engl. transl.); La Vallée Poussin, *Bouddhisme,* 1909; Sénart, *Origines bouddhiques* (in *Conf. Guimet,* 1907, p. 115).—A. Fouché, *L'Art gréco-bouddhique du Gandhâra,* 1905 *et seq.* (*cf.* Perrot, *Journ. des Sav.,* 1906, p. 345).

25. Sénart, *La légende de Bouddha,* 1876 (1882); *cf.* Renan, *Journ. des Sav.,* 1883, p. 177.

27. Sénart, *Castes dans l'Inde,* 1896 (1927); Bouglé, *Régime des castes* (in *Année sociol.,* 1900).

31. Edmunds, *Buddhist and Christian Gospels* (Tokyo), 1905; Seydel, *Die Buddhalegende und das Leben Jesu,* 2nd ed., 1897 (*cf.* L. de la Vallée Poussin, *Rev. bibl.,* July 1906); E. Kuhn, *Barlaam u. Joasaph,* 1897 (*cf.* Saintyves, *Les Saints,* 1907, p. 178); E. Watson Burlingame, *Buddhist legends,* 1921; S. Lévi, *Revue des Etudes grecques,* 1891, p. 98 (edicts of Asoka).

33. Stan. Julien, *Voyages des pèlerins bouddhistes,* 3 vols., 1853-1858; Vincent A. Smith, *Asoka,* 1901.

34. Edkins, *Chinese Buddhism,* 1893.

35. Grünwedel, *Mythol. du bouddhisme en Tibet et en Mongolie,* 1900; *Der Lamaismus* (in *Die oriental. Religionen,* 1906, p. 136); L. de Milloué, *Le Tibet* (in *Conf. Guimet,* 1901, p. 1); Goblet d'Alviella, *Moulins à prières* (in *Rev. Univ. Brux.,* 1895, p. 641); D. Macdonald, *Land of the Lama,* 1927.

36. L. Feer, in *Annales du Musée Guimet,* vols. ii and v.

37. Barnett, *Hinduism,* 1906; Monier-Williams, *Brahmanism and Hinduism,* 4th ed., 1891; A. Lyall, *Asiatic Studies,* 1899, 1907.

38. Dahlmann, *Das Mahâbhârata,* 1895 (*cf.* Barth, *Journ. des Sav.,* 1897, p. 221); Jacobi, *Das Râmâyana,* 1893; E. W. Hopkins, *The Epic of India,* 1903.

42. A. Macauliffe, *The Sikh Religion,* 1909.

43. G. d'Alviella, *L'évol. relig. chez les Hindous,* 1884; L. de Milloué, in *Conf. Guimet,* 1901, p. 81; S. Lévi, *Ibid.,* 1907, p. 193; Auzuech, in *Rev. clergé français,* June 1, 1908, p. 563; J. N. Farquhar, *Modern Relig. Movements in India,* 1915.

II. Geiger and Kuhn, *Grundriss der iranischen Philologie,* 1895-1904; J. Darmesteter, *Ormazd et Ahriman,* 1876; *Le Zendavesta,* 3 vols., 1892; V. Henry, *Le Parsisme,* 1905; A. V. W. Jackson, *Persia,* 1906.

1. First appearance of the Aryans: *L'Anthropologie,* 1908, p. 314.

3. Bréal, *Le Zendavesta,* in *Journ. des Sav.,* 1894, p. 5; Meillet, *Les Gâthas,* 1925.

5. W. Jackson, *Zoroaster,* 1899; R. Pettazoni, *Zarathustra,* 1920.

8. Söderblom, *Les Fravashis,* in *Rev. hist. relig.,* 1899.

12. Söderblom, *La vie future d'après le mazdéisme,* 1901.

15. Cumont, *Mystères de Mithra,* 2 vols., 1890-1896; also an abridg-

ment 1902; by the same, the articles *Mithra*, in Roscher and in Saglio.

18. The morality of Mithraism: S. Reinach, *Cultes*, ii, 220.

19. Burkitt, *The Religion of the Manichees*, 1925; H. Schrader, *Die Manichäer*, 1927.

27. V. Brandt, *Die mandäische Religion*, 1889; M. Lidzbarski, *Ginza*, 1925; S. A. Pallis, *Mandæan Studies*, 1927; J. Behm, *Die Mand. Relig. und das Christentum*, 1927; Reitzenstein, *Vorgesch. der Taufe*, 1929 (ritual of *Mandæan baptism*).

CHAPTER III

THE GREEKS AND THE ROMANS

I. Myths and rites. Ægean and Mycenæan religions. Crete. The invasion of the Dorians. Greek anthropomorphism. Animism. Personifications. The worship of the dead. Belief in a future life. Totemism. Metamorphosis. Metempsychosis. Orpheus. Sacrifice of the god. Actæon, Hippolytus, Phaeton, Prometheus. Lamentations over the dead gods. Harvest rites. Magic. Hierogamies. Masquerades. The influence of works of art on myths. Sublimated epithets. Alien gods in Greece. Greek intolerance; the death of Socrates. Priests and wizards; oracles. Incubation. Sacrifices. Purifications. Festivals. Mysteries.

II. Romans and Etruscans. Greek influences. Animism. Multiplicity of gods. The Lares and Penates. Personifications. Fetiches. Sacred trees and animals. Taboos. Secret names. Magic. Temples. The Roman Pantheon; the twelve great gods. Belief in a future life. Funeral rites. Colleges of priests. Sacrifices. The Sibylline books. Introduction of alien divinities. The affair of the Bacchanalia. The influence of Oriental sacerdotalism. The religious and nationalist reaction under Augustus; Emperor worship. Babylonian astrology and Roman paganism. Mysticism.

I. The Greeks or Hellenes

1. The religions of Greece are known to us by texts and monuments for a period of over twenty centuries. It may therefore be supposed that they varied greatly and that it is easier to relate their history than to give a general picture of them.

2. Ever since Homer and Hesiod, poets have endeavoured to embellish the fictions of the past, mythographers to coordinate them, philosophers to explain or destroy them; but the actual basis of religion is long anterior to literature. It is revealed to us by primitive works of art, and still more clearly by the analysis of religious customs, of rites which often survive the conceptions of which they are the echo, and remain immutable, even in their transformation. These rites themselves, becoming unintelligible in their turn, give birth to new myths. This has happened everywhere, but more es-

SACRED OFFERINGS TO HERMES

pecially in Greece, because the Greek, curious and ingenious by nature, attempted to explain the customs he no longer understood by legends, and often invented very charming ones.

Detailed examination of these myths, due to the imagination of poets and the subtlety of mythographers, must be left to the literary historian. A knowledge of those Greek fables from which literature and art still draw inspiration is indispensable to every educated man; here I must be content to note a few examples in passing.

3. The excavations at Troy, Mycenæ, Amorgos, Melos, and Crete, carried out from 1870 to this day, have thrown some light on the religious ideas which prevailed in Greek countries many centuries before the Homeric epos (850). It is of little consequence whether the men of this remote period spoke Greek or some other tongue; their beliefs were not lost to their successors, any more than those of the inhabitants of Canaan to their Hebrew conquerors.

4. Some little flat statues of a nude goddess, in marble, have been found in tombs dating from about 3000 B.C.; they have been considered (quite arbitrarily) as images of Earth the Mother. A similar figure appears on Babylonian cylinders, on a smaller scale than the other personages, and raised upon a pedestal; I think these represent a statue taken by some victorious Babylonian king from a people of Asia Minor, and brought to Babylon with other spoils.

5. At Troy, in some of the very ancient strata (*c.* 3000 B.C.), clay vases have been found, ornamented with a head surmounting very rudely carved breasts; the head is so like that of an owl that it suggested to Schliemann the epithet applied to Athene in Homer: "the goddess with the face of an owl," *glaukópis*. A much later heifer's head in silver was exhumed at Mycenæ, which, in like manner, recalls the Hera *bo-ôpis* of Homer "with the eyes or the face of a heifer." Other images and numerous texts indicate a survival of the worship of animals, as in Egypt, where divinities with animal heads and human bodies were long represented by art.

6. Crete and the adjacent islands have yielded many engraved stones dating from about 2000 B.C., on which figure

demons with the heads of animals. Some of these types persisted down to the classic period; I may instance the Cretan Minotaur, the Sirens and the Centaurs, images of partially humanised animals.

7. A later advance emancipated man from the animal, and transformed the latter into the companion or attribute of the god; this was the case of a Cretan goddess between two lions, analogous to the classic Cybele, of another who holds two serpents, like the Arcadian Artemis, of a third who was attended by two doves, like the Aphrodite-Astarte of Cyprus. The worship of trees and of sacred pillars is attested in the islands of the Archipelago and in Phœnicia; the column between two lions which crowns the gate of Mycenæ is perhaps one of those divinities without human features known as *aniconic*.

8. In the palace of Cnossos in Crete, sacred pillars have been found which do not support anything; on them are engraved double axes; the same object has been found elsewhere, sometimes painted or engraved, sometimes in metal. The double axe was called a *labrys;* it has been suggested that the famous Labyrinth of Cnossos was "the palace of the double axe." The name reappears in Caria, where, until the triumph of Christianity, the worship of Zeus with the double axe, the Zeus of the sanctuary of Labranda in Caria, flourished. It has even been suggested that the name and symbol of the axe *labrys* were the originals of the *labarum*, or standard of the cross given by Constantine to his troops in A.D. 312.

9. A chapel in the palace of Cnossos contained an equilateral cross in marble, a token of the religious character of this symbol more than fifteen centuries before Christ. Another form of cross, known as the gammadion or *svastika* (a Sanscrit word), is frequent at Troy (on votive objects) and at Cyprus; it reappears on Greek pottery about the year 800, then on archaic coins, and becomes rare in the classic period, to show itself again in the Christian era in the catacombs of Rome and on the funeral stelæ of Asia Minor. The *svastika* is also frequently employed in the Buddhist art of India and China. This mystic sign, to

which Indian literature attributes a magic power, may perhaps have been formed by the conventionalisation of the image of a large bird, like the stork, which has so far preserved its sacred character even in our own countries that it is never killed. In Northern Greece at the time of Aristotle, it was a capital offence to kill a stork.

10. The excavations in Crete have further revealed the existence of sacred grottoes, of altars adorned with horns like those described in the Book of Exodus, of tables of offerings, of clay and metal (*ex votos*). The sacrifices comprised the burning of the offerings. The most usual funeral rite was burial. The royal tombs discovered on the Acropolis of Mycenæ were full of precious objects, attesting, like the adjoining tombs with cupolas, the religious care with which the dead were guarded.

11. Towards the year 1100 B.C. the invasion of northern tribes, the most warlike of which were the Dorians, put an almost sudden end to the brilliant civilisation which is known at the beginning as Ægean, at its apogee as Minoan or Cretan, and towards the end as Mycenæan. It is beyond question that the elements of the Homeric poems go back to the Mycenæan period, though they did not receive their definitive form till about 850 B.C. The invasions caused a long eclipse of the plastic arts. The first Greek idols of about 750 B.C. are almost as rude as those of Troy, carved some twenty centuries earlier. Two centuries and a half after the new dawn of art, Greece was already producing masterpieces under the influence of the tribes, which, driven out of Greece by the invaders, had preserved, on the coasts of Asia and in Cyprus, some traditions of Mycenæan art, and also under the influence of Egypt, whose little clay and bronze idols were disseminated throughout the Greek world by commerce.

12. Greek religion from the time of Homer was distinguished by what is called anthropomorphism. The gods have human forms and mingle familiarly with mortals. Even when irritated, they are not inexorable, and although superhuman, they are not monstrous. The stories told of them represent them as benevolent and sociable. There are, cer-

tainly, exceptions to this rule, sanguinary or grotesque myths, an unwillingly accepted legacy from remote ages; but generally speaking the Greek beliefs are those of mild and reasonable men, who perform their ancestral rites conscientiously, are averse from all sombre fanaticism, and seem always to be saying to their gods what Voltaire's Spinoza says to his:

Mais je crois, entre nous, que vous n'existez pas.[1]

13. We must, however, be careful not to judge the Greek religion as a whole from the writings of the poets and philosophers of the literary period. As we have seen, it did not begin with anthropomorphism, and though it became deeply imbued with art and rationalism, it was originally a faith without images and without gaiety, a true primitive religion.

14. When we explore the earliest bases of the Greek religions in the light of survivals and ancient rites, we are amazed to find that they are identical with those of all other religions, even the most savage. But where the Australian remained, the Greek merely passed by.

Here, as elsewhere, the elements of religion and mythology are animism, totemism, and magic.

15. Animism gives a soul and a will to mountains, rivers, rocks, trees, stones, the heavenly bodies, the earth and the sky. A tree, a post, a pillar, the hollow of a rock are the seat or throne of invisible spirits. These spirits are conceived and figured at a later stage under animal form, and then under human form. A spring was a horse; it was Pegasus, Apollo's horse, who caused the Hippocrene spring to gush from Parnassus. A river is a bull with a human face, though in general the Greeks did not like these ambiguous images. The laurel was Daphne, whom Apollo had pursued; the oak was Zeus himself, before being the tree of Zeus, and Dionysos was supposed to live in the tree, after he had ceased to be himself the tree. The earth was Gæa, emerging from the soil in the shape of a woman who implores the sky to water her. The sky was Uranos, the son of Time and the father of the gods.

[1] "But, between ourselves, I think that you do not exist."

16. Seconded by art, Greek animism gave "a body, a spirit, a face" even to the most abstract conceptions, and this tendency persisted until the end of paganism. It was Greece which created the images of Peace, Concord, Mercy, &c. After having endowed all bodies with thought, she endowed all thoughts with bodies.

17. The idea of soul divorced from matter is a result of animism. The Greeks imagined the souls of the dead as little winged beings, such as birds, serpents, and butterflies (the Greek word for soul, *psyche*, also means butterfly). They had contradictory ideas as to the fate of the dead, which, however, were not developed simultaneously. The most ancient seems to have been that the dead still lead an obscure existence underneath the earth, and that this must be made agreeable to them, lest their spirits should become maleficent. Familiar objects were placed beside them, their arms, carved or painted representations of their life on earth; above all, libations and sacrifices were offered to them, and this homage rendered to ancestors became the bonds of the family and of the city. The dead remain the friends of their heirs, and give them counsel; the first oracles were delivered near the tombs of chieftains or ancestors of powerful families. The dead, who were invoked as Christians invoke their saints, were called *heroes*. The funeral rites continued to imply that they were still inhabiting their tombs, even when other ideas had prevailed, assigning them more distant dwellings.

18. The soul, liberated from the body by the fire of the funeral pyre, mounts heavenwards, to the stars; or else begins a long voyage under the earth, conducted by Hermes Psychopomp (the conductor of souls); or flies in the form of a bird towards a distant region in the west, where the sun sets, and where are the Fortunate Islands. A widely spread belief was that it entered the infernal regions after crossing the river Styx in the boat of the old ferryman Charon, who exacted as the fare an obolus, which was placed in the mouth of the dead person. In the infernal regions it appeared before the three judges of the place, Minos, Eacus and Rhadamanthus, who were, in their lifetime, equitable judges; if condemned for its crimes, it had to suffer in Tar-

tarus; if rewarded for its virtues, it would inhabit the Elysian Fields, which are sometimes supposed to be under the earth, near the infernal regions, sometimes in a remote spot where perpetual spring reigns. The Greeks even invented a Limbo, the abode of children who had died in infancy, and a Purgatory, where a certain mild chastisement purified souls. They had many other ideas of the future life, but they never reduced these to a doctrinal code, perhaps because when they had become capable of so doing, they had ceased to believe seriously in a future life.

19. Totemism left something more than traces in Greece. We note, first of all, the familiar animals of the gods, which, at an earlier stage, had been themselves the gods—the eagle of Zeus, the owl of Athene, the hind of Artemis, the dolphin of Poseidon, the dove of Aphrodite, &c. The sacred animal usually became the companion of the god, but occasionally it figures as his enemy or his victim. Thus Apollo Sauroctonos is, as the name indicates, the slayer of lizards; but in the beginning it was the lizard itself which was divine. We have already seen that the boar, before becoming the slayer of Adonis, was Adonis himself. An animal was sometimes sacred to several gods, each of which had inherited several cycles of animal legends. Thus the wolf was the animal both of Apollo and of Ares; the bull was the symbol both of Zeus and of Dionysos. The Greeks apportioned the old totems among their more recent gods.

20. Greek mythology contains many legends of gods and heroes transformed into animals, trees and stones; these were what are called metamorphoses. Metamorphoses are religious history reversed, as it were. Thus, according to the tradition, Zeus took the form of a swan to seduce Leda, who gave birth to eggs. This fable must have arisen in a group of tribes which had the swan for their totem, attributed a sacred character to it, and believed that a divine swan might be the father of a human child. Leda's twins, the Dioscuri Castor and Pollux, cleave the air on winged horses and appear suddenly among men; this was because they were originally imagined as swans, and the tales of their *theophanies* (appearances) bore the impress of their primitive nature.

Daphne, pursued by Apollo, was changed into a laurel; this was because Daphne, the divine spirit of the laurel, the leaves of which excite the prophetic delirium, was closely connected with the worship of Apollo. Niobe, weeping for her children, became a rock from which tears were always oozing; this was because the rock Niobe, on Mount Sipylos, was a divine rock which exuded moisture, and anthropomorphism had to invent a reason for its apparent grief.

21. Finally, we find that not only did many Greek clans on becoming nations bear the names of animals—like the Myrmidons, or ants, the Arcadians, or bears—but that Greece preserved traditions of tribes which believed that they were related to certain noxious creatures, and were supposed to be immune from attack by them. The Ophiogenes of Phrygia declared themselves the descendants of a serpent-hero, and claimed the power of healing the bites of serpents. Many Greek legends describe helpful animals, such as the dolphin which saved Arion. Even after the triumph of anthropomorphism, Greek art represented certain divinities, as the Egyptians habitually did, with a head, a body or the skin of an animal, which indicates their particular nature. The Tritons have the bodies of fish; the Phigalian Demeter has a horse's head; Herakles, imagined as a lion in Lydia, wears a lion's skin, just as the fox, Orpheus, wears a fox-skin (*alôpekis*).

22. The idea of metempsychosis, the extreme consequence of totemism, existed in Greece as in India, at least as a popular belief. It found in Orphism mystic and poetical expression and a philosophic formula in the sect of Pythagoras. This strange personage, who in some respects resembles the medicine-men of the Redskins, declared that he could remember his former incarnations; among other forms, he had inhabited that of a peacock. Orpheus, whom the Greeks considered an earlier poet than Homer, was in their eyes a civilising hero, who had induced the Thracians to renounce cannibalism and had taught them the useful arts. He was in reality an old totemic god of Northern Greece, whose violent death and resurrection were the articles of faith of a mystic form of worship. This worship had an extraordinary suc-

cess; not only did it spread throughout the Greek world and into Southern Italy, but it inspired philosophers like Pythagoras and Plato, who gave a more or less scientific form to its conceptions.

23. Orphism held the doctrine of original sin. The soul was enclosed in the body as in a tomb or prison, to punish a very early crime committed by the Titans, the ancestors of man, who had treacherously slain the young god Zagreus.

24. Long poems, among others a *Descent into Hell*, were hawked about under the name of Orpheus. Initiation into the Orphic mysteries, performed by priestly sorcerers and healers, was supposed to spare souls the "cycle of reincarnation," an idea identical with that of Buddhism, though it does not necessarily imply Greek influence in India. To avoid new birth, certain magic formulæ were learnt by heart; the dead man was allowed to drink the water of a living spring, whereupon he cast off his carnal nature in which sin inhered, and thus purified "reigned among the heroes." These ideas, which have been held to be Christian, are expressed in Virgil's Fourth Eclogue, and more definitely still in fragments of some little poems engraved on golden tablets which were discovered in Crete and in Southern Italy beside skeletons of the initiated. There is an evident analogy between these tablets, the guides of the dead in his journey beyond the tomb, and the verbose Egyptian *Book of the Dead*. But, here again, we need not accept the theory of influence. The road of charlatanism is so narrow that travellers may meet here without seeking one another.

25. The primitive sacrifice of the god, generally accompanied by eating his flesh (communion), was perpetuated in ritual, and becoming incomprehensible, gave rise to numerous legends. To understand their genesis, it is essential to bear in mind two characteristic elements of totemic rites: *masquerade* and *adoption of a name*. As the object of the sacrifice of the totem was to deify the faithful who took part in it, and to assimilate them to the god as closely as possible, the faithful sought to embrace this resemblance by taking the name of the god and covering themselves with the skins of animals of the same kind. Thus the Athenian

maidens who celebrated the worship of the Bear-Artemis, dressed as, and called themselves, she-bears. The Mænads, who sacrificed the fawn Pentheus, dressed themselves in the skins of fawns. Even in later forms of worship we find the devotees of Bakkhos taking the name of Bakkhoi.

26. There is a whole series of legends which can be explained now as ancient semi-rationalist interpretations of the communion sacrifice. Actæon was a great stag sacrificed by women, who called themselves the great doe and the little does; he became the imprudent hunter, who, having seen Artemis bathing, was transformed into a stag by the goddess and devoured by her dogs. These *dogs* are a euphemism; in the primitive legend, it was the devotees of the sacred stag who tore him to pieces and ate him. Such religious repasts of raw flesh were called *omophagies* in Greece; they subsisted in mystic rituals, long after man had given up eating uncooked meat. Orpheus (the *frowner*), who appears in art with a fox-skin on his head, is merely a sacred fox torn in pieces by the women of the Tribe of the Fox; these women are called in the legend Bassarides: now *bassareus* is the ancient name of the fox. Pentheus was a fawn killed in the same manner; stories were invented at a later period to explain how he had incurred this punishment; but the discrepancies of these stories suffice to show that they were late inventions and that the only certain fact is that attested by the ritual, the killing and eating of the god. Zagreus was the son of Jupiter and Persephone; to escape the Titans who were incited against him by the jealousy of Hera, he changed himself into a bull; the Titans, the worshippers of the divine bull, killed and ate him. In the ritual of Zagreus, he continued to be invoked as "the goodly bull," and when Zagreus, by the grace of Zeus, was born again under the name of Dionysos, the young god bore on his brow horns in token of his animal origin.

Hippolytus in the fable is the son of Theseus, who repulses the love of Phædra, his stepmother, and dies, the victim of his terrified horses, because Theseus, deceived by Phædra, had invoked the anger of a god against him. Now Hippolytus means in Greek "torn by horses." Hippolytus was himself a horse, whom the worshippers of the sacred horse, disguised as horses, tore to pieces and ate.

Phaeton ("the brilliant") was the son of Apollo who begged to be allowed to drive the chariot of the sun, drove it unskilfully, nearly set the world on fire, and ended by falling into the sea. This legend was the echo of an ancient rite of Rhodes, the island of the sun, where every year a white horse and a burning chariot were cast into the sea, to be the assistants of the weary sun; the annual fall of Phaeton into the sea was explained by a legend, that is to say, by the invention of a unique event, localised in space and time.

Prometheus was a cunning Titan who stole fire from heaven and presented it to man. Zeus punished the thief by nailing him to a rock where an eagle devoured his liver, which was perpetually renewed. But in primitive mythologies, the eagle was the bird who mounted to the sun and took fire from it to give to man; on the other hand, the eagle was immune from thunderbolts, and was nailed to the summits of buildings to serve as a lightning conductor. Hence the name of eagles (*aetoi*) given to the pediments of Greek temples; hence also the legend of Prometheus, which corresponds to the following ingenuous dialogue: "Why was this eagle crucified?"—"To punish him for stealing fire from heaven." Originally, the legend was that of the eagle's chastisement. When for the eagle, *prometheus* (the far-seeing, a name given to the eagle as a bird of augury), men substituted the Titan, Prometheus, the eagle remained in the legend, but as executioner instead of victim. I might multiply instances, but those I have cited suffice to indicate the method, which may be applied with surprising facility, as I have shown, in a great many cases.

27. A divine animal when sacrificed never died completely; for after a few days of mourning a successor was found, another animal of the same kind, which remained sacred and intangible for a year. This explains the resurrection of so many gods and heroes, the fact that their tombs were preserved, that they were honoured in a ritual, and represented as living among the gods. Such was the case in all the instances I have given; in many tradition has preserved the

lamentations which followed their deaths, and the joy with which the news of their resurrection was hailed. When we compare these facts with the observances in Europe between Good Friday and Easter Day, we understand that the idea of a god who had died and risen again was the more easily accepted, because it was already very familiar in the lower and more religious ranks of society.

28. Anthropomorphism had the effect of weakening the idea of the immolation of the god, and bringing into prominence that of sacrificing a victim in the guise of a present or expiation. The sacrificial present is the form that prevails in classic Greek religion; the communion sacrifice was no longer celebrated, save in some of the ancient forms of worship, and then always in secret among the initiated. In the most famous of the Greek mysteries, those of Eleusis near Athens, there are vestiges of a communion feast, consisting, not of the consumption of an animal, but in the ritual absorption of a sacred flour and a divine drink. Perhaps at some anterior period, when men were ignorant of the culture of cereals, the faithful or the initiated ate and drank the flesh and blood of sacred sucking-pigs; the sacrifice of sucking-pigs still figured prominently in the ritual of the Eleusinian divinities at the classic period. Strange as it may seem, Demeter and her daughter Persephone, like the Astarte of Byblos, were originally sows.

29. When the ancestors of the Greeks became agriculturists, the totemic rites of the nomads and shepherds did not disappear, but they received a new interpretation. Thus, harvesters took the last animal that had found shelter among the last sheaves, or fashioned a simulacrum of such an animal with straw, killed it, burnt it, and scattered the ashes with the idea that the *spirit of harvest*, thus preserved from the decay of winter, would remain in the fields as a fertilising force. Animals thus sacrificed, whether in reality or in effigy, were ancient totems, and the custom of bewailing them after killing them, and recalling them to life by prayers, still persisted. The credit of having demonstrated the prevalence of these rites throughout Europe, and even beyond, belongs to Mannhardt (*d.* 1876); collated with the rites

of totemic sacrifice, as expounded by William Robertson Smith (*d.* 1894), they throw light upon a great number of religious usages which were incomprehensible to our predecessors.

30. In Greece, as elsewhere, magic was the principle of worship; the forms of worship of the classic period were merely magic ceremonies, refined on the one hand by rationalism, and on the other, modified in details by the relatively recent conception of the sacrificial gift. But magic was also the mother of legend. A curious example is furnished by the myth of Danae, the princess who was shut up in a tower by her father, and whom Jupiter visited in the form of a golden rain. An allegory! it used to be said, showing that with gold one can force all bolts and bars. Those who accept such prosaic explanations should not meddle with mythology. Danae in Greek means the earth, or the goddess of the earth. Even in the present day, in Roumania, in Servia, and in certain parts of Germany, when rain has been long withheld, it is solicited by means of rites which owe their origin to sympathetic magic: a young girl is stripped and water is poured over her ceremonially. Nature, stirred to emulation, treats the thirsty earth as men have treated the young girl. This rain from heaven is indeed a golden rain: Zeus (Heaven) has in this liquid form visited Danae (the earth). In ancient times, no doubt in Argos, the young girl thus ritually besprinkled was called the Earth, Danae, in order that conformity of name might be added to that of the rite to solicit rain from heaven. Here, as in the totemic rites, we may have an example of name-adoption.

31. Many other agrarian rites were inspired by sympathetic magic. The marriage of a god and goddess, represented by priest and priestess, constituted an annual hierogamy, the example of which would not, it was supposed, be disregarded by Nature. Thus at Athens, the wife of the archon-king pretended to marry the priest of Dionysos, to ensure the fecundity of the vine. Something analogous took place at Eleusis and at other places; myths were derived from these rites, as, for instance, that of the union of Demeter, wandering in search of her daughter, with local

heroes of Attica. The ancients believed, and the moderns long believed, that the rites commemorated myths, whereas in reality many myths were invented to explain rites, when their primitive significance had been lost.

32. One of the processes of imitative magic is simulation or masquerade; the hierogamies (ritual marriages) of which I have just spoken were simulacra. In Australia, the children who are to be initiated into the mysteries of the tribe are the objects of a simulacrum of sacrifice. They retire into the bush, whence they return some time afterwards, pretending that they have died, and have been born again, and that they must learn to speak afresh. Baptism was originally a simulacrum of drowning. When a Christian priest says to children after a first communion, or to a young couple newly married that they *are born to a new life*, he uses a conventional formula which has lost its profound meaning; but primally, every initiation comprised two acts, apparent death and resurrection. The "taking of the veil" by the novice, the veiling of brides and dying persons have a like significance. In spite of the scantiness of our information concerning the Greek mysteries, it is certain that at Eleusis the initiated were shrouded in darkness, frightened by dismal visions of death, and then suddenly inundated with brilliant light and recalled to life, as it were. This, it was said, was an image of inevitable death and of a glorious life to follow it, but it was not merely an image. Initiation included certain gestures, certain words which had to be pronounced after death, and ensured the salvation of the soul. Pindar and Cicero tell us that those who came back from Eleusis brought with them hopes that sustained them in death; under the direction of priestly charlatans, the initiated served their apprenticeship to death and to future life. The Orphic mysteries had a similar object, with this difference, that they gave the credulous magic receipts to evade new birth in a different body.

33. Another factor in mythology among an artistic people like the Greeks was the work of art, the statue or picture, the primitive significance of which has been obscured. This was what Clermont-Ganneau called "iconological

mythology"; even in the Middle Ages images gave rise to pious legends. Thus the legend of St. Denis carrying his head is due to the representation of this saint as a decapitated man carrying his head, in allusion to the manner of his martyrdom, just as St. Lucy, whose eyes were put out, is painted carrying her eyes on a dish, and St. Apollonia, whose teeth were extracted, carries her teeth. In Greece, legends arose from the interpretations given to Egyptian and Phœnician works introduced by traders, and also from the explanations given by *ciceroni*, or guides, of old pictures preserved in the temples. Why, from the Homeric period onward, was it said that Sisyphus in the infernal regions was condemned to roll a huge stone which always fell back before he had reached the top of the hill? or that the Danaides were compelled to fill up vases with holes in them, through which the contents immediately ran out on to the ground? The *ciceroni* had invented moral explanations: Sisyphus had dishonoured himself by robbery, the Danaides had killed their husbands. These are mere old wives' tales. There is, I think, a more rational explanation: Sisyphus is supposed to have built a huge edifice *almost* at the summit of Acrocorinthus; he is represented rolling a stone up this mountain. The Danaides had, no doubt by magic processes, procured a rainfall in Argos; they were represented watering the earth by means of vases with holes in them. These pictures intended to glorify the deceased figured in the temples, and were copied by those who painted pictures of the infernal regions, that is to say, gatherings of the illustrious dead. When the idea that man was subjected to expiatory sufferings after death gained ground, these images of *beneficent activity* were explained as *eternal penances;* hence the idea of Sisyphus vainly rolling his stone, and the Danaides ceaselessly plying their perforated vases. These graphic misunderstandings, it must be noted, were more ancient than Homer; the pictures which gave rise to them must therefore have dated from the Mycenæan period, when painting, as recent excavations have shown us, was a highly developed art.

34. Many other causes contributed to the birth of myths.

We have already seen that Phaeton, "the brilliant," an epithet applied to the sun or the solar horse, ended by becoming, in mythology, the son of Apollo. This is the type of a process numerous examples of which might be quoted. Adjectives show a tendency to separate themselves from the divine names they qualify, and to take on an individual existence; an unappropriated ritual epithet, in search of a body, became a hero or even a god.

35. Although Greece was very rich herself in gods and heroes, she showed herself hospitable to the gods of the stranger. Egypt, Assyria, Syria, Phœnicia and Persia presented divinities to her; she also received them more especially from the less civilised countries of Asia Minor, where Hellenism did not triumph till the end of the Roman period, and whence—an important point in this connection—the majority of slaves for the Greek markets were brought. With these alien gods, the Greeks received forms of worship, which, unlike the official religion, were accessible to foreigners, slaves and women. Societies called *thiasi* were formed for their celebration, in which imaginations were fired by mysterious ceremonies. As early as the fourth century B.C. Athens took alarm at this invasion, and Phryne, the famous model of Praxiteles, was brought to trial on the charge of affiliation to these alien forms of worship. But such causes as the influx of foreign traders, the increase in the number of slaves, the decadence of rationalism under the impact of the ignorant lower classes, proved more powerful than the restrictions of the law. Athens was invaded by the Phrygian Sabazios, the Syrian Aphrodite, the Thracian goddess Cotytto. Their worship, at once noisy and mysterious, justified suspicion, and was charged, no doubt baselessly, with immorality. Things went from bad to worse after the conquest of Asia by Alexander, which might more correctly be described as the conquest of Greece by Asia, for it threw Greece open to Oriental influences even more than it made way for Hellenism in Asia. This invasion by Oriental faiths must not be judged too severely. It satisfied the religious needs of the piously inclined masses, just as the worship of the official gods had sufficed for the cultivated rationalistic

classes, which cared nothing for enlightening the poor folk. These classes suffered the punishment due to their indifference and selfishness. Their chastisement was complete when Christianity, which had entered Greece in the wake of the Oriental faiths, decreed, by the pen of Theodosius' sons, the destruction of the temples, and when in 529 Justinian closed the school of Athens, the last refuge of Hellenic philosophy and free thought.

36. In general, the Greeks were extremely tolerant; religious persecution occupies no space in their history. Nevertheless Anaxagoras was tried for having doubted the gods, and Socrates was condemned to die by the hemlock for having ridiculed them. The death of Socrates is a stain on the history of Athens; but dogmatic intolerance seems to have had little part in it. The official religion was a matter of convenience; the priests and the temples subsisted on the sacrifices; the peasantry, who were sure of a market for their cattle among those who offered these sacrifices, found it a profitable arrangement. The first person who publicly attacked Socrates, Aristophanes the comedian, was, as M. Croiset has shown, the mouthpiece of the rural classes of Attica, to whom his comedies were played. Men cannot tolerate doctrines which imperil their interests, but they do not ostensibly attack them on these grounds; they seek and easily discover others. We see St. Paul persecuted by those who sold devotional objects at Ephesus, the Christians of Bithynia denounced to the Roman Governor, Pliny the Younger, because they had caused stagnation in the cattle-market, and finally in our own times, Zola pursued by the implacable hatred of monks because he spoke direspectfully of the trade at Lourdes. Something of the same sort happened no doubt at Athens. Socrates was the victim of commercial priests, and of those who are now called Agrarians.

*
* *

37. There was always a very marked tendency in Greece to subordinate the spiritual to the temporal, the priest to the magistrate. The first kings were also priests; magistrates and heads of families continued to perform religious

rites; but although at the time of Homer princes still carried out certain rites there were already priests attached to the temples, who had no power but that derived from the supposed protection of their god. In the Greek states of the classic period there were priests and priestesses who were always the ministers of a god, never associated in communities, neither ambulant, like the priests of unrecognised creeds, nor set apart as instructors like the Druids of Gaul. There were no seminaries for the education of priests; each priest learnt the ritual of a god by serving him. Thus the Greek priests never constituted a clergy like those of India, Persia or Gaul; the only attempt at such a constitution was the one Grote has compared to the foundation of the Society of Jesus, the confraternity formed in Southern Italy by Pythagoras, which was a failure.

38. The Athenian priest had to be a citizen enjoying all his rights, physically perfect and morally pure. Sometimes celibacy was exacted; but even the priestesses were often married. For certain offices young girls were chosen, who ceased to be priestesses when they married. If a priest or priestess lost a child, they became *taboo*, and had to resign their office that they might not sully the altar.

39. There was no fixed rule for ordination. Functions were transmitted by heritage or purchase, or by election and casting lots. Many important religious dignities were hereditary in great families; among these were the offices of the priests of Eleusis.

40. The costumes of the priests were prescribed by ritual. Often the priest represented the god himself, took his name, and imitated his appearance: this was a survival from a very ancient order of things, which is closely related to totemism among the North American Indians.

41. The priests were greatly revered. Their revenues, often very considerable, were derived principally from sacrifices, from the sale of the skins and flesh of the victims, the profits of which they shared with the State.

42. Divination was practised in the temples by accredited priests and priestesses, and elsewhere by itinerant soothsayers, who are not to be confounded with the priests. There

were two kinds of divination; in one the will of the god was directly revealed, in the other the interpretation was drawn from contingent manifestations. At Dodona, the oracle of Zeus, the god made his will known by the rustling of the oaks in the wind, or by the sound emitted by a brass vessel when struck by a thong. The priestesses or prophetesses of Dodona were called *doves*, just as those of the Artemis of Ephesus were called *bees;* this shows that these oracles were originally founded on observations of the flight of doves and bees, and also, no doubt, that they had their origin in totemic forms of worship of which these creatures were the objects.

43. The most famous oracle of antiquity, that of Delphi, was interpreted by a young girl called *Pythia*, who, inspired by Apollo, prophesied in fits of delirium. Earlier still, those who came to consult the oracle placed themselves upon the tripod, and received inspiration from the god with the vapours which exhaled from the prophetic cavern. No doubt it was found later that a sickly young girl was a surer medium for the suggestion of the god and his priests than their clients themselves.

44. Every manual of Greek antiquities gives the necessary details of the different kinds of soothsayers, of enchantments and of sorcery. I need say but a few words here of *incubation*, a proceeding which consisted in sleeping in a temple, or in a dormitory adjoining a temple, in order to enjoy visions and receive counsel or benefits from the god. Incubation was practised on the bare earth, the abode of spirits, or on the skin of a sacred animal. Long inscriptions discovered at Epidaurus describe a great number of cures obtained by sick persons, thanks to the nocturnal intervention of Asklepios and the animals proper to his worship, the dog, the serpent and the goose. "Euphanes, a child of Epidaurus, suffered from the stone; he fell asleep and the god appeared to him. 'What wilt thou give me if I cure thee?' asked he. The child replied: 'Ten knuckle-bones.' The god laughed and said he would cure the child. On the following day he left the temple, cured." In several cases, those who expressed doubts, or scoffed at the ex-votos of the sufferers, were afflicted with additional distempers, or con-

demned by the god to give a more costly offering; on the other hand, faith was a virtue that was highly appreciated, and the god did not fail to reward it. We recognise the well-organised industry of the priests who act upon the sick by suggestion, but also give them sensible advice occasionally. At the period when the inscriptions of Epidaurus were engraved, the science of healing had long been secularised by Hippocrates; but the old sacerdotal medicine, from which lay medicine had issued, continued to make dupes to the end of antiquity. We know that it still does so.

45. Sacrifices were differentiated from offerings by the destruction of the object offered, either by burning it whole —holocaust—or merely killing it. Men sacrificed to the gods to thank them, to render them propitious, to appease their anger. The general idea, at the classic period, was that of a feast to which the god was bidden; but there were certain rites in which the animal sacred to the god was sacrificed to him, indicating the primitive form of the sacrifice of the divine animal, eaten ritually by its worshippers. These totemic sacrifices were originally exceptional rites surrounded by minute precautions, the memory of which was preserved in certain forms of worship. At the Athenian Bouphonia, sacred wafers were presented to the ox (in reality, perhaps, to enhance his sanctity) so that by eating them he might seem to deserve death; after the immolation of the ox the sacrificer was subjected to a fictitious trial; then it was declared that the axe or knife alone was guilty, and this was thrown into the sea. At Tenedos stones were hurled at the priest who offered a young bull to Dionysos; at Corinth the annual sacrifice of a goat to Hera was performed by strange ministers, engaged for the purpose, and these arranged the knife in such a manner as to suggest that the victim had killed herself by accident. But a detailed account of Greek sacrifices would carry me too far; I must restrict myself to these rapid indications.

46. Running water was much in favour for purifications; sea-water was considered still more efficacious; in default of this, salt was thrown into fresh water. Purification was also carried out by means of smoke, ventilation, and suspension

in the air, which was even practised in the infernal regions, it was said. The sound of brass was supposed to have a purifying effect, hence the use of gongs and, later, of bells. Among many savage tribes it is usual to make a hideous din during eclipses of the moon, to drive away the demons who are attacking the planet. The custom was not unknown among the Greeks and Romans. The idea of "scaring demons" was always present in the minds of those who practised these noisy rites.

47. The festivals were either common to all Greece or peculiar to each people. The Pan-Hellenic festivals were called Olympics at Olympia, Pythian games at Delphi, Nemæan games at Nemæa, Isthmian games at Corinth. Every city had also its local festivals, such as the Panathenæa, the Eleusinia and the Dionysia at Athens. The Greek theatre arose from the Dionysiac celebrations. Originally, these rites circled round the sacrifice of a totemic goat, otherwise Dionysos himself; his death was bewailed, and then his resurrection was celebrated with transports of joy. The lamentations gave birth to tragedy, the rejoicings to comedy. The same evolution may be traced in the Middle Ages, when the modern theatre developed out of the *Mysteries* of the Passion.

48. The Greek mysteries were essentially initiations. Some of them, such as those of Eleusis, were under the protection of the State. The mysteries that still subsisted during the classic period were apparently mere survivals, for originally the admission of every male to the worship of his tribe was preceded by probation, the communication of gestures or formulæ under the seal of secrecy. The object of these primitive forms of worship was to exercise a stimulating action upon some natural phenomenon; even in the mysteries of the classic period, we find that in addition to the initiation which was to ensure the salvation of individuals, there were magic rites of more general interest, designed to promote the fertility of the fields. At Eleusis, these figured the union of the god and goddess (Pluto and Demeter), whose symbolic fruit, an ear of corn gathered in silence, was presented by the hierophant to the initiated.

II. The Italians and Romans

1. The Roman religion was an old Italic faith enlarged rather than modified in the course of twelve centuries by contributions from Etruria, Greece proper, and the East.

2. The only people to whose rule Rome once submitted, the Etruscans, did not impose their religion upon her. All she received from them was a false science, aruspicy, or divination by inspection of the entrails of animals, perhaps the conception of the goddess Minerva, and the idea of a council of the gods. Etruria was so thoroughly impregnated with Hellenic influences that the ideas she brought to Rome were rather those of Greece than her own. Thus we find no trace among the Romans of the civilising Etruscan god, Tages, who came into the world with white hair. Indeed, the sombre and mystical character of the Etruscan religion, in which Oriental elements are perceptible, was not calculated to attract the ancient Romans.

3. Towards the year 1200 B.C., or even earlier, Sicily and Southern Italy had been visited by the Cretans; there was a legend according to which Dædalus, the builder of the Labyrinth of Cnossos, had appeared in Sicily and at Cumæ, and Virgil calls Crete the cradle of the Roman people. Modern science in its turn recognises analogies between the worships of Crete, Arcadia and Rome, between the religious institutions attributed to the pious king Numa, and those which in Southern Italy were ascribed to the philosopher Pythagoras. If the legend of the Trojan Æneas arriving at Lavinium and founding Alba will hardly stand the strain of criticism, the same cannot be said of the traditions of Evander the Arcadian and the Ætolian Diomedes, whose landing in Italy was recorded in Greek history. It is therefore probable that at the very dawn of history, Central Italy was subjected to influences coming from Greece and the islands of the Archipelago, perhaps even from the coasts of Phœnicia, whose navigators traded with the Etruscans.

4. The Italic basis of Roman religion is mainly known by its rituals and sacred legends. Fragments of Salian and Arvalian songs have come down to us; the ritual of the

Umbrian confraternity of Iguvium has been preserved in seven long inscriptions; finally, we have calendars of festivals, for which Ovid's *Fasti* furnish an excellent commentary (through six months of the year), and considerable extracts from the great work of Varro on *divine things* (*c.* 50 B.C.). Varro was both a scholar and a theologian; there is nothing scientific in his theology, but the passages borrowed from him by St. Augustine and the Roman grammarians constitute some of the most precious relics of antiquity.

5. Italian animism is differentiated from that of the Greeks by an entire absence of imagination. Instead of gods and goddesses, it created powers, *numina,* without genealogical connections or history. For us these are hardly more than names, the sterile exuberance of which is uninstructive. Rome was all the more prepared to adopt the legends of the Greek gods, because she had so few of native growth.

6. "There is no spot without its genius," wrote Servius, and this same grammarian, inspired by Varro, said that special gods presided over each act in life. These gods form long lists of epithets, imperfectly personified, which figured in prayers and litanies: *Cuba* watched over the child in his bed, *Abeona* taught him to walk, *Farinus,* to speak. Every man had a *genius,* every woman a *Juno;* under the Empire, the genii of the Emperors were worshipped, and men even talked of the genii of the gods. The genii of the fields and of the house were called *Lares;* the familiar *Lar* was that of the hearth and family; at a later period, the imperial *Lar* was worshipped. The *Penates* were the genii of the larder (*penus*). The genii of the dead were their *Manes* (signifying "the good," no doubt a euphemism), the chief objects of family worship; before inhabiting tombs outside the house, they served as guardians of the house itself, for the dead were buried under the hearth in primitive times. The *Larvæ* and *Lemures* were of the same nature as the *Manes*, but they were held to be more or less hostile; they were spirits which had to be appeased by offerings, or kept at a distance by magic rites.

7. The State, like the family, had also its Penates, the

worship of which was celebrated in the temple of Vesta, the guardian of fire, *i.e.*, of the public hearth. This fire was never allowed to be extinguished; virgins called Vestals tended the flame. They were the brides of the fire and belonged to it absolutely. They could only marry after obtaining their dismissal. Those who broke their vows were buried alive and condemned to die of hunger.

8. Personifications such as Health, Fortune, Youth, belong to a class of genii without any legends, products of animism and of the tendency to abstraction. These are not altogether lacking in Greek mythology, but that of the Romans is positively overburdened with them. The reverses of coins struck under the Empire form a veritable museum of cold abstractions.

9. A material object inhabited by a spirit is a fetich. Primitive Rome had fetiches instead of idols. A lance was the first image of the god of war, a flint that of Jupiter. With a flint the Fetiales sacrificed a pig to ratify a treaty, just as to declare war they threw a lance upon a hostile territory. The mysterious object called the Palladium of Rome, which more or less resembled an armed Minerva (*Pallas*), was a fetich confided to the care of the vestals; later, a tradition grew up that it had been brought from Troy by Æneas.

10. The Roman legends which Titus Livius and Dionysius record as history attest the sacred character of the fig-tree, the onion and the bean. There were trees which formed sacred woods, like those of the Arvales and the goddess of Nemi. Among animals, the wolf was the one held in the highest veneration. The association of this beast with Mars, in the character of "favourite victim," leaves no doubt as to the original nature of the god himself. It was a wolf which served as guide to the Samnites when they were seeking for territory on which to settle, and these Samnites were called *Hirpi* or *Hirpini*, that is to say, wolves. Romulus and Remus, the sons of the wolf Mars and the she-wolf Silvia (the forest nymph) were suckled by a wolf. The ancient god Silvanus (the forester) was probably a wolf in the be-

ginning; later on, he was regarded as a hunter of wolves and was clad in a wolf-skin.

11. The horse, which was sacrificed and cut up at Rome in the month of October, was a divinity no less than the white bull, immolated during the Latin Feria and distributed in fragments among the cities of Latium.

12. The Romans declared that they kept geese on the Capitol to honour the vigilance of these birds, which had frustrated a nocturnal attack attempted by the Gauls; this was a later explanation of a custom founded on the sacred character of the goose. Fowls, which the insular Britons of the time of Cæsar kept in the same way without daring to eat them, were also sacred in Rome, as we see from the part played by the sacred fowls in divination; even during a campaign, food was offered to them, and if they refused to eat, reverses were anticipated. All the augural animals of the classic period were originally sacred animals; the totem was the protector and guide of the tribe. The wolves, boars and eagles which crowned the Roman standards had a similar origin. Tacitus was aware that the animals on the standards were sacred. Of course these were merely survivals of totemism, but it is impossible to contest their origin. In like manner the existence of Roman families called Porcii, Fabii, &c., is easily explained if we admit that the boar and the bean (*porcus, faba*) were the totems and mythical ancestors of these clans. The Pythagoreans considered it a crime to eat or even to tread upon a bean. At Rome, where it was supposed that Numa had been a disciple of Pythagoras, the worship of the bean has left its traces, particularly in the ancient ceremony of the Lemuralia; the father of the family, fearing the Lemures, threw beans behind his back, that these demons might eat them, and leave him and his in peace.

13. The Latin word *sacer* is the exact equivalent of *taboo*, for it signifies both sacred and impure. Everything that was *sacer* was withdrawn from common use; when it was said of a man "Let him be sacred," this meant that he should be withdrawn from society, exiled, or put to death. A person or object was rendered sacred by the rites of the

consecratio, and *desecrated* by *profanatio*, which, in its original sense, does not imply anything impious. There were tabooed days, on which nothing was to be undertaken; the calendar called them *nefasti*, because on them the sacramental words of worship and of justice could not be pronounced (*fari*); the days when this was permitted were called *fasti*. During the festivals (*feriæ*) all work was suspended; certain gods might not be mentioned by name. The priest of Jupiter, *Flamen dialis*, and his wife, the *Flaminica*, were subjected to numerous and vexatious taboos. The *flamen* might neither eat nor touch a bean, nor touch a horse, nor wear a ring which was not broken, nor tread upon a vine. The spoils taken from the enemy were *taboo;* it was long the custom to pile them up on a sacred spot of the Capitol, the Tarpeian rock, and this accumulation of shields and other arms gave rise to the legend of the virgin Tarpeia, who was crushed beneath a heap of arms for having betrayed the Capitol to the enemy. At the classic period, the spoils of war were hung upon sacred oaks, and on the walls of temples and houses; save in cases of extreme peril, it was unlawful to touch them. This was because they bore the weight of the maledictions pronounced against the enemy at the beginning of the war; every war was originally a religious one.

14. The true names of the divinities were taboo, because had they been revealed, it would have been possible for hostile magic to attract them. This is why our knowledge is confined in the main to epithets, which do duty for divine names. Rome itself had a secret name, used in the most solemn invocations. The secret of this name was so well kept that we do not know it to this day.

15. The most ancient secular code of Rome, that known as the law of the Twelve Tables, dealt very severely with magic, with malevolent magic, that is to say, the object of which was to injure a fellow-creature. This *black* magic was continually repressed and as constantly practised; the State only had recourse to it when formulæ of execration had to be pronounced against a rebellious citizen or an enemy. But sympathetic magic was the very essence of

Roman worship. Small images were thrown into the Tiber to bring about a rainfall; to render women prolific, the priests known as Luperci (*lupus, hircus*) flogged them with thongs, perhaps of wolfskin. Cato the Elder, who was so opposed to all innovations, has left us a large collection of magic formulæ which were used in agriculture and medicine, and esteemed highly efficacious.

16. The first temple built at Rome, under Tarquin I., was that of Jupiter Capitolinus, the seat of the three divinities, Jupiter, Juno and Minerva, the *Capitoline Triad.* Up to this time, says Varro (*c.* 50 B.C.), Rome, for a space of one hundred and seventy years, had had neither temples nor images. The word *templum* in the archaic tongue did not mean a building, but a sacred spot set apart by the augurs for the performance of certain religious acts.

17. The constitution of the Roman Pantheon began about 550 B.C. Jupiter, the god of heaven and thunder, was at once the protector of Rome and the guardian of the prescribed faith; Mars or Quirinus was the god of war; Faunus presided over the raising of cattle. Janus, the two-faced god, had a temple the gates of which were thrown open at the beginning of a war, for this vigilant god was supposed to sally forth with the warriors. We have already spoken of Vesta, the goddess of the hearth. This first Pantheon was modified by the identification of the Roman gods with those of Greece, which seems to have been accomplished before 200 B.C. The twelve gods are enumerated in these two verses of Ennius:

Juno, Vesta, Minerva, Ceres, Diana, Venus, Mars,
Mercurius, Jovis, Neptunus, Volcanus, Apollo.

Jovis (Jupiter) was the celestial Indo-European deity, *Zeus pater;* Apollo was borrowed from the Greeks, Minerva from the Etruscans; the other gods correspond approximately only to the Greek deities, Hestia, Demeter, Artemis, Ares, &c. Venus, a mere abstraction indicating Desire, emerged from her obscurity when it became necessary to find a pendant for the Greek Aphrodite, who, according to the Æneas legend, was the ancestress of the Romans.

18. The twelve great gods, to whom banquets or *lectisternia* were sometimes offered, were considered a divine council (*di consentes*). Rude copies of the wooden statues of these gods, which stood in the Forum, have come down to us on a Gallo-Roman altar at Mavilly (Côte-d'Or). Diana is shown holding serpents, like the goddess at Cnossos in Crete and the old Arcadian Artemis; the motive is unknown in Greek classic art. Mars also figures as the Etruscan Mars, and Mercury has wings at his back, after an Etruscan and not a Greek model. But the most curious figure is that of Vesta, hiding her eyes with her hands to shield them from the smoke of the altar, in the attitude which Ovid ascribes to the statues of Vesta in a temple at Alba, and notes without understanding its significance.

19. The Romans adopted not only the myths of the Greeks, but their ideas as to the origin of the world and of another life. On this last subject they had certain popular conceptions which have survived to this day. Orcus, the devourer of corpses, perhaps a wolf originally, became the *Orco* of the Italians, the *ogre* of our fairy-tales. The Roman Pluto, *Dis pater*, is represented with a mallet, wherewith to stun the dead, probably in imitation of the Etruscan Charon, who was rather an executioner than a ferryman. As Dispater is also clad in a wolf-skin, I am inclined to see in him another example of an infernal wolf. In literature, the Greek legends became predominant, but they do not seem to have received much credence; Lucretius scorns them, and Juvenal tells us that in his time, only young children not as yet admitted to the public baths believed in the subterranean world and Charon's boat.

20. The funeral rites were cremation and burial, the latter tending to prevail from the third century of the empire, under the influence of the imported Oriental creeds. Children of tender years were never to be burnt, but laid in the earth, whence it was believed they were born again in new bodies. Certain other traces of the doctrine of metempsychosis are to be traced in the popular beliefs of Italy.

21. The official form of worship was a dry and positive ritualism, closely related to political life. As religion was a

matter not of sentiment but of the State, there was no conflict between temporal and spiritual interests. The three great colleges of priests, charged with the conduct of public worship, were the pontiffs, the sacrificing decemvirs, and the augurs. The college of pontiffs further included the king of the sacrifices, on whom the ancient sacerdotal functions of the king had devolved, the flamens and the vestals. The name of the pontiff was obviously derived from the construction of bridges (*ponti-fex*); but was the reference to the first bridges thrown across the Tiber, like the Pons Sublicius, or to those more ancient bridges which, in the square encampments of prehistoric Italy, spanned the moats that enclosed and guarded them? The pontiff presided over the entire national worship, and in addition superintended private worship, offerings to the dead, and marriages. The head of the college of pontiffs was originally the king, then a high priest, Pontifex Maximus. From Augustus to Gratianus all the emperors had claimed this dignity, and even Constantine, the protector of Christianity, wished to be invested with it.

22. The decemvirs (later quindecemvirs) of the sacrifices were the priests of the alien gods and of the Greek rites. The augurs were charged with divination by means of birds; the aruspices examined the entrails of victims at the bidding of the pontiffs. Other colleges less important, but no less revered, directed the worship of Mars (the Salii), of the Dea Dia (the Arvales), of Faunus Lupercus (the Luperci). The Salii or *Jumpers*, the flamines of Mars, guarded the *ancilia* or sacred shields, the first of which, the model of the rest, had fallen from heaven into Numa's palace. We know the shape of these shields, which was identical with that of the 8-shaped shields of the Minoan period; here again the influence of prehistoric Greece, or that of a common origin, is revealed in the Rome of the kings.

23. Certain forms of worship had devolved on families (*gentes*) and public or private confraternities. The professional corporations had a religious character and a common form of worship. The funerary colleges ensured the honourable sepulture of its members; De Rossi suggested

that the first Christians formed associations of this kind to perform their rites under the protection of the law.

24. In the sacrifices, a thousand puerile details, such as the sex and colour of the victims, were minutely prescribed by ritual. Sacred flour and salt were sprinkled on the head of a victim to consecrate it to the god. This *deified* it, or assimilated it to the god by a preliminary rite; consequently it was the god who was sacrificed, and the inspection of the entrails was the more instructive, in that it was directed to a divine body. These practices of inspection passed perhaps from Babylonia to Etruria, then from Etruria to Rome. As in Babylonia, it was the liver of the animal which was most carefully examined. The principal sacrifice consisted of a pig, a sheep and a bull; the order in which these animals are enumerated, attested by the ancient word used to designate this group of victims, *suovetaurilia*, is very significant, for it clearly indicates the religious importance of the pig, that is to say, the wild boar.

25. Tarquin II., called the Proud, was supposed to have bought the Sibylline Books, the oracles of the fate of Rome, which were confided to the decemvirs, and consulted on grave occasions, by order of the Senate. They were destroyed in 82 B.C., when the Capitol was burnt; a new collection was then formed in Asia and Egypt. The little we know of the later texts shows that they were for the most part Greek verses manufactured by Hellenistic Jews, full of veiled threats against the Empire. This explains why Stilicho ordered their destruction on the eve of the great disasters (A.D. 405). The Sibylline oracles which now exist were freely circulated, and were quoted as inspired texts by certain Fathers of the Church; they are still accepted as such in the Catholic funeral service (*teste David cum Sibylla*). They are nevertheless for the most part forgeries at second-hand, Judæo-Christian imitations of those Jewish forgeries which formed the official Sibylline Books of the Empire; hatred of Rome is freely expressed in them, as in the Apocalypse of St. John.

26. In the no less fraudulent collection of oracles destroyed in 82, it was supposed from time to time that pas-

sages had been discovered, enjoining the introduction into Rome of Hellenic deities, and the construction of temples for them. The Dioscuri were thus admitted in 488, Apollo about 430, Asklepios (Æsculapius) about 290; Cybele, the great Asiatic mother of Ida, arrived at Rome from Pessinus in 204. At the time of Mithridates, the sanguinary goddess Comana was introduced from Cappadocia, and assimilated to the Italic Bellona, with her cortège of frenzied priests, and dancing and howling dervishes who were called *fanatici* (from *fanum*, a temple). Thus fanaticism, so distasteful to the Romans, entered Rome under the auspices of the Senate. As time went on, it flourished only too well on that soil.

27. When the Senate had not itself taken the initiative, it showed great uneasiness at the introduction of new forms of worship, not from religious intolerance, but from fear that pious confraternities might be a cover for political associations. This explains the persecution directed against the Bacchanalia (186 A.D.). These rites of Dionysos, which were very widely practised in Southern Italy, had gained a large number of devotees in Rome, especially among women. It was alleged by suborned witnesses, that the ceremonies were a pretext for immoralities and crimes of every kind. The Bacchanalia were prohibited in Italy; thousands of men and women were put to death for having taken part in them. As a fact, the Senate wanted to weaken Italian Hellenism at a moment when this seemed to threaten danger; the crimes imputed to the initiated were no less imaginary than those with which the Romans of the Empire charged the Christians, or those which the Christians in their turn attributed to schismatics and infidels. Even if the priests of Bacchus were lunatics or impostors, the policy of the Roman Senate against them was a policy of murder and fraud.

28. In spite of these cruelties, which were followed by others, alien creeds invaded Italy, and were eagerly accepted by the masses; they satisfied those yearnings for fervour and mystic piety which the official forms of worship could not content. Not only were the priests of these official faiths sceptical—Cato said that two aruspices could not look at each other without laughing—but they were functionaries

charged with the performance of certain rites, who cared no more about the matter when their task was duly accomplished. What a difference between these men and the Oriental priest who went straight to the believer, called him his brother and treated him as such, aroused and nourished his impulses of devotion, taught him ecstasy, the hope of a better world, resignation to the miseries of this life! These itinerant priests found a ready following in the foreign population, either enslaved or poor, which was swelled by a continual stream of immigration from the East. Juvenal complains that the Orontes of Syria had emptied itself into the Tiber; he might have said the same of the Nile, the Jordan and the Halys. Asia Minor and Egypt, imperfectly Hellenised except upon the coasts, had remained the two great religious countries of the antique world. The Roman Empire was filled with the worshippers of Attis, Isis, Osiris, Serapis, Sabazios, Zeus Dolichenos and Mithra. The strangest customs, imbued with a sombre mysticism, replaced the cold and severe Roman practices. In the sacrifice of the *taurobolium*, which took place in the worship of Cybele, a priest immolated a bull. Its blood was made to drip between the boards of the floor upon the head of the person who made the offering, and was supposed to render him divine. It was in vain that Augustus and Tiberius took measures against the Egyptian worships, and that several emperors prosecuted the Chaldæan and Syrian astrologers. Caligula authorised the worship of Isis at Rome, Commodus was initiated into the mysteries of Mithra, and Oriental superstition was installed in the very palace of the Cæsars when Bassianus, priest of the Black Stone of Emesa, became emperor under the title of Heliogabalus.

29. Heliogabalus was no exceptional case. The dynasty of Syrian emperors from Septimius Severus (A.D. 193-235) threw open the gates of Rome to all the Oriental creeds favoured by the devotion of the empresses. The emperors themselves were not averse from faiths which flattered their despotic instincts; for the worship of deified emperors had been borrowed from the East at the beginning of the empire. This indulgence was enhanced by the superstitious

tendency to conciliate and amalgamate religions, due to the idea that there might be some good in all the gods. Alexander Severus had in his private chapel images of Apollonius of Tyana, of Orpheus, and of Jesus; he even thought of building a temple to the god of the Jews. The progress of Christianity, implanted at Rome from about the year A.D. 50, was so rapid at this period that the subsequent persecution, the work more especially of the military emperors, served but to hasten the development of the crisis in favour of the more active and, in the towns at least, the more numerous party.

30. It is remarkable that the worships of Gaul, of Germany, and even of Northern Africa (with the exception of Egypt), found little favour at Rome. The only Gallic divinity which became popular there, thanks to the cavalry of the legions recruited in Gaul, was Epona, the protectress of horses. The reason of this fact must be sought in the world of slaves and freedmen. Gauls, Germans and Africans were employed in rural cultivation; the Orientals, male and female, more refined and gentle, attached themselves to the family, propagated their ideas, and converted their mistresses, if not their masters. It must be noted further that the East provided a perpetual stream of enthusiastic missionaries. Among these was Apollonius of Tyana (*d.* 97), who claimed to have been the pupil of the Indian Brahmans. In the third century Philostratus wrote an edifying biography, full of miracles, perhaps with the intention of setting up this thaumaturgus as the rival of Jesus.

* * *

31. The old religion was already so decrepit at the time of Cæsar that it is surprising it should have lasted four centuries longer. This survival was due to its national and political character. The worship of the Roman divinities became a form of patriotism, especially after the reaction inaugurated by Augustus. Himself a free-thinker like Cæsar, he exerted himself to the utmost to revive a reverence for the past and combat the subversive tendencies of his day. He found auxiliaries in serious men such as Virgil and Titus

Livius, and even in epicureans like Propertius, Horace and Ovid. The *Æneid*, which has become the national epic of Rome, was a religious poem; Livy's *Decades*, Horace's *Carmen Sæculare* and Ovid's *Fasti* are inspired by a kindred spirit, and simulate a kind of piety that supplies the place of faith. The throne looked to the altar for support; the orthodox gentleman, the "homme bien pensant" who believes in nothing, but sends his servants to church, dates from the time of Augustus. Finally, the public worship accorded to the emperors, especially to deceased and deified emperors, for which the Senate had prepared the way by building a temple to Cæsar, was associated with the worship of the goddess Rome, and became in the provinces the religious formula of loyalism. It was because they refused to participate in this worship that the Jews and Christians were always looked upon with suspicion by the powers; the Christians more particularly, because they did not constitute the remnants of a conquered nation, but a State within the State. "We are but of yesterday," wrote Tertullian about A.D. 200, "and already we fill the world! We have left you only your temples."

32. Before it finally died out, Græco-Roman paganism was vivified by Babylonian astrology. A kind of solar Pantheism, compounded of scientific and mystical elements, replaced the worship of the old gods in the upper classes. Astrology supplanted the grosser methods of divination and helped to silence the oracles. As early as the time of Augustus, the poet Manilius had set forth the doctrines of astrology; in the third and fourth centuries, all the aristocracy of paganism professed them with great ardour. It was, in the main, an application of the idea of universal sympathy; the sovereign power was attributed to the planets, which were supposed to govern and dominate the world from the heavens. The result of this teaching was fatalism, which has remained endemic in the East. Christianity itself has contributed to it to some extent, by the conception of grace. To escape the compelling power of the horoscope, a refined and pseudo-scientific magic was called into play, which stood on the same footing as the official astrology and that of the

wayside astrologers. All this, as Franz Cumont has shown, contributed rather to advance than to check the progress of Christianity, for on the one hand, astrology finally discredited the ancient forms of worship and national rites, and on the other, it had a tendency to monotheism in the preponderant place it assigned in the system of the world to the heavenly God as manifested in the sun.

33. The history of philosophic doctrines does not belong to our subject; but it is impossible not to say a few words of the mystic schools, and especially of Neo-Platonism, which from the time of Plotinus the Alexandrian (*d.* A.D. 290), and more especially of his disciple Porphyry (*d.* 305), unconsciously contributed to the diffusion of Christianity by their abuse of dogmatic constructions and their hostility to rationalism. The action of these schools was parallel with that of the Oriental religions and of astrology, to whose influence indeed they themselves were subjected. Thus rationalism became rare in the second half of the second century; even Plutarch (*d.* 140) is half a mystic. The writers of the eighteenth century imagined that Julian and Constantine were unbelieving politicians, the one hostile, the other favourable to Christianity; they were, as a fact, devotees, the one of the Sun, the other of all the religions through which he had hopes of his salvation, which had been imperilled by a long series of crimes. Christianity had not to triumph over official Roman paganism; this had long been dead or effete; its rivals were the other Oriental religions. The product, in part, of Jewish prophetism, it was superior to these by its simplicity and purity; these were the qualities which ensured its victory, and have preserved it to the present day.

BIBLIOGRAPHY

All questions bearing on the religions of Greece and Rome are treated in Saglio's Dictionary, Pauly-Wissowa's *Real-Encyclopedie,* and more particularly in Roscher's *Lexikon der Mythologie* (from 1882). Most of the ideas indicated in this chapter are more fully worked out in my five volumes, *Cultes, Mythes et Religions* (1904-1923); see also, for a survey of religious institutions, Gardner's *Manual of Greek Antiquities,* 1895, and Stuart Jones' *Companion to Roman History,* 1912.

I. Farnell, *Cults of the Greek States*, 4 vols., 1896-1907; P. Decharme, *Mythol. de la Grèce*, 2nd ed., 1886; O. Gruppe, *Griechische Mythologie*, 1906 (very important); P. Stengel, *Griech. Sakralalterthümer*, 2nd ed., 1899; J. Harrison, *Religion of Ancient Greece*, 1905; *Themis, Social Origins of Greek Religion*, 1912; Nilsson, *A History of Greek Religion*, 1925; J. Girard, *Le sentiment religieux en Grèce*, 1869 (first rate).

2. Decharme, *Traditions religieuses des Grecs*, 1904 (*cf.* Cumont, *Journ. des Sav.*, 1908, p. 113).

3. Hogarth, *Ægean Religion*, in Hastings' *Encycl. of Religion*, vol. i (1908); Evans, *Mycenæan Tree and Pillar Cult*, 1901; Burrows, *Discoveries in Crete*, 1907; R. Dussaud, *Les civilisations préhelléniques*, 2nd ed., 1914; Nilsson, *Minoan and Myken. Religion*, 1927.

4. S. R., *Les déesses nues dans l'art oriental* (in *Chron. d'Orient*, vol. ii).

7. The Arcadian Artemis and the goddess with the serpents: S. Reinach, *Cultes*, vol. iii, p. 210.

9. G. d'Alviella, *Migration des symboles*, 1891; S. R., *Oiseaux et swastikas* (in *Cultes*, vol. ii, p. 234).

15. De Visser, *Die nicht menschengestaltigen Götter der Griechen*, 1903; C. Bötticher, *Baumcultus der Hellenen*, 1856.

17. Fustel de Coulanges, *La cité antique*, 1865 (Engl. transl.); E. Rohde, *Psyche*, 2nd ed., 1898; Dieterich, *Nekyia*, 1893.

20. Leda and the Dioscuri; S. R., *Cultes*, vol. ii, p. 42.

22. Burnet, *Early Greek Philosophy*, 1892. The standard work on Orphism (in Latin) is still A. Lobeck's *Aglaophamus*, 2 vols., 1829; see also art. *Orpheus* by Gruppe in Roscher's *Lexikon;* S. Reinach, *Cultes*, vol. ii, p. 85 (death of Orpheus); G. W. Dyson, *Speculum religionis*, 1929, p. 19, and recent books by Maass, Eisler, Kern, Boulanger, etc. For Zagreus, see, in addition to Lobeck, S. Reinach, *Cultes*, vol. ii, p. 58. Orphism in Virgil: *ibid.*, vol. ii, p. 66. The Orphic formulæ: *ib.*, vol. ii, p. 123, and Jane Harrison, *Prolegomena to the Study of Greek Religion*, 1903 (texts and complete translations).

26. Actæon: S. R., *Cultes*, vol. iii, p. 24.—Hippolytus: *Ibid.*, vol. iii, p. 54.—Phaeton: *Ibid.*, vol. iv, p. 45.—Prometheus: *Ibid.*, vol. iii, p. 68.

28. Foucart, *Les mystères d'Eleusis*, 1914; Anrich, *Das antike Mysterienwesen*, 1904; R. Pettazoni, *I misteri*, 1924; O. Kern, *Griech. Mysterien*, 1927.

30. Hubert, art. *Magia* in Saglio.

33. Sisyphus in Hell: S. R., *Cultes*, vol. ii, p. 159.

35. P. Foucart, *Assoc. relig. chez les Grecs*, 1873.

36. M. Croiset, *Aristophane et les partis*, 1906. The explanation of the trial of Socrates is my own.

37 *et seq.* See Schœmann, Gardner, Hermann, &c., on Greek antiquities.

43. Bouché-Leclercq, *Hist. de la divination*, 4 vols., 1879-1881.

44. Deubner, *De incubatione*, 1900; Lechat and Defrasse, *Epidaure*, 1896; P. Stengel, *Opfergebräuche der Griechen*, 1910.

47. A. Mommsen, *Heortologie*, 1883; *Feste der Stadt Athen*, 1898; M. P. Nilsson, *Griechische Feste*, 1906; Foucart, *Le culte de Dionysos en Attique*, 1904.

II. 2. *Etrusci* in Pauly-Wissowa and in Saglio.

6. Art. *Indigitamenta* in Saglio's Dictionary.

7. R. Cagnat, *Les Vestales* (in *Conf. Guimet*, 1906, p. 61); S. R., *Cultes*, vol. iii, p. 191 (on Vesta).

9. Wissowa, *Relig. der Römer*, 2nd ed., 1912; Toutain, *Cultes paiens dans l'Empire romain*, vol. i, 1907; W. Fowler, *Relig. Experience of the Romans*, 1911.

23. M. Besnier, *Les catacombes de Rome,* 1908, p. 44 (funerary colleges).

24. Warde Fowler, *The Roman Festivals* (republican era), 1899.

27. Bacchanalia: S. R., *Cultes,* vol. iii, p. 254.

28. Cumont, *Religions orientales dans le paganisme romain,* 1907; *Astrology and religion,* 1912.

30. S. R., *Epona,* 1895, and *Cultes,* vol. iv, p. 54.

31. G. Boissier, *Religion romaine d'Auguste aux Antonins,* 2 vols., 1874; Beurlier, *Le culte impérial,* 1891.

32. Boll, *Sphära,* 1903; Cumont, *op. cit.* (28); Bouché-Leclercq, *Astrologie grecque,* 1899.

CHAPTER IV

CELTS, GERMANS AND SLAVS

I. The Conquests of the Celts. The first inhabitants of Gaul. The art of the cave-dwellers; its magical origin. Bones coloured with red ochre. Dolmens, menhirs and cromlechs. The worship of the axe. The rarity of idols. The worship of mountains, rivers, and trees; the mistletoe. The worship of animals and the survival of totemism. The taboo on the spoils of war; the martial taboo. Esus, Teutates and Taranis. The Jupiter with the wheel. Dis pater, the god with the mallet. Ogmios. Mothers, or matrons. Celtic Triads. Celtic and Roman divinities. Names and epithets. Emperor worship. Temples. The Druids and sacrifices. Belief in a future life. The decay of Druidism; Druidism in Ireland. Irish mythology; survivals from Celtic religions.

II. The religion of the Germans as described by Cæsar. Sun worship. The Moon identified with Diana. The religion of the Germans as described by Tacitus. The days of the week. The gods of the Germans. The worship of Mars, Mercury and Hercules. Goddesses. Witches. Animism. Sacred animals. The worship of the horse. Kings and priests. Idols. Irminsul. Funeral rites. Iceland and Norway. The poems of the Skalds and the Runes. The Edda, poetry and mythology of the Vikings. The Voluspa; the Twilight of the Gods. Anglo-Saxon and Germanic poems of the Middle Ages.

III. The religion of the Slavs as described by Procopius. The Slav Jupiter. The horse-god. Many-headed idols. The god of flocks. The god Trajan. The Black God. Nymphs. The domestic gods. Sacred trees. The worship of the dead. Voracious demons and epidemics.

I. The Celts or Gauls

1. The Celts spoken of by the classic historians were conquering tribes who, coming from the right bank of the Rhine, successively invaded Gaul, part of Germany, the Britannic Isles, Spain, the north of Italy and the valley of the Danube; some of their warlike septs penetrated into Asia Minor and there occupied a province to which they gave their name (Galatia). These Celts, Gauls or Galatæ did not take possession of uninhabited regions; in each case they found more ancient races than themselves, whose civilisation, including no doubt their religious ideas, they adopted. It is impos-

sible to determine what they added of their own; perhaps very little. When therefore we speak of Celtic religions, we must bear in mind that this means religions the essential elements of which were certainly anterior to the Celts of history, religions which might just as fitly be termed Ligurian, Iberian, or even to use a more comprehensive phrase, the religions of Western Europe.

2. At the period of the mammoth and the reindeer, many thousand years before our era, Gaul already possessed artists who, in Périgord and the Pyrenean region, carved and engraved figures of animals, and painted them on the walls of the inhabited caves. These animals were of a particular kind; they are mostly comestible and desirable; very few beasts of prey are represented. Sometimes the animal is depicted pierced by arrows, prefiguring a successful hunt, or rather perhaps with the idea that the reality would be brought about by the image. We find the same conception in the Middle Ages, when a spell was cast upon an enemy by striking pins into a waxen image made in his likeness.

3. Here we lay hold of the magic origins of art, the object of which was to attract the animals, which served the tribe for food, by a sort of fascination. It is quite possible that these animals were the totems of the different clans, that the caves were the scenes of totemic ceremonies, and that the engraved or sculptured objects made of reindeer horn and called commanders' bâtons played a magic part in the worship. We even have, at Montesquieu-Avantès (Ariège), the figure of a wizard in animal disguise and the traces (also found in Spain) of sacred dances in caves.

4. Certain graves dating from the quaternary period and many others of a later age have been found to contain skeletons which before burial were exposed to the air till the flesh dropped off, the bones being then painted over with a layer of red ochre. Evidences of this custom are to be found from Spain to Russia; its existence in Oceania and in South America has also been established. It has certainly some connection with a religious idea, red being the colour of life, as opposed to the pale hue of death. Bodies have also been found with the head severed from the trunk, perhaps for fear of

THE POEMS OF THE SKALDS

the "vampire." This seems to be the explanation of the singular discovery made at Milan in A.D. 386 of a grave containing two great decapitated skeletons painted red. St. Ambrose, then Bishop of Milan, believed and made others believe that they were the bones of Christian martyrs of the time of Nero, Gervase and Protasius, still red with the blood shed at their execution. As if organic matter like blood could have retained its colour for three centuries! This pretended discovery of the bodies of the two martyrs was exploited as a miracle in the interests of the Catholic faith, which was menaced at the time by a sect claiming to be adherents of Arius, and protected by the Empress Justina.

5. In the latter part of the Polished Stone Period, Gaul, Spain and the British Isles were covered with dolmens, menhirs, and cromlechs. The dolmens, huge tombs of undressed stone, attest the worship of the dead; they also attest the domination of a sacerdotal aristocracy sufficiently powerful to impose painful labour on the masses. The dolmens contain articles of use and luxury, arms, amulets, evidences of belief in a future life analogous to that of Greece and Rome. Among the amulets are roundels taken from skulls trepanned before, or after, death; these were sometimes placed in other skulls. Some of the dolmens are closed by means of a perforated slab; this is a peculiarity to be found in the dolmens of the Crimea, Syria and India, and may have some connection with the belief in the periodic emergences of spirits. The menhirs do not appear to have been funereal monuments; but they often indicate the proximity of dolmens, and when they are set side by side in large numbers, forming circles (cromlechs) or avenues, they mark the site or the limits of a sacred territory dedicated to the performance of religious rites. When they are isolated, they recall those upright stones, the domicile of an ancestral spirit or a god (Bethels), mentioned in the Bible and by the Greek writers. The menhirs remain to this very day the object of a popular reverence which the Church has sought to render inoffensive by surmounting them with a cross. This worship is attested as early as the Roman era by a passage in Cæsar which calls the menhirs "simulacra of Mercury," and by the

existence of a menhir at Kernuz in Brittany, on which figures of gods were carved in relief about the first century.

6. Certain monuments of large stones, notably in Brittany and Ireland, are engraved with signs of a religious character, axes, serpents, and spiral lines which resemble the creases in the fingers of the hand. At this period, when metals were unknown, or very scarce, the polished axe was an implement of common use, but, like many other weapons among both ancient and modern peoples, it was an object of worship and perhaps a talisman against thunderbolts. The worship of the axe is attested in Babylonia, Asia Minor, Crete and Rome; it also existed in Gaul. Axes are engraved on the walls of the funeral grottoes in the Petit Morin valley (Marne), where there is also the rude image of a female divinity in relief. Later, about the middle or end of the Age of Copper, primitive statues were fashioned, a kind of anthropoid menhirs representing half-draped women; examples have been found in the Aveyron and the Tarn; they have been compared with the feminine idols of the Ægean (p. 81). But these are rarities; the representation of the human figure did not develop in Gaul before the Roman conquest. About 280 B.C. the Gallic chief Brennus scoffed at the idols of marble and bronze he saw in the temple of Delphi. Does this indicate the existence of some religious prohibition analogous to that which obtained among the Jews and the Musulmans? As the ancients recognised affinities in the doctrines of the Druids and the Pythagoreans, it is possible that Druidism may be responsible for the almost total absence of statues in ancient Gaul, from the middle of the Bronze Age. We have already seen that the "simulacra of Mercury" of which Cæsar speaks, were probably only menhirs, analogous to the sacred pillars which the Greeks called *hermai* (§ 5).

7. Of all the religious literature of the Celts, which was, indeed, rather oral than written, no single line has come down to us; our information, which is derived from classic texts, from sculptures and from inscriptions, dates almost entirely from the era of Roman Gaul. If, however, we subtract the Roman elements, and invoke auxiliary sciences,

such as the etymology of proper names, we can form a fairly definite idea of the religions of Gaul before the conquest. These religions were very various and essentially local; there was neither a single creed nor a centralised government. I may add that the primitive creeds of Gaul, like those of all other countries, were animistic and totemic in origin; anthropomorphism developed late, under Roman influence.

8. The Gauls worshipped high mountains, the St. Bernard, the Donon, the Puy-de-Dôme. Rivers and springs were sacred in their eyes. Certain Gauls, dwellers on the banks of the Rhine, plunged their new-born infants into its waters; if they floated, they, in their turn, were accepted as descendants of the Rhine, protected by the common ancestor, and hence as legitimate offspring. This was one of those *ordeals* which the Middle Ages retained under the name of *Judgments of God.* Many of the rivers and springs were styled "divine," hence the frequent occurrence of such names as *Dive* and *Divonne.* Thermal springs were the abodes of genii called *Bormo* or *Borvo* (meaning "boiling"); hence the name Bourbon, Bourbonne, Bourboule, &c. The activity of a gushing fountain suggested the idea of a sacred animal, sometimes a bull, sometimes a horse. The bull became the attribute of Apollo, the god of healing. The name of the goddess Epona, signifying an "equine spring," is exactly comparable to that of the fountain of Parnassus which Apollo's steed, Pegasus, brought forth (Hippocrene, from *hippos, kréné*).

9. There were in Gaul sacred forests, consisting principally of oaks, the trees of which were protected by a religious reverence. These forests served as meeting-places and temples; their "spirits" were worshipped. Among these were *Abnoba,* the Black Forest, and *Arduinna,* the forest of the Ardennes. The oak was held in such veneration that a Greek writer makes it the supreme god, the Zeus of the Gauls. The mistletoe of the oak, which is a somewhat rare parasite, was gathered with great ceremony by the Druids, dressed in white robes; they detached it with a golden sickle, after sacrificing a white bull to the gods, and caught it in white cloths as it fell from the tree. To this day the mistle-

toe is the object of a superstitious reverence in England. Another plant, the brook-weed, a remedy for the diseases of animals, had to be gathered fasting, with the left hand; the person who gathered it was forbidden to look at it. In the neighbourhood of the Pyrenees, Latin dedications have been found to the gods *Robur*, *Fagus*, and *Sexarbor;* we also hear of a Mars *Buxenus*, that is to say, a god of the sacred box-tree, identified, I know not why, with the Roman Mars.

10. The worship of animals has left traces in Celtic nomenclature. First, in the names of some tribes: the *Taurisci* are the people of the Bull, the *Brannovices* those of the Raven, the *Bibroci* those of the Beaver; then again in names of towns and of individuals: *Tarvisus*, the city of the Bull; *Deiotarus*, the divine Bull; *Artogenos*, *Brannogenos*, the descendants of the Bear and of the Raven. In the third place, we have the Gallic ensigns surmounted by the image of a boar. The reverses of coins struck in Gaul, from about 250 B.C. onwards, bear the images of horses, bulls and boars, the sacred character of which is evident. We have already seen that the goddess Epona was a mare before she became an equestrian; the Gauls had also a stallion-god, *Rudiobus*, a large image of which, without a rider, was found near Orleans together with images of boars and one of a stag.

11. A number of little bronzes are in existence representing supernatural bulls with three horns; there is also a bronze boar with three horns. When anthropomorphism prevailed in Gaul the sacred animals were identified with gods, and thenceforth these animals were represented as the companions of the gods, or the god was depicted with the horns and the skins of animals. Thus the goddess *Artio* (she-bear), found near Berne, is accompanied by a she-bear; a goddess analogous to the Roman Diana, discovered in the Ardennes, bestrides a boar; the Gallic god of the Reims altar, between Apollo and Mercury, wears stag's horns; a horned god on a Parisian altar is called Cernunnos, that is, "the horned" in the inscription. On altars of the Roman period, the sacred animal still figures alone occasionally, but this is exceptional; the altar discovered at Notre Dame de Paris shows a bull with three cranes (and the inscription:

Tarvos Trigaranus). Although a similar bas-relief was dug up near Treves, we do not know the exact significance of the bull with the three cranes; but it is evident that the crane was no less sacred than the bull, for cranes appear as religious emblems on Gallic shields, among the triumphal reliefs of the Roman arch at Orange.

12. On an altar of the first century after Christ carved with the figures of the twelve Roman gods, there is also a serpent with a ram's head, no doubt an important Gallic god; the same fantastic animal figures elsewhere as an attribute of Mercury, a proof that there were later attempts to identify it with this deity, after a first assimilation of it to Mars.

13. Alimentary prohibitions are always derived from totemism. We know of none in Gaul proper, unless the great repugnance of the Celts to horse-flesh may be referred to some such cause; but the insular Britons of the time of Cæsar kept fowls, geese, and hares which they did not dare to eat. The sacred character of the cock, the hen and the chicken are attested by many customs in Italy and Gaul; I may instance the sacred chickens of the Roman augurs, and the cocks on our steeples, where they are supposed to avert thunderbolts. The goose was sacred on the Roman Capitol. As to the hare, we know it was used in Britain in forecasting the future, that is to say, as an augural animal; now all augural animals, as well as the animals used as emblems on standards, were, at least originally, totems.

14. Among the other interdictions or *taboos* which prevailed in Gaul there are two which deserve mention. The spoil taken from the enemy was interdicted; it was piled in heaps which no one was allowed to touch under pain of death; or it was thrown into lakes, like the famous treasures which the Roman Cepio fished up out of the ponds of Toulouse, a sacrilege which he expiated shortly after by defeat and death. A strange prohibition, which belongs to the class of *taboos of majesty*, forbade a child to approach its father armed; the result was that boys were brought up in strange families or by the Druids, a curious custom which persisted for a long time in Ireland; the English and French

institution of boarding schools may be a survival of this practice.

15. I have already spoken of several Gallic divinities, which, as they have no equivalents in Greece and Rome, may be considered indigenous. Here are a few other examples. On that same altar of Notre Dame on which is the bull with the three cranes, we find a divine woodman, named Esus, associated with the Roman gods Jupiter and Vulcan. This Esus is mentioned by Lucan (*c.* A.D. 60), together with Teutates and Taranis; according to the poet, they were three sanguinary deities, who exacted human sacrifices. It has been wrongly supposed that these three gods constituted a sort of Celtic Trinity; in reality, as the passage in Lucan proves, they were deities venerated by a few tribes to the north of the Loire, among others the Parisii. Esus seems to be the same word as the Latin *herus* and perhaps the Indo-Iranian *Asuras*. Teutates was the god of the people, Taranis the god of thunder. The reason for representing Esus as a woodman is not yet apparent.

16. In Gallo-Roman works of art, Jupiter sometimes appears carrying a wheel, or with a wheel at his feet; this wheel is no doubt a symbol of the sun. On some of the Pyrenean altars we find the wheel associated with the svastika, which seems also to have symbolised the sun or fire in Gaul. Some little bronze wheels which were used as amulets have been discovered, and no doubt their origin was the same. Even in these days, at the rustic festival of St. John (June 24), a fiery wheel represents the sun; it is rolled to a neighbouring river and submerged, perhaps that it may serve as an auxiliary to the heavenly fire.

17. The Druids taught that the Gauls had for their common ancestor an infernal or nocturnal god whom Cæsar calls *Dis pater*. This god, of whom there are many images, is represented wrapped in a wolf-skin and holding a mallet with a long handle. The mallet recalls that of the Etruscan Charon. A bas-relief at Sarrebourg in Lorraine showed that one of the titles of this Gallic god was *Sucellus*, meaning "the good striker." The wolf-skin suggests that this nocturnal god was originally a wolf, a beast which prowls

about and commits its ravages at night. During the Roman period he was also identified with *Silvanus* (the forester), himself originally a wolf, who was supposed to be a hunter of wolves. Thus the Gauls, or at any rate a certain proportion of them, had a national legend identical with that of the Romans; like Romulus, they were the "children of the wolf," and this perhaps was why the Arverni called themselves the brothers of the Latins.

18. Lucian (*c.* A.D. 170) speaks of a Celtic Hercules, Ogmios, represented as an old man with white hair carrying a lion-skin, a club, and a bow, and dragging after him a number of worshippers by little chains of gold and amber; the chief chain hung from the god's tongue, symbolising eloquence. Ogmios is a title closely akin to the name of Ogme, who is supposed in Ireland to have been the inventor of oghamic writing. The Hercules-Ogmios, of whom Lucian or the author he follows may have seen an image among the Allobroges (Dauphiné), was a "civilising hero"; certain texts suggest that a similar character was ascribed to the Celtic Hercules, the founder of Alesia.

19. From many monuments we learn of the existence of mother-goddesses, generally grouped in threes, who were called *Matres* or *Matronæ,* and who bear a variety of local names, Celtic or Germanic. They correspond with the *fairies* of Celtic folklore, and the Latin form of this word, *fatæ* (French *fée*), is sometimes applied to them in inscriptions.

20. This grouping of divinities by threes seems to have been familiar to the Celts. I have already spoken of Esus, Taranis and Teutates, of the horned god between Apollo and Mercury; on several monuments we find a three-headed god, identified at a later period with Mercury, who seems to constitute a triad in himself. The triad was also a religious formula, and Diogenes Laertius attributes this triple precept to the Druids: "Honour the gods, do no evil, be brave." The literary form of the triad was highly developed among the Britons of Wales; local scholars in the eighteenth century fabricated long litanies composed of philosophical and moral triads on models known to them by tradition. The

triad, sky, earth and sea, is used in the formula of a Celtic oath. On the other hand, many of the Gallic gods were associated with goddesses, not in triads but in couples; thus Sucellus is mated with Nantosvelta, Mercury with Rosmerta, Borvo with Damona, Apollo with Sirona, Mars with Nemetona. We do not know whether these goddesses figured in legend as the mothers, wives or sisters of the gods; we prudently describe them as their companions or *paredræ*.

21. Cæsar says that the Gauls were a very superstitious people; yet in his history of the war against the Gauls he ignores their religion. A free-thinker himself, he secularised his history, so to speak, thus creating an impression which Camille Jullian, the historian of Gaul, has very rightly attempted to modify.

22. In a famous passage (vi, 17) Cæsar tells us that the Gauls had much the same ideas as other nations respecting the gods: that their principal god was Mercury, inventor of the arts and guide of travellers; that next to him they honoured Apollo, the healer of disease, Mars, the god of war, Jupiter, the god of heaven, and Minerva, the protectress of industries. These summary statements must not be implicitly accepted. Cæsar says himself (i, 1) that the Gallic tribes differed from each other in language, manners and laws; he seems therefore to contradict himself when he attributes to them a well-defined Pantheon of five gods. Besides, it is quite certain that the identification of certain Gallic gods with the Roman gods was a result of the conquest, and not antecedent to it. Cæsar expressed himself very briefly, and summed up the general impression left on his mind by the religions of Gaul for the benefit of his Roman readers. He found in that country a great number of gods, some of them analogous to those of the old Roman religion, from which the Roman Pantheon had been selected under the influence of Greece. Indicating, and by this very means producing, a similar evolution, he grouped the divinities under five principal heads. His example was so well followed that in the inscriptions of Roman Gaul, we find precisely these five collective names of gods, followed by epithets sometimes local, sometimes characteristic of the functions

of native gods. Thus in the epigraphic texts Mars appears with forty epithets, Mercury with twenty, Apollo with twelve, Jupiter and Minerva with three or four only. On the monuments, Mercury appears much more frequently than Mars. The latter, who represented the group of martial divinities, was naturally held in greater honour at the time of Celtic independence; but, from the time of Cæsar, Gaul had become peaceful and wealthy, and Mercury, the god of commerce, came to the fore; his importance increased the more rapidly under the Roman domination, in that the Romans did not look upon him with suspicion. The Celtic Mars was assimilated to the Mars of the Capitol, which made him inoffensive, *romanised* him in fact, whereas the thrifty Mercury was still often represented in the character of a Gallic god.

23. Cæsar was right in ascribing to the Gauls a medical Apollo; he was the god of the thermal springs, whose Roman name appears in conjunction with numerous epithets such as *Bormo* or *Borvo* (the boiling), *Grannus* (the brilliant), *Maponus* (the child), *Toutiorix* (the king of the people), &c. The Apollo of Noricum (on the Danube) was called *Belenus;* under the empire the soldiery propagated his worship, as well as that of *Grannus*, whom Caracalla worshipped in A.D. 215, and that of the equine goddess, Epona.

24. We see that the so-called names of the Gallic deities, of which we know several hundreds, were really nothing but epithets; if these gods had actual names, we can only conclude that they were kept secret.

25. The organisation of the Gallo-Roman religion, on the model of the Roman Pantheon, was a result of the political organisation of Gaul and also of the activity of the image-makers, which developed very rapidly. Specifically Roman divinities such as Neptune, Vesta, Tutela, Concordia, were introduced into Gaul; merchants and soldiers brought in alien forms of worship, such as those of Isis, Mithra, Attis and Belos. All these creeds were dominated by the political worship of Rome and of Augustus, which was instituted in the year 12 B.C. at the confluence of the Rhône and the Saône at Lyons. The loyalty of the Gauls, like

that of other conquered races, was also affirmed by the addition of Augustus to the names of their divinities, as, for instance, in the formula "dedicated to Mercury Augustus," which occurs frequently in inscriptions.

26. Whereas before the conquest only Cisalpine Gaul and Provence possessed temples, from the beginning of the first century Transalpine Gaul began to raise sumptuous buildings, such as the sanctuary of Mercury Dumias on the Puy-de-Dôme, the colossal bronze statue in which was the work of the Syrian Zenodorus. It is needless to enlarge here on the Gallo-Roman religion; the details of its organisation, its priests and its festivals belong to the domain of manuals of antiquity.

27. The Druids were the national Gallic clergy; they were found in the British Isles and in Gaul, but not in Cisalpine Gaul, Germany or Galatia. The name appears to mean *dru-vid*, "the far-seeing"; the etymology which derives it from the Greek name of the oak, *drus*, is now discredited. According to Cæsar, the Druids came from the island of Britain, and it is often held that they only penetrated into Gaul as missionaries some five hundred years before Christ. To this it may be objected that the megalithic monuments attest the power of a priesthood at an earlier period and that though the centre of the Druidical association may have been in Britain at the time of Cæsar, it does not prove that the Druids came to Gaul from this island at a recent date. I am inclined to believe that Druidism first flourished in the neolithic period, especially in Ireland, that its influence soon spread to the continent, and that the Druids rejoined their Irish *confrères* after the Roman conquest, and came to an end where they had begun.

28. The Druidical clergy were recruited among the flower of the nation's youth; the novitiate lasted twenty years, and entailed tremendous efforts of memory, as the sacred literature of the Druids was oral. The Arch-Druid, who was nominated for life, was replaced by election. The doctrine comprised theology, divination, astrology, a knowledge of nature and of history. It was said that human sacrifices were demanded by the worship; but these may have been merely

simulacra of sacrifices; the priests took a few drops of blood from the victim, or the victim was represented by a wicker dummy which was set on fire. It is certain, however, that criminals, traitors, and rebels were sometimes enclosed in these effigies.

29. The Druids had a monopoly of sacrifices both public and private; they were exempt from military service; they adjudicated in disputes between tribes and between individuals, and excommunicated those who refused to accept their judgments by excluding them from the sacrifices. Soothsayers, magicians, and doctors, the Druids gathered the mistletoe of the oaks, for which they claimed magical virtue; they attributed similar properties to a number of other plants and to fossil echinodermata, which were called serpent's eggs (no doubt sacred serpents). We know but little of their ideas concerning the gods; the ancients suspected that they did not believe in the deities of the vulgar. If we are to credit a certain (very late) Irish text [1] the Druids taught that three of their number had created heaven and earth, and that from these the gods had issued; perhaps we should take this as an allusion to the creative power of sacrifice, akin to the belief that prevailed in India. The Druids no doubt taught metempsychosis in the beginning, a doctrine which they afterwards reduced to the migration of souls towards a region in the West; death was thus but an incident between two lives, and the Gauls were so convinced of this that they were in the habit of borrowing with a promise to repay in a future life. According to the Druidical cosmogony, which in this respect was analogous to that of the Greek Stoics, the world we inhabit will perish by fire and water.

30. According to Cæsar, the Druids and knights formed the two classes of the Gallic aristocracy; the plebs were of no account. He often speaks of an Æduan, Divitiac, without saying that he was a Druid, a detail we gather from Cicero, who celebrates his knowledge of presages. Although Cæsar tells us that the Druids were very powerful, he does not attribute any part to them during the conquest. Am-

[1] *Revue archéologique,* 1878, i, p. 384.

mianus Marcellinus, translating the Greek Timagenes, compares the Druidical associations to the Pythagorean confraternities, which implies not only an analogy of doctrines, but a kind of cenobitic life. Cæsar gives no hint of anything of the sort. The point is open to controversies, which have been freely waged around it. I think we must, first of all, distinguish between the nobles who had received a Druidical training, like the Divitiac above mentioned, and the sacerdotal body properly so called, which was governed by a very severe discipline, and held its annual conferences in the region of Chartres, the religious centre of Transalpine Gaul. Were these Druids married? Did they live in communities? We cannot say. But it seems perfectly evident that at the time of Cæsar, the power of the Druids had already declined; Gaul was no longer a theocracy.

31. In connection with the Druids, two Greek writers mention the Bards, of whom Cæsar says nothing, but who are also to be traced in Ireland. The priest of local worship in Gaul was called *gutuater*. It is not certain that there were priestesses, at least in Cæsar's time, for the prophetesses of the isle of Sena, witches and sorceresses, may very well have been a poetic myth recounted by the geographer Mela. As to the Druidesses of whom there is occasional mention under the Empire, they were mere vulgar fortune-tellers; there is nothing to show that women played any part in the Druidical institution before its decline.

32. This decline was not the result of a religious persecution, but of police measures by which the Empire prohibited Druidical sacrifices, and of the foundation of the great Roman schools, such as that of Autun, which deprived the Druids of their pupils. After a last effort under Vespasian, at the time of the burning of the Capitol, in which they saw a presage of the overthrow of the Roman power, the Druids emigrated to Great Britain, and then to Ireland, where they subsisted for four centuries longer. In Ireland, they had their places at table side by side with the kings, whose children they educated; a king did not dare to speak before a Druid; they were sorcerers, soothsayers and councillors of State. Even after the triumph of Christianity, Irish Dru-

idism held its own against the Christian clergy; it did not disappear until about A.D. 560, after the abandonment of Tara, the capital of the supreme king of the island.

33. All that we know of the Irish Druids comes to us from the epic and historic literature of Ireland, transmitted to us in a much revised state by manuscripts, the earliest of which date from the eleventh century only. These texts have preserved legends very much earlier in date and certainly pagan, which have been pressed into the service to complete the little we know of the mythological traditions of the Celts. Scholars admit that *Nuadu*, the king with the silver hand in the Irish legend, is identical with the Mars *Nodon*, known by a Roman inscription found in Great Britain; it may be that the name of the god *Lug*, artist and physician, reappears in that of the Celtic genii called (in the plural) *Lugoves*, if not in those of the towns called *Lugdunum*, though a Greek writer explains the word *Lug* as "crow."[1] D'Arbois has interpreted certain figured monuments of Gaul by the aid of Irish mythology. Thus, in a bas-relief found in Paris, the woodman is Cûchulainn, who cuts down trees to impede the enemy; the bull is the divine animal who is called *Dorn* in Ireland, and the three cranes are three forms of a goddess, who comes to warn the bull of the danger that threatens him. It cannot, however, be said that the demonstration is complete; points of contact much more numerous and definite were to be expected and have not as yet been found.

34. The Irish epics comprise three cycles. The first records the invasion of the island by a goat-headed race, the *Fomore*. The second describes the carrying off of a divine bull and of the cows to whom he is a kind of chief; the principal personages are King Conchobar, his nephew the hero Cûchulainn, the son of Lug and of a mortal, and Queen Medb (Shakespeare's Mab). The manners described are very similar to those of the Homeric heroes; the warriors fight in chariots. The third cycle is that which, passing from Ireland to Scotland, there gave birth to the so-called *Ossianic* literature. In 1760-63, Macpherson published an

[1] The true explanation, given by Heric, seems to be *mons lucidus* (*cf.* *Cler-mont*).

English version of poems attributed to the aged blind bard Ossian, which celebrate the deeds of Finn mac Cumail (Fingal) and his *Fianna* or Fenians. Ossian (Ossin) was the son of Finn. These poems, which purported to be translations from the original Gaelic, had an immense success. Goethe, Napoleon, and Chateaubriand read them with passionate interest; Musset and many others imitated them; but it is now attested that though the matter of these poems is Irish, all that the nineteenth century thought so sublime in them was the work of Macpherson.

35. In the cycle of Cûchulainn, there are very archaic elements, which the Christian modifications have not altogether suppressed, although they eliminated all mention of pagan worship. The sacred bull is the seventh incarnation of a swineherd of the gods, who had been successively a crow, a seal, a warrior, a ghost and a worm;[1] this is a curious vestige of Celtic metempsychosis. The name Cûchulainn means the dog of "Culann," a smith whose dog Cûchulainn had killed; the Irish hero may not eat dog, and this is probably a totemic taboo. Although equally pagan in origin, the Ossianic cycle has preserved fewer traces of the old belief, though it contains allusions to the Druids. The heathen tradition waxes still fainter in the Welsh romances called *Mabinogion* (twelfth century).[2] Yet magic and metamorphoses play a great part in them. Although it has been modified considerably, this literature is not fraudulent. The same cannot be said of the pretended "bardic mysteries" published by some Welshmen in the eighteenth century, which deceived Michelet and Henri Martin. The latest literary fraud committed in the Celtic domain was the *Barzaz-Breiz*[3] published by Hersart de la Villemarqué in 1839. It is not an unmitigated forgery; but most of the interesting passages are interpolations or frauds.

36. This rapid sketch of the religions of Gaul would be too incomplete if I omitted some brief allusion to the pagan survivals, which, despite the prohibitions of councils (from A.D. 567 onwards), and the efforts of the Church, have per-

[1] *Revue celtique,* 1907, p. 17.
[2] *Mabinogi,* children's tales (*narratio puerilis,* Zeuss).
[3] *Barzaz-Breiz,* songs of the Bards of Brittany.

sisted in country districts. Sylphs, gnomes, will-o'-the-wisps, elves, dwarfs, *crions*, *poulpiquets*, fairies, bogeys, &c., are so many living souvenirs of the Celtic and even the pre-Celtic past; the most familiar of the French giants, Gargantua, is probably a Celt, and the popularity he owes to Rabelais is merely a revival. Stones, springs and animals have their legends, sometimes intermixed with Christian elements, but retaining an obviously pagan basis. Sacred oaks, herbs gathered on Midsummer's Eve, the ex-votos hung on branches, cures effected by passing through a hole in a stone or a cleft in a tree, all these, with a thousand other beliefs of the same order, prolong the tenacious illusions of the past. When peasants jump, or make their animals jump, through the bonfires kindled on Midsummer's Eve, they are performing an ancient Celtic rite, just as did the inhabitants of Paris in the sixteenth century when they threw cats into the flames, or those of Tours, who, as recently as 1900, burnt a straw effigy called a *babouin* on the same festival. The Roman Pantheon is really dead, because its life was always an artificial one; but the polydemonism of old Gaul remains vital, because it struck deep root into the soil.

II. The Germans and Scandinavians

1. Germanic paganism survived Celtic paganism by five centuries; we are therefore much better informed as to the former. Unfortunately, the quality of our documents leaves a good deal to be desired, especially for the final period, when they are most abundant.

2. These documents may be divided into three groups; (1) the texts of classic authors, especially Cæsar and Tacitus; (2) the works which set forth Scandinavian or Norse mythology, *Sagas* and *Eddas;* (3) popular customs and traditions, some collected and observed at a relatively recent period, others known by prohibitions of the Church, and by a species of interrogatory compiled for the use of priests who received the confessions of German converts to Christianity. They were asked: "Have you done or believed such and such a thing, observed such and such a pagan rite?"

These penitential manuals are very instructive; they enable us to watch German paganism at work, so to speak, in all its popular tenacity surviving Christian preaching.

3. Cæsar knew of but three German gods, the Sun, the Moon and Vulcan. As the warrior god of the Celts was sometimes identified with Vulcan, it is probable that Cæsar had heard of the Germanic Mars, to whom we shall return presently. Sun-worship among the Germans is attested by a very ancient bronze group discovered in the island of Zeeland; it represents a horse harnessed to a car, on which a large disc ornamented with incisions is placed vertically. This ex-voto of local manufacture was evidently thrown into the marsh to serve as auxiliary to the sun, like the white horses which were thrown into the sea at Rhodes.

4. Germans and Celts agreed in the practice of helping the sun by lighting brands, especially at the beginning of spring and in the solstices, and by carrying about and finally immersing fiery wheels. The fire on the hearth was assimilated to the sun and participated in his sanctity; in the event of an epidemic it was extinguished, and replaced by a *new fire*, produced by rubbing two pieces of wood together.

5. The moon was identified with the Diana of the Romans, the nocturnal huntress and queen of sabbaths. One of the questions put by Burchard, Bishop of Worms, in the year 1000 A.D., ran thus: "Hast thou believed in the existence of a certain female who, like her whom the folly of the vulgar calls Holda, rides about at night on certain beasts, in company with demons transformed into women? This is affirmed by certain creatures deceived by the devil." The question is repeated in other catechisms, with this difference, that Holde—the *Frau Holle* or *Holde* of German legends—is called "Diana, goddess of the heathen." *Hold* in German means "benevolent" or "propitious"; but this is a euphemism akin to that which gave the name Euxine (or "hospitable") Sea to the Black Sea, or "benevolent goddesses" to the terrible Greek Eumenides. In the popular texts, Holle is a genius of water and the atmosphere. At noon in summer she may be surprised, like the Greek Artemis, bathing in a spring; in winter she causes snow to fall by shaking the eiderdown

of her bed. But she is more especially a witch, the queen of witches, terrible and cruel, who carries off the souls of unbaptized children. In this character she was also identified with Herodias, the stepdaughter of Herod, who caused the death of John the Baptist. Burchard speaks of her in these terms: "Certain wretched women, seduced by the sorcery of demons, believe that during the night they ride abroad with Diana, goddess of the heathen, or with Herodias and a host of other women, and that they traverse immense spaces." A bishop writes in 1280: "Let no woman be suffered to pretend that she rides abroad at night with Diana, goddess of the heathen, or with Herodias, also called *Bensozia*." This latter name is perhaps a corruption of *Bona Socia*, "good companion." About A.D. 680, when St. Kilian was labouring to convert the Franks, their chief, Gozbert, repeatedly asked him if the god he preached was "better than his own Diana."

6. Tacitus, following Cæsar in his account of the Gauls, identified the Germanic gods with those of the Græco-Roman Pantheon. The principal god of the Germans, according to him, was Mercury: "On certain days they offer victims to him. They also worship Hercules and Mars, but these they appease by less barbarous offerings." The medieval chroniclers say that the German Mercury was called *Vodan, Woden, Odin.* The names given to the days of the week are very significant in this connection. The week of seven days called by the names of the planets had been generally adopted throughout the Roman Empire by the end of the second century; the Germans adopted it in the fourth century, substituting the names of the Germanic divinities for those of the Roman gods. The *dies Martis* became *Tuesday* in English (the day of *Tiu* or *Tyr*, the Germanic Mars); the German *Dienstag* is derived from a surname of this god, *Thingsus,* which is found in Latin dedications by German soldiers. The *dies Mercurii* is in English *Wednesday,* the day of Woden; the Germans say *Mittwoch,* "the middle of the week." *Jovis dies,* in English *Thursday,* in German *Donnerstag,* attests that Thor or Donar, the god of thunder, was identical with Jupiter. *Veneris dies* (*Friday, Freytag*), proves that Freya was identified with Venus. It must

not be forgotten, however, that these identifications were *assimilations*, and do not reveal the primitive nature of the Germanic gods.

7. In the Eddas, Tyr-Mars is the son of Odin-Mercury, and, like him, a warrior god. It has been shown that the name of Tyr (*Tiw* in Anglo-Saxon, *Ziu* in High German) is etymologically identical with the Sanscrit *Dyaus* and Greek *Zeus;* he was therefore originally the celestial god. As to Woden, his name, analogous to that of the wind in German (*Wind*) shows that he was a god of the wind and no doubt at an earlier stage the god of spirits and the guide of the dead after the manner of the Greek Hermes Psychopomp. The army of spirits, led by Odin, pass through the air, and the noise they make suggests the idea of a "wild chase." At night when there is a gale the peasant still says that "the wild hunters are in the sky." Odin is therefore at once an atmospheric, a nocturnal, and an infernal god. If we remember that according to Cæsar the Gauls believed themselves to be the descendants of a nocturnal god approximating to Pluto, it is difficult not to trace a connection between this Celtic conception and that of the Germans.

8. In a certain number of tribes, Tyr-Mars must have taken precedence of Odin-Mercury. Thus Tacitus (*Ann.* xiii, 57) relates the conclusion of a war between the Hermunduri and the Catti; the vanquished army was massacred in consequence of a vow made to Mars and to Mercury (note that here Mars leads the way). Again, in the *Histories* of Tacitus (iv, 64), the Tenchtheri address their thanksgivings to Mars, the "first of the gods." In a large uncentralised country which had as yet neither clergy nor written literature, such divergences are not surprising.

9. In chap. xxxix of his *Germania*, Tacitus gives a description of the ceremonies performed in the worship of Mars. He lays the scene among the Semnones, the most ancient and noble of the Suevi. "They have," he says, "delegates, who meet at stated periods in a venerable wood" (thus we see there were sacred forests and devotional gatherings of a political character). "None may enter the wood without being bound, in token of his dependence and his pub-

lic homage to the power of the god. If he fall, he is forbidden to rise or to be helped from the ground; he has to leave the wood rolling himself along the ground. . . . In this wood, the cradle of the race, the sovereign divinity resides." In these all too brief lines we discern the idea that the Germans believed themselves to have been the offspring of their sacred trees, an idea to be met with among other races, and also the belief that contact with Mother Earth is beneficent, for the description evidently applies to persons who deliberately fall and roll on the ground, not to persons who do so accidentally. We know, moreover, that among the Germans a new-born infant was laid on the bare ground, and that its father took it up, as if it had just emerged from the earth, the common mother of mortals.

Tacitus does not tell us that Mars was the god of the Semnones; but as the Suevi called themselves *Cyuvari*, that is, worshippers of Ziu, it is probable that he was the god in question.

10. In addition to Mercury and Mars, Tacitus distinguishes a third great god whom he identifies with Hercules, saying nothing of Jupiter. It is certain that the same German god, Thor or Donar, was assimilated sometimes to Jupiter, sometimes to Hercules. Thor in the Eddas is a redoubtable warrior, a slayer of monsters, of extraordinary height, vigour and appetite, like Hercules; his sacred hammer, Mioellnir, recalls the club of the Greek hero, who was himself the son of Zeus, the thundergod. On one occasion Donar, in spite of his long red beard, disguised himself as a woman, like the Greek Herakles; not, it is true, to humour the whim of an Omphale, but to regain by stratagem his stolen hammer.

11. The Latin documents of the Middle Ages generally attribute to Jupiter all that the Germanic documents attribute to Thor. The oak of Jupiter is the *Donares eih*, which St. Boniface caused to be cut down at Geismar. Saxo gives the name *lapides* or *mallei joviales* (stones or hammers of Jupiter) to those polished axes which were looked upon as "thunder-bolts," and which the Greeks, for this reason, called *Ceraunia;* the Germans still call them "thunder-

hatchets" (*Donnerkeile*), and imagine them to be talismans against thunder-bolts. Finally, the plant called *Donnerbart* in Germany is the French *Joubarbe* (*Jovis barba*); it was supposed that it protected the walls on which it grew from thunder-bolts.

12. In addition to Mercury, Hercules and Mars, Tacitus believed that the goddess Isis was to be found among the Germans (*Germania*, ix). A portion of the great tribe of the Suevi offered sacrifices to this alien divinity, according to him; he adds that the ship which was her symbol attests the fact that she came from beyond the seas. Tacitus was evidently thinking of the "bark of Isis" which was offered annually to the goddess in the Roman worship of this Egyptian divinity. Similar customs are to be found among the Germans of the Middle Ages (twelfth century). The people, dancing and singing, followed a ship mounted on wheels, "which contained," says a chronicler, "I know not what evil genius." The hypothesis of the introduction of Isis-worship into Germany must be left to Tacitus; the ceremony described was one of those "sacred processions" on a car or in a boat which recur in various countries, as, for instance, in the Græco-Roman worship of Cybele. A goddess of Abundance, adored on the sea-coast, might very well have had for her emblem a boat or an oar, like the Germanic Nehalennia, whose carved altars have been discovered in Holland, near the mouths of the Rhine.

13. Tacitus speaks of another divinity who was drawn in a car (*Germ.*, xl): "In an island of the ocean there is a sacred wood, and in it a covered car, destined for the goddess. Only the priest has a right to touch it; he knows the moment when she is present in the sanctuary; she sets out, drawn by white heifers; he follows with profound veneration. Joyful days follow; high festival is held in all the places she deigns to honour with her presence. Wars are suspended (the *Truce of God*); all weapons are carefully laid aside. This is the only time during which the Barbarians agree to rest and it lasts until the goddess, having had her fill of human intercourse, is taken back to her temple by the same priest. Then the car and the veil that covers it, and also,

if we are to believe what we are told, the goddess herself, are bathed in a lonely lake. Slaves perform this office, upon the conclusion of which they are at once thrown into the lake. Hence a religious terror and a pious ignorance concerning this superstitious object, to look upon which is death."

The visual taboo, the progress, and the bath of the goddess—a rite designed to call down rain—are ideas of frequent occurrence. The Roman calendar notes a bath of the Mother of the Gods (*lavatio Matris deum*) on the sixth day of the Kalends of April. Ovid describes a priest, dressed in a purple robe, washing a goddess and sacred objects in the Almo.

14. Tacitus has given the name of this goddess of Sleswig; she was called *Nerthus* (the subterranean) and the Roman historian rightly identifies her with the Earth Mother, the Cybele or Mother of the Gods of the Asiatic Greeks. Her procession was in the nature of an agrarian festival, designed to promote the awakening of Nature in the springtime. Similar rites are still observed in Germany; the beneficent divinity is represented by effigies, the king and queen of the May, who are greeted with dance and song. In the time of Tacitus it is probable that the goddess was supposed to be present, but that there was merely a seat without an idol on the car. Analogies are found in other cults. There is an engraved Mycenæan stone which represents a procession of women advancing to an empty throne. The *worship of the throne*, analogous to that of the Ark among the Hebrews, has been fully explained in its connection with archaic Greece. Thus it has been shown that the accidents of the ground, called the "thrones" of gods or heroes, as, for instance, the rock called the "throne of Pelops" near Smyrna were merely ancient places of worship. Reichel has very ingeniously demonstrated the evolution of the natural throne into the portable throne, on which the divinity, localised by the worship offered him, accompanies the tribe in its migrations. Herodotus, describing the army of Xerxes coming out from Sardis, mentions a car drawn by eight white horses; this car was empty, but none might mount upon it, for it belonged to the master of the gods.

15. The Germanic Freya, the wife of Odin, identified with Venus in the name of Friday (*Veneris dies, Freytag*), is probably merely a goddess of fecundity, and the Nerthus of Tacitus and the so-called Isis are perhaps her local designations or epithets.

16. Tacitus further mentions a few secondary gods, for instance, in a sacred wood of the Waldgebirge (*Germania*, xliii): "The direction of the ceremonial," he says, "is confided to a priest dressed as a woman. The objects of this cult are gods who, in the Roman Olympus, would be Castor and Pollux. There are no statues and no traces of a foreign influence; but the gods worshipped are certainly two young brothers." Diodorus says that the "Celts on the Ocean coast" (*i.e.*, the Germans) worshipped the Dioscuri. A similar divine pair existed in Gaul, for figures of the Roman Dioscuri, associated with Gallic gods, are to be seen on a Parisian altar of the time of Tiberius. The name Alcis, given by Tacitus to the German Dioscuri, has not yet been explained.

17. We know hardly anything of other Germanic divinities, such as the *Tanfana* and *Baduhenna* of Tacitus, and the numerous mother-goddesses with barbaric names which occur by the dozen in inscriptions found in the Rhine Valley. Those in which the letter *h* occurs are certainly Germanic and not Celtic; but the conception of these goddesses, generally grouped in threes, seems to have originated in Gaul, where fairies played an important part, and whence they passed into German folk-lore.

18. On the other hand, the Germans believed firmly in witches. Tacitus says that they attributed a certain sanctity to women, and referred to them for counsel. This does not imply, as has been supposed, a chivalrous respect for the weaker sex, but rather the widely spread and disastrous belief that women have a natural gift for prophecy and magic. Velleda, who incited the Batavians against the Romans in A.D. 70, is the most famous of the German prophetesses. After they had become Christians, the Germans continued to listen to their witches; but the Inquisition taught them to burn them. German Dominicans wrote the

infamous book called *The Hammer of Witches*, and it was more especially for Germany and against the German witches that Innocent VIII. launched a bull, a solemn and infallible affirmation of the power of witches, the signal for a hideous carnage extending over two centuries, in the course of which over a hundred thousand innocent women were burnt alive.

19. According to Tacitus, the Germans thought temples and statues unworthy of their gods; they were content to adore them. But he tells us nothing of the German worship of rivers, mountains and rocks, and he makes but a passing allusion to their worship of trees and animals, a much more important feature than their Pantheon. The Germans were profoundly animistic. All nature to them was peopled with genii, elves and trolls; those of the waters were nixies, those of the mountains giants and dwarfs. The genius of the Riesengebirge was the famous giant Rubezahl. The giants were the architects of colossal buildings, fortresses or castles of the gods. The dwarfs (*Zwerge*) were cunning smiths, and forged the weapons of the gods; their chief was Wieland, the smith. As the souls which were said to wander in the air were assimilated to the winds, and as the winds blow from the mountains, the latter were supposed to be the abodes of spirits; it is in a mountain, the Kyffhäuser, that the Emperor Frederick I. sits in a magic sleep, and there he will some day awake. This accounts for the funeral sacrifices offered on summits, in spite of the prohibitions of the Church. The worship of springs and rivers was as fully developed among the Germans as in Gaul; offerings were thrown into them, and even human victims, it is said. To obtain rain, water was poured out, sometimes over a naked girl. The springs were held to be inhabited by spirits, male and female, the nixies, who showed themselves in the form of bulls and horses and lured men maliciously into the abyss. The feminine demon of the sea was *Ran*, whose husband was *Ægir;* the sea which surrounds the world was in the form of an immense dragon. In the sacred forests, every tree had its genius, which took the form of an owl, a vulture or a wild cat. The guardian spirit of a family inhabited a tree near the dwelling; the gods of the Edda had their own sa-

cred tutelary tree, Yggdrasill. He who cuts down a tree destroys a genius.

The sacred animals play an important part. Plutarch speaks of a bull on which the Cimbri swore, Tacitus of augural horses and wild boar standards; other standards were surmounted by serpents and dragons. Men and women could transform themselves into serpents, wolves and bears to injure their fellow-mortals. The wolf-bogey of the Germans is the masculine pendant of the witch; in Norway there is also a bear-bogey. Witches, giants and trolls, disguised as crows or ravens, ride on the storm-clouds. During sleep or at the moment of death the soul comes out of the mouth in the form of a serpent or a mouse; as a ghost it could take the form of a quadruped or a bird. The spirits of cultivated fields are materialised in the form of wolves, bulls, dogs and boars; any of these animals caught among the last sheaves of harvest in which they had sought refuge were considered sacred. But we have still more decisive evidences than these of the old Germanic totemism.

20. At the beginning of the eighth century, Popes Gregory III. and Zacharias enjoined Boniface, the apostle of the Germans, to see that his converts abstained from the flesh of horses, jays, crows, storks, beavers and hares. To eat horse is a filthy and execrable crime, adds Gregory. It is evident that the Popes were concerned, not for the hygiene of the Germans, but for their religion. The meats they proscribe are those of sacred animals, which were eaten ritually. Now we know that the Icelanders, until their conversion in A.D. 997, ate horse "on certain occasions"; we know also that the Germans sacrificed horses, that they placed the heads of these victims on the trunks of trees; that white horses, exempted from work, were kept in the sacred woods as augural animals, and that a white horse was supposed to carry the god in the military expeditions of the Germans. Every nine years the Danes of Zeeland sacrificed horses, dogs and cocks. These sacrifices were followed by sacred feasts, at which the food was the flesh of the victims, and the object, the sanctification of the faithful by communion. The Christian Normans called the Swedes "eaters of horses"; the giants and

witches of German legend were reputed hippophagi. These facts attest the survival in Germany of totemism but thinly disguised; and they do not stand alone.

21. According to Bede (*c.* 700), the first chiefs of the Anglo-Saxons were called *Hengist* and *Horsa,* and were descended from Odin, to whom horses were sacrificed. Now *Hengist* means a stallion and *Horsa* a horse, and Grimm has pointed out that in Bede's lists, the other mythical kings have names derived from an Anglo-Saxon word meaning horse (*vicg*). It would seem therefore that these old genealogies, going back to the god Odin, imply the existence of clans whose mythic ancestor was a horse-god, like the Poseidon Hippios of the Arcadians; this is an obvious indication of totemism.

22. Cæsar remarks that there were no Druids in Germany. In primitive times the king was also the priest, and was supposed to be an incarnation of the deity. When Nature seemed irritated, the king was blamed, just as now in times of scarcity and commercial depression people say: "It is the fault of the government." A king might be killed for *magical incapacity* and replaced by a younger chief. Tacitus knew of priests in Germany; they seem to have been nominated for life, and invested with very great authority. The priest presided over popular assemblies, and prescribed penances, as the executor of the divine will. He offered sacrifice, the German name of which, *Opfer,* derived from the Latin *operari,* reveals a Latin influence where we should least expect to find it. The first temples, replacing the sacred groves, were built in Germany but a short time before the triumph of Christianity. Idols were also installed in them. In the second half of the fourth century a Greek historian relates that Athanaric, the King of the Goths, wishing to arrest the progress of the new religion, caused the image of a pagan deity to be taken about on a chariot. Gregory of Tours makes Clotilde say to Clovis, trying to convert him: "The gods you worship are wood and stone." In 612, at Bregenz, St. Columba and St. Gall saw three images of gilded bronze to which the people offered sacrifices, looking upon them as their patrons. At the bidding of the evan-

gelists stones were thrown at these statues to break them, and their fragments were cast into the lake. They may have been Roman statues; but there were certainly statues of native manufacture among the Saxons in the sixth century. Widekind of Corvey records the victory of the Saxons over the Thuringians in 530, and in connection with their triumph speaks of three statues representing Mars, Hercules and Apollo. In the eleventh century, Adam of Bremen, describing the pagan temple of Upsala, also mentions three statues, of Thor, Wodin and Fricco, the husband of Freya.

23. Frankish chronicles of the year 772 relate that Charlemagne, the conqueror of the Saxons, destroyed a centre of their worship at Heresburg, which was called *Ermensul.* A more precise account is given by the chronicler Rudolf of Fulda: "The Saxons," he says, "worship in the open air a very large tree-trunk; this they call *Irminsul,* which means the column of the world, the column which sustains everything." This explanation, which attributes to *Irmin* the signification "universal," seems to be correct. The name of the king of the Goths, Ermanaric, is probably identical with *irmin-rix,* meaning "the supreme king." A relation would seem to have been established between the Irminsul and the god Mercury, either on account of the analogy of names (the Greek Hermes), or because the classic Mercury was sometimes worshipped in the form of a pillar. On the other hand, as Odin was the Germanic Mercury, we must suppose that Odin was represented in the form of a tree-trunk supporting the world. We find an analogous conception in the Eddas, the great cosmic tree, the ash *Yggdrasill.*

24. In North Germany, towards the end of the Middle Ages, we find allusions to the "columns of Roland"; in Sweden there were "columns of Thor"; among the Anglo-Saxons, "columns of Athelstan." These are so many survivals and variants of the primitive worship of the tree and the pillar, which are also to be found among many other people in Greece and in Italy as well as in Gaul.

25. The funeral rites of the Germans, with their oblations to the dead, resembled those of their neighbours. The

dominion of souls was sometimes under the earth, in the kingdom of Hel, the daughter of Loki, sometimes in a northern country or in a distant island, and more frequently in the air. The souls of the dead revisited mankind more especially during the great autumnal gales; it was therefore necessary to propitiate them by rites which the Church has Christianised in the observance of All Souls' Day. In France, the wind which blows in the early part of November and whirls the dead leaves about is still called the *wind of the dead*. The Church forbade the celebration of these rites by masquerades in which the participants dressed up in the skins of animals, another indication of a totemic survival.

∴

26. A single victory in 872 made Harald Harfagri the master of Norway. A number of the petty chiefs of this country fled to Iceland, which became a centre of the old Germanic spirit and remained independent till the thirteenth century. From 900 to about 1250, active relations existed between Norway and Iceland. About the year 1000, King Olaf Tryggvason, who had converted Norway to Christianity, sent missionaries to Iceland. The mission was successful, but the Icelanders retained their attachment to their own traditions. The poetry of the Skalds, born in Norway, flourished longer and with greater splendour in Iceland than anywhere else. A classic prose sprang up side by side with the national poetry; this was the origin of Norse literature, which in its later developments has exercised so strong an influence upon the literatures of Europe.

27. The poems of the Skalds which have survived are chiefly eulogies of the Viking princes, the sea-kings of the North. This courtly poetry is far from simple. One of its favourite formulæ, the *kenningar*, consists in repeating the same thing two or three times in a complicated form. The Skalds gave one hundred and fifteen epithets to Odin; he is the patron of poets, to whom he presented the divine nectar, the *met*, which he stole in the form of a serpent from the daughter of a giant. In spite of its subtlety, the poetry of

the Skalds preserves marks of its magical origin; the *lied*, like the Roman *carmen*, was originally an incantation. The first written characters used in Scandinavia, the *runes*, an invention attributed to Odin, long served as a magic script, and are still engraved on talismans.

28. What is currently taught on the subject of the Edda, from which the literature of the Skalds is inseparable, is as follows:[1] In the twelfth century, when Christianity finally triumphed in Iceland, Sæmund Sigfusson collected the songs which served as theology and literature to the pagan ancestors of his people. Sæmund was a priest who died in 1133. He called his collection the *Edda*, which means the *grandmother*, as if the whole had been related by a grandmother. In the following century Sæmund's example was followed by Snorri Sturluson, the author of a prose Edda which is at once a commentary on the first Edda and a compendium of the poetic science of the Skalds, the authors of the *Sagas*.

29. All this needs revision. In the first place, the Edda in verse, supposed to have been written by Sæmund about 1130, was not discovered till 1643 by Bishop Brynjolf Svenisson, who attributed it to Sæmund on no other grounds than the great reputation for learning ascribed by tradition to this priest. The prose Edda was discovered in 1628, and for this the title of Edda is correct; it is also certain that it was the work of Snorri Sturluson, who died in 1241. But all the supposed facts relating to the poetic Edda are, as Bugge has shown, vitiated by errors, for the following reasons:

30. The Icelandic scholars of the seventeenth century took a great interest in the works of Snorri, to which his school had given the name of *Edda*, meaning poetic. Now in the prose Edda certain fragments of poetry are quoted, which are found, together with many others, in MS. 2365 in the Copenhagen Library. These poems were accordingly published under the title *Edda Sæmundi*, in the belief that Edda meant *grandmother*. Here we have a double confusion, for a collection of poems does not constitute a system of

[1] Heinrich, *Histoire de la littérature allemande*, vol. i, p. 6.

poetics, and the attribution of the collection to Sæmund is a perfectly gratuitous hypothesis.

31. None of the poems of the Edda were transcribed before 1250; none appear to be earlier in date than 900. They are the poetry of the Vikings, not of the ancient Germans. And as the Vikings had relations of all sorts with Great Britain and Ireland, it is natural that we should find in their poetry elements borrowed from neighbouring civilisations, and even from classic traditions preserved more especially in British and Irish monasteries.

32. Must we conclude therefore, as certain scholars have ventured to do, that students of Germanic mythology must leave the Edda altogether out of account? Most certainly not; but it must be handled cautiously. It does not mark the dawn of Germanic mythology, nor its apogee; it is Scandinavian mythology, which received its present form under the influence of foreign conceptions. It may be compared with the art of the Vikings, which remains the most perfect product of the Northern arts, in spite of the Græco-Roman motives which have been noted in it. Sophus Bugge has shown that the greater part of the mythological literature of the Edda was composed by poets of the Norwegian Court in the British Isles, especially in the north-west of England, and that it passed thence, by way of Scotland and the Hebrides, to Iceland, where it was supplemented.

33. Among the songs of which the Edda consists, the most important celebrate the glory and the exploits of the god Odin. One of these songs, the *Voluspa,* put into the mouth of a prophetess, contains a veritable cosmogony.[1] In the beginning there was Chaos, between the regions of fire and darkness, *Muspillheim* and *Nifflheim.* The hoar-frost which came out of Nifflheim was fertilised by the sparks that burst from Muspillheim, and thus was born *Ymir*, the father of the maleficent giants. The melting ice gives birth to a divine cow; she feeds by licking the snow in the hollows of the rocks and four rivers of milk flow from her udders. On

[1] Heinrich, *Histoire de la littérature allemande,* vol. i, p. 7 *et seq.* (textual excerpts). Voluspa means the "prophecy of the (female) soothsayer" (*volva*).

the first day she discovers a mass of hair under the snow, on the second a head, on the third a body; this was the god *Bure*. Bure's grandchildren were *Odin*, *Vili* and *Vé*, the gods of the new age.

34. Odin was a horseman, swift as lightning; he rode escorted by two wolves, and preceded by two crows. Active and beneficent, he attacked and killed Ymir. The body of the giant, cut into pieces, formed the world; the earth was his flesh, the water his blood, the rocks were his bones, the vault of heaven was his skull. But the victory of the gods was not complete. One of the sons of Ymir, Bergelmer, had escaped, and further, the worms which had gnawed the flesh of Ymir had given birth to the race of dwarfs who lurk in caverns and guard hidden treasure. The gods decided to people the earth. They pulled up an ash and an alder. The first human couple emerged from the ash and the alder.

35. Satisfied with his work, Odin retired into the sacred city of Asgard, where he reigned in company with the Ases, his children. Enthroned beside him were Thor, the god of thunder, and Freyr, the god of abundance, who form a trinity with him. Other gods peopled his court: Tyr, the god of thunder; Manni, the god of the moon; Sunna, the goddess of the sun; Freya, the Scandinavian Venus.

36. But the race of Bergelmer had multiplied and the giants had accomplices at the court of Odin. The god Loki plotted the death of the Ases with them. Heimdall, the most vigilant of the gods, was obliged to be perpetually on the alert, standing on the rainbow, a trumpet in his hand, ready to call the Ases to the combat. He slept no more soundly than a bird and heard the grass grow in the valleys.

37. Under the great ash Yggdrasill, the trunk of which forms the axis of the world, lived three Virgins, the guardians of destiny, the Norns. They had declared that the power of the Ases was bound up with the life of Balder, the most beautiful of the sons of Odin. The mother of the young god, Frigga, summoned the four elements and made them swear to spare her son. Only a single plant, the mistletoe, was overlooked and did not take the oath. The traitor Loki gathered it and placed it in the hands of Bal-

der's brother, Hoeder, who was blind. Meanwhile the assembled gods made trial of Balder's invulnerability; Hoeder advanced, struck in his turn, and Balder was slain. He descended to Hela, the dark goddess of death. The gods tried to ransom him, but Hela demanded as his ransom a tear from every living creature. Gods, men, the very stones themselves all wept for Balder, save one cruel daughter of the giants, who would not give a tear—and Hela kept her prey.

38. So destiny had to be accomplished. The giants invaded Asgard and slaughtered the gods. A vast fire devoured the world and annihilated the human race. The giants triumphed; this was the catastrophe predicted by the prophetess and called by her the Twilight of the Gods (*Götterdämmerung*).

39. But a mysterious power restored order. A new world, fair and verdant, emerged from the waves. The gods come to life again and Balder with them. They meet at interminable banquets, where they talk of their battles, and meditate on the oracles of the supreme god. Thus all ends, or rather all continues for the best.

40. Balder, whose resurrection ensures the happiness of the world, recalls Jesus, but he may be an original conception; as to the other personages, they are all warriors, bearing the rude impress of the Vikings. Odin himself, the father of wise counsels, was above all a god of war. A troop of warlike goddesses, the Walkyries, followed in his train. Their mission was to choose the warriors who had fallen in battle and admit them to the banquet of the gods in the halls of Walhalla. To die in his bed was considered a disgrace to a warrior. These ideas have little indeed of the Christian spirit.

41. This Scandinavian mythology has certain points in common with the Germanic conceptions which we know from earlier texts. First of all the names: Odin, Tyr, Thor, Freya, and perhaps too the idea of Yggdrasill, which resembles the Irminsul of the Saxons. Then the idea that the world will perish by fire is found in Celtic mythology; it may therefore have been borrowed by the Germans at an early

date from the Celts. The rest is isolated or may be partly explained by Christian legends, grafted on to the old Scandinavian trunk. Thus Loki does not recall the Christian Lucifer by his name only; Balder seems to have borrowed certain traits from Jesus; the blind Hoeder is modelled on the Longinus of legend, the blind soldier, who pierced the Saviour with his lance. The story of the fatal mistletoe is Celtic and British, not Norwegian, for there is no mistletoe, or hardly any, in Norway. Nevertheless it is going much too far to see throughout the *Voluspa* an echo of the Apocalypse of St. John. Certain Scandinavian scholars of the nineteenth century yielded to a kind of inverted chauvinism. Whereas their country can boast an original civilisation, the finest polished stone, the most beautiful bronze swords, the incomparable decorative art of the Vikings, they have been at pains to seek the origin, and as it were the patents of nobility of all the admirable manifestations of Norse genius in the south of Europe. Yet it would seem enough that this genius should have been strangled by a semi-Oriental, semi-Roman religion, the Oriental elements of which it retained after getting rid of the Roman elements in the Reformation. It might at least be conceded the honour of having given the world the Æschylean conceptions of the *Voluspa*, to which there is nothing comparable before Dante in all the Middle Ages of the West.

42. Of the old Germanic poems collected by Charlemagne not a line has come down to us; but certain compositions have survived, which, though compiled later, make use of some fairly ancient elements. The first in date is the Anglo-Saxon *Beowulf* (tenth century), the narrative of a struggle undertaken by the Gothic hero Beowulf against the demon of the waters, Grendel, who had carried off and devoured thirty of the King of Denmark's companions. Grendel was overcome; Beowulf then attacks a dragon, the guardian of treasures in a cave, and dies of a wound received while killing the monster. A breath of fresh morning air seems to pass through the austere simplicity of this poem. Later, at the beginning of the thirteenth century, we find the essentially Germanic epics, the outcome of six epic cycles inter-

mingled with Christian elements: that of Siegfried who fights a dragon, delivers Grimhild and dies in the flower of his age; that of Dietrich of Berne, who was the King of the Goths, Theodoric; that of Etzel, who was the King of the Huns, Attila; that of Hettel, King of the Hegelings, and of his daughter, Gudrun; and finally the Lombard cycle of King Rother. The first three cycles have formed the poem of the Nibelungen, the fifth that of Gudrun. As to the beautiful legends of Parsifal and of his son Lohengrin, the Knight of the Swan, which Wagner has made so popular, they are not of Germanic origin. The legend of the Holy Grail, the central motive of Wolfram of Eschenbach's Parsifal (thirteenth century), was first Celtic and then French; Wolfram himself indicates the Provençal Guyot as his source. Parsifal was a French knight, Perceval; Lohengrin is nothing but the Knight from Lorraine. Interesting as these legends may be for a history of religious ideas, they must not detain us here, any more than those French and Provençal *chansons de geste* of which they are the echo.

III. The Slavs

1. The Baltic Slavs, the Northern Slavs, the Poles and the Russians occupy an immense area to the east of Europe. Like the Germans and Celts, they had no single national religion in primitive times, and their local religions are very imperfectly known to us, as all the pagan literature of the Slavs has perished. The priests who converted them, from the ninth century onward, are our most trustworthy sources of information; but among the more recent texts there are some which are not above suspicion of fraud.

2. Folk-lorists have worked assiduously in this domain, and have collected a mass of material bearing upon the legends, the superstitious rites and the magic of the Slavs. This last is still a potent factor; the influence of the Mongolian *chamans* has, no doubt, something to do with this. In the summary I am about to make, I shall suppress naturalistic and popular forms of worship, in order to avoid repetition of what I have already said in connection with the Celts and

the Germans; I shall restrict myself to a rapid survey of the Slav gods, the forms under which they have been represented, and the mode in which they have been adored.

3. The words denoting god (*bog*), demon (*besu*), prayer (*modliti*), and paradise (*raj*) are common to all the Slav tongues. The word *bog* (Persian *baga*, Sanscrit *bhaga*) implies the conception of wealth and power; *besu* is derived from the root *bi*, to strike; *modliti* is akin to *modla*, which means both *prayer* and *idol*. Among the Russians, the priest is "the sacrificer"; the magician is "he who mutters words," "he who casts spells," or "he who traces signs" (*cf.* the Scandinavian runes).

4. "The Slavs," says Procopius, "believe that there is a god who forges thunder-bolts and is the sole master of the universe; they sacrifice oxen and all kinds of beasts to him. They know nothing of Destiny. . . . When they are in danger of death they promise, if they escape, to offer a sacrifice, and they think they can ransom themselves by these means. They also worship rivers and nymphs and other divinities, and practise divination at their sacrifices." In a treaty concluded in A.D. 945 between the Slavs and the Greeks, the supreme god is called *Perunu* and the god of flocks *Volusu*. About the year 980 there was at Kieff a wooden idol of Perunu, with a silver head and a golden beard, holding in his hand a thunder-bolt, and surrounded by other idols; human sacrifices were offered to these gods, and a perpetual fire was maintained in their honour. Wladimir, who was converted to Christianity in 988, caused the image of Perunu to be tied to the tail of a horse and dragged in the Dnieper.

5. Among the Baltic Slavs, the name of Thursday (*Jovis dies*) is *Perendan*, which implies a name akin to Perunu for the god of heaven and of thunder. Is Perunu to be identified with the Lithuanian storm-god, *Perkunas?* It seems doubtful; but the fact remains that the supreme god of the Slavs, mentioned by Procopius, was a god of thunder-bolts, a god who struck (from *pera*, I strike). We know, on the evidence of a Galician text which mentions an *oak of*

Perkunu as the land-mark of a field, that the oak was his sacred tree. Louis Léger argued that among the Russians, the Servians and the Bulgarians, St. Elias, who figures as the lord of thunder, rain, and storm, inherited the legend of Perunu.

6. Helmold, a priest of Lubeck (*c.* 1150), says that the principal god of the Slavs was *Svantovit*, whose temple and image in the island of Rügen he describes. Judging by the details he gives of the worship here practised, this Svantovit was a horse-god. According to Helmold, Svantovit was a corruption of Saint Vit, the patron saint of Corvey, whose worship had been established by Louis II. at Rügen in the ninth century, prior to the last offensive return of Slav paganism. This hypothesis is quite inadmissible, though it is frequently put forward, for if we accept it, how are we to account for the names of certain Slav gods which are akin to that of Svantovit, such as Porevit, Rugievit, and Herovit? It was the monks who claimed to have discovered their *Sanctus Vitus* in Svantovit, whose name seems to have meant "the mighty oracle."

7. We hear of many-headed idols among the Baltic Slavs. Saxo (*c.* 1170) describes a certain god *Porenutius* at Rügen, whose idol had four faces, and a fifth on his breast. He also tells of the idol of Svantovit in the temple of Arcona at Rügen, with four necks and four heads; it held in one hand a bow, in the other a drinking-horn, which the priest filled every year with wine; he predicted the future harvests from the state of preservation of the wine. Near the idol were a saddle and bridle destined for the white horse of the god, which only the priest might mount. It was supposed that the god rode this steed to fight against the enemies of the Rugians, and that he did so at night, for the horse was often found covered with mud and sweat in the morning. This horse also served as an augural animal, a form of divination which is known among other Slav tribes. The priest alone might enter the sanctuary: while he swept it, he had to hold his breath (like the Parsees). We also hear of a triple god called *Triglav*, of a *Rugievit* with seven faces,

of a *Porevit* with five heads, &c. Triglav, like Svantovit, had a sacred oracular horse at Stettin; his saddle, preserved in the temple, was of gold and silver.

8. Certain rude stone idols, representing gods holding horns, are found in museums; the most interesting of these is a large cubic stone discovered in a river and preserved at Cracow. These idols are akin to the carved menhirs of the Aveyron, and still more to the numerous figures called *Kammenaia baba*, stone statues of men and women holding a drinking-horn, which are common in South Russia.

9. *Volusu*, the god of flocks, identified by Russian folklorists with St. Blasius, is called *Veles* in Czech, and in the fifteenth century meant the devil. *Dazbogu*, of whom there was an image at Kief, was a solar god; his name means "the god who gives." In Servian, *Dabog* is the devil.

10. The Balkan Slavs had a god *Trojanu*, who was obviously the Emperor Trajan. The Roman ruins of the Danubian region attributed by popular tradition to Trajan were supposed, like all ruins, to be inhabited by demons; the name of the Emperor was given to one of these. His worship was transmitted to the Russians, and various texts, from the twelfth to the sixteenth century, associate the name Trojanu with that of Perunu.

11. Helmold speaks of a Slav god called *Zcernoboch*, "the black god." The chronicler says further that at their banquets the Slavs handed round a cup, pronouncing certain words over it "in the name of the good god and the evil god." The black god must have had a counterpart in a white god, *Bielbog*, whose name has survived in the names of certain places. Here we note traces of dualism, due perhaps to Persian influences.

12. The nymphs mentioned by Procopius were the *Vilas*, common to all save the Baltic Slavs. The Vilas, who inhabited the clouds, the earth and the waters, were pretty girls who passed their time dancing and hunting. Though sometimes benevolent and healers of sickness, they were often maleficent, raising tempests, killing or blinding those who surprised them bathing, and inflicting fits of delirium, like the Greek nymphs. Their life-principle was contained in

their golden hair; if a hair was plucked from the head of one of them, she instantly died. There are analogous legends in classic antiquity: a golden hair was treacherously snatched from the head of Nisus, king of Megara, by his daughter Scylla (Ovid); to ensure the death of Dido on the pyre, Proserpine had to pull out her one golden hair (Virgil). Some of the legends indicate the animal nature of the Vilas, who are represented as serpents, fish, or swans, and sometimes riding on stags (in Bulgaria). Even at the present day the Southern Slavs make offerings to them, shreds of stuff, flowers and cakes.

13. Among the Russians and Bulgarians there were Vilas called *Rusalkas,* a name which has been connected with the Græco-Byzantine *Rousalia,* the Feast of Roses. In some countries they were supposed to be the souls of young girls who had died before marriage.

14. The domestic gods play an important part in Slav folklore. The Russian equivalent for the Roman *Lar familiaris* is an old man, called the grandfather of the house, who hides behind the stove during the day, and comes out at night to eat the food prepared for him. This genius is the soul of an ancestor; invocations and sacrifices are offered to him and when the peasant changes houses, he invites the *domovoj* to follow him to his new abode.

15. We have seen that the Baltic Slavs had temples; but there were probably none in Russia, where it was the custom to set up idols in high places. The assertions of Christian chroniclers concerning human sacrifices must not be unreservedly accepted, but sacrifices of oxen, horses and sheep are well authenticated. Sacred woods played the same part as in Germany; the sacred trees were more especially the oak and the walnut. Springs and mountains were also worshipped; at least we hear of a sacred mountain in Silesia.

16. The worship of the dead is attested by thousands of pagan graves, in which the dead were surrounded by familiar objects that had belonged to them. The word *raj,* common to all the Slavs, must have meant the other world before it was used to designate the Christian Paradise. The rites of burial and of cremation were both practised; Slav widows,

like those of the Hindus, were sometimes burnt on their husbands' funeral pyres. Banquets were given in honour of the dead, who were supposed to eat the remains. There is still a survival from this custom: at the end of a banquet a formula is pronounced which sends the "holy ancestors" back to their own place. The demon of illness is even more voracious than the deceased; during recent cholera epidemics, the unhappy *moujiks* prepared veritable banquets for the monster at night, hoping he might spare them if he were well gorged. Dying of hunger themselves, they dared not touch the provisions destined for the dreaded devourer of men. Such is the state of enlightenment in which ten centuries of Christianity has left them!

BIBLIOGRAPHY

I. 1. Holder, *Altkeltischer Sprachschatz,* 1896-1908 (important); Renel, *Les religions de la Gaule,* 1907; Dottin, *Manuel de l'antiquité celtique,* 1906; MacCulloch, *Celtic Mythology,* 1918; S. R., *Cultes et mythes,* 5 vols., 1904-1923; *Bronzes figurés de la Gaule,* 1894; C. Jullian, *Histoire de la Gaule,* 1907 *et seq.;* Toutain, *Cultes païens,* vol. iii, 1920.

3. Art and Magic: S. Reinach, *Cultes,* vol. i, p. 125.

4. Reddening of corpses and the affair of St. Ambrose at Milan: S. R., *L'Anthropologie,* 1907, p. 718.

5. Déchelette, *Manuel d'archéol. préhistorique et celtique,* vols. i-iv, 1908-1914.

6. Plastic Art and Druidism: S. R., *Cultes,* vol. i, p. 146.

10. Totemism among the Celts: S. R., *Cultes,* vol. i, p. 30.

11. Tarvos Trigaranus: *Ibid.,* vol. i, p. 233.—Altar of N.-D. de Paris: *Ibid.,* p. 234; of Treves: *Ibid.,* pp. 236, 237.

12. Altar of Mavilly and Vesta: *Ibid.,* vol. iii, p. 191.

13. The Pythagorean cock: *Ibid.,* vol. i, p. 31.

14. Taboo of spoil: *Ibid.,* vol. iii, p. 223. The military taboo of the Celts: *Ibid.,* vol. iii, p. 119.

15. Teutates, Esus, Taranis: *Ibid.,* vol. i, p. 204.

17. The God with the mallet: *Ibid.,* vol. i, p. 264; Sucellus: *Ibid.,* vol. i, p. 217.

20. Windisch, art. *Keltische Sprachen* in Ersch and Gruber's Encyclopædia.

22. Mercury tricephalus: S. R., *Cultes,* vol. iii, p. 160.

27. D'Arbois, *Les Druides,* 1906; S. R., *Cultes,* vol. i, p. 188; iv, p. 188; v, p. 216.

29. *Orbis alius* of the Druids: S. R., *Cultes,* vol. i, p. 184.

31. The Virgins of Sena: *Ibid.,* vol. i, p. 195.

34. D'Arbois, *Cycle mythologique irlandais,* 1884; *Epopée celtique en Irlande,* 1902, and other works by the same author on the Celts; Windisch, *Keltisches Britannien,* 1912; G. Dottin, *L'Epopée irlandaise,* 1926.

II. J. Grimm, *Deutsche Mythol.,* 4th ed., 3 vols., 1875-1878; E. H. Meyer, *Germanische Mythol.,* 1891; Eug. Mogk, *Germ. Mythol.,* 1906 (the same subject in much greater detail in the *Grundriss der Germ. Philol.* by Paul); A. Geffroy, *Rome et les Barbares,* 1874; Montelius and S. R., *Temps préhist. en Suède,* 1895.

9. A. Dieterich, *Mutter Erde,* 1907.

14. Reichel, *Vorhellenische Göttercuite,* 1897 (*cf.* S. R., *Rev. crit.,* 1897, vol. ii, p. 389).

18. Witches: Lea, *Hist. of the Inquisition,* vol. iii; Gummere, *Germanic Origins,* 1892, p. 143.

20. Horse taboo: S. R., *Cultes,* vol. iii, p. 129.

25. All Saints' Day was fixed on Nov. 1 in 835 (Saintyves, *Les Saints,* 1907, p. 83).

26. Translation of the Edda by Bergmann, 1853; Vigfusson and J. Powell, *Corpus poeticum boreale,* 2 vols., 1883; M. Cahen, *Vocabulaire religieux du Vieux-Scandinave,* 1921; S. Bugge, *The Home of the Eddic poems,* 1899; B. S. Phillpots, *The elder Edda,* 1920; Craigie, *Rel. of ancient Scandinavia,* 1906; Pineau, *Vieux chants populaires scandinaves,* 1897, 1901 (*cf.* G. Paris, *Jour. des Sav.,* 1898, p. 385); art. *Eddas* in Hastings' *Encycl. of Religion,* 1912. On S. Bugge's theories, see Bréal, *Journal des Savants,* 1889, p. 622; Duvau, *Ibid.,* 1899, p. 695. On the figurative mythology of the Edda, see the same, *Ibid.,* 1901, p. 575.

42. On Beowulf, Parsifal, &c., see Karpeles, *Allgemeine Geschichte der Litteratur,* vol. ii (1891), pp. 129, 307, 316, 412; on the Legend of the Holy Grail (1180-1220), see Thurston, *Rev. du clergé, déc.* 1908, p. 556, and *Rev. archéol.,* 1921, i, p. 183.

III. L. Léger, *Mythologie slave,* 1901; *Les anciennes civilis. slaves,* 1921; Lubor Niederle, *La race slave* (French transl.), 1911.

CHAPTER V

CHINESE, JAPANESE, MONGOLIANS, FINNS, AFRICANS, OCEANIANS, AND AMERICANS

I. The tolerant spirit of the Chinese. Rationalism. The ***King***. Confucius and Laotse. Taoism. ***Feng-shui***. Optimism and Pessimism.

II. Lack of deep religious feeling in Japan. Shinto. Sacred animals. Temples and ritual. Belief in a future life. Buddhism and the Shinto reaction. Tolerance in Japan.

III. Mongolian Shamanism. Dualist doctrine. The ritual use of blood. Popular Finnish Songs.

IV. Kaffirs and Negroes. The Religion of the South African natives. Negro Fetichism. Ancestor-worship and human sacrifices. Totemism in Africa.

V. Taboos and totemism in Oceania. Rites of initiation. Polynesian cosmogony. Secret rites and societies. Mana.

VI. American totemism. The great Manitou. Mexico. Toltecs and Aztecs. Human Sacrifices. Sun-worship in Peru. Totemism and magic among the Mexicans of to-day.

I. The Chinese

1. There are or were[1] three principal religions in China, setting aside Christianity, Islamism and Judaism; these are: Confucianism, Taoism and Buddhism. The last of these came from India, where it no longer exists, except in Ceylon. The Chinese do not like the Christian missionaries, who sow discord among them and were accused of protecting converted criminals; nor do they like the Musulmans, since the revolt of the latter which took so long to suppress (1853-1872); but as a rule they are tolerant, taking what suits them from the three religions of the empire, and refraining from proselytism. Confucianism is the religion more especially of the cultured, Taoism or Buddhism that of the populace.

2. Chinese rationalism has to a great extent effaced the

[1] Since the Chinese revolution (1911) and the civil wars which have ensued, the conservative religions of China have suffered an almost total eclipse; I speak of China before the overthrow of the monarchy.

traces of primitive religion, a peasant cult of fertility; but such traces subsist in popular customs and beliefs, which are profoundly animistic, and offer a great variety of religious traits. These, as J. M. de Groot has shown, have exercised a considerable influence on the learned religions and philosophical systems of China.

3. The five sacred books called *King* were prior to the great sage Kong-tse, or Confucius (571 to 478 B.C.). These writings contain poetry, rules of etiquette, historical facts and even religion. This last consists in the worship of heaven and earth, of the Great Spirit and of inferior spirits; it is an animism tending to monotheism, dominated by the social idea of the harmony between the course of Nature and the conduct of man. When Nature shows irritation, it is man who is in fault; the government should intervene for improvement. The spirits of earth and heaven include those of ancestors, who are always present, and whose worship is the essential feature of Chinese religion, although ideas as to the manner in which they survive are somewhat vague. The Emperor alone may offer the great sacrifice to Heaven; but every one sacrifices to his ancestors. There are no clergy, only functionaries charged with the performance of rites.

4. The honest Confucius took part in the political life of his day. After holding office as a minister, he was exiled and persecuted, and finally recalled. His teaching was temperate, a doctrine of practical virtues and social etiquette. He was the least mystic of religious law-givers. But he set great store on learning, and the excessive influence exercised in China by men of letters is due to him. He is adored there as the "throneless king," "the perfect sage"; his adherents invoke him and offer sacrifices to him. Though he put the duties of filial piety and family sentiment first in his moral code, he did not forget what man owes to his neighbour. "Do unto others as ye would men should do unto you" was a precept Confucius had no need to borrow from our Scriptures.

5. Laotse, an older man than Confucius, whom he is said to have known, lived in retirement. There is a book by him,

the *Tao-te* (way of truth), which treats of duty and politics in an obscure style; the doctrine it teaches is a kind of mystic Pantheism. His morality is ascetic, almost Christian. *Tao* is Reason, which governs the world and should inspire man; meditation is more important than knowledge to this end.

Laotse condemns violence and war; he would reduce the intervention of the State to a minimum. "Repay evil with justice and unkindness with kindness." This precept again was not borrowed from our Scriptures.

6. The religion founded on the Tao is known as Taoism; it has greatly degenerated. Buddhist influences and a complicated system of magic have impaired its character. Taoism has exorcists, celibate monks and nuns, a religious head who is a kind of pope (without any temporal power). The rites are more archaic than the doctrine, for they are of popular origin. At the Spring festivals, fires are kindled, and the Taoist priests, half-naked, throw rice and salt into the flames and run through them with bare feet; this is a survival of sun-worship. Water is personified by the King of Dragons, to whom temples are built on the banks of lakes and of rivers. The repose of the dead in their tombs must be ensured, or they will molest the living. The choice of sepulchres is governed by very minute rules, and elaborate precautions are taken to prevent their violation. All this forms a science known as *Feng-shui*, to which the devout Taoists were the more attached, because it put obstacles in the way of our engineers and their works.

7. In addition to her religious law-givers, China has had philosophers, some of whom preach the love of pleasure, and others abstinence, while others again deal with politics and magic. The great philosopher of the school of Confucius was Meng-tse, called Mencius (371-288 B.C.). His doctrine, instinct with optimism, admits the primitive goodness of human nature; to be good, man has only to remain so. There has been no lack of pessimists to contradict him, nor of eclectics to harmonise the two points of view.

II. The Japanese

1. The present population of the Japanese archipelago comprises Shintoists, Buddhists and Christians. Buddhists and Shintoists live in perfect accord. Japanese who have presented their children in the Shinto temple are occasionally buried with Buddhist rites.

2. This intelligent race is by no means religious, in spite of assertions to the contrary. Its one strong religion, its sole strong passion, is patriotism. This is the final expression of ancestor-worship, for in the fatherland, as has often been said since Comte, there are many more dead than living.

3. According to a competent writer, nine Japanese out of ten, if questioned concerning the old national religion called *Shinto* (the way), will reply that it is ancestor-worship. This is hardly the case, historically speaking. Although the sacred books of Shinto only date from the eighth century of our era, they show that the basis of this religion is animistic and naturalistic, with totemic survivals. Shinto enumerates myriads of spirits or gods, among which are the goddess of Earth, the solar goddess, the lunar god, the god of fire; the god of heaven, who plays so important a part in China, is unknown. The sun is feminine in Japan, whereas in China it is masculine; this difference is not unimportant when we recall the considerable part played by women in ancient Japan. Old Chinese books call it "the land of queens"; there were queens among the first Mikados.

4. Many animals, such as the white horse, the fox, the dog, the rat and the cock continue to be the attributes of divinities. That of the solar goddess is a bird; it is from her that the Mikados claim descent. There are also sacred trees. Another essential element of the Shinto Pantheon are the heroes, men who are deified because they deserved the gratitude of their countrymen. These, if I may so express it, are the *élite* of the ancestors; ancestors of any kind are held in honour, however, but less stringently than in China, and this veneration is less irksome for the living.

5. The temples are the abodes of the gods. Beds and

pillows are prepared for them in these buildings. In addition to the priests there are priestesses who perform in the pantomimes that form part of the worship. In Japan, as elsewhere, these soon gave birth to the profane drama. The priestesses quit the service of the temple when they marry.

6. Pilgrimages to the great religious sanctuaries are enjoined, and the Mikado himself sets the example. Purification—by fire, salt, and rice—divination and maleficent spells worked by means of effigies are practised. The offerings are comestibles of various kinds; they are never burnt. The worship of fire is attested by the fires which are lighted in the courts of the temples in November, by the renewal of the sacred fire at the beginning of the year, and by the very widely spread custom of "passage through fire," a purification which has become an ordeal.

7. Human sacrifices are said to have formed part of the funeral rites of former times; the servants and horses of warriors were immolated. From the first century, clay statuettes were substituted for servants and horses; a similar substitution is believed to have taken place in Greece, a country with which Japan has some interesting analogies. The soul of the dead is supposed to be shut up in a wooden casket; it is invoked in domestic worship; but belief in the future life is as vague as in China.

8. From the sixth century of our era, Buddhism penetrated into Japan and has mingled with Shinto. In the eighteenth century, a patriotic reaction restored pure Shinto to its pristine honours; this reaction had a certain influence upon the political revolution of 1868, which reaffirmed the power of the Mikado, the descendant of the Sun-goddess, and drove out Buddhist rites and monks from the Shinto sanctuaries. But harmony was soon restored and Japan, disregarding the evil example of Europe, has found strength and union in toleration.

III. The Mongolians and the Finns

1. The steppes of the north are the domain of magic. Those among the Mongolians who have not embraced Bud-

dhism or Islamism are Shamanists; but Shamanism has subsisted side by side with these more enlightened creeds, and has even intermingled with them, notably among the Manchus.

2. The Shamans are ecstatic priests, chosen from among epileptics or from among those who by the use of drugs and exercises are able to throw themselves into a state of delirium. They practise all kinds of sorcery to the accompaniment of music and dancing, sell talismans, offer sacrifices, and claim to be able to act as guides to souls in the other world, which they paint in the most gloomy colours.

3. The doctrine of these jugglers is dualist. The universe is peopled with spirits; each mortal has two, one good and one evil. In the world, the good spirits are in the air, the evil ones on earth. It is therefore of primary importance to conciliate the earth. Sacrifices of horses are offered to both good and evil spirits; these must be eaten without spilling the blood or breaking the bones, like the Paschal lamb of the Jews. The souls of ancestors inhabit the third heaven, in company with seven gods of an inferior order.

4. To drink blood together, or to drink blood drawn from the arm of another person and to offer him one's own in the same manner, are sacred rites of alliance. These rites are very ancient, and are to be found among other races as well as among the Tartars; their object is to establish artificially what we still call "blood-brotherhood."

5. The Finns, a mixed race of Europeans and Mongolians, have an epic literature, or at least two famous collections of popular poems, the *Kanteletar*, published in 1840, and the *Kalewala* (1849). The *Kalewala* in its present form is no earlier than Charlemagne. It records the birth of the world from a bird, the marriage of a young girl to the Wind. The god of heaven, originally a thunder-god, is called "the old man"; there are divinities of the earth, of water, of forests and of the sun. It is a Pantheon in its infancy, with a superabundance of spirits and genii. The worship of ancestors is less in vogue than magic. An immense oak, springing from a magic acorn, invaded heaven;

destroyed by a water-spirit, a dwarf, it fell, shaking the world; those who collected the fragments possess the secrets of magic. The weapon of the hero of the *Kalewala* is a magic harp, and the chief episode in this embryonic epopee is the theft of a sacred object, which has suspicious analogies with the Holy Grail.

IV. The Africans

1. Africa, so far as it is neither Musulman nor Christian, comprises two great ethnical divisions which present very diverse religious phenomena: Kaffirs, Hottentots and Bushmen in the south; Negroes in the centre, the east and west. There are further marked differences between the Negroes of the Soudanese or western group and those of the Bantu or eastern group; but I must restrict myself here to summary indications.

2. The religion of the South Africans seems poor and sterile, perhaps because it has been but imperfectly studied hitherto. Trees and animals are held to be the ancestors of man, and it is chiefly in animal forms that the dead appear to the living. The worship of the dead comprises sacrifice. Death entails taboo; a Hottentot *kraal* in which a death has taken place must be abandoned. There are wizards who form confraternities and are also soothsayers and healers. Fetichism does not exist. Various mutilations, performed upon the teeth and other parts of the body, indicate affiliation to the religious life, which is also the political life of the tribes.

3. Among the Negroes, Fetichism, or as it may be called in the basin of the Niger *Jujuism* (from *juju*, a fetich), is predominant. The fetich is a material object, natural or artificial, in which the ancestral spirit, which has become the protecting spirit of a group or tribe, has taken up its abode. Fetichism is so deeply implanted in the souls of the Negroes that they even adapt to it the more enlightened creeds taught them, such as Christianity or Islamism; this is seen more especially in the United States and the Antilles. The priests of Fetichism are magicians who offer sacrifices,

utter oracles, conduct law-suits, arbitrate in quarrels and accusations of murder, control rain and fine weather, and heal the sick; the authority of the great fetichists is such that they dispose of the life and the goods of individuals. As sickness and death are looked upon as the effects of maleficent spells, the fetichist is continually called upon to discover the evil-doer, suspects are put to the ordeal of poison, instances of which are to be found elsewhere, notably in India. A suspect may, however, justify himself and this is the more easily done if he makes a little present to the fetichist. Secret societies, which are very numerous among the Negroes, have their special fetiches; tattoo-marks attest the dependence of the devotee on his fetich. Among the Dahomeyans and the Ashantis, ancestor-worship was attended by horrible human hecatombs offered to the spirits of deceased chiefs. It is said that these sacrifices are still frequent in the regions of the Lower Niger, and that the victims, resigned to their fate, undertake to bear messages from the living to the dead.

4. The Bantu Negroes, who live in the regions of the great lakes, are divided into totemic clans; the members of a clan may neither kill their totem, nor marry a wife of their own clan. Totemism is also to be found in British East Africa and in Madagascar, with a strongly developed system of magic.

V. The Oceanians

1. In my introduction, I spoke at some length of the taboos and the totemism which are found throughout Oceania. Taboos are of the essence of religion in Polynesia and Melanesia; a totemism comparable to that of the North American Indians, but presenting individual traits, has been studied among the Aruntas of Central Australia. These blacks draw animals and imitate them in their dances to attract them; they eat their totem (from which they generally abstain) ritually; they believe that the souls of their ancestors inhabit ornamented wooden slabs which they hide carefully in the depths of their forests. They band

themselves together in religious societies, imposing complicated initiatory rites and cruel mutilations on adults. The young man who is initiated is supposed to die and to be born again to a new life. Marriage is subject to severe restrictions, for no one may take a wife of his own blood, even a cousin in the twentieth degree. A great part of the year is spent in ceremonies the object of which is to ensure abundance of game. Poverty and superstition do not prevent these people from thinking themselves happy and loving life.

2. In Polynesia and Malaya, where the culture of cereals and domestic animals are known, religion is naturally more highly developed. The Polynesians believe in a divine creator and have legends as to the origin of the world, how it was fished up out of the sea, or hatched from an egg. The god of the Maoris (of New Zealand) is not only the fisher of the world, but the bird who stole fire from heaven, the beneficent hero. In Java, at the beginning of the rainy season, the marriage of Heaven and Earth is celebrated, and at seed-time, the marriage of Rice. Souls are supposed to migrate from one island to another; presents are offered to them for the journey. The ideas of a subterranean abode of souls and of the tutelary spirits of ancestors are to be found everywhere. Secret societies abound in Polynesia; males are admitted to these at the end of a novitiate, with long ceremonies comprising dances, music, acting and scenes representing the history of the gods. Tattoo-marks are the visible evidences of alliance with the god of the tribe; it is rare among women, but obligatory for men. The patterns often represent totem animals. Belief in the common origin of men and animals is further manifested in tales of metamorphosis; in Borneo more especially, men can transform themselves into tigers, and become tiger-bogeys.

3. A quasi-philosophical idea, also found elsewhere, that of *mana*, completes the wide-spread notion of taboo in Melanesia and Polynesia. *Mana* is the principle of magic; it is the latent power in a person, a thing, even in a word. He who can evoke this energy and make it subserve his ends is a clever man. In modern language, this means that there are

reserves of force everywhere and that we should use them for our needs. If taboo is the principle of morality and decency, mana is that of the applied sciences. All honour then to *taboo* and *mana!*

VI. The Aborigines of America

1. Garcilasso de la Vega, son of one of Pizarro's comrades and an Inca woman, records the existence of totemism in Peru as far back as the sixteenth century; at the beginning of the eighteenth century, the Jesuit Lafitau discovered it among the North American Indians. The religion of these Indians and of those of Mexico has been minutely studied by the ethnographers of the United States in our own times. Thanks to them, we are thoroughly well informed concerning totemic ceremonies, dances with animal-masks, and spirit-worship. If taboo has been more perfectly preserved in Polynesia than elsewhere, North America is the favoured land of totemism. Every reader of Cooper and Aymard knows that the Redskin tribes adopt the names of animals, that the chiefs are proud of these names, and display corresponding emblems in their costume.

2. The world of spirits itself has a chief; this is the Great Manitou, commonly incorporated in an animal. The Great Manitou created the world as the result of a struggle with the waters, an idea analogous to that of the Babylonians: it has given rise to myths in which missionaries have traced the story of Noah's deluge. With regard to men, it was an accepted theory that they were the progeny of trees and that they were raised to higher conditions by civilising heroes or demi-gods. A Peruvian legend made them the offspring of stones and rocks; but here again the civilising hero plays his part.

3. Before the Spanish conquest, Mexico and Peru had achieved a high degree of culture. The Mexicans had temples, pyramids, tombs, palaces, a solar calendar and hieroglyphic writing which is but partially decipherable. Although they worshipped gods in animal form, birds and serpents, they also adored some in human form. The prin-

cipal god of the Toltecs, a civilising hero, was, like the Egyptian Osiris, the friend of men, who taught them to live in peace; then he disappeared, but with a promise to return some day. The god of the Aztecs was a sort of Mars, warlike and implacable, who exacted human sacrifices. Their religion, at once cruel and ascetic, must have pleased the Spaniards, especially as monastic associations, both male and female, abounded. The conquerors were greatly struck by a ceremony analogous to their own communion. On the occasion of the winter festival, an image of the god was made in dough; he was then put to death in effigy and the dough was distributed to those present to eat. Young nobles were also sacrificed; they were chosen a year beforehand and assimilated to the god by rites before being put to death. The idea of the eminent dignity of the victim thus deified in preparation for sacrifice is very wide-spread in both worlds; but to the Spaniards, these rude analogies with Christianity were only to be explained as a device of the devil.

4. Peru was less advanced than Mexico, for the inhabitants were ignorant of writing; they corresponded by means of *quipos*, small cords with knots of different colours. Yet the Peruvians had made certain astronomical observations; they had solar and lunar calendars. The government was purely theocratic. The dominant tribe, the Incas, exercised both religious and political power; the Temple of the Sun only opened to them. They claimed to be descended from a civilising couple, the children of the sun, Manco Capac and Mama Oello. The reigning Inca was the incarnation of the planet; he was the pope of the solar kingdom. There were convents for noble maidens, the brides of the sun, who, like the Roman Vestals, were dedicated to his worship. This worship was milder than in Mexico; the sacrifices were chiefly tame llama goats and birds of prey. The vestiges of totemism which had survived in the sixteenth century were subordinate to the religion of the Sun.

5. Among the still semi-barbarous tribes of Mexico, Central America, Brazil, &c., travellers both ancient and modern have observed customs and beliefs derived from totemism

AMERICAN TOTEMISM

and magic. Nothing could be stranger, to quote but one instance, than the prayer-magic of the Huichol Indians of Mexico; to represent a divinity is, in their opinion, one of the most efficacious ways of praying to him; even to speak of the gods, and to relate their legends, is to pray to them; every ex-voto placed in a temple is a prayer, incorporated in a material object. Another Mexican tribe, the Zuñis, furnishes the most striking example of totemism complicated by fetichism, for the fetich is the intermediary, the mediator between the Zuñi and his animal god. The Zuñis have also a cosmogony, a history of the creation of the world, and elaborate initiations or mysteries which have even been compared with those of the Greeks.

BIBLIOGRAPHY

I. J. de Groot, *The religious systems of China*, 1892 *et seq.;* by the same, *Die Religionen der Chinesen* (in *Orientalische Religionen*, 1906, p. 162) and *Religion in China*, 1912; Chavannes, *Le T'ai Chan*, 1910; Granet, *La religion de Chinois*, 1922; Maspero, *La Chine antique*, 1927.

3. Barth. S.-Hilaire, *Les livres sacrés de la Chine* (in *Journ. des Sav.*, 1894, pp. 65, 509).

4 *et seq.* R. V. Douglas, *Confucianism and Taoism*, 1889; Ab. Rémusat, *Lao-tseu*, 1820; Eitel, *Feng-shui*, 1873.

II. Aston, *Shinto*, 1907; K. Florenz, *Die Religionen der Japaner* (in *Orientalische Religionen*, 1906, p. 194); W. E. Griffis, *The Religions of Japan*, 1895.

III. W. Radloff, *Das Schamanentum*, 1885; W. Sieroszeweski, *Du chamanisme* (in *Rev. hist. relig.*, 1902).

5. Comparetti, *Der Kalewala*, 1892; Krohn, art. *Finns* in Hastings; English translation of *Kalewala* by J. M. Crawford, 1889.

IV. 1. Delafosse, *Les nègres*, 1927; W. Schneider, *Die Religionen der afrik. Naturvölker*, 1891; J. Macdonald, *Religions and Myth* (Africa), 1893; art. *Africa and Bantus* in Hastings.

2. G. Fritsch, *Die Eingeborenen Süd-Afrikas*, 1872.

3. F. Schultze, *Der Fetishismus*, 1871; Mary Kingsley, *West African Studies*, 1899; A. Bros, *Le problème de la mort chez les non-civilisés* (in *Rev. clergé français*, Oct. 1, 1908, p. 46).

4. A. van Gennep, *Tabou et totémisme à Madagascar*, 1904.

V. A. Réville, *Relig. des peuples non-civilisés*, 2 vols., 1883; J. Deniker, *Races et peuples*, 1900; A. Bros, *La relig. des peuples non-civilisés*, 1907.—Codrington, *The Melanesians*, 1891; Howitt, *The Native Tribes of S. E. Australia*, 1904; Spencer and Gillen, *The Native Tribes of Central and Northern Australia*, 2 vols., 1899, 1904 (important); C. Strehlow, *Aranda und Loritjastämme*, 1907; Grey, *Polynesian Mythology*, 1855; A. van Gennep, *Mythes et légendes d'Australie*, 1906; W.

Skeat, *Malay Magic,* 1900; M. Mauss, *Pouvoirs magiques dans les sociétés australiennes,* 1904; Durkheim, *Système totémique en Australie,* 1912.

3. For *Mana,* see Hubert and Mauss, *La magie* (in *Année sociol.,* vol. vii, 1904); Saintyves, *La force magique,* 1914; R. Marrett, *The Threshold of Religion,* 1911.

VI. D. Brinton, *Myths of the New World,* 3rd ed., 1896; *Religions of primitive Peoples,* 1897; Dellenbaugh, *The North Americans of Yesterday,* 1901; F. Boas, *The Indians of British Columbia,* 1898, and other works by the same writer; Beuchat, *Manuel d'archéologie américaine,* 1912.

2. Winternitz, *Flutsagen des Alterthums und der Naturvölker,* 1901.

3. A. Réville, *Les religions du Mexique et du Pérou,* 1885; L. Spence, *The mythol. of ancient Mexico and Peru,* 1907; Lehmann, *Mexican Research,* 1909; Hamy, *Croyances et pratiques des premiers Mexicains* (in *Conf. Guimet,* 1907, p. 43); G. Raynaud, *Les Panthéons de l'Amérique Centrale* (in *Etudes de critique,* 1896, p. 373).

5. H. Cushing, *Zuñi Creation Myths,* 1896; C. Lumholtz, *The Huichol Indians,* 1898, 1900; *Unknown Mexico,* 2 vols., 1903; Hubert and Mauss, *Mélanges d'hist. des relig.,* 1909.

CHAPTER VI

THE MUSULMANS

Arabia before Islam. Djinns. Allah and Al-Lât. Fetiches and totemic sacrifices. Christians and Jews in Arabia. The Life of Mahomet. Religious institutions of Islam. Fatalism. "Young Turkey." The Koran.—Rapid progress of Islamism. Musulman tolerance. The Shiite schism. Shiite sects; Sufism. Secret societies; the Mahdi. Liberal tendencies. Freemasonry in Turkey. Babism in Persia.

1. Classic texts and, to a still greater degree, inscriptions have thrown some light upon the nomad populations of Arabia before the Musulman era, Minæans, Nabatæans and Himyarites or Homerites. The last-named became partially converted to Judaism, and showed great hostility to Christianity, which increased considerably in the Yemen (Arabia Felix) during the fourth century, encouraged by the Christians of Abyssinia.

2. The religion of Arabia before Mahomet was a polytheistic animism, which developed into monotheism without losing the characteristics of its former stages. The Arabs located their spirits (*djinns*) in trees, stones, rude images, the sun, the moon and the stars; but among all these gods, they had a clear conception of a supreme deity whom they called Allah (*Al ilâh*), and upon whom they looked as the guardian of moral order. Three goddesses were worshipped as "the daughters of Allah" from the time of Mahomet; one of these, Al-Lât (the goddess) had already been mentioned by Herodotus (B.C. 450), under the name of a female Allah, *Alilat*.

3. Mahomet did not create the monotheism of Islam; he merely got rid of Allah's satellites, male and female, whose prestige had already suffered considerably from that of the god.

4. There were no temples, but sacred enclosures sur-

rounding fetiches and images. All creatures living in these sacred precincts, or even straying into them by accident, were taboo and became the property of the god. Sacrifices consisted of offerings of sheep and camels. St. Nilus (fifth century) has left us an elaborate account of the sacrifice of a camel among the Saracens, Arab nomads of the peninsula of Sinai, which has all the character of a totemic communion feast. The uncooked blood and flesh of the animal had to be entirely consumed by the faithful before daybreak.

5. The Christians were numerous in the north-west of Arabia (Sinai) and in the Yemen; the Jews were scattered throughout the country. The influence of these monotheists no doubt counted for something in the discrediting of idols, and also in Mahomet's reforms, although his knowledge of Christianity and Judaism was very imperfect. It is said that on many occasions in his youth he conversed with Jews and with Christian monks, notably in the course of a journey to Bostra (Syria). He even adopted a Christian slave, Zaid, the *Séide* of Voltaire's *Mahomet*, whose name has become in French a synonym for fanatical devotion. But an illiterate man, talking with half-educated men, cannot learn much from them beyond the elements and the superficial phenomena of their religion.

6. Besides the Koran, which contains numerous allusions to events in the life of Mahomet, we have several detailed biographies of the Prophet written in Arabic, the earliest of which (*c.* 768) is known to us only in a revised version of 833. The marvellous, more especially the intervention of angels, predictions, &c., play an important part in it; it must therefore be consulted with caution.

7. Mahomet, or more correctly Mohammed (the praised one), was born at Mecca about 571, of a humble family, the social status of which was a good deal magnified in after years. During his youth he was engaged in various callings, among them those of a camel-driver and of a shepherd. Having improved his fortunes by marriage with a rich widow fifteen years his senior, Khadîdja, he conceived the idea of reforming the religious faiths of his country by simplifying them (612). Mecca was an important town, where a great

THE DANCE OF THE DERVISHES

annual market was held; a volcanic stone, set in the Ka'ba (cube), called the House of Allah, was a point of pilgrimage where the religion of Allah developed. Mahomet was soon in conflict with the greatest family of the city, the Koreischites; after ten years of struggle, during which he gained but few adherents, he gave up the unequal contest, and left for Yatrib, which has since taken the name of Medina (the *city* of the Prophet). Here there was a Jewish community well disposed to the cause of monotheism. This retreat of Mahomet was the Hegira, the beginning of the Musulman era (July 16, 622). Mahomet was then fifty-one years old. He was an eloquent man of handsome appearance, but subject to epileptic or hysterical attacks, which he also simulated at convenient moments. He was almost entirely without literary education.

8. From Medina, Mahomet led predatory raids against the merchants of Mecca. He even dared to attack a caravan during the month of the great market when the Bedouins observed the "truce of God." After his victory at the battle of Bedr (624), he cruelly massacred many prisoners. "Who will take care of my children?" exclaimed one of these. "The fires of Hell," replied the energumen.[1] The following year, fortune deserted him, but his persistence, seconded by the military talents of his best lieutenant, Omar, was not discouraged by reverses. In 629 he made a pacific entry into Mecca, and there converted even the bitterest of those opponents against whom he had preached the "holy war," which has remained one of the principles of Islamism. He destroyed idols everywhere; if he preserved the Black Stone, it was because, by a pious fraud, he associated it with an incident in the life of Abraham. An attack he attempted against the Byzantines on the Syrian frontier was unsuccessful; but when he died at Medina, on June 8, 632, on his return from a "last pilgrimage" to Mecca, he was the master of nearly all Arabia, and was revered almost as a god.

9. Ferocious against the heathen, that is to say, the worshippers of idols, Mahomet showed rather more tenderness

[1] Quatremère, *Journal Asiatique,* n.s., vol. xvi, p. 57 (from the *Kitab-Alagâni*); *cf.* C. de Perceval, *Histoire des Arabes,* iii, p. 70.

towards the "holders of the Scriptures," Jews, Christians, Parsees and Mandæans. He considered Moses and Jesus prophets, inspired by the same God as himself. But at an early period of his career he had come into conflict with the Jews at Medina, who accused him of plagiarising from the Bible and corrupting what he stole. He called them "asses loaded with books." In the course of his guerilla warfare against the inhabitants of Mecca, Mahomet attacked a Jewish tribe, put all the men to the sword, and reduced the women and children to slavery. He spared but one beautiful Jewess, whom he kept in his house, but who scornfully refused to become his wife.

10. If Mahomet's personal successes are to be explained by his unscrupulous energy and his lucid if uncultured intelligence, the astonishing progress of his doctrine is due to its simplicity. One God, the God of the patriarchs of Israel, worshipped without images; an immortal soul, destined to material rewards or penalties in a future life—these are its essential elements. The creation and the fall of man are taken from the Bible and recounted with certain variations. There is very little ritual; one month of daily fasting (*Ramadân*), with permission to feast during the night; ablutions; five prayers a day, repeated with the face turned towards Mecca. The Koran says nothing of circumcision, an old Arab rite which the Musulmans adopted. It contains very few prohibitions; the forbidden things are: the blood of animals, pork, fermented drinks, games of chance and images. The Musulmans have no clergy, only a director of public prayers (*imâm*), and a herald (*muezzin*), who announces the hour of prayer. As belief in djinns could not be altogether abandoned, Mahomet made them subordinate to the angels of post-Biblical Jewish tradition, the messengers of God or beneficent guardians of individuals. The fallen angel, Satan, was called Iblis (from the Greek *diabolos*). The reformer did no violence to the customs of the Arabs, whose predatory instincts he flattered by the doctrine of a holy war to be waged against infidels. Though he restricted polygamy by allowing only four legitimate wives, he himself set the example of a composition with the

law by taking nine wives after the death of Khadîdja. The Musulman woman continued to be half a slave, compelled to veil herself before strangers, learning nothing, and taking hardly any part in public worship; but the facilities of divorce were somewhat checked by the obligation of paying a dowry, which was imposed on the husband who put away his wife. The rest of Musulman morality is borrowed from Judaism and Christianity; it includes the principle of human fraternity, which was proclaimed rather than applied; but Mahomet, who had been poor himself, showed a special solicitude for the poor by making alms-giving no less obligatory than religious observances.

11. The duty *par excellence* is obedience and submission to God (*Islam*), which no other religion has formulated so rigorously. This naturally engendered fatalism. When overtaken by misfortune, no matter how undeserved, the Arab says: "It was written!" or "Allah is great!" Such a discipline makes heroic soldiers, patient and resigned workers; but does it make pioneers of progress? History gives the answer.

12. The "Young Turks," who conquered political power in July 1908 and deceived Europe by affected liberalism, maintained that the doctrines of modern civilisation are perfectly compatible with the Koran. But they did not evolve them from the Koran. Western civilisation is the daughter of the sixteenth-century Renaissance, which reinstated the wisdom of the Greeks. Every new victory of civilisation extends the moral domain of Hellenism and restricts that of the Oriental faiths. These may come to terms with it, but on condition that they develop, as Judaism and Christianity have done, in a manner directly opposed to that of the old theocracies.

13. The Koran (*El Qur'an*, reading) consists of one hundred chapters or *Surates*, which record the pronouncements and speeches of the Prophet without much system, in language which has become classical. During the life of Mahomet, they were transcribed in part (he himself could not write). The definitive edition of these fragments was published in 650, under the Caliphate of Othman. Though the

general authenticity is unquestionable, there is now reason to believe that the text has been seriously tampered with.

14. From the literary point of view, the Koran has little merit. Declamation, repetition, puerility, a lack of logic and coherence strike the unprepared reader at every turn. It is humiliating to the human intellect to think that this mediocre literature has been the subject of innumerable commentaries, and that millions of men are still wasting time in absorbing it.

∴

15. "Allah is the only God, and Mahomet is his Prophet!" This *credo* of Islam once threatened to become the faith of the world. The successors of Mahomet (*Caliphs*, which means Vicars) conquered in less than a century Syria, Egypt, Babylonia, Persia, Turkestan, Spain, the islands of the Ægean, northern Africa, Sicily, Southern France; they made Constantinople tremble, and resisted the furious onslaughts of the Crusaders. Although the Arab empire was divided as early as the eighth century, Arab civilisation, the heir of the vanquished races, flourished both at Bagdad and in Spain; the Arab religion, despite its schisms, retained all its expansive vitality. The Ottoman Turks, natives of Central Asia, conquered Asia Minor, and destroyed the last remnant of the Roman Empire by the capture of Constantinople in 1453. The whole of the Balkan peninsula, nearly all the islands, and the Crimea, fell into the hands of the Musulmans, who conquered Syria, Egypt, the Yemen, and North Africa during the sixteenth century. The great Musulman Empire of the Moguls was also established in India at about the same period.

16. The political decline of Islam was first manifested in Spain by the fall of the Arab kingdom of Granada (1492), to which events had long been tending; but religious Islamism never ceased to make progress in Asia and Africa. It now numbers over one hundred and sixty million adherents, sixty millions of whom are in British India, and it seems likely to take a further development among the African Negroes, to whom its simplicity, its fatalism and its promises

of sensual joys are much more attractive than the theological subtleties and the moral restraint of Christianity.

17. Wherever Islam has been introduced by conquest, as a rule the native populations have neither been massacred nor forcibly converted; the Arabs and the Turks have been content with extortion. During the first centuries after the Hegira, conquest would not have been so rapid if the Arab *régime* had not been preferable to that of the Byzantines or the Persians.[1] In spite of the menaces of the Koran, the vanquished were often treated with indulgence, and even with consideration. When Omar took Jerusalem in 636, he ensured the free exercise of their religion and the security of their persons and their goods to the inhabitants, both Jews and Christians. But when the Crusaders took Jerusalem in 1099, they massacred all the Musulmans and burnt the Jews alive; it is said that seventy thousand persons were put to death in less than a week to attest the superior morality of the Christian faith.

18. After the death of the Caliph Othman (656), Ali, the son-in-law and adopted son of Mahomet, was excluded from the succession by the intrigues of the governor of Syria. Ali died at Mesched and his son Hoseïn was murdered in 680; but their partisans founded a sect (*Shia*) which became the Shiites. The Shiites, who revere Ali and Hoseïn almost as much as Mahomet, reject the written tradition concerning the Prophet known as the *Sunna*, which the Orthodox, or Sunnites, accept as the natural complement of the Koran. The Shiites do not proscribe the use of wine and the representation of living creatures with the same rigour as the Sunnites; the more educated, influenced by Persian and Buddhist ideas, incline to an amiable Pantheism. Shiite Islamism has been the official religion of Persia since 1499; it is also very widely diffused in India. The Shiites never recognized the authority of the Sheikh-ul-Islam of Constantinople, the Vicar of the Commander of the Faithful, or Sultan of Turkey.

[1] In Syria, the invasion of the seventh century had been prepared by the incessant infiltration of Arab tribes from the Roman epoch onwards.

19. The Shiite sect was divided in its turn. The Ismailians are almost free-thinkers; the Druses of Lebanon, who are not content either with the Koran or the Bible, live in expectation of a new prophet. From the eleventh to the thirteenth century, Asia Minor was terrorised by the sectaries called Haschischim, because they intoxicated themselves with *haschisch* (hemp), sanguinary robbers who gave the word *assassin* to our modern languages. The most important of the Shiite sects is that of the mystics known as *Sufi* (from the Arab *sûf*, meaning wool, because of the woollen garments worn by the faithful); it was inspired by a woman, Râbia (*c.* 700). Their doctrine developed in Persia in the ninth century; Musulman convents, which Mahomet abhorred, were founded by its devotees, and thus asceticism penetrated into Islamism. The Sufites believe that the soul is an emanation from God, and that it is its destiny to reunite with him by love. It was this divine love, curiously intermingled with human love and scepticism, which inspired those great Persian poets we still read, Omar Khayyâm and Hafiz.

20. Ever since the twelfth century, Islam, perhaps influenced by India, has had its frenzied ascetics and charlatans, its dancing Dervishes, howlers, dancers, eaters of worms, scorpions and serpents—*illuminati* or deceivers who form confraternities and live by imposture. About 1880, a Dervish of the Egyptian Soudan, the founder of a Negro state, proclaimed himself the *Mahdi* ("led by Allah"), and roused fanaticism to such a degree that Egypt lost Nubia and the Upper Nile (1885). The victory of the English at Omdurman (1898) put an end to this tragi-comedy. But even now, secret societies maintain a perpetual fermentation in the lower strata of Islamism; one of the most active of these in North Africa is that of the Sanussya (*Snoussi*) founded by the Sheikh Sanus (1813-1859).

21. Liberal tendencies have not failed to show themselves in the bosom of orthodox Islamism; the *Motazilites* (Separatists) have introduced rationalism and attempted to purify their religion. But their influence was confined to the schools. A bolder attempt to lead back Islamism to its

primitive simplicity was made in the eighteenth century by Abd-ul-Wahhâb, an Arab of Nedjed, founder of the sect of Wahhâbites. It was primarily a reaction against the worship of the tombs of saints and of relics, against the luxury and corruption of manners, and even against the use of tobacco. These reformers began a struggle against the Turks about 1800; they seized Mecca and Medina, overthrew the Black Stone, and devastated the tomb of Mahomet. The Viceroy of Egypt, Mehemet Ali, was charged by the Sultan to subjugate them, and succeeded in 1818; but the Wahhâbites survived as a sect, rigidly faithful to the Koran alone, and exercised a certain influence on the insurrections of Arabia, which finally became independent of the Turkish Empire (1916). After having retaken Mecca, the Sultan of the Wahhâbites assumed the title of king (1926).

22. European Freemasonry penetrated into the Empire in the nineteenth century. It was mainly in the Lodges frequented by Turkish doctors and officers that the revolution was elaborated which put an end to the bloody *régime* of Sultan Abd-ul-Hamid (July 1908). But the so-called Young Turks, by their infamous cruelties against Armenians and Syrians, soon showed that their pretence of civilisation was a sham; they achieved the moral and material ruin of Turkey, and were in turn persecuted by the new nationalist *régime* which issued from the Great War and still endures.

23. Reform was preached in Persia from 1840 onwards by a pretended descendant of the Prophet, who called himself the *Mahdi el Bâb* (Gate of Truth). He was shot in 1850, but his disciples continued his propaganda of reaction against the ignorance and corruption of the Shiite clergy (the *mollahs*). Babism, although mystic and Sufite, assumed the character of a party of political reform, recruiting its adherents among the poor and oppressed, but also attracting various great personages. The government responded by ferocious executions, which failed to arrest the movement. The morality of the Babists is purely secular, and hostile to asceticism; it demands the suppression of polygamy and the veil, restrictions on divorce, the admission of women to ceremonial worship. In general, the Bab-

ists are men of progress, in so far as Musulmans without European culture can be, and there is reason to believe that they will contribute to the regeneration of Shiite Persia, which is laboriously accomplishing itself under our eyes.

BIBLIOGRAPHY

R. Dozy, *Essai sur l'hist. de l'islamisme,* French transl. from the Dutch, 1879; Hartmann, *Der Islam,* 1909; A. Bertholet, *Gestalt des Islam,* 1926; R. Bell, *Origin of Islam,* 1926; H. Lammens, *Islam,* 1926 (Engl. transl.).

2. Dussaud, *Les Arabes en Syrie avant l'Islam,* 1907; J. Wellhausen, *Reste arabischen Heidentums,* 2nd ed., 1897; Rob. Smith, *Kinship and Marriage in early Arabia,* 2nd ed., 1904; Th. Nöldeke, art. *Arabs* in Hastings, *Encycl.,* 1908.

7. W. Muir, *Life of Mahomet,* 4th ed., 1912; Renan, in *Etudes d'hist. relig.,* 1864; H. Grimme, *Mohammed,* 1895; Cl. Huart, *Hist. des Arabes,* 2 vol., 1913; Casanova, *Mohammed et la fin du monde,* 1912; E. Dermenghem, *Vie de Mahomet,* 1929.

13. George Sale, *The Koran,* English trans., 1734; latest edition, 1877; Max Müller, *Sacred Books of the East,* vol. v; Th. Nöldeke, *Geschichte des Korans,* 2d ed., 1909.

15. T. W. Arnold, *The Preaching of Islam,* 1896.—Art. *Khalifen,* by A. Müller in Ersch and Gruber (1884).

19. S. de Sacy, *Exposé de la religion des Druses,* 1838; Dussaud, *Religion des Nosaïris,* 1900; Nicholson, *Origins and Developments of Sufism* (in *Journ. Roy. Asiatic Society,* 1906); Goldziher, *Vorlesungen über den Islam,* 1910.

20. J. Darmesteter, *Le Mahdi,* 1885.

23. E. G. Browne, *A Year among the Persians* (Babism), 1893, and art. *Bâb* in Hastings; A. de Gobineau, *Les religions dans l'Asie centrale,* 1865; A. L. M. Nicolas, *Le Bâb,* 1908; E. D. Ross, *Babism,* 1902; H. Dreyfus, *L'œuvre de Baha-oullah,* 1924 (the successor of the Bâb and founder of *Behaism*).

CHAPTER VII

HEBREWS, ISRAELITES AND JEWS

Hebrews, Israelites, Jews. The mythical character of their primitive history. The Scriptural Canon; translations of the Bible. Inspiration and concordism. The moral value of the Old Testament. Names of the divinity. The creation and original sin. Polytheism and Jahvism. Baal, Sabaoth, Teraphim. Taboos. Totems. Magic. Eschatology. Festivals. The Pentateuch. The Prophets. Messianism. The Psalms, Proverbs, Job. The Restoration and the end of Jewish independence. Judaism since the destruction of the Temple.

1. The Hebrews made their first appearance in history as nomad Bedouins, worshippers of *djinns* or spirits, and fetiches. Their supreme god was the fulgurant God of Sinaï, who led them to the conquest of Canaan. They then became agriculturists, and partially adopted the religions of those they had vanquished; but sacerdotalism tended to impose on them the worship of its exclusive god. Its auxiliaries in this task were the preachers or prophets, who combated the polytheistic tendencies of kings and people. After the fall of the kingdom of Judah, prophetism got the upper hand definitely, and at the return after the Captivity, a theocratic *régime* was established in Judæa. But triumphant Jahvism was insidiously undermined by Græco-Alexandrian Judaism, which was inspired not by nationalist but by universalist ideas, and by obscure survivals of popular cults. This dual influence reveals itself in the Hellenistic mysticism of St. Paul, and is reflected in all the subsequent history of Christianity.

2. Israel ("God combats"?) was the name given by God to Jacob after the mythical episode of his encounter with the patriarch (Gen. xxxii, 28). The twelve tribes took the collective name of Israelites (Ex. iii, 16); at a later period it was applied to the tribes who, after the reign of Solomon, formed the kingdom of the north, or kingdom of Israel. The

Hebrews who returned to Judæa from Babylon took the name of Israelites, though they belonged mainly to the tribe of Judah.

3. Jew (in Hebrew *Jehoudi*) is the ethnic designation of the inhabitants of the Southern kingdom, or Judah. After the return from the Captivity, although the nation in general were termed Israelites, individuals called themselves Jews; their descendants are still so called. The name Judæa, applied to the country of the Jews, is posterior to the Exile; strictly speaking, it means the region to the west of the Jordan and to the south of Samaria.

4. The Hebrews are, or claim to be, the descendants of Abraham; their appellation became synonymous with Israelite, but we still say the Hebrew language or Hebrew, and not the Israelitish or Jewish tongue. Etymologically, the *Hibri* are "the people from beyond," the immigrants from the other side of a river, Euphrates or Jordan; this name was given to them by the natives of Canaan, who spoke a language akin to Hebrew.

5. Authentic history begins for the Israelites with the constitution of Saul's monarchy (*c.* 1100 B.C.). All that precedes this—the Deluge, the dispersal of mankind, Abraham, Jacob, Joseph, the captivity in Egypt, Moses, Joshua, the conquest of Canaan—is more or less mythical; but this mythology is interwoven with historical traditions, and the proportion of these becomes considerable from the date of the Exodus of the Hebrews out of Egypt.

6. The religion of the Israelites before Jesus Christ is known to us through the medium of their religious literature, which forms part of the Bible and is called the Old Testament. Bible is the Greek *biblia*, "the books" (*par excellence*), a designation we find in use from the fifth century after Christ. In France the term Bible, meaning the Jewish Bible, is often incorrectly used in opposition to the New Testament. The distinction between the Old and New Testaments, the Old and the New Law, is founded upon a passage in St. Paul's writings; but the Latin *testamentum* in Tertullian (*c.* 200) is an incorrect translation of the Greek *diathêkê*, which means both *testament* and *covenant*. The

THE JEWS

real distinction is between the books of the old and of the new covenant made by God with man.

7. The word Canon (from the Greek *kanôn*, rule), applied to the Old Testament, means the official collection of books composing it. There are several Canons, which differ as to the number and nature of the books they include. The Jews and the Protestants accept fewer books than the Roman Catholics. The Jewish Canon comprises those so-called sacred books of which the Synagogue possessed Hebrew texts about a century before our era. About 150 B.C. the sacred books of the Jews were translated into Greek for the use of those Egyptian Jews who could not read Hebrew. This translation is called the *Septuagint*, from a tradition that seventy or seventy-two translators had worked upon it. It is from the Septuagint that the quotations from the Old Testament are usually taken in the New Testament. The Septuagint includes books which the Jews and the Protestants reject as apocryphal, *i.e.*, uninspired, such, for instance, as the books of *Tobit* and of *Judith*. The canon of the Roman Church, based on the Latin translation of the Bible called the *Vulgate* (*c.* A.D. 400), is almost identical with that of the Greek Bible or Alexandrian Canon, which was itself somewhat lacking in precision. It includes the books of Tobit, Judith, Wisdom, Ecclesiasticus, Baruch, and the first and second books of the Maccabees (but not the last two). The Council of Trent, in 1546, explicitly forbade any question as to the divine inspiration of these works.

8. Our earliest manuscripts of the Hebrew Bible date only from the tenth century A.D.; but the texts had been carefully preserved in the synagogues. We have very much older manuscripts of the Greek and Latin translations. Among the translations made in other languages, I may mention the Syrian *Peschitto* ("simple version"), perhaps anterior to the Christian era, and the Gothic version due to Bishop Ulfilas (fourth century), who suppressed many of the narratives of battles, thinking that the Goths were in no need of any such examples.[1]

9. The Hebrew manuscripts of the Old Testament, and

[1] Philostorgius, *Hist. Eccles.*, ii, p. 5.

more notably those in other tongues, abound in slight variations; but in its main lines the text is authentic everywhere, save where it had already been corrupted before 200 B.C. The Greek translators made nonsense of some of the difficult passages of the Hebrew text, and similar lapses are not infrequent in St. Jerome's Latin version, the Vulgate, which is, nevertheless, a splendid achievement, declared "authentic" by the Council of Trent and accepted as authoritative in the Roman Church.

10. At the time of Jesus Christ, three divisions of the Old Testament were recognised: the Law, the Prophets and the (other) Scriptures.[1] The Law comprised the five books attributed to Moses (Genesis, Exodus, Numbers, Leviticus, Deuteronomy); the works of the Prophets included, not only the books of the three Greater Prophets (Isaiah, Jeremiah and Ezekiel), and of the twelve Minor Prophets, but also the books of Joshua, Samuel and Kings.

11. The first five books or volumes (scrolls) were called by the Greeks *Penté teuché;* hence Pentateuch. They are, as a fact, inseparable from the Book of Joshua, and modern commentators therefore speak of the *Hexateuch* (*hex,* six, and *teuché,* volumes) as the first section of the Old Testament.

12. The attribution of the first five books to Moses himself, although they contain the account of his death, was accepted by the Israelites as early as the fifth century B.C., and has been maintained by the Synagogue. The Christian Church followed on the same path, and the Roman Catholic Church still upholds this view, though it allows that Moses may have made use of documents already existing, and may even have employed "secretaries." From the seventeenth century onward, serious scholars have rejected this theory; the French Oratorian, Richard Simon, who was very unjustly attacked by Bossuet, was one of the first to put forward reasons for doubting it, though he himself did not venture to go so far.

13. The Jewish Synagogue and the various Christian Churches further hold that the Old Testament is a collection

[1] Or hagiographers (sacred writers).

of works "inspired" or, as others say, "dictated" by God. Opinions differ as to the nature of this inspiration; a moderate hypothesis, rejected by Rome in 1893, limited inspiration to questions of "faith and morals," without, indeed, defining these two terms. The orthodox thesis therefore remains in force, and to this a liberal theologian can only say: "If God himself wrote the Bible, we must believe him to be either ignorant or untruthful."[1] As critics have pointed out a host of errors, contradictions, and manifest absurdities in the Old Testament, orthodoxy, to safeguard the authority of the sacred text, has invented *Concordism*, a false science which consists in finding, at any cost, "a perfect harmony between modern science and the knowledge possessed by God's people."[2] Thus we are told that the *days* of creation were not days at all, but *periods*, although the sacred text speaks of the morning and the evening of each day. Independent science can only meet Concordism with contempt. Further, there are in the Old Testament a number of passages where God is represented in a manner unworthy of the conceptions of modern religion, as, for instance, walking in the cool of the evening, showing his back to Moses, ordering abominable massacres and punishing chiefs who had not killed enough people. To justify these texts, orthodoxy has sometimes resorted to sophisms, and sometimes urged that God spoke to men in accordance with the customs and ideas of their times. Such subterfuges are the negation of historical criticism. The texts in which the God of Israel differs widely from the ideals evoked by his name in our days must not be explained away, but taken literally; they are of the greatest interest to the historian, for they enable him to study the evolution of the idea of God. The Deity is inaccessible to man; but at the various epochs traversed by civilisation, humanity has made God in its own likeness, and the gradual idealisation of this image is an essential part of the history of humanity itself.

14. As the Old Testament was the work of a large number of authors who lived at different periods and made use

[1] Loisy, *Quelques réflexions*, p. 228.
[2] Houtin, *Question biblique au XIXème siècle*, p. 35.

of earlier documents, it is puerile to judge this collection as a whole, and to exalt or depreciate it as such. Every impartial reader will admit that the story of Joseph is beautiful, that the Book of Job has sublime passages, that the Psalms and the Prophets contain some of the most magnificent pages ever produced by human genius. But it is no less manifest that the rest is disfigured by a good deal of Oriental bombast, incoherence and absurdity, that the narrative lacks logic and precision, that the marvels recounted are often ludicrous or grotesque. Yet if we compare the Bible to any other collection of sacred books, Hindu, Persian or Arabian, we recognise that it is more readable, more instructive, less infected by mysticism and declamation, less in bondage to hieratic prejudices, in a word, more human and secular. It may fairly be said that it contains the germ of all the great ideas of modern civilisation, and, checking it by history, we see how deeply modern civilisation is indebted to it. Anglo-Saxon society, and the society which was born of the French Revolution in Western Europe, are its offspring. Salvador and Darmesteter were able to maintain, without paradox, that the two great ideas of our age, that of the unity of forces and of unlimited progress—not only in material well-being but in mercy and justice—were already familiar to the prophets of Israel, under the, as yet, unsecularised forms of divine unity and Messianic hope. It is true that the study of history, especially after the triumph of Christianity, shows but too plainly the calamities and ravages caused in the world by religious exclusiveness, by that fanaticism—the Christian heritage from the Jewish Bible—of which the Greeks and Romans were innocent. But against this we must set the sense of human dignity, of solidarity, of charity, of the equality of men before God transmitted by the Old to the New Testament, and still propagated by their means among us. This "Book of books" is responsible for much good and for much evil; but we should have to condemn all the civilisation of Christian countries, which would be to uphold an absurd contention, if we denied that the good has been in excess of the evil. It was the Bible, not the somewhat disdainful philosophy of Greece, which was the first educative force in Europe, which prepared her to assimilate Hellenism after the Renaissance, and, by opening wider vistas before her, has gradually enabled her to dispense with its guidance.

∴

15. A French physician of the eighteenth century, Astruc, was the first scholar to point out that the two principal designations of God in Genesis, *Elohim* and *Jahveh*, are not used arbitrarily. If we place side by side the passages in which God is called Elohim and those in which he is called by the other name, we get two perfectly distinct narratives, which the author of the Pentateuch as we possess it has juxtaposed rather than fused. This one discovery suffices to discredit the attribution of these books to Moses, who could not have been an unintelligent compiler, and also the theory of the divine inspiration of the Bible text. A comparison of the two narratives shows that all which relates to the creation of Eve, the garden of Eden, and Adam's transgression, exists only in the Jehovist text. (See the parallel passages on inset pages.) This text does not seem to have been held in much esteem by the ancient Hebrews, for there is not the slightest allusion to the fall of Adam in the Prophets, the Psalms, the historic books, or even in the Gospels, although St. Paul constructed his whole theory of the redemption of man by Jesus Christ on this popular legend.

16. Thus it is evident that two versions of the Creation are given in Genesis. But there are traces in the Old Testament of a third legend, akin to that of the Babylonians, in which Marduk creates the world by virtue of a victory over the waters of chaos (Tiamat). When, in Racine's *Athalie*, the High Priest says:

> Celui qui met un frein à la fureur des flots
> Sait aussi des méchants arrêter les complots . . .[1]

he alludes to well-known passages of Scripture which enshrine the memory of the Eternal's conflict with the sea.

[1] "He who puts a check to the fury of the waters, can also stop the plots of the wicked."

THE TWO NARRATIVES OF THE CREATION

Elohist

i. 1. In the beginning Elohim created the heaven and the earth. 2. And the earth was without form and void . . . and the spirit of Elohim moved upon the face of the waters. 3. And Elohim said: Let there be light; and there was light. 4. And Elohim saw the light, that it was good; and Elohim divided the light from the darkness. 5. And Elohim called the light Day, and the darkness he called Night. And the evening and the morning were the first day. 6. And Elohim said: Let there be a firmament in the midst of the waters. . . . 9. And Elohim said: Let the waters under the heaven be gathered together unto one place, and let the dry land appear. . . . 11. And Elohim said: Let the earth bring forth grass . . . and the fruit-tree yielding fruit after its kind. . . . 14. And Elohim said: Let there be lights in the firmament of the heaven to divide the day from the night. . . . 20. And Elohim said: Let the waters bring forth abundantly the moving creature that hath life, and fowl that may fly above the earth. . . . 21. And Elohim created great whales, and every living creature that moveth, which the waters brought forth abundantly after their kind, and every winged fowl after his kind. . . . 22. And Elohim blessed them and said: Be fruitful and multiply and fill the waters in the sea, and let fowl multiply in the earth. . . . 24. And Elohim said: Let the earth bring forth the living creature after his kind. . . . 26. And Elohim said: Let us make man in our image, after our likeness. . . . 27. So Elohim created man in his own image . . . male and female created he them. 28. And Elohim blessed them, and said unto them: Be fruitful and multiply and replenish the earth and subdue it. 29. And Elohim said: Behold, I have given you every herb bearing seed . . . and every tree in the which is the fruit of a tree yielding seed . . . to you it shall be for meat.

ii. 1. Thus the heavens and the earth were finished, and all the

Jehovist

ii. 4. In the day that Jahveh Elohim made the earth and the heavens . . . and every plant of the field, and every herb of the field . . . Jahveh Elohim had not caused it to rain upon the earth, and there was not a man to till the ground. . . . 6. But there went up a mist from the earth and watered the whole face of the ground. 7. And Jahveh Elohim formed man of the dust of the ground, and breathed into his nostrils the breath of life. 8. And Jahveh Elohim planted a garden eastward in Eden, and there he put the man whom he had formed. 9. And out of the ground made Elohim to grow every tree that is pleasant to the sight, the tree of life also in the midst of the garden, and the tree of knowledge of good and evil. . . . 15. And Jahveh Elohim took the man and put him into the garden of Eden to dress it and to keep it. 16. And Jahveh Elohim commanded the man, saying: Of every tree of the garden thou mayest freely eat. 17. But of the tree of the knowledge of good and evil, thou shalt not eat of it; for in the day that thou eatest thereof thou shalt surely die. 18. And Jahveh Elohim said: It is not good that the man should be alone; I will make him an help meet for him. . . . 21. And Jahveh Elohim caused a deep sleep to fall upon Adam . . . and he took one of his ribs, and closed up the flesh instead thereof. 22. And the rib which Jahveh Elohim had taken from man, made he a woman and brought her to the man.

iii. 1. Now the serpent was more subtil than any beast of the field. And he said unto the woman: Yea, hath Elohim * said: Ye shall not eat of every tree of the garden? 2. And the woman said unto the serpent: We may eat of the fruit of the trees of the garden; 3. But of the fruit of the tree which is in the midst of the

* The sequel of the narrative shows that here the whole name, Jahveh Elohim, must be restored. The same remark applies to three other passages.

ELOHIST—*continued*

host of them. 2. And on the seventh day Elohim ended his work
. . . and he rested on the seventh
day. . . . 4. These are the generations of the heavens and of the
earth when they were created.*

* Evidently quoted from an ancient lost book.

JEHOVIST—*continued*

garden, Elohim hath said: Ye shall
not eat of it, neither shall ye
touch it, lest ye die. 4. And the
serpent said unto the woman: Ye
shall not surely die; 5. For Elohim
doth know that in the day ye eat
thereof, then your eyes shall be
opened, and ye shall be as Elohim,
knowing good and evil. 6. And
. . . the woman . . . took of the
fruit and did eat, and gave also
unto her husband with her, and
he did eat. . . . 8. And they heard
the voice of Jahveh Elohim walking in the garden in the cool of
the day. . . . 11. And he said:
. . . Hast thou eaten of the tree
whereof I commanded thee that
thou shouldest not eat? 12. And
the man said: The woman whom
thou gavest to be with me, she
gave me of the tree, and I did eat.
13. And Jahveh Elohim said unto
the woman: What is this that thou
hast done? And the woman said:
The serpent beguiled me, and I
did eat. 14. And Jahveh Elohim
said unto the serpent: Because
thou hast done this, thou art
cursed . . . upon thy belly shalt
thou go, and dust shalt thou eat
all the days of thy life. . . . 15.
And I will put enmity between
thee and the woman, and between
thy seed and her seed; it shall
bruise thy head and thou shalt
bruise his heel.† 16. Unto the
woman he said: I will greatly multiply thy sorrow and thy conception; in sorrow thou shalt bring
forth children. 17. And unto
Adam he said: . . . In sorrow
shalt thou eat all the days of thy
life. 19. In the sweat of thy face
shalt thou eat bread, till thou return unto the ground . . . for dust
thou art and unto dust shalt thou
return. . . . 22. And Jahveh Elohim said: Behold, the man is become as one of us, to know good
and evil: and now lest he put
forth his hand and take also of
the tree of life, and eat, and live
for ever: 23. Therefore Jahveh
Elohim sent him forth from the
garden of Eden to till the ground
from whence he was taken.

† *Cf.* S. Reinach, *Cultes*, ii, p.
396.

Thus in Job xxvi, 10: "He hath compassed the waters with bounds"; Job xxxviii, 8, 11: "who shut up the sea with doors . . . and said, Hitherto shalt thou come but no further, and here shall thy proud waves be stayed." Jeremiah also (v. 22) speaks of the sea as subdued and controlled by Jehovah. This conception of a conflict between the Creator and hostile forces was contrary to the monotheistic thesis, and has disappeared from our two versions of Genesis; but the suppression sufficiently proves that it was very ancient, and had long been accepted.

17. The name *Elohim* is a plural (singular *Eloah*, "he who is feared"?) meaning the *gods*. This sufficiently proves that the Hebrews were originally polytheists, though it has been explained as a "plural of Majesty." Again, in another passage of Genesis, God is described as saying: "Let us make man in our image" (i, 26), and further on: "The man is become as one of us" (iii, 22). It is childish to interpret these plurals as allusions to the Trinity, though even Bossuet did so. Another favourite name for the deity is El, meaning perhaps "the chief." The mysterious name of God, which was never to be pronounced, is written by means of four consonants (the *tetragram* of the Greeks): between these the vowels of *Adonai*, the Lord, were conventionally inserted, producing the name *Jehowah* or *Jehova*. The idea that the name of God is taboo, and should not be uttered, is found among many races. It is explained partly by the superstitious awe inspired by that name, partly by fear lest the enemy might learn it and invoke it. The knowledge of a sacred name gives a hold over the being to whom it is applied. This is one of the principles of magic.

18. There is reason to believe that the true pronunciation of the tetragram was *Jahwé*, with *Jahu* as a secondary form. The etymology, which has been much disputed, may be the radical HWH, "to be." ("I am that I am," said God to Moses.) But it has been pointed out that God revealed himself to Moses on Sinaï, which long remained the centre of his worship. He was therefore perhaps a local god of Sinaï, whose name was derived not from Hebrew, but from some other language.

19. The divine name *Baal* (plural *baalim*) is reserved in the Bible for the gods of the heathen; but as it occurs in Hebrew proper names such as Meribaal, the son of Jonathan, it is evident that at a certain period the Hebrews worshipped *baalim* like their neighbours.

20. Another interesting expression is that of *Sabaoth*, a plural meaning "the armies," which was affixed to Jahveh or Elohim, whence the locution "Lord of hosts," which has passed from the Bible into current language. Did it mean the god of the warring Israelites, or the god of the celestial armies (angels or stars)? The point is doubtful.

21. The *Teraphim*, the etymology of which is unknown, were little portable idols which seem to have been the Lares of the ancient Hebrews. David owned some (1 Sam. xix, 13-16), and the prophet Hosea, in the eighth century before Christ, seems still to have considered the *teraphim* as indispensable in worship (Hos. iii, 4). They were used for divination. Here we have formal evidence of the persistence of polytheism and fetichism in the people of Israel, whose claims to have been faithful from their earliest origin to a spiritualistic monotheism will not bear critical examination.

∴

22. The idea of taboo, common to all primitive races, has left numerous traces in the Bible. The tree of the knowledge of good and evil was *taboo;* God forbade man to eat the fruit thereof, without saying why, and the penalty of disobedience was death. If we find that Adam, after disregarding the taboo, did not die, it is because the Jehovist text is a compilation from earlier texts, one of which probably recorded the sudden death of the first man. Theologians, following the exegesis of the Jewish rabbis, from about the year 200 B.C., have taught that Adam was created immortal, and that to chastise his disobedience God had deprived him of eternal life, though he allowed him to live to the age of 930. But there is nothing at all about this in the Book of Genesis. If, as St. Paul declared, death entered into the world by Adam's sin, how could the newly created

Adam have understood the divine threat: "In the day that thou eatest thereof, thou shalt surely die." Besides, Adam was not expelled from Eden because he had eaten the forbidden fruit, but because the gods were afraid he would become as one of them by eating also of the fruit of the tree of life—another magic tree. If the gods feared lest he should become immortal, he cannot have been created so. All the traditional interpretation of the fall in Genesis is founded on dogmatic errors, deliberately upheld to give philosophical colour to a childish tale, repugnant to our moral ideas, which St. Paul made the doctrinal basis of Christianity.

23. Another object of *taboo* was the ark of the covenant. It was a wooden chest, perhaps containing fetiches, in which divine power was supposed to reside. I have already spoken of it in my Introduction (§ 10), to which it will suffice to refer the reader.

24. The legislation and the morality of the Pentateuch are also impregnated with taboo; it is interesting to see moral ideas evolving from it and remaining in touch with it. The Sabbath was originally a taboo day, that is to say, an unlucky day; no one was to work on that day, nor to make his servant or his beast of burden work, for they would run the risk of hurting themselves or spoiling their work. But in the Bible we see this crude idea developing; the idea of a day of rest is evolved, with its implied kindness, its pity for the fatigue of others. In the midst of the prohibitions of the Decalogue we find this injunction: "Honour thy father and thy mother, that thy days may be long in the land" (Ex. xx, 12). This is, as it were, the reversal and modification of an ancient taboo: "If thou strikest thy father or thy mother, thou shalt die [at once]." But the taboo thus becomes a law of morality. In Deuteronomy xii we read: "Thou shalt not plow with an ox and an ass together." Touching pity for animals! say the preachers; the ass, which is weak, should not be made to perform the same task as the ox. But this interpretation is absurd. We need only read the precepts laid down in the context: "Thou shalt not sow thy vineyards with divers seeds; lest the fruit of thy seed

which thou hast sown, and the fruit of thy vineyard, be defiled," *i.e.*, taboo; here we have a taboo laid upon *intermixture*. "Thou shalt not wear a garment . . . of woollen and linen together" (the same taboo). Note that all these prohibitions have the same imperative tone; all this was held to be necessary to the purity, the presumed interest of the faithful, who were not to subject themselves to the defilement resulting from a violated taboo. Here we lay a finger upon the origin of the moral codes which still govern humanity. At the birth of all these systems, there is a confusion between the ordinances we call moral and those for which superstition alone is responsible. Where there is a confusion of things essentially different, and resting upon a different logical basis, it is inevitable that classification and selection should ultimately take place. The idea of social utility, verifiable by experience, intervenes; all that corresponds to the real needs of society is retained as law; the residue becomes the arsenal of etiquette and of vain superstitions.

25. Before a tribe went forth to war, its priests or magicians pronounced terrible imprecations against the enemy. After victory, the enemy and all belonging to him were taboo; all prisoners were to be killed, all booty burnt or destroyed. This taboo of the spoils is to be found among the Hebrews as among all other races of antiquity; in Rome all the enemy's shields were piled up at a certain point of the Capitol, a custom which gave rise to the legend of Tarpeia, crushed under the shields of the Sabines for her treachery in giving up the citadel. The most typical example in the Bible is that of the taking of Jericho by Joshua. A magic circle was drawn round the city; its walls fell down at the magic blast of the Hebrew trumpets. Although the conquerors were poor and homeless, they neither appropriated the booty nor reduced the inhabitants to slavery. At the command of their god, they destroyed all, both persons and things, and when one of their number, Achan, was convicted of having kept "some silver and gold and a goodly Babylonish garment" he was stoned and burnt with all his family and his belongings. In time these savage proceedings were modified by cupidity and good sense; metal objects were

preserved, but to purify them from the taboo that weighed upon them they were passed through fire and water.

26. Among the Jews, as among the Polynesians, contact with a corpse rendered a person taboo; at the end of seven days, the impure person washed his clothes, bathed himself in water and became clean (Numbers xix, 11-22). A young Jewish mother was taboo, like a young Polynesian mother (Levit. xii). Among the Israelites there were men and women called *Nazirs* or *Nazarites* who had made vows to the Eternal which are detailed in the Book of Numbers (vi). *Nazir* means "separated" or "dedicated," which is the exact significance of "taboo." To release a Nazarite from his vows, ceremonies were performed identical with those which take off a taboo in Polynesia. The Nazarite shaved his head at the door of the sanctuary, and the priest placed food in his hands. This does not imply that the Mosaic code was known in Polynesia, but that the universal conception of the taboo may produce the same effects in different countries.

27. Totemism left traces among the Hebrews no less than taboo. The very idea of Jehovah's covenant with Israel is one that is to be found everywhere in connection with totemism, where a clan or tribe form an alliance with an animal or vegetable species. The Hebrews abstain from killing or eating animals such as the pig, whose ancestors (wild boars) had been the totems of their forefathers or of the earlier peoples of Palestine. These animals are designated either as sacred or unclean, two over-precise terms, which, if traced back to their origins, will be reduced to the idea of *taboo*, or prohibition. At a much later period it was suggested that the flesh of these animals was unwholesome, or that those who ate it might contract vices of character. The Mosaic law merely formulates prohibitions which were already ancient; the Jews themselves believed these prohibitions to have been anterior to the Flood, for when Noah is about to take refuge in the Ark, the Eternal orders him to take with him two couples of every unclean beast and seven couples of every clean beast, without explaining what these words meant (Gen. vii, 2). Another evidence of the sacred character of the animals described as unclean was the

clandestine custom reprobated by Isaiah (lxvi, 17): "They that sanctify themselves and purify themselves in the garden . . . eating swine's flesh, and the abomination and the mouse, shall be consumed together, saith the Lord." Here we have evidently the survival of one of these periodic sacrifices of totems, in which men sought to sanctify themselves by eating some sacred meat, the general use of which was forbidden.

28. I will not insist on those names of men and tribes which are compounded of the names of animals, for it may always be objected that these were merely nicknames; but the worship of the bull and of the serpent among the Hebrews is an indubitable survival of totemism. It seems very probable that Jehovah was long represented by a bull. Portable gilded images of bulls were consecrated by Jeroboam (1 Kings xii, 28); the prophet Hosea inveighed against the worship of the bull in the kingdom of Israel (Hos. viii, 5; x, 5). The famous golden calf of the Israelites, the object of Moses' anger, had nothing to do with the bull Apis, which was a live animal; it was a totemic idol of a kind commonly found in the land of Canaan, where the bull was the symbol, that is to say, the incarnation of a Baal. Although the law of Moses was hostile to every kind of idolatry, the worship of the serpent was practised by Moses himself, who transformed his magic wand into a serpent (Ex. vii, 9-12) and made a brazen serpent to heal the people of the bites of serpents (Numbers xxi, 9). A brazen serpent, perhaps a totem of David's family, was worshipped in the temple of Jerusalem and was only destroyed by Hezekiah about 700 B.C. (2 Kings xviii, 4).

29. The prophetess Deborah, whose name means a bee, was no doubt like those priestesses of Diana of Ephesus who were called bees (*melissaï*), the ministrant of a totemic worship of this insect. Samson, the lion-slayer, was probably a lion, whose strength lay in his luxuriant tawny mane. This lion was identified with the sun, as in Babylonia, hence the analogy of Samson's name with that of the Babylonian solar god, *Shamash*. I might multiply these examples, and speak of Balaam's eloquent ass, which may be compared with the

Greek tradition of an ass-headed god worshipped by the Israelites—possibly those of Samaria—and the part played by the ass in Zechariah ix, 9, and in the account of Christ's entry into Jerusalem. The dove which descended from Heaven upon Jesus at his baptism was also an ancient Syrian totem. I have already mentioned the fish, a Syrian totem adopted by the Jews, and the early Christians (p. 21). Of course these are all *survivals* only; the Jews were unconscious totemists. Like all other peoples, they must have ceased to be totemists, in the strict sense of the word, as soon as they owned domestic animals. Totemic worship is generally incompatible with the possession of cattle.

30. In opposition to the heathen races who surrounded Israel and whose practices were constantly alluring them, the Jewish priesthood, the authors of the Old Testament, were hostile to all magic, and also to the popular belief in a future life, which was likely to result in the evocation of the dead or necromancy. But this strategy of animism is so natural to man that the Bible nevertheless contains numerous instances of it. Moses and Aaron were magicians who rivalled Pharaoh's magicians (Ex. vii, 11-20). Balaam was a magician who pronounced incantations against Israel, and afterwards passed over to the service of Jehovah (Numbers xxii *et seq.;* Micah vi, 5). Jacob resorted to a kind of sympathetic magic to procure the birth of speckled sheep (Gen. xxx, 39). Divination, which is the use of magic to discover the will of spiritual beings, was practised by means of *Urim* and *Thummim*, perhaps a kind of dice enclosed in a sacred receptacle called an ephod.[1]

"Thou shalt not suffer a witch to live" is written in Exodus xxii, 18. Fatal words which the Christian Churches have obeyed only too faithfully! They offered at once an affirmation of the reality of witchcraft, and a tendency which still survives even in these days to look upon witchcraft as an appanage of the weaker sex. Both churches and secular tribunals have burnt far more witches than wizards.

. . .

[1] See articles ***Ephod*** and ***Urim*** in ***Encycl. Biblica.***

31. After the centralisation of national worship at Jerusalem (620 B.C.), the great Jewish festivals of *Mazzoth* (Azym), *Shabuoth* (Weeks or Pentecost) and *Sukkoth* (Tabernacles), were artificially related to events in the ancient history of the Hebrews: the Exodus, and the life of the Israelites in the desert. Before this era, they were agrarian festivals of no fixed date, commemorating the beginning of barley-harvest, the end of wheat-harvest fifty days later —hence the name Pentecost from the Greek for fiftieth—and the vintage. They were old Canaanitish festivals which the Hebrews adopted when they settled in the land of Canaan. At the Feast of Azym, unleavened bread was eaten for a week, because it was a festival of first-fruits, and the fermented dough of the new year had not yet been made. At the Feast of Sukkoth, it was the custom to live for a week in booths made of green branches; at Jerusalem these were set up in courtyards or on the housetops. This solemnity comprised processions and dances, in which the faithful carried palms and flowering branches likes the Bacchic *thyrsi* of the Greeks; hence the excusable error made by Plutarch, who assimilates this festival to the Bacchanalia, and ascribes the worship of Dionysos to the Hebrews.

32. The Feast of Azym was originally distinct from that of the Passover (*Pesach*), but soon became merged in it. Pesach ("the passage of the god"?) was the feast of the first-fruits of the flocks; a lamb or a kid was sacrificed and eaten in haste by the household, who were dressed as for a journey; the bones of the victim were not to be broken, and it was to be entirely consumed. The god was supposed to be present at the feast, and to take his portion of it, which was the blood of the animal, sprinkled upon the door of the house. At a later period, this festival was brought into relation with the exodus from Egypt: God had slain the first-born of the Egyptians, but had spared those of the Israelites, whose doors were marked with the blood of the lamb. It was further explained that in their haste to depart, the Israelites had carried away their bread in the form of unleavened cakes, and this was why unleavened bread was eaten with the lamb. All these were sacerdotal inventions. The Pass-

over, among the sedentary Canaanites, was the oblation of a kid to the local god, who, as the master of everything, had a right to a tribute. In early times there was a communion feast in which the god took part, and earlier still—perhaps in the clan of *Rachel*, as this name means a sheep—it was the totemic repast, at which the sacred lamb was eaten to renew and fortify the sanctity of the clan. This old idea was so vital that it reappears in Christianity. Jesus was the Paschal Lamb, sacrificed at the time of Passover, whose flesh and blood is perpetually partaken of by the faithful in the Eucharist.

33. The custom of sprinkling blood upon the door and the threshold reflects a superstition of savages; as demons are eager for blood and are attracted by the smell of it, the faithful need not fear their gluttony, which is appeased on the threshold. Even in the refined worship of Jehovah, the blood of animals is forbidden to men; it is the portion of the god.

34. At the time of the Maccabees, the feast of *Purim*, which was supposed to celebrate the overthrow of Haman, was added, or rather adopted. This word means "lots"; it was remembered that Haman had drawn lots to fix the date of his savage projects against the Jews. This is a concocted explanation, and a very foolish attempt to explain the name of the festival. As a fact, this name is only Hebrew in appearance. It is probably that of an Assyrian festival, *Puhru*. The names *Esther* and *Mordecai* are so closely akin to those of the Babylonian gods *Istar* and *Marduk* that the story of Esther has sometimes been supposed to be the echo of some Babylonian legend.

35. Among the other Jewish festivals which, like the above, are regulated by the lunar calendar, I may mention the first day of the year, or of the month Tishri (*Rosh-ha-shanah*); the Day of Atonement (*Yom-ha-Kippurim*), a day of fasting and absolute cessation from work, consecrated to the expiation of faults, the cleansing of the secret defilements of the year; and the Dedication (*Hannukah*), commemorating the dedication of a new altar after the entry of Judas Maccabæus into the Temple (1 Mac. iv, 59).

36. The majority of the Jewish festivals were marked by rejoicings, processions and dances; they often attracted large crowds of people, each family coming to offer a victim at the Temple and bring presents to the priests. The most solemn sacrifices were those in which the victim was burnt (holocausts); it was then an offering to Jehovah in its entirety, whereas in ordinary cases he had to be content with the blood sprinkled upon the altar. After the destruction of the Temple the Jews gave up these sanguinary offerings, not in consequence of a religious reform, but because the Deuteronomic law forbade the celebration of sacrifices elsewhere.

37. Among the nomad Arabs, the only clergy are the custodians of the temples and those who deliver the oracles; worship is generally conducted by the head of the family. The same customs probably prevailed among the Hebrews, whose name for a priest (*kohen*) is identical with that of soothsayer in Arabic (*kahin*). The great temples had *kohanim*, together with prophets, *nebiim*, and both were reputed to be inspired. Thus the Hebrew priesthood began by divination. At a very early period there was a tendency to reserve the office of soothsayer for Levites of the family of Moses, considered as the descendants of a tribe of Levi (Gen. xxix, 34) whose very existence is ill authenticated. The Levites finally formed a caste who had no territory of their own, but received a portion of the offerings and held jurisdiction in forty-eight townships. They were very powerful after the return from the Babylonian exile, but for some obscure reason their power declined to such an extent that they are barely mentioned in the New Testament.

38. According to the author of the Book of Numbers (xvi, 33), the descendants of Aaron played an important part in the Biblical hierarchy; they alone might approach the altar. The personality of Aaron himself is probably mythical; it has been pointed out that *hâ ârōn* means the sacred ark in Hebrew.

39. The historical part of the Pentateuch comprises many very ancient fragments, some of them quite incomprehensible and lacking any relation to the context (such

as the song of Lamech); others attesting a very primitive state of civilisation (cave-burial, ignorance of the horse, &c.). The same may be said of the Book of Joshua, in which the ferocity of manners depicted is in itself an indubitable evidence of archaism (see more especially the episode of Jericho). To suppose that all this was written about five hundred years before Christ and even later is the more absurd, in that traces of the utilisation of more ancient documents very unskilfully strung together are visible throughout; sometimes earlier sources are even quoted (*the book of the wars of Jehovah*). But if we are inquiring when the Pentateuch in its present form was *published*, there is every reason to suppose that this was not till after the Captivity. St. Jerome himself seems to suggest that the Pentateuch might be attributed to Moses *or to Esdras*, the organiser of the Jewish State after the return from Babylon.

40. We have an important text bearing on the publication of the Book of Deuteronomy. In the reign of Josiah, it was said that a very ancient document, which had long been lost, was discovered in the Temple. It was solemnly promulgated. These stories of the "discovery" of ancient manuscripts are always suspicious; it is probable that this text was not unearthed, but manufactured at this period, and Voltaire, followed by Renan, has suggested that Jeremiah had a hand in this fraud. There are in fact in Jeremiah numerous allusions to Deuteronomy, notably to the passage which concerns the liberation of slaves and the resentment this measure aroused among the rich. As to the other Prophets, they never quote the written law, and the inference is that they were ignorant of it. It is no less certain that many of the *historic* episodes related in the Books of Judges and Samuel are in conflict with the Mosaic code, which cannot have been accepted as authoritative at this period. I have already said that the Prophets were quite ignorant of the myths of the Creation and the Fall, and that they make allusions to another legend of the Creation, which the so-called Mosaic Genesis has not preserved (p. 187).

41. The date given by the text quoted above (2 Kings

xxii) for the compilation of Deuteronomy is the only one as to which we have some degree of certainty. I cannot here enter into a discussion of the various hypotheses relative to the other strata of the Pentateuch. Scholars are not agreed on this subject; but it cannot be said that their theories are mutually destructive, for they are at least almost unanimous in denying the homogeneity, the Mosaic authorship, and the great antiquity of the Pentateuch. It is generally admitted that the Book of Leviticus is posterior to the Captivity and to Ezekiel; the theocracy, *i.e.*, the sacerdotal domination, is more strongly emphasised than in Deuteronomy, and the point of view is religious rather than national. This does not, of course, imply that the whole body of the so-called Mosaic legislation is posterior to the Exile; this, as it has come down to us, is founded upon very ancient customs, many of which, strongly impregnated with heathen superstitions, are anterior to the supposed period of Moses and even to that of Hammurabi (2100 B.C.).

42. The Book of Genesis (*Genesis kosmou*, the birth of the world, in Greek) relates the mythic traditions of the Hebrews from the creation of the world to the death of Joseph. Throughout these narratives there are charming episodes, full of simplicity and freshness. The dominant idea is that of a close covenant between God and the seed of Abraham. God does not demand a complicated form of worship from the faithful, but obedience and faith, and in return he promises them the land of Canaan. We have seen that it is possible to isolate at least two of these sources of information, the Elohist and the Jehovist, and this applies not only to the account of the Creation, which I took as typical, but to the whole Book of Genesis. Modern exegesis even thinks it possible to distinguish three sources, called by scholars E. P. (Elohist sources, an early and a later one) and J. (Jehovist). It seems probable that E. was compiled in the Kingdom of Israel, and J. in that of Judah, both some considerable time before the destruction of the former (721 B.C.), and both from sources of much greater antiquity. There are certain allusions to the complete submission of the Canaanites and to the subjugation

of Edom, which show the compilation to have been posterior to David (1016 B.C.). The difficulties of criticism are increased by the fact that many passages were inserted at a later period.

43. It would be going too far to deny any historic basis for these legends. Abraham, Jacob and Joseph, often supposed to have been tribal gods, may have been real persons. The Book of Genesis places Abraham in the reign of a king called Amraphel (Gen. xiv, 19), possibly identical with Hammurabi, who reigned in Babylonia about 2100 B.C., and whose code has been discovered at Susa in our own times. In the legend of Joseph there are authentic Egyptian traits which point to the period of the Hyksos kings, and the account given by Manetho of the expulsion of the lepers from Egypt under the leadership of the priest Osarsiph may well refer to the Exodus, as may the name Osarsiph to Joseph. But if there are a few fragments of history in Genesis, they are mere grains of gold in a heavy alluvial stratum. It requires a singular simplicity of mind to accept the details of these stories, or to believe the legends of the Flood, the dispersal of mankind in consequence of the confusion of tongues, &c. Eighteenth-century criticism disposed of these illusions, which reappeared, to the discredit of the nineteenth century, but only to fall into final disrepute.

44. The Book of Exodus (*Exodos Aiguptou*, "the coming out of Egypt") first relates the multiplication of the family of Jacob and the succession of a Pharaoh hostile to the Hebrews, who ordered that all their new-born infants should be thrown into the Nile. The infant Moses, saved by Pharaoh's daughter, grew up at the court of the monarch. Then, having killed an Egyptian who was ill-treating a Hebrew, he fled to the desert, where God appeared to him in a burning bush, and commissioned him to save his people, and to establish them in the "promised land" of Canaan. In company with his brother Aaron, Moses asked Pharaoh to liberate the children of Israel, but after vain attempts to dazzle Pharaoh by his skill as a magician, he met with an obstinate refusal. Hereupon, the Eternal inflicted ten plagues upon Egypt, the last and most terrible being the

death of all the first-born in the land. The Hebrews were spared by the destroying angel, because, in accordance with the divine instructions, they had celebrated the Passover. Finally, the Israelites quitted Egypt, carrying away with them the gold and silver of their oppressors, and they entered the desert, guided by a pillar of cloud and a pillar of fire. The magic art of Moses enabled them to pass dry-footed through the Red Sea, whereas the Pharaoh who was pursuing them was engulfed with his whole army. The Israelites began to murmur in the desert, in spite of the manna which fell from heaven to feed them, and the water which Moses caused to gush from the rock of Horeb by striking it. On arriving at Sinaï, Moses received the commandments of God in the midst of lightnings and thunder; he communicated them to the Hebrews assembled at the foot of the mountain, and they agreed to observe them. Here we have a first outline of the code (chapters xx-xxiii). The end of the book contains minute details concerning the erection of the Tabernacle, a kind of portable sanctuary in the centre of which was the Ark of the Covenant. The description is interrupted by the account of the revolt of the Hebrews, who took to worshipping a golden calf and were chastised by the Levites at the command of Moses. Then the prophet, who in his anger had broken the first tables of the Law, is called up to Sinaï with new tables, on which God again inscribes the same text, and confirms his covenant with Israel. Finally, the Tabernacle is set up; Aaron and his sons are invested with the hereditary right to offer sacrifices to the Lord.

45. It was suggested as long ago as 1834 that the country from which the Hebrews migrated was not *Misraim* (Egypt), but *Musri*, a region to the north of Arabia. However, a *stela* discovered by Flinders Petrie in 1896 seems to establish the fact that about 1300 B.C., in the reign of Menephthah, the Egyptians devastated the territory of *Isiraal* and chastised several of the cities of Canaan. Names of tribes akin to *Joseph-el* and *Jacob-el* (*Isphal* and *Iakbal*) figure on the lists of Thotmes III. as having lived in Palestine. These Josephites and Jacobites were Bedouins who

may have been driven by famine into Egypt, where they were well received at first, but finally expelled.

46. The existence of Moses (*Mosé*, perhaps the Egyptian *mesu*, child) is not demonstrated by the Biblical books which are falsely ascribed to him; but we have no right to deny it. It is and must remain merely doubtful. No religion is the work of one man; but neither can one conceive the full flight of a religion without the impetus of a powerful will, of a genius such as Moses, St. Paul or Mahomet. Moses may have been a worshipper of Jehovah, who for a time caused the worship of his god to triumph among the tribes subjected to his influence. He may have been a statesman and soldier who grouped a number of tribes and inflamed them with his own enthusiasm. The details of his history are manifestly mythical. The legend of the child cast upon the waters is to be found from Germany to Japan, passing through Babylonia. Moses before Pharaoh descends to the level of a vulgar sorcerer, armed with a magic wand, whose performances make us smile. The passage across the Red Sea and the drowning of Pharaoh are romantic incidents, not only unknown to the Egyptian texts, but to the earliest of the Hebrew prophets. The promulgation of the law at Sinaï may have a historic basis, if Jehovah was really the local god of the mountain, the god of the clan of Moses, and no universal god; but who, as Wellhausen asks, can seriously believe that Jehovah wrote the ten commandments with his own hand upon the stone? And which are the true commandments, those of Exodus xx or those of Exodus xxxiv, two texts which differ considerably? If the Hebrews went to Sinaï, it was on a pilgrimage, to sacrifice to Jehovah, and not to receive a code from him. Finally, the long sojourn of forty years in the desert seemed somewhat incredible even to the Jewish writer, who, to modify its improbability, invented the stories of the manna and of the quails which fell from heaven; but even these inventions testify that the tradition was very ancient. Some thousands of Hebrew shepherds (not six hundred thousand, as the Bible states) may have wandered in the desert for a considerable time before conquering Canaan; Moses was the religious and political

chief of these Bedouins; this is the maximum that we can retain and affirm.

47. The third book of the Pentateuch has been called Leviticus, because it contains mainly the legislation relating to the clergy, or caste of the Levites. This legislation is very complicated; it provides for a vast number of details connected with sacrifices, purifications, &c.; and insists very strongly upon unclean animals, acts, and states, in other words, upon taboos and the magic rites necessary for their removal. The use of blood is rigorously prohibited; the unity of the sanctuary is prescribed (chap. xvii, 4), the institution of the sabbatical year and of the quinquagenarian jubilee are added to that of the Sabbath. The historical part records the erection of the Tabernacle before Sinaï, the consecration of Aaron and his sons, and the oblation of the first sacrifices.

48. Here is a specimen of the minutiæ God is supposed to have dictated to Moses (chap. xiv, 25): "The priest shall take some of the blood of the trespass offering and put it upon the tip of the right ear of him who is to be cleansed, and upon the thumb of his right hand, and upon the great toe of his right foot, and the priest shall pour of the oil into the palm of his own left hand, and shall sprinkle with his right finger some of the oil that is in his left hand seven times before the Lord."

49. The sources of Leviticus are very ancient in parts; but in the state in which it has come down to us, it is not earlier than Ezekiel, to whom indeed it has been attributed by several critics on account of some analogies of style.

50. The Book of Numbers records two numberings of the Israelites, whence the Greek name (*Arithmoi*). It is made up for the rest of a chaotic series of civil and religious prescriptions. The historical portion dwells upon the insubordination of the Hebrews, which draws down upon them many severe chastisements and causes God to condemn them to wander for forty years in the desert before entering the Promised Land; the generation which came out of Egypt was doomed to perish first, Moses himself being included in this judgment. Miriam, the sister of Moses and Aaron, dies

before him. One of the most curious episodes in the book is that of Balaam the prophet, whose ass seems to have been an echo of the worship of the ass, considered as an oracular animal. The tendency of Numbers is clearly sacerdotal; the importance and privileges of the priesthood are brought into strong relief.

51. The fifth book of the Pentateuch bears the name of Deuteronomy, which means in Greek the second Law, or the recapitulation of the Law. It contains the last injunctions of Moses to the Hebrews before passing over Jordan and the account of his last days. It was the discovery of this book (or a portion of it) in the Temple which was the mainspring of the reforms in the reign of Josiah (622 B.C.). This king, enlightened by the new text, extirpated alien religions and destroyed all the altars and high places, preserving only the sanctuary of Jerusalem (2 Kings xxii). Numerous interpolations were made in the Book of Deuteronomy after the Captivity, in the interest of the sacerdotal caste. The author was not acquainted with the whole of the so-called Mosaic legislation, although he was familiar with the primitive code, Exodus xxi-xxiii (the book of the covenant). The work claims to be by Moses (chap. xxxi, 9), but the evidence proves it to have been very much later. It reflects a civilisation that had long been sedentary, and the existence of monarchical institutions (chap. xvii, 14-20). The unity of the sanctuary is but briefly prescribed in Leviticus, but in Deuteronomy it is perpetually insisted upon; now Jerusalem was not one of the most ancient holy places of the Israelites; it was the sanctuary of the Jewish kings and more especially of the Jewish State restored by Nehemiah. The Jewish colony of Elephantina in Egypt, which, according to the evidence of a recently discovered papyrus, had constructed a temple on the model of that of Jerusalem about the year 500 B.C., cannot have accepted the Book of Deuteronomy. The influence of this book in Jewish literature is manifest after Jeremiah; it does not appear in the prophets of the seventh century B.C.; hence the unproven hypothesis of Voltaire and others that Deuteronomy was the work of Jeremiah himself, and that it was written at Jerusalem (§ 40).

52. The Hebrew prophet (*nabi*) was not only a visionary, a healer and a soothsayer who could cause lost objects to be found (1 Sam. ix, 9); he was the champion of intransigeant monotheism against the idolatry which was often protected by the kings; he made himself the interpreter of the conscience of the people in its loftiest and purest impulses. "Prophetism among the Hebrews was what the evangelical ministry is among Christian nations." [1] There were doubtless many charlatans among them, like those howling prophets who came down from the high places in companies, escorted by musicians playing different instruments (1 Sam. x, 5); but we need only look into the Books of Isaiah, Jeremiah and Ezekiel to feel that the Hebrew prophet was no mere dervish. Pagan antiquity has left us nothing more eloquent than these exhortations to justice, equality, and moral purity. Their authors are rather apostles than prophets, and it may truly be said that their apostolate is still alive, so mightily have the ideas they formulated borne fruit in the world. "Prophetism is still one of the forces of the future in the religious regeneration of Europe," wrote the great scholar James Darmesteter.

53. It is remarkable that the Prophets do not mention the Books of the Law, nor a divine code, nor the legends of the Book of Genesis, such as the fall of Adam. This alone suffices to falsify those modern theories which have attempted to bring down the works of the Great Prophets to the fourth century B.C., and to show that the names of Isaiah, Ezekiel, &c., were usurped by forgers. Such forgers would not have failed to bring forward Elijah and Elisha, who play so prominent a part in the historic books of the Old Testament. As a fact, the supposed teaching of Moses was transmitted in the *schools* of the prophets before the period when it was published by Esdras, and the prophets give us an echo of that interpretation of the Jewish religion, moral rather than ritual, which obtained in those little congregations.

54. The earliest of the prophets, Elijah and Elisha, had preached in Israel and taken part in its internecine strug-

[1] M. Nicolas, *Ancien Testament,* i, p. 339.

gles. Treated with great severity by the kings, they found few successors, although the first prophets whose utterances have come down to us, Amos and Hosea, also preached in the northern kingdom. From the year 800 B.C. onwards, prophetism flourished more especially in the kingdom of Judah. Preaching at this period took on an almost exclusively moral character, and waged war against formalism and hypocrisy no less than against idolatry and oppression. The Eternal, says Hosea, desires mercy rather than sacrifice (Hos. vi, 6); he rejects the oblations of the wicked, says Amos (Amos v, 21-25); Micah and Isaiah express the same thought: "Wash you, make you clean; put away the evil of your doings from before mine eyes; cease to do evil, learn to do well; seek judgment, relieve the oppressed, judge the fatherless, plead for the widow." (Is. i, 16, 17.) Jeremiah goes even further, and seems to proscribe holocausts and sacrifices altogether (chap. vii, 21-23). Ezekiel really preaches "an anticipatory gospel" when he makes the Eternal say: "Cast away from you all your transgressions . . . and make you a new heart and a new spirit. . . . For I have no pleasure in the death of him that dieth, said the Lord God; wherefore turn yourselves and live ye" (Ezekiel xviii, 23, 24). Thus formalism, which was to increase more and more in Israel during the last five centuries before Christ, was denounced by the Prophets, in spite of the priesthood who lived by it, and who even incited other prophets to defend it (Jer. vii and xvii).

55. Isaiah was preaching in Judah when Samaria was taken by the Assyrians (721 B.C.), who put an end to the kingdom of Israel. Down to this time he had inveighed against "the greed of the rich, the iniquity of the judges, the hollowness of the worship." After the catastrophe, he hailed with enthusiasm the reign of Hezekiah, who seemed destined to realise the hopes of prophetism in Judah. He welcomed the king as a hero of God, a prince of peace; Hezekiah became the Messiah and the texts referring to him have been supposed to foretell the reign of Jesus (Is. ix, 2; *cf.* Matt. iv, 16). Isaiah further predicts the ruin of Assyria, the end of war and hatred: the wolf was to dwell with the lamb, the calf, the lion, and the sheep were to feed together, and a little child was to lead them (Is. xi, 6). Unfortunately, Hezekiah died, leaving a son of twelve, Manasseh, whose minority and long reign were marked by a "libertine" reaction.[1] Isaiah was reduced to silence by the executioner.[2]

56. The compilation which has come down to us under the name of Isaiah (740-710 B.C.) comprises a considerable section (chap. xl to lx) which modern criticism has withdrawn from this prophet and ascribed to a later author, the *second* Isaiah. The second Isaiah speaks to the Jews who are exiles in Babylon; Jerusalem and the other towns are in ruins; but the prophet announces the arrival of Cyrus, who will take Babylon and deliver the Jews. As we cannot suppose this to be anything but a prophecy after the event, the second Isaiah cannot have flourished before 538 B.C. It was in vain that the Biblical commission of the Vatican decreed in 1907 that no second Isaiah was to be recognised, and that consequently Cyrus had been mentioned by name and his actions had been predicted before his birth:

> Dieu fit choix de Cyrus avant qu'il vît le jour.[3]

Orthodoxy itself has laid stress on the theological as distinct from the historical character of this pronouncement, an ingenious manner of excusing its absurdity; liberal commentators have merely smiled. The case has long been decided.

The second Isaiah is perhaps the most eloquent of all the prophets and the one "whose voice has carried farthest." There is nothing more sublime than the song of triumph in which he acclaims the mercy of God to his people: "Sing, O ye heavens, for the Lord hath done it, shout, ye lower parts of the earth; break forth into singing, ye mountains, O forest and every tree therein, for the Lord hath redeemed Jacob and glorified himself in Israel" (chap. xliv, 23). Several chapters deal with the ideal "just man," the servant of

1 Darmesteter, *Prophètes,* p. 65.
2 According to a late Jewish tradition.
3 Racine, *Esther:* "God chose Cyrus before he saw the light of day."

Jehovah, whose sufferings and death are to hasten the victory of God. "The programme of the servant of Jehovah," says A. Loisy, "is almost identical with that of Jesus; his idea of the kingdom of God seems to be purely spiritual, all political and national preoccupations being set aside." When Jerusalem was restored, the work of prophetism was accomplished; during the period of the second Temple, we hear of only three Minor Prophets, Haggai, Zechariah and Malachi.

57. "Jeremiah," writes Darmesteter, "generally passes for the prophet of the *jeremiads;* he owes this reputation to a little collection of elegies on the fall of Jerusalem which are not by him. During his forty years of prophetism, he preached, he acted, he cursed, but he wept very little." Jeremiah was the first prophet who was also a priest; "but in him, as in Isaiah, it was the prophet who predominated, the reformer of the moral life, of social life, of political life." Jeremiah saw Jerusalem fall into the hands of Nebuchadnezzar, and witnessed the end of the kingdom of Judah (586 B.C.). He had counselled his countrymen not to resist an enemy greatly superior in strength to themselves; but he preached hope and faith in the future to the exiled survivors.

Ezekiel, a priest like Jeremiah, was deported to Babylon, where he became the great prophet of the Captivity, rebuilding in imagination the Temple of Jerusalem, and breathing life into the dry bones of his people (Ezekiel xxxvii).

58. Unlike the other prophecies, those which form the Book of Daniel are written partly in Aramaic, partly in Hebrew. According to the narrative with which this book begins, Daniel was taken captive to Babylon (604 B.C.); he was brought up at the court of Nebuchadnezzar, and predicted the downfall of Belshazzar. He saved Susannah, unjustly accused by elders, exposed the imposture of the priests of Bel, and came out unscathed from the den of lions into which he had been thrown by order of Darius.[1] Not only

[1] The story of Susannah and that of the priests of Bel are Greek additions, later than the Aramaic original.

are these tales fables, but the whole of the book attributed to Daniel is fraudulent. Professing to date from about 550 B.C., it makes transparent allusions to events which took place some hundred and sixty years before Christ; these pretended prophecies, although they have been accepted by the whole body of Christian theology, can no longer deceive any thinking person.

59. Another prophet to whom Christian authors have given great prominence, to whom Jesus compared himself, and who has been described as one of his antetypes, is Jonah, famous for his sojourn in the belly of the whale and for his revolt against the Eternal. Nineveh, menaced by the prophecies of Jonah, repented; the Lord pardoned it, and the prophet dared to reproach God for his mildness. He went to sleep in the shade of a tree which a worm devoured in the night, and again reproached God for having destroyed this tree. "Then said the Lord, Thou hast had pity on the gourd . . . and should not I spare Nineveh, that great city wherein are more than six score thousand persons that cannot discern between their right hand and their left hand, and also much cattle" (Jon. iv, 11). This short and very singular composition is erroneously included among the series of the Minor Prophets. Jonah has been assimilated to the fish-god Oannes; his miraculous preservation has been interpreted as figuring that of Israel, devoured by the Assyrian dragon, and restored to life again; finally, the last episode has been construed as a criticism of the narrow and splenetic nationalism of the Israelites after the return from exile. All these are as yet rudimentary interpretations.

60. The idea of the coming of a Messiah, that is to say, one *anointed* by the Lord (in Greek *Christos*, from *chriein*, to anoint), manifests itself already in the writings of the great prophets and exercised a decisive influence on the fate of Christianity. It was long supposed that the Messiah was to be a triumphant warrior of the race of David, who would appear with great glory and restore the fortunes of Israel. But side by side with this conception, discredited by the course of history, there arose the idea of a humble

and suffering Messiah, the *servant of the Lord*, whose advent would purify rather than exalt Israel.[1] The so-called Messianic texts, which are supposed to prefigure Jesus in the Old Testament, have all been either misunderstood or deliberately misinterpreted. The most celebrated is that in Isaiah (vii, 14), which predicts that a Virgin shall bear a son, Emmanuel; but the word *almah*, which the Septuagint rendered virgin, means in Hebrew a young woman, and the passage merely deals with the approaching birth of a son to the king or the prophet himself. This error of the Septuagint is one of the sources of the legend relating to the virginal birth of Jesus. As early as the second century A.D. the Jews perceived it and pointed it out to the Greeks; but the Church knowingly persisted in the false reading, and for over fifteen centuries she has clung to her error.

* * *

61. There are numerous pieces of poetry scattered throughout the Bible, such as the song of Lamech, the song of victory over the Philistines, the song of Deborah, "that gem of the patriotic poetry of Israel."[2] We have even a collection of love-poems, the *Song of Songs*, attributed without any sort of reason to Solomon, in which all sorts of pious allegories which do not exist have been discovered. But with the exception of these fragments, all the secular poetry has perished; what has come down to us is the religious poetry, over-rich in imagery, often incoherent, but showing a very deep moral sense. This poetry is contained in the Psalms, the Proverbs and the Book of Job. The Greek copyists divided it into verses in translating it, which the ordinary Bibles do not do. The rules of this Hebraic poetry are still a matter of controversy. All that can be said is that it possesses assonance and rhythm, and that the end of the strophe is sometimes indicated by a refrain.

62. The Psalms (in Greek *psalmoi*, from *psallein*, to sing to an accompaniment) form a collection of one hundred and

[1] The humble Messiah is predicted in Zechariah, ix, 9; for *the servant of the Lord* see especially Is. xl, xlii and liii.

[2] Reuss, *La Bible*, vii, p. 5.

fifty poems, and were the hymn-book of the Synagogue. This somewhat monotonous literature, in which the ideas of humility, resignation, and hope in God occupy a large place, has exercised an immense influence on the civilisations and the thought of Christian Europe. Nearly half of the Psalms are attributed in their superscriptions to King David, and tradition, agreeing with the earliest Christian texts (Acts iv, 25; Hebr. iv, 7) ascribes the whole Psalter to him. This is a complete error. The Psalter is a collection which was gradually formed, and in which there are repetitions and double versions; it was modified and added to up to the time of the Maccabees, or even later. Though some psalms may be very ancient, others contain allusions to the oppression of Israel, to destroyed synagogues, to the introduction of symbols of idolatry into the sanctuary (Ps. lxxiv). Those psalms which are believed to allude to the history of David contradict what we know of this history and all the exigencies of historical probability, *e.g.*, Psalm li, where David is supposed to ask God to rebuild the walls of Jerusalem. The fact that tradition made David a poet-musician (1 Sam. xvi, 18) sufficiently explains the attribution of ritual hymns to this warlike chieftain who had become a king; but this was only possible long after his own age, when the rude characteristics of his personality were effaced.

63. The Lamentations are five little poems relating to the taking of Jerusalem in 586 B.C., attributed to Jeremiah. Modern critics have shown that they are the work of several writers.

64. The Book of Proverbs consists of exhortations and moral sentences, inspired by a knowledge of the world and by piety. The collection is due to several authors, who repeated and imitated one another. The attribution to Solomon is based on a text of the First Book of Kings (v, 12), according to which this wise prince pronounced three thousand *mashal;* it is contradicted by the contents of the collection itself. The Book of Proverbs reflects a state of civilisation in which there is no longer either polytheism or polygamy, and this points to the period of the Restoration. The personification of Wisdom (chap. viii) is a trait quite

alien to the prophetic and legislative writings of the Old Testament; it even suggests a Greek influence.

65. The Book of Job is a didactic poem, with narrative portions in prose, the object of which is to show how the just should endure. A rich and honourable man, Job, is tried by the Lord, who allows one of his angels to take all his possessions from him. He resigns himself and blesses God. The evil angel, called the Accuser (in Greek *diabolos*, hence the name *devil*), further insists on striking Job in his body, which becomes covered with ulcers; his wife blasphemes, but Job does not imitate her. His friends come to see him and remain mute before his misery. Then Job, losing patience, bursts out into lamentations, and curses the day when he was born. His friends reply that his misfortunes are perhaps deserved, and address to him reproaches which exasperate him; another personage intervenes, censuring both Job and his friends. Finally the voice of Jehovah makes itself heard in the storm and glorifies the intelligence which governs the world. Job repents of his impulse of revolt and God restores all his possessions, which he henceforth enjoys during a long life of one hundred and forty years.

66. The importance ascribed to the evil angel who argues with God suffices to show that this book belongs to a late period, after the Captivity, when the Persian idea of Satan (Ahriman) had crept into the religious thought of the Jews. On the other hand, the popular basis of the legend is very ancient, for, in the first place, Job "the just man" is mentioned in Ezekiel (xiv, 14), and in the second place, Job neither invokes nor receives any consolation founded on belief in another life. A gross error of translation in the Vulgate (xix, 25) caused it to be believed that Job spoke of his own resurrection and of the expected Messiah; but this obscure passage only deals, as a fact, with a terrestrial compensation.[1] The whole work would have no point were there any conception in it of rewards beyond the grave, a thought quite alien to orthodox Jewish literature before the third century B.C. It should be added that the text is very corrupt, and that there are serious interpolations.

[1] Reuss, *La Bible,* viii, 76.

67. The Hebrews were not molested during their enforced sojourn in Babylon. When Cyrus by an edict permitted them to return to their country, only the tribes of Judah and Benjamin set out; the descendants of the others became merged in the population that surrounded them. The new exodus, directed by Zerubbabel, a descendant of David, and the high priest Joshua, was not fortunate; nevertheless, the rebuilding of the Temple began about 535 B.C. in spite of the intrigues of the Samaritans, who denounced the ambition of the Jews to the Persian king. It required the religious ascendancy of Esdras (Ezra) about 458 B.C., and thirteen years later the political tact of Nehemiah, who had held high office at the Persian court, to give the Jewish people a solid organisation. This organisation was essentially theocratic; Judæa was governed by a High Priest, assisted later on by a Sanhedrin or Council. Mosaism, hitherto an ideal, became a reality for the first time. There were no more lapses into polytheism, no more prophets, but doctors of the law or scribes, schools of theology, and an essential novelty in the shape of oratories or synagogues, where laymen met to read the sacred books and exchange ideas concerning them. It was from the synagogue and not from the Temple that Christian teaching was to emanate.

The most important events of this period were the promulgation of the Law by Ezra, and the schism of the Samaritans, who set up a sanctuary on Mount Gerizim in rivalry to the Temple of Jerusalem. At a later period, a second sanctuary was established in Egypt by Onias, which was also considered schismatic (150 B.C.). After Alexander the Great, Judæa belonged for a century to the Ptolemies (320 B.C.), and then to the Seleucidæ (189 B.C.). Antiochus IV. persecuted the Jews, who retaliated by an insurrection, the leader of which, Judas Maccabæus (the Hammer?), one of the sons of the priest Mattathias, gained some striking successes. The struggle lasted for a long time, under the Asmonæan pontiffs (so called from the great-grandfather of Mattathias), members of the numerous family known as the Maccabees; finally one of them, Simeon, took the title of prince of the Jews (142 B.C.). His successors, Hyrcanus,

Aristobulus, and Alexander Jannæus, were at once kings and high priests. Under Hyrcanus II. Jerusalem was taken by Pompey, and Herod of Idumæa, the son of a minister of Hyrcanus, obtained the crown from the triumvir Mark Antony. After his death, his kingdom was divided into three tetrarchies, and given to his three children, to whom the Roman procurators left but a semblance of power. After many local uprisings, directed against the Romans and the Jewish aristocracy subservient to them, a general revolt broke out under Nero (A.D. 66) which was brought to an end under Vespasian by the taking of Jerusalem and its destruction (A.D. 70). The Temple was burnt down, the inhabitants massacred or sold as slaves. A fresh insurrection, led by the false Messiah Barcochba, was not more successful. Bether, the last Jewish fortress, fell into the hands of the Romans, and Hadrian founded the colony of Ælia Capitolina on the ruins of Jerusalem (A.D. 136).

The dispersal of the Jewish nation was then finally achieved. It was this dispersal which the Roman Senator Rutilius Namatianus, writing shortly after the taking of Rome by Alaric (A.D. 410), condemned as the source of all the evils which had befallen the Empire; for every Jewish community soon sheltered a nascent Christian community, and marked a stage in the conquest of the antique world by Christianity. "Would to Heaven," says Rutilius, "that Judæa had never been subjugated by the wars of Pompey and the arms of Titus! The evil spreads its contagion all the further for being uprooted, and the conquered nation oppresses its conquerors." A little before this, in evident allusion to a saying of St. Paul's, he calls Judaism "the root of madness" (*radix stultitiæ*). Titus had already, according to Tacitus, declared that the Temple of Jerusalem must be destroyed, because Christianity had sprung from Judaism, and that, if the root were torn up, the branch would perish the more certainly.[1] Titus can hardly have said this in A.D. 70; but Tacitus may well have thought it thirty years later.

[1] Tacitus, fragment in Sulpicius Severus, Chron. ii, 50.

68. During the five centuries which elapsed between the return after the Captivity and the Christian era, Christianity was evolved in the Jewish world by an intermingling of Mosaic, Persian and Greek doctrines. Jerusalem was naturally the religious centre where hostile and, indeed, confused tendencies, difficult to define nowadays, were represented by the Sadducees (from *saddik*, righteous, or from the family of a priest named Sadok) and the Pharisees (from *Peroushim*, "those set apart"). The Sadducees denied the resurrection and angels, which the Pharisees recognised (Acts xxiii, 8). Among the novel doctrines of the Judaism of this period there are some which seem Persian, such as that of the spirit of evil (Satan), of archangels and angels; others are Hellenic, perhaps Orphic and Platonic, like those of asceticism, of future rewards and punishments, and of original sin. The invasion of Hellenic ideas was favoured by the existence of large Jewish colonies in Egypt (especially at Alexandria) and in Cyrenaica. It was for these Jews who had forgotten their own tongue that the Old Testament was translated into Greek; it was they who, following the example of the Stoic philosophers, attempted to explain all the more incredible elements of the Biblical legends by giving them an allegorical meaning. Their ideas are made known to us by Philo, an Alexandrian Jew contemporary with Jesus. The infiltration of Hellenism is clearly attested even in Palestine; the Jewish doctors took Greek names and spoke Greek. As early as the second century before Christ there was a "Hellenic peril"; the alliance between Jews and Greeks, preached by St. Paul, had long been prepared.

69. An asceticism similar to that of the Pythagoreans inspired the Essenes of Palestine and the Therapeutists of Egypt,[1] who lived in little laborious communities, had no slaves, and held all their possessions in common. They practised a kind of baptism, offered no sacrificial victims, held chastity in high esteem, and refused to take oaths; John the Baptist sprang from this sect. According to Josephus they believed that souls are attached to the body as to a

[1] If the name of *Therapeutists* (healers) is the Greek translation of *Essenes*, this latter may be derived from the Hebrew *asah*, to heal.

prison, that those of the good went after death to the islands beyond the ocean, that the others were given over to eternal torment under the earth. If Josephus was rightly informed on these points, the Hellenic origin of the sect is beyond question. The Essenes had also certain secret doctrines which they swore not to reveal; perhaps these have been rightly regarded as the source of the speculations of the Jewish Kabbala ("tradition"), known to us by certain Hebrew books of the Middle Ages, such as the *Zohar* (book of splendour). The Kabbala is a magical and pantheistic doctrine, in which the numerical values of letters, legions of angels and demons, and the emanations of light play a large part. Though one of the worst aberrations of the human intellect, it has preserved many followers to this day, even among non-Jewish mystics since the Renaissance.

70. The Book of Ecclesiastes (in Hebrew *Koheleth*, the preacher), which claims to be the work of King Solomon, but really dates only from the third century B.C., deplores the multiplicity of books; unfortunately, none of this literature has come down to us. The preacher declares that all is vanity, and draws therefrom the epicurean moral that we should enjoy life. Ecclesiasticus, or the Wisdom of Jesus, son of Sirach, is a collection of well-intentioned little discourses; the author (*c.* 200 B.C.) had some knowledge of Greek philosophy. The Book of Esther (*c.* 150 B.C.) is a didactic tale which attests a certain familiarity with Persian things, but in its present state it presupposes that the Persian Empire had long ceased to exist. The name of Israel does not occur in it, nor does that of God; its general tone is coarse and materialistic. The Book of Daniel (see p. 208), those of the Chronicles, of Ezra, of Nehemiah and of the Maccabees, belong to this period. The historic value of the first two books of the Maccabees is considerable; that of the last two almost *nil.* The fourth is a homily rather than a history; it is remarkable for the development of ideas concerning the immortality of the soul, and future rewards and punishments. The Book of Tobit (*c.* 150 B.C.) is a romance like that of Esther, saturated with Persian ideas; Satan plays a part in this fable which is absolutely

non-Mosaic. Finally, the book called The Wisdom of Solomon (*c.* 50 B.C.) seems, like the three last books of the Maccabees, to have been written at Alexandria in a pagan centre which was hostile to Judaism, and not on religious grounds alone.

71. A word must be said about three other curious compositions. The Apocalypse of Esdras, called in the Vulgate the Fourth Book of Esdras, was written in Egypt after the destruction of the Temple, in the reign of Domitian. It purports to contain the revelations and visions of Esdras during the Captivity; the Messiah is predicted; he will be the Son of God and will live for four centuries, after which will come the Resurrection. The Book of Baruch the prophet, the friend of Jeremiah, is of the same period, though some critics have assigned it to the third and even to the fourth century before Christ. The Book of Enoch, which was lost about the period of Charlemagne, was found again in 1773, in an Ethiopian translation. It is a kind of Apocalypse attributed to the patriarch Enoch, containing visions of the fall of the Angels, the fate of souls after death, and the Messiah, who, as in the Book of Daniel (vii, 13), is called the Son of Man, a designation Jesus often applies to himself in the Gospels. This book is composed of fragments of five other books, connected in a very arbitrary fashion; the material dates from the period of the Syrian domination, between 200 and 170 years before our era. We are still far from a clear understanding of this rhapsody, which, like that bearing the name of Esdras, has received various interpolations, probably of Christian origin.

72. About the beginning of our era, the greatest Jewish doctor at Jerusalem was Hillel, born at Babylon, whose grandson Gamaliel was the teacher of St. Paul. The little we know of Hillel's teaching from the Talmud breathes a spirit of mildness and love for humanity. To a pagan who, wishing to embrace Judaism, asked him for an abstract of his religion, he replied: "Do not unto others what thou wouldest not they should do unto thee, this is the whole of the Law; the rest is only commentary." This is almost identical with the code of Jesus (Matt. xxii, 39; Mark xii,

31; Luke x, 27). Hillel also insisted much on the idea that man was made in the image of God and deduced man's duty to himself from this belief. He says elsewhere: "My soul is a guest on earth, towards whom I must fulfil the duties of charity." "Judge not thy neighbour until thou hast been in his place" (*cf.* Matt. vii, 1). "My humility is my exaltation, my exaltation is my humility." "Where there are no men, strive to show thyself a man." As Hillel was a Pharisee, it is difficult to understand the hostility of Jesus to this sect, whose ideas were in such close agreement with his own (Mark xii, 26-34). Our Gospels must have been written by men who, ignorant of a previous state of things, confounded all the doctors of the Law with the narrower and more rigid Pharisees. The antagonism shown by the Pharisees to Christianity of the school of St. Paul perhaps explains the odious part assigned to them in the New Testament.

. . .

73. Since they ceased to be a nation, the Jews have lived among other nations, nearly always scorned and persecuted, but steadfast in their faith. The Church might have annihilated them as she did the Arians and Manichæans; she preserved them as the depositaries of the Ancient Law, the witnesses to the Gospel, and it was even at Rome itself that they were least rigorously treated. Excluded from nearly all functions of the State, from most of the professions, and from agriculture, they developed commercial qualities which enabled them to live, but enhanced the odium in which they were held, partly because of the wealth they acquired, partly because of that which was popularly ascribed to them. Their great title to honour is that they alone of almost all Europe down to the Reformation upheld the doctrine of divine unity and refused to accept the irrational creed of Nicæa. But the characteristic doctrines, or rather the subtle disquisitions of their doctors upon the Law, which compose the Talmuds of Jerusalem (first to fourth century) and of Babylon (third to fifth century) have not much contributed to the sum of human knowledge. Although the

greatest Jewish philosopher, Moses Maimonides of Cordova (A.D. 1135-1204), was a liberal, indeed almost a rationalist, it was not until the eighteenth century that religious liberalism really penetrated into Israel; indeed, a universal obscurantist reaction prevailed in the Jewish communities from the sixteenth century. Even in these days, the majority of the 11,000,000 of Israelites are less advanced than the Christians in this respect, because they rigorously observe the Sabbath, and many absurd alimentary prohibitions. The Jewish religion is an easy creed only to those who profess but do not practise it. The internal emancipation of Judaism will be the most urgent of its duties when once its political and social emancipation, as yet imperfect, shall have been procured by law and public opinion.

74. In the Roman Empire, the Jews, with few exceptions,[1] had no political rights, and they paid a special tax; save for this, they were free, but they were forbidden to proselytise. They had made a great number of converts in the Greek dominions since the reign of Alexander; some of these were received without reserve, others were admitted only to certain rites (these were known as *proselytes of the gate*). The Christian Emperors began to persecute the Jews and to attempt to convert them forcibly. In the barbarous kingdoms of the West, they lived amicably with the inhabitants, who looked upon them more or less as magicians. In Spain, the Visigoth kings, incited by the clergy, made slaves of them (A.D. 694), but they regained their freedom at the time of the Arab conquest (A.D. 711), and distinguished themselves in medicine and astronomy; they also translated many Greek and Arabian works, thus making them accessible to the West. Their influence in France and Germany alarmed Agobard, Bishop of Lyons, who wrote diatribes against them (A.D. 820); popular excesses directed against them took place as far back as the end of the ninth century. But the real persecutions, of the most atrocious and savage description, began with the Crusades. The first Crusaders massacred all the Jews they encountered, considering them

[1] St. Paul was a Roman citizen; some Jews even held the rank of knights.

"Deicides"; and at Jerusalem burnt thousands of them in their synagogues. England expelled them root and branch (1290), and her example was followed, first by France (1306 and 1395), then by Spain (1492) and by Portugal (1497). Driven out of Spain, the Jews took refuge in Morocco and in Turkey, the latter the only country which received them kindly; they retained the Spanish tongue in their new abode, notably at Salonica, where there are now over 60,000 of them. The French Jews passed into Germany, Hungary and Poland. All the cruelties perpetrated upon the Jews, murder, ill-treatment and spoliation, were inspired by the fanaticism of the clergy and the greed of kings in want of money, like Edward I. and Philip Augustus. To give some apparent justification for these odious excesses, the accusations brought by the pagans against the early Christians were revived as charges against the Jews; it was declared that they killed children to mix their blood with the Passover bread; these absurd accusations, not one of which was ever judicially established, have been periodically renewed down to our own times. It was further asserted that the Jews were in the habit of desecrating the sacramental wafers, that they ruined the Christians by usury, and that they were in secret league with the Infidels. When an epidemic broke out, it was the Jews who had poisoned the wells; thus the Black Death of 1348-1350 caused the massacre of thousands of Jews from Provence to Austria. It was, always and everywhere, "the fault of the Jews," a good pretext for pillage and butchery.

75. In those countries where the Jews were tolerated, as in Italy, in Poland, and a part of Germany, they were allotted special quarters (*ghetto*, in Italian), and forbidden to quit them after certain hours; they had also to wear a distinctive dress to prevent them from having any relations with Christians.

76. All the laws against the Jews were applied with more or less rigour. Princes, when they wanted money, recalled the Jews by means of finance; then, when they thought their activity had enriched them again, they expelled them afresh, in order to confiscate their possessions.

77. Such of the Jews as were converted voluntarily, or by force and stratagem, especially in Spain, came under the jurisdiction of the Inquisition by the mere fact of baptism. Then, if the converts observed, or appeared to observe Judaic rites, they were declared renegades and burnt alive. This was the fate of innumerable poor wretches who were called *Neo-Christians* or *Marranos;* of these the Spanish Inquisition made jubilant bonfires, after having expelled from Spain those who refused to be converted.

78. This is not the place in which to dwell on the martyrology of the medieval Jews; but it is impossible not to recall the heroic victims burnt at Troyes in 1288, those of the massacres in London and Norwich in 1190, and of Spires, Worms and Frankfort in 1350. As late as 1510, in the Mark of Brandenburg, forty Jews, accused of having desecrated a sacramental wafer, were burnt at the stake on the same day.

79. In the seventeenth century they were no longer massacred, except occasionally in Spain as *Marranos*, but they were robbed more or less everywhere; the taxes and exactions to which they were subjected were more severe than those of the villeins. Nevertheless the Jews achieved a certain measure of prosperity in Holland, in England, and in the west of Germany. In the Musulman countries there was far more tolerance, but the security of the Jews was very precarious. A false prophet, Sabbataï Sevi, appeared at Smyrna, gave himself out as the Messiah, inflamed a number of the Jews of the Ottoman Empire, and finally became a convert of Islamism (1666).

80. The era of toleration was inaugurated by the Rationalists of the eighteenth century. A Berlin Jew, Moses Mendelssohn (1719-1786), contributed to this by modernising his co-religionists and reconciling them to the civilisation about them. The first benevolent measures were passed by the enlightened Emperor Joseph II. (1781); but the decisive reform, the legal emancipation, was the work of the French National Assembly, exhorted to tolerance by the Abbé Grégoire (1791). The arms of Napoleon carried liberal ideas into Germany; they lapsed again at the Restora-

tion, especially in Prussia, where till quite recently no Jew could be either a diplomatist or an officer. Nevertheless the impulse had been given, and legal emancipation took place in due course (Prussia, 1847; Italy, 1848; Austria, 1867). The Constitution of the United States of America admitted no distinctions founded on differences of creed; this country has remained the great refuge of the Jews who have suffered persecution in Russia and Roumania. In England, complete emancipation was only given in 1860, when the Houses of Parliament and the magistrature were thrown open to the Jews. In Russia, where there are 7,000,000 Jews, persecution was almost continuous, in spite of the tolerant tendencies of Alexander II. (1855-1881). The accession of Alexander III. was marked by scenes of pillage, in consequence of which the minister Ignatieff promulgated the so-called provisional laws of May 1882, which aggravated the hardships of the Jews, who were already restricted to certain provinces. The new decree forbade them to live outside the towns (and, consequently, to practise agriculture); those who had not become naturalised Russian subjects were expelled from the country. These laws, which were applied more particularly since 1891, produced an immense flood of emigration. But the situation became still worse under Nicholas II., who, like his father, was advised by the Procurator of the Holy Synod, Pobedonoszew, whom Mommsen has styled "the modern Torquemada." With the tacit complicity of the government and the active co-operation of the police, the Jews, suspected of revolutionary tendencies, were slaughtered in crowds at Kichineff, at Odessa, at Kieff, and in a hundred and twenty other towns and villages; women and children were hacked to pieces. Europe, which had allowed Abdul Hamid to massacre three hundred thousand of his Armenian subjects in time of peace (1896), was content to refrain from applause of these new butcheries. A noble-hearted man, Count Ivan Tolstoy, a former minister of Nicholas II., demanded the equality of the Russian Jews before the law, in a book he published in 1907; he demanded it in the interests of Russia herself, where the exceptional laws against the Jews perpetuated corruption and injustice. But the legal emancipation of the Russian Jews had to await the fall of Czardom (1917).

81. In Roumania, the situation created for the Jews was so cruel that in 1878 the Congress of Berlin insisted that they should receive their rights of citizenship. Roumania promised this, but failed to keep her word; she invented a prolonged system of naturalisation, in which each case was to be ratified by a double vote in Parliament. Eight hundred Jews who had served in the war against the Turks were naturalised at one stroke, but the benefit was refused to nearly all the rest (about 280,000), although they were compelled to serve in the army. To consider people incorporated in the army aliens, although they cannot claim any other country, was an enormity without any parallel in public law. Citizenship was not granted to the Roumanian Jews until the end of the Great War (1918).

82. After the emancipation of the Jews in Western Europe, their adversaries shifted their ground of attack from the religious to the nationalist domain. German chauvinism, over-excited by the war of 1870, hurled anathemas against the "Semitic race," which was adjudged inferior to the "Germanic race," as if the term race, applied to sub-varieties of the white race, were scientifically defensible. This new Anti-Semitism, masquerading as patriotism, was first propagated at Berlin by the court chaplain Stöcker, with the connivance of Bismarck (1878). At Vienna, it found an energetic representative in Lueger, a clerical who called himself a Christian Socialist, and posed as the champion of the humble Austrian, petty trader or workman, against the Jew. From Germany the movement spread into France (about 1883), where, encouraged by the Jesuits and Assumptionists, it succeeded beyond all expectations for about ten years. Algeria, whose Jewish population had been naturalised *en bloc* by the Jewish minister Crémieux (November 1870), executing a project which had, indeed, been matured under the Empire, gave way for a time to all the excesses of Anti-Semitism. In France the Dreyfus affair, after enhancing the credit of the Anti-Semitic party immensely for a time, ended by opening the eyes of the Republicans to the true object of this

propaganda, directed against one of the fundamental ideas of the Revolution, that of tolerance, and indeed against the Revolution itself. But this long campaign, which was carried on even after the rehabilitation of Captain Dreyfus (1906), was not unfruitful; prejudice has reappeared in all classes of society, and now a Jew who aspires to position of any sort requires greater talent and more strenuous efforts than his fellow-citizens of other confessions.[1]

83. The Jewish religion has developed with its surroundings. Maimonides formulated a *credo* in thirteen articles, comprising the immortality of the soul and the resurrection of the body, which is as remote from Biblical Judaism as is the Catholicism of the Council of Trent from the Gospels. Among the educated Jews of all countries, rationalism predominates, with a certain reverence for their ancestors which stands in the place of faith. Liberal synagogues have been founded in Germany, England, the United States and even in France; in Galicia, in Poland, in Palestine, orthodoxy is still very powerful, and is often complicated by thaumaturgy. This is more especially true of the 400,000 *Hassidim* or devout persons, whose mysticism in the eighteenth century was a reaction against Talmudic formalism. In Galicia, Poland and Lithuania they constitute communities hostile to the modern spirit; their noisy and disorderly form of worship has all the appearance of a religious frenzy.

On the other hand, the Russian and Turkish sect of the Karaites, founded about the year 800 A.D., is opposed to all mysticism, rejects the Talmud, and relies almost exclusively upon the Bible. As Catherine II. granted certain privileges to the Russian Karaites, they have never been molested; but no Jew was allowed to become a convert to Karaitism.

84. One of the results of persecution was the renewal of the old idea that the oppressed Jews should return to Palestine and restore the Kingdom of David as a part of the Ottoman Empire. But the Turkish government was opposed to that scheme, in spite of the eloquent propaganda led by a Hungarian Jew, Theodore Herzl (*d.* 1904). England offered to settle many Jews in Uganda; that was not *Zionism*,

[1] *Grande Encyclopédie*, art. *Juifs*, at the end.

but, as it was styled, *Territorialism*, and did not appeal to the masses. Later on, when England, during the Great War, conquered Palestine, and the Arabs threw off the Turkish yoke, the cause of Zionism was taken up by British policy. The Balfour declaration (Nov. 2, 1927), approved by the Allied Powers and the United States, recited that they "view with favour the establishment in Palestine of a National Home for the Jewish people." The words "a Jewish state," which the Arabs would have objected to, were thus carefully avoided. The Balfour declaration was inserted in the treaty of Sèvres and Great Britain accepted a mandate for Palestine on behalf of the League of Nations (April 1920). But Palestine offers no sufficient resources for the settlement of a large number of Jews, though the colonies founded there by Edmond de Rothschild have become fairly prosperous.

Other less ambitious schemes served to alleviate the misery of the Oriental Jews. The *Alliance israélite universelle* (Paris, 1862), and analogous societies in London, Berlin and Vienna devoted themselves to the elevation of the Oriental Jew by means of schools; an English society, founded by the rich financier Maurice de Hirsch, created colonies for the persecuted in the Argentine Republic, in Brazil and in Canada. The emigration to the United States—now checked by law—has been so considerable since 1881 that New York, with its 1,100,000 Israelites has become the veritable metropolis of Judaism.

85. The Jews make no proselytes, but many are made among them. Those who embrace Christianity are either cunning beggars, who undergo the rite of baptism several times, or poor but industrious young men, prevented by iniquitous laws or prejudice from frequenting the schools and earning their bread; or again, rich people, who believe in nothing, and who purchase by baptism the privilege of a cool reception in the fashionable world. Their children are generally Anti-Semites.

BIBLIOGRAPHY

The richest sources of information are the Biblical encyclopædias and dictionaries of Smith, Cheyne, Hastings and Vigouroux, Hauck's *Realencyklopädie für protestantische Theologie* (3rd German ed.) and the *Jewish Encyclopædia.* S. Munk's work, *La Palestine,* although old (1845), is admirable and indispensable. There is an English illustrated *Dictionary of the Bible,* in one volume, published by Piercy in 1908. Students may keep abreast of contemporary knowledge by reading the *Revue biblique* and the *Revue des Etudes juives.*

E. Meyer, *Die Israeliten und ihre Nachbarstämme,* 1906; R. Kittel, *Gesch. des Volkes Israel,* 1912; Piepenbring, *Hist. du peuple d'Israël,* 1898; E. Renan, *Hist. du peuple d'Israël,* 1887-1894; Wellhausen, *Prolegomena zur Geschichte Israëls,* 5th ed., 1904 (*cf.* Renan, *Journ. des Sav.,* 1886, p. 201; *Israel und jüd. Gesch.,* 7th ed., 1924; Rob. Smith, *The Religion of the Semites,* 3rd ed., 1904; Loisy, *Le religion d'Israël,* 2nd ed., 1908; Kreglinger, *La religion d'Israël,* 1926; K. Budde, *Altisrael. Religion,* 3rd ed., 1912; Frazer, *Folklore in the O. T.,* 3 vols., 1918.

6. E. Reuss, *La Bible,* 17 vols., 1877-1881 (translation, with introduction and commentary); L. Gautier and others, *La Bible du cinquantenaire,* 1911 *et seq.;* E. Kautzsch, *Die heiligen Schriften des A. T.,* 3rd ed., 1908; *Die Apokryphen und Pseudepigraphen des A. T.,* 2 vols., 1900 (German translations); Nowack, *Hand Commentar zum alten Testament,* 1901; L. Gautier, *Introd. à l'A. T.,* 2nd ed., 1914.

7. Loisy, *Histoire du canon de l'Ancien Testament,* 1890.

8. Art. *Bibelübersetzungen* (translations from the Bible) in Hauck.

12. T. K. Cheyne, *Founders of Old Testament Criticism,* 1893; F. Stummer, *R. Simon,* 1912.

13. Houtin, *La critique biblique au XIX*e *siècle,* 1902; *au XX*e *siècle,* 1906.

14. Darmesteter, *Les Prophètes* (*Coup d'œil sur l'hist. du peuple juif*), 1892.

15. Fr. Lenormant, *Les origines de l'histoire,* vol. i, 2nd ed., 1880.

16. Gunkel, *Genesis,* 3rd ed., 1910; Loisy, *Mythes babyloniens et Genèse,* 1901. Recent excavations at Kish and Ur show that there occurred a local "deluge" in Mesopotamia about 3400 B.C.

17. Art. *Elohim, Jahve* and *Polytheismus* in Hauck.

21. Art. *Teraphim,* in Hauck.

22. S. R., *Cultes,* vol. i, p. 3; vol. ii, p. 32; vol. iii, p. 343.

24. *Ibid.,* vol. ii, p. 443.

25. *Ibid.,* vol. iii, p. 223.

26. Frazer, art. *Taboo,* in the *Encyclop. Britannica,* 9th ed.

27. S. R., *Cultes,* vol. i, p. 15; vol. ii, p. 12.

29. Worship of the ass and fish: *Ibid.,* vol. i, p. 342; vol. iii, p. 43.

30. W. Davies, *Magic, Divination and Demonology among the Hebrews,* 1898; Grüneisen, *Der Ahnenkultus und die Urreligion Israels,* 1900. On *Urim* and *Thummim,* see *Rev. critique,* 1918, ii, p. 422.

31. Art. *Feasts,* in Cheyne; and *Festivals* in *Jewish Encyclopædia.*

32. Th. Reinach, *La fête de Pâque,* 1906.

34. Art. *Purim,* in Cheyne; Frazer, *Golden Bough,* 2nd ed., vol. iii, p. 153.

37. Art. *Priest,* in Cheyne.

40. A. Pukko, *Das Deuteronomium,* 1910.

45. Art. *Mizraim,* in Cheyne; *Amraphel, Jacob* and *Joseph,* in Cheyne and Hastings.

46. K. Budde, *Die Religion des Volkes Israel,* 1890.

51. I. Lévi, *Le temple du dieu Jahou et la colonie d'Eléphantine* (in *Rev. études juives,* 1908, vols. liv and lvi); E. Meyer, *Papyrusfund von Elefantine,* 1912; S. A. Fries, *Jahvetempel ausserhalb Palästinas,* 1914.

52. Rob. Smith, *The Prophets of Israel,* 1882; Darmesteter, *Les prophètes d'Israël,* 1892; A. Causse, *Les Prophètes,* 1903.

54. J. Touzard, *Le livre d'Amos,* 1909.

56. Condamin, *Le serviteur de Jahvé* (in *Revue biblique,* 1908, p. 162); art. *Servant of the Lord* in Cheyne; A. Loisy, *Le second Isaïe,* 1927.

57. F. Ch. Jean, *Jérémie,* 1913.

58-60. Art. *Daniel* and *Jonas,* in Cheyne and Hastings.

61. R. H. Charles, *Jewish Eschatology,* 1899; I. Loeb, *Littérature des pauvres dans la Bible,* 1891; Lagrange, *Le Messianisme chez les Juifs,* 1909; A. Berthollet, *Daniel und die griechische Gefahr,* 1907; Dussaud, *Le Cantique de Cantiques,* 1919.

62. A. Causse, *Les vieux chants de la Bible,* 1926; S. Mowinckel, *Psalmenstudien,* 1921-1924 (see *Rev. hist. relig.,* 1925, p. 16).

64. W. O. E. Oesterley, *The Book of Proverbs,* 1927.

65. M. Jastrow, *The Book of Job,* 1920; K. Budde, *Das Buch Hiob,* 2nd ed., 1913.

67 *et seq.* E. Schürer, *Geschichte des jüd. Volkes im Zeitalter Jesu,* 3rd ed., 1901 (Engl. transl.; a capital work); J. A. Montgomery, *The Samaritans,* 1907; Th. Reinach, *Textes d'auteurs grecs et romains relatifs au judaïsme* (translation and commentaries), 1895.

68. There is a transl. of Philo in the Bohn Library (3 vols.).

69. Art. *Essenier* in Hauck; Moses identified with Pythagoras, *Rev. arch.,* 1927, ii, p. 307; Is. Lévy, *Légende de Pythagore,* 1927; T. Loeb, art. *Cabale* in the *Grande Encyclopédie.* There exists a French translation of the Zohar, 1906 (see *Rev. biblique,* 1908, p. 588).

70. E. Podechard, *L'Ecclésiaste,* 1912; Isr. Lévy, *L'Ecclésiastique,* 1901.

71. G. Charles, *The apocrypha of the O. T.,* 1913; *The book of Enoch,* 2nd ed., 1913; W. Bousset, *Die jüdische Apokalyptik,* 1903; *Die Religion des Judentums im N. T. Zeitalter,* 1903; F. Martin and others, *Les apocryphes de l'A. T.,* 1905 and foll.; Vaganay, *Le quatrième livre d'Esdras,* 1906.

72. Friedländer, *Synagoge und Kirche,* 1908.

73. H. Graetz, *Gesch. der Juden,* 11 vols., 1853-1874 (Engl. transl.); Th. Reinach, *Histoire des Israélites,* 3rd ed., 1903; G. Foot Moore, *Judaism in the first Centuries,* 1927; J. Abrahams, *Jewish life in the Middle Ages,* 1896; art. *Talmud* in *Jew. Encycl.;* S. R., *Emancipation intérieure du judaïsme,* in *Cultes,* vol. ii, p. 418.

74. Juster, *Les Juifs dans l'Empire Romain,* 1914; Strack, art. *Antisemitism* in Hastings' *Encycl. of Religion;* Vacandard, *Etudes,* vol. iii, 1912 (the accusation of *Ritual Murder*); Anat. Leroy-Beaulieu, *Israël chez le Nations,* 1893.

77. E. N. Adler, *Auto de fé and Jew,* 1908.

80. Errera, *Les juifs russes,* 2nd ed., 1903 (Engl. transl.). The best source of information is the *Bulletin de l'Alliance israélite,* 1862-1913.

83. Cl. Montefiore, *Liberal judaism,* 1903; Isr. Abrahams, *Judaism,* 1907; Bricout, *L'union libérale israélite* (in *Revue du clergé,* Nov. 1, 1908); art. *Hassidim* and *Karaïtes* in *Jew. Encycl.*

84. Art. *Alliance, Jewish Colonization* in *Jew. Encycl.;* art. *Zionism* in *Brit. Encycl.* and supplementary vol. xxxii; Nahum Sokolow, *Hist. of Zionism,* 1919.

85. Art. *Mission unter den Juden* in Hauck.

CHAPTER VIII

CHRISTIAN ORIGINS

Myth and history of Jesus. The Canon of the New Testament. The orthodox tradition as to the Evangelists. The conclusions of criticism on this point. The date of our Gospels. The synoptical Gospels. Testimony of Papias. The composition of the synoptic Gospels. The fourth Gospel. The lack of historic authority for the Gospels. The idea of the Messiah. The miracles and the resurrection. Chronological difficulties. The testimony of Tacitus. The letter of Claudius to the Alexandrians. Incredible story told by Tertullian. The Docetes. Doubts as to the existence of Jesus. The testimony of Josephus and the Slavonic text of the *Jewish War*. Jesus as leader of a revolt against the Romans. The 22nd Psalm. The supposed fulfilment of prophecies. The morals of the Gospels. The apocryphal Gospels. The Epistles of St. Paul. Chronology of St. Paul's apostolate. The Catholic Epistles. The Epistle of St. John and the verse of the "three witnesses." The Apocalypse of St. John. The Apocalypse of St. Peter. Various Epistles. The Pastor of Hermas. The Symbolum and the Doctrine of the Apostles. The pseudo-Clementine writings. Simon Magus. Antichrist.

1. The beginning of every history is shrouded in legend; Christianity is no exception to the rule. The churches insist that the legends of Christianity are pure history; if this were so, it would be the greatest of miracles.

2. Christianity belongs to a group of religions quite different from the official creeds of Judæa, Greece and Rome. The essential feature of the former group consists in an initiation into the cult of a Saviour-god, who assumed human form, taught, suffered, died and rose from the dead; the reward of the initiated is salvation. Such were the religions of Osiris, Dionysos, Orpheus, Adonis, Attis and the like; such were no doubt many obscure creeds practised in Greece, Asia Minor and Syria of which we know very little, because they are hardly mentioned in literature. Christianity is the most recent of its class, the only perfectly moral and decent one, and the only one that has triumphed and survived. But it differs from all others in a very striking peculiarity: the Saviour-god of the Christians lived in historical times, not in

THE DOCTRINE OF THE APOSTLES

a remote and unattainable past. So what we may call, for analogy's sake, the *myth of Christ*, the evolution of which can be clearly traced from the time of St. Paul and of the Fourth Gospel, must be distinguished from the *history of Jesus:* a most difficult task, the more so as our earliest documents relating to Jesus are already steeped in miracle and in myth.

3. Twenty-seven little Greek compositions, all the work of Christian writers, compose what is known as the Canon or rule of the New Testament. They are: the four so-called canonical Gospels [1] (the Gospels according to Matthew, Mark, Luke and John), the Acts of the Apostles, twenty-one letters attributed to the Apostles (Paul, Peter, John, James and Jude), and the Apocalypse or Revelation attributed to St. John.

4. This Canon was practically established about 350 A.D., after the Council of Nicæa (A.D. 325), and was confirmed for the Western churches by St. Augustine in 397; the only doubtful item was the Apocalypse, and this was still considered not above suspicion in France during the eighth century. But the first idea of a Canon dates from A.D. 150; it was the famous heretic, Marcion, who then formed the first collection of the kind, which included an abridged Luke and the majority of the Pauline epistles. Down to this time all quotations from "the Scriptures" in the works of the Apostolic Fathers (or early orthodox Christian writers) refer exclusively to the Old Testament.[2]

5. A mutilated Latin catalogue, discovered at Milan by the learned scholar Muratori (1672-1750) and dating from about 150 to 200 A.D., enumerates all the essentials of our Canon, but adds the Apocalypse of St. Peter, which has been discovered in Egypt in our own times. This catalogue was probably the Canon of the Roman Church in the second century.

[1] *Evangelion* (Greek), *i.e.,* "good news."

[2] "It may be confidently asserted that these writers [Christians of the first half of the second century] did not know our Gospels, or, if they did know them, that they never mention or quote them, which comes to the same thing for us." (Michel Nicolas, *Études sur la Bible,* vol. ii, p. 5.)

6. It is supposed that the definitive Canon was formed of the collected writings which were read in the majority of the large churches, and considered in harmony with the average opinion of Christendom. There could, of course, have been no question in those days of a scientific criterion, based on the origin and history of these writings. "If it be true that the Church applied a certain critical judgment to the choice and acceptance of the sacred books, it was not the critical judgment of the modern historian, but an opinion inspired by faith and based upon the value of these writings from the point of view of faith." [1]

7. Matthew or Levi was, according to tradition, a publican or tax-gatherer who attached himself to Jesus. Mark is said to have been the secretary of Peter, whom he accompanied to Rome, and the founder of the Church of Alexandria. A companion of St. Paul, Luke, a physician of Antioch, wrote the Acts of the Apostles as a sequel to his Gospel. John the Evangelist, the son of Zebedee, was one of the twelve Apostles, the one to whom Jesus commended his mother from the Cross. After living at Ephesus, he was banished to Patmos, and there he is supposed to have written the Apocalypse in his old age.

Thus, if the tradition were well founded, we should possess the writings of two eye-witnesses of the life of Jesus, Matthew and John, and of two intimate friends of Peter and Paul. It matters little that the Gospels purport to be *according* to St. Matthew, *according* to St. Luke, &c.; the prologue to St. Luke's Gospel sufficiently shows that he claims to be the author, not the inspirer of his book.

8. The tradition of the Church is no longer tenable. Not one of the Gospels is the work of an eye-witness; we need only read them attentively to be convinced of this. It is true that certain verses seem to suggest the converse, and it is therefore necessary to examine them here. John xix, 35 (a soldier has pierced the side of Jesus with a spear): "And he that saw it bare record, and his record is true; and he knoweth that he saith true, that ye might believe." This means that the witness invoked is John, whom the Fourth

[1] Loisy, *Simples Réflexions*, p. 33.

Gospel calls "the disciple whom Jesus loved," and who was the only one of the Apostles present at the Passion. But this mode of expression is obviously inappropriate to the author of the book; it is an appeal to the testimony of another person; and the writer of the Gospel cannot have been an eye-witness of what he describes. The second passage is to be found at the end of the same Gospel, and is, indeed, an addition to the original text (xxi, 24): "This is the disciple which testifieth of these things, and wrote these things, and we know that his testimony is true. And there are also many other things which Jesus did, the which, if they should be written every one, I suppose that even the world itself could not contain the books that should be written." Here it is even more evident that a *compiler* is attesting the veracity of the disciple; for, "if this disciple had been known to all as the author of the Gospel, it would not have been necessary to affirm the fact."[1] Thus we find that these two texts prove the exact opposite of what they are supposed to demonstrate, and further suggest the presumption of a pious fraud on the part of the ultimate compiler.

9. In the narrative of the arrest of Jesus as related by St. Mark (xiv, 51, 52) we read of the flight of the disciples, and of a young man who followed Jesus, "having a linen cloth cast about his naked body; and the young men laid hold on him, and he left the linen cloth, and fled from them naked." It was long supposed that this young man was Mark himself, and this passage has been compared to an artist's signature hidden away in the corner of a picture. Were this the case, it would give immense authority to Mark's narrative, such as none of the Gospel texts possess. But the source of this episode is a prophecy by Amos (ii, 16): "And he that is courageous among the mighty *shall flee away naked in that day*." Here we have a detail, apparently characteristic, because it seems insignificant, which was inserted in the narrative to mark in the most puerile fashion the fulfilment of a prophecy. The same preoccupation caused the insertion of numerous episodes in our Gospels.

[1] Loisy, *Quatrième Evangile*, p. 250.

What confidence can we feel in texts which have been so tampered with?

10. The conclusion of liberal exegesis in this delicate matter has been formulated as follows by the Abbé Loisy: "To allege that the earliest testimony as to the origin of the Gospels is certain, precise, traditional and historical is to falsify its character entirely; it is, on the contrary, hypothetical, vague, legendary and partisan; it shows that at the period when the Gospels were brought forward to check the extravagances of Gnostic heresy, only the vaguest information existed as to their origin."[1]

11. Why are there only *four* canonical Gospels? "Just as," says St. Irenæus (*c.* 170), "there are four cardinal points." This reply cannot be taken seriously. There were a great many writings called Gospels. The Church finally adopted four, guaranteeing their inspiration and absolute veracity, no doubt because they were in favour in four very influential churches, Matthew at Jerusalem, Mark at Rome or at Alexandria, Luke at Antioch, John at Ephesus. When the Canon was constituted, these Gospels were so well known that it was not practicable to make an abstract from them in the shape of a single narrative, at the cost of destroying the sources. Such a single narrative—known as a *harmonised Gospel*—would have greatly facilitated the task of a Church embarrassed by four Gospels claiming to be inspired, which are contradictory and irreconcilable. If then we have four Canonical Gospels, and the inception of the Canon dates from A.D. 150, our Gospels are evidently earlier than this in date, a conclusion which does not, however, exclude the hypothesis of later modifications.

12. It is possible to fix the approximate date of our Gospels in the form in which they have come down to us. Matthew makes Jesus predict the destruction of Jerusalem (xxiv, 29-31), and as its sequel, the coming of the Son of Man in the clouds. This can only have been written a very short time before or after the catastrophe of A.D. 70, when it was still possible to believe in the speedy advent of Christ in glory, heralded by the great upheaval. In Luke (xxi,

[1] Loisy, *Quelques Réflexions*, p. 127.

9-24) the second coming (called *Parousia*, presence) is foretold for a later period. "These things must first come to pass," said Jesus, "but the end is not by-and-by." Here we are between A.D. 80 and 100, and nearer to the second than to the first of these dates. The parallel passage in Mark (chap. xiii) is valueless, for in it Jesus predicts the sufferings of the Apostles and the propagation of the Gospel among all nations; it is an obvious interpolation. But as the material in Mark was evidently used by Matthew, we may date it between A.D. 60 and 70. As to the Gospel of St. John, if it is by the same hand as the Apocalypse, which dates from A.D. 93, we may place it towards the end of the first, or the beginning of the second century; but it is probably somewhat later (A.D. 130).

13. The diffusion of our Gospels in Christian communities was a slow process. With the possible exception of Papias (*c.* 120), who speaks of a narrative by Mark, and a collection of sayings or oracles made by Matthew, no Christian writer of the first half of the second century quotes the Gospels or their reputed authors (§ 4). It is true that St. Justin (*c.* 150) mentions the Memoirs of the Apostles, but the extracts he gives from these are never textually identical with passages in our Gospels. Some of them come from unrecognised gospels, called apocryphal, others from unknown sources. The teaching of Jesus was still in a confused state, comprising those numerous narratives mentioned by Luke in his preamble, and a still more considerable body of oral tradition, which was transmitted by preaching. It is probable that our Evangelists acquired the authority faith has retained for them when the Church came into conflict with the Gnostic sects, which based their teaching upon books hardly less historical, but certainly much more extravagant than the Gospels.

14. The three Gospels of Matthew, Mark and Luke relate more or less the same facts in a similar order; they may be printed side by side in three columns;[1] this collation or synopsis of the three works has caused them to be known as

[1] See the convenient edition published by Chastand and Morel, *Concordance des Evangiles,* Neufchâtel, 1901 (with colours).

the *synoptical Gospels.* The Gospel of St. John does not lend itself to any comparative study of this sort, and must be examined by itself.

15. Here we are confronted with the most difficult question of Gospel exegesis. When the three synoptical writers relate the same facts, they do not usually describe them as taking place under the same circumstances. When they *do* agree, it is not in a general way, but often literally, in every detail of a series of long phrases. These documents must therefore have had a common source, or several common sources. But this well-spring cannot have been a lost Gospel, richer in details than those we possess, for in that case we should not find in one or the other of the three *lacunæ* and important variations in a narrative of the same event. There must have been several sources, which we must endeavour to trace. We have, to help us in this task, two very important evidences: Luke's preamble, and certain fragments by Papias, transcribed about 350 A.D. by Eusebius, Bishop of Cæsaræa. Papias' own work is lost.

16. This is Luke's exordium: "Forasmuch as many have taken in hand to set forth in order a declaration of those things which are most surely believed among us, even as they delivered them unto us, which from the beginning were eye-witnesses and ministers of the word; it seemed good to me also, having had perfect understanding of all things from the very first, to write unto thee in order, most excellent Theophilus,[1] that thou mightest know the certainty of those things wherein thou hast been instructed." This clearly means that when St. Luke wrote his Gospel, many evangelical narratives based on the testimony of the Apostles existed, but that they lacked co-ordination. Luke was therefore a compiler, working from written documents. If everything important in Matthew and Mark were to be found in Luke, we should suppose that he had referred to these two Gospels; but, on the contrary, certain essential episodes, such as the Massacre of the Innocents and the Flight into Egypt, are found only in Matthew, and a few

[1] The epithet *kratiste* applied by Luke to this unknown personage has suggested the idea that he was a converted Roman official.

others only in Mark, about an eighth part of whose Gospel belongs exclusively to himself. It is evident therefore that Luke cannot have known either *our* Gospel according to St. Matthew or *our* Gospel according to St. Mark. We now perceive that Luke was not an eye-witness, and that our Matthew and Mark are not the narratives of eye-witnesses, but are based upon records no longer in existence.

17. Let us now examine the texts of Papias, Bishop of Hierapolis in Asia about 120 A.D., who had known *presbyters* or *elders* said to have known the Apostles. "An elder said this: Mark, the mouthpiece of Peter, carefully wrote down all he could remember, but he did not write all that Jesus did and said in proper order, for he had not heard or followed the Lord; but at a later period, he had followed Peter, who gave instruction as occasion arose, but did not set forth the Lord's discourses [or oracles] in due order; Mark is therefore not to be blamed for having written down certain things from memory, for he was careful not to omit anything he had heard, and not to introduce any errors. . . . Matthew had written down the dominical oracles in Hebrew, and each one interpreted them as best he could."

In spite of the obvious mediocrity of the writer, these texts are of the utmost importance. They prove, in the first place, that the Mark referred to by the elder who gave this information to Papias was not *our* Mark, whose Gospel shows no lack of order, but merely one of the sources drawn upon by *our* Mark; and further, that *our* Matthew was not the original Matthew, which consisted of certain sacred texts [1] recorded in Hebrew, and in a somewhat obscure manner. There is no reason whatever to doubt the good faith of Papias' informant.

18. A careful comparative study of the synoptical writers authorises, I think, the following propositions, as to which, however, critics are not entirely agreed:

a. The passages common to Matthew and Luke, which are absent from Mark, are derived from a Greek translation

[1] I am inclined to believe, with an anonymous writer (1894), that Matthew compiled a series of Old Testament prophecies, supposed to be related to the Lord. See Rendel Harris, *Testimonies,* 1916, p. 131.

of the sayings of Jesus. This collection further included certain narrative passages serving to connect the sayings, but it did not include the Passion. It is designated by the letter Q (the initial of the German word *Quelle*, source).

b. *Our* Mark, the conclusion of which (xvi, 9-20) is an addition made at the end of the first century, and not to be found in the earliest manuscripts, is a compilation from two older texts; the first was perhaps written in Aramaic; the writer of the second was acquainted with Q; the writer of *our* Mark was acquainted with Matthew and even with Luke.

c. *Our* Matthew is based upon Q, a collection which was enlarged and recast several times, notably by the help of the second version of Mark.

d. *Our* Luke is perhaps a second and more complete edition, due to the same writer as the first, of a text owned by Marcion in A.D. 150. The Fathers of the Church (Tertullian, Epiphanius, &c.) accused Marcion of having mutilated the text of Luke, and pointed out various passages he had *abridged.* In reality, he seems to have possessed the original Luke, compiled from a revised edition of Q, an ancient copy of Mark, and perhaps Paul's First Epistle to the Corinthians, together with other lost documents. *Our* Luke attests a knowledge of Josephus' *Antiquities,* published A.D. 93. It is notable that entire passages given by Matthew, but not by Mark (*e.g.,* xvii, 24; xx, 1-16) are not to be found in Luke, and that not a single discourse in Matthew is reproduced in Luke.

e. The Church has always called Matthew the First Gospel, and Mark the Second Gospel. As a fact, the basis of Mark is earlier than *our* Matthew, but the basis of Matthew may be earlier than *our* Mark.

f. The Fourth Gospel, called that of St. John, is the work of a Hellenistic Jew, inspired by Philo of Alexandria. He is rather a mystic theologian than a historian. Nevertheless, an unprejudiced reader understands that he pretends to write history, and that he does so not ignoring the synoptical gospels, but disbelieving in much that they say. The Egyptian Jew Cerinthus, an enemy of St. Paul, was thought by some to be the author of the Fourth Gospel, in which traces of recasting and remodelling have been detected.

19. Those who are disquieted by the discrepancies between the three synoptical writers, and of their three Gospels with that of John, are generally assured that the "Gospels complete each other." This is not true. Far from completing, they contradict each other, and when they do not contradict, they repeat each other. The Christ of Mark is, however, compatible with the Christ of Matthew and Luke; but the Christ of John is a totally different person. "If there is one thing above others that is obvious, but as to which the most powerful of theological interests has caused a deliberate or unconscious blindness, it is the profound, the irreducible incompatibility of the Synoptical Gospels and the Fourth Gospel. If Jesus spoke and acted as he is said to have spoken and acted in the first three Gospels, he did not speak and act as he is reported to have done in the fourth."[1] It is only necessary to have an open mind, and to be able to read, to convince ourselves of this.

20. Broadly speaking, our Gospels tell us what different Christian communities believed concerning Jesus between the years 70 and 100 A.D. They reflect a legendary and expository labour carried on for at least forty years in the bosom of the community.[2] As John has little historic value and Luke comes to us at third hand, there remain the sources of Mark and of Matthew, notably Q, and the basis of Mark. Thus all that may be sound in these two documents is derived from the last two sources, of whose authority we have no guarantee. It is, indeed, certain that the basis of Mark cannot go back to Peter, an eye-witness, for all that relates to Peter in Mark is entirely vague. As to the sayings in Q, it is obvious that no one had transcribed them at the moment; at most we can only see in them an echo of the words that the disciples of Jesus repeated long after his death, and that more skilful men, influenced by the preaching of

[1] Loisy, *Quelques Lettres* (1908), p. 130.

[2] The Gospel was preached before it was written. Preaching to the Jews, the followers of Jesus used a *Book of Testimonies* from the Old Testament, which underlies the so-called "fulfilled prophecies" in our Gospels; preaching to the Gentiles, they used the *Collection of the Sayings of Jesus* (Rendel Harris, *Testimonies*, 1916, p. 54).

St. Paul, arranged, completed and transcribed. To speak of the authenticity of the Sermon on the Mount (the mountain itself being a fiction, intended to serve as a pendant to Sinaï), is hardly consistent with serious criticism. Nay, more; there are words such as those Jesus is supposed to have uttered during the slumber of the Apostles (Matt. xxvi, 39; Mark xiv, 35; Luke xxii, 42), of which it may safely be said that they were neither heard nor put on record by any one. "I should not believe in the Gospel," wrote St. Augustine, "if I had not the authority of the Church for so doing."[1] The situation is unchanged, although science has defined it with singular emphasis. The Gospels, stripped of the authority of the Church, are documents which cannot be utilised for a history of the real life of Jesus. They can and should only serve to teach us what the primitive churches thought of him, and to acquaint us with the origin of the immense influence those opinions exercised on the human race.

∴

21. Collation of our Gospels, and perception of the successive strata which compose them prove that even the legend of Jesus as taught by the Church is not supported in all its details by the texts adduced. The miraculous birth is not mentioned in Mark; it seems to have been deliberately ignored by John, who accepts the Philonian doctrine of the incarnation of the Word, "the first-born God, the second God, the intercessor between God and man,"[2] making, however, an essential addition of his own by identifying this "Word" with the Messiah. In Matthew and in Luke the miraculous birth is recorded with conflicting details. Jesus himself never alludes to it, and his parents do not understand him, when they find him in the Temple and he speaks of his "Father's business" (Luke ii, 50). The fact that Matthew and Luke give two genealogies (irreconcilable one with

[1] St. Augustine, against the epistle entitled: *Of the Foundation*, § 5 (ed. Vives, vol. xxv, p. 435): *Ego vero Evangelio non crederem, nisi me catholicæ ecclesiæ commoveret auctoritas. . . . Ego me ad eos teneam, quibus præcipientibus Evangelio credidi.*

[2] Expressions used by Philo.

another), which trace the descent of Jesus from King David through Joseph, is a sufficient evidence that the idea of the miraculous birth was introduced rather late into the tradition. These genealogies, and no doubt others no longer extant, were composed to confirm the Jewish belief that the Messiah would be of the family of David; the story of the miraculous birth, frequent in the legends of paganism, was, in its turn, introduced when the idea of the divinity of Jesus had become familiar.

22. The Gospels speak with great simplicity of the brothers and sisters of Jesus. According to Matthew (i, 25), he was the eldest of the family. The notion that these brothers and sisters were cousins or children of Joseph by a former marriage is a mere theological subtlety. "Belief in the virginity of Mary has forced ecclesiastical writers to explain or rather to eliminate the relationship."[1]

23. The idea that Jesus was the Messiah and that he was God is clearly formulated in the fourth Gospel, but in the first three Gospels it appears in embryo only. The essential feature of the preaching of Jesus in the Gospels is the announcement of the reign of God, the speedy coming of which is indicated (Matt. xvi, 28; Mark ix, 1; Luke ix, 27). Jesus calls himself the Son of Man, which in Hebrew is synonymous with man, and Son of God, which means inspired by God. He forbids his disciples to call him Messiah (Matt. xvi, 20), and he reproves the scribes for teaching that the Messiah would be a descendant of David (Mark xii, 35), a proof that the Davidic affiliation is no less an excrescence than the supernatural affiliation. In the speech ascribed to St. Peter in the Acts (ii, 22) Jesus is described as a divine man whom God has raised from the dead. Finally, there is no trace of the Jews having accused Jesus of claiming to be God. "It is only in the Gospel of John that the sayings and the acts of Jesus tend to prove his supernatural mission, his celestial origin and his divinity. This peculiarity indicates the theological and non-historic character of the Fourth Gospel."[2]

[1] Loisy, *Quelques Lettres,* p. 155.
[2] Loisy, *Réflexions,* p. 69.

24. Jesus did not institute Peter the head of his Church, he did not "found the Papacy." The passage in Matthew (xvi, 18): "Thou art Peter and upon this rock I will build my Church . . . and I will give unto thee the keys of the kingdom of heaven," &c. is obviously an interpolation, made at a period when a Church separated from the Synagogue already existed. In the parallel passages in Mark (viii, 27-32) and in Luke (ix, 18-22) there is not a word of the primacy of Peter, a detail Mark, the reputed disciple of Peter, could hardly have omitted if he had known of it. The interpolation is posterior to the compilation of Luke's Gospel.

25. Jesus taught no dogma of any sort, nor anything resembling the sacraments of the Church. Himself baptized by St. John, he baptized no one. The famous words: "This is my body, this is my blood," do not belong to the primitive tradition touching the last Sacrament. "Jesus simply gave bread and wine to his disciples, telling them that he would not eat and drink with them again, until they were together in the kingdom of heaven."[1] The doctrine of sin and justification is also absent from the teaching of Christ in the Gospels.[2] The idea of redemption appears only in the passages interpolated under the influence of St. Paul's preaching.

26. The miracles attributed to Jesus by evangelical tradition are exorcisms (casting out devils), or allegories (the multiplication of the loaves and fishes, the transformation of water into wine at the marriage-feast of Cana). The most unequivocal of the miracles, the resurrection of Lazarus, whose body was already decomposed, is itself allegorical; and besides, it is only recorded in the fourth Gospel. If this had been an actual fact, or even a fact embellished and transformed by ancient tradition, it would be inexplicable that the Synoptic Writers make no reference to it.

27. The miracle of Christ's resurrection is related by the Synoptic Writers with irreconcilable discrepancies. The discovery of the empty tomb is the less credible in that Jesus,

[1] Loisy, *Réflexions,* p. 90.
[2] Loisy, *Evangile et Eglise,* p. 199.

once put to death, would have been thrown by the Roman soldiers into the common grave of malefactors. The end of Mark's Gospel (xvi, 9-20) is, as we have seen (p. 236), a later addition, which is not found in the best manuscripts. "The tradition followed by the author of the first Gospel is that of the authentic Mark, according to which the principal appearances took place in Galilee; the appearances in Jerusalem on the day of the Resurrection notified by Luke and John are simply ignored."[1] The Abbé Loisy went so far as to say that the author of the Third Gospel tampered with the testimony of Mark (corroborated by Matthew), touching the appearances of Jesus in Galilee[2] in order to bring the disciples together on the day of the Resurrection and to keep them at Jerusalem—until the Feast of Pentecost. Even in the revised form in which our texts have come down to us, it is evident that if the Resurrection of Jesus was accepted by the early Christian communities and St. Paul, it was known to them as a pious belief and not as an historic fact.

28. Is it even possible to extract the elements of a biography of Jesus from the Gospels? It is contrary to every sound method to compose, as Renan did, a life of Jesus, eliminating the marvellous elements of the Gospel story. It is no more possible to make real history with myths than to make bread with the pollen of flowers. The very little we know concerning the historic Jesus comes from a quite different source, and though underlying the legend of Christ, is more contradicted than confirmed by it. Obvious interests, both religious and political, have been at work to distort the truth.

29. The earthly existence of Jesus does not seem to have been questioned in ancient times, though very little was known about him outside the Church; even there, the chronology of his life and death was most uncertain. According to Luke, Jesus was only six months younger than John the Baptist; but many works of early Christian art, describing the Baptism in the Jordan, depict Jesus as a child and John

[1] Loisy, *Quelques Lettres,* p. 226.
[2] *Ibid.,* p. 190.

as an elderly man. Matthew places his birth in the reign of Herod, that is to say, at latest in the year 4 B.C. Luke dates it at the time of a census which took place ten years after, in 6 A.D. Luke makes the ministry of Jesus last only a year and a half, whereas, according to John, it lasted three and a half years. Luke recounts an episode of the boyhood of Jesus, whereas the other Evangelists know nothing of this period of his life. Luke says that Jesus was thirty in the fifteenth year of the reign of Tiberius, 29 A.D., the year to which he assigns the baptism of Jesus by St. John; but the fourth Gospel makes the Jews say to Jesus: "Thou are not yet fifty years old," from which certain early churches inferred that he was about forty-nine at his death; but, in that case, if he was born in 4 B.C., he must have died A.D. 45, not under Tiberius, but under Claudius, and indeed one of the reports attributed by the Christians to Pilatus is addressed to Claudius. The founder of the library in Jerusalem, about 210, even contended that Jesus had died in 58 under Nero! Finally, there is a very important passage in Eusebius (*Eccles. Hist.*, ix, 5), which gives a quite different and earlier date. He reports that the pagans had concocted "acts of Pilatus and of our Saviour full of blasphemies" and that Emperor Maximinus Daïa, about 311, had ordered those forgeries to be sent throughout the East, placarded in the towns and villages, read and taught by schoolmasters to the children. Eusebius, unfortunately, refused to publish that document, or it was suppressed from his text. He had mentioned it in an earlier part of his work (i, 9) with the following words: "So we can clearly recognize the forgery of those who recently published the Acts against our Saviour, because their chronology is wrong. Those events are said to have happened in the first Consulate of Tiberius and seventh year of his reign (21 A.D.). Now, at that time, Pilatus had not yet arrived in Judæa, *at least if we may trust Josephus*, according to whom Pilatus became procurator in the twelfth year of Tiberius." So Eusebius has no disproof of his own; he opposed his text of Josephus (which, as we know, had been already tampered with) to an official publication, taken from the imperial archives, no doubt the very report sent to Tiberius by Pilatus, which put the death of Christ in 21 A.D. The many forged reports attributed to Pilate by Christians and which we possess were made to counteract the publication of Maximinus, which may still some day be discovered in Egypt. The later date adopted by the Church was perhaps devised to harmonise with the total eclipse of the sun as recorded by the Gospel narrative (Mark xv, 33).

30. A crude Jewish legend, already familiar to the pagan philosopher Celsus (173 A.D.), made Jesus the son of a Roman soldier; another one stated that he was the son of a rabbi who fled to Alexandria and, on his return to Palestine, founded a sect of apostate Jews—about 70 B.C.! If, as we may suppose, there was some serious information in Jewish documents, the medieval censor, enlightened by converted Jews, must have suppressed it.

31. The Jewish philosopher Philo, the contemporary of Jesus in Alexandria, never mentioned him, nor any Messianic agitator, perhaps for fear of displeasing the Romans. The same may have been the case with the Jewish historian Justus of Tiberias, whose silence about Jesus was attributed by Photius (*c.* 850 A.D.) to "malevolence"; but it may be also that the text read by Photius had been curtailed by the Christian censorship, a very early and exacting institution. Of Josephus and his important testimonies I will speak hereafter. The famous passage in the *Annals* of Tacitus (xv, 44), the authenticity of which has been absurdly questioned, runs thus: "The emperor [Nero] inflicted cruel tortures on men hated for their crimes, called by the vulgar *Christians.* Christ, from whom they took their name, had been put to death under Tiberius by the procurator Pontius Pilatus. Repressed for a time, this detestable superstition broke out again, not only in Judæa, the fount of the evil, but at Rome, whither all irregularities and infamies tend to gravitate." This was written about 117 A.D. A few years earlier, Tacitus' friend, the younger Pliny, had met with Christians in Bithynia (see chap. ix, § 4) and may have awakened the interest of Tacitus in that sect.

32. Suetonius, another friend of the younger Pliny, de-

scribing in 120 A.D. events of the year 50, says that the emperor Claudius banished the (or *certain*) Jews from Rome because they continued to breed disorder at the instigation of a Messiah (*impulsore Christo*). The import of that passage has only been realised thanks to the publication (1920) of a letter written in 41 A.D. by Claudius, preserved on a papyrus in the British Museum. Greeks and Jews had been coming to blows in Alexandria. Claudius bids them keep the peace and be mutually tolerant. Then, suddenly, as if flying into a passion, he upbraids the Jews: "Do not introduce or invite Jews who sail down to Alexandria from Syria or Egypt, thus compelling me to conceive the greater suspicion; otherwise I will by all means take vengeance on you as fomenting a general plague for the whole world." I submitted (1924) that such an outburst was intelligible only if Claudius had heard from his Jewish friends in Rome, especially from King Agrippa, that the Messianic agitation, both anti-Roman and anti-social, was brooding mischief in the East and even in Rome. A few years later, as the agitation continued and gained ground, Claudius banished from Rome not *all* the Jews, but those who took part in the disturbance.

Claudius' words are probably alluded to in *Acts* (xxiv, 5) where Tertullus accuses St. Paul: "We have found this man a pestilent fellow and a mover of sedition among all the Jews throughout the world." The imperial letter must have been widely circulated and served as a warning to the Messianic Jews.

33. Official documents about Jesus are never quoted by Christian writers; but Tertullian (*c.* 197) gives this incredible story, which occurs again in Eusebius, Orosius and Gregory of Tours: "Tiberius, having received intelligence from Palestine of events which had clearly shown the truth of Christ's divinity, brought the matter before the Senate, with his own decision in favour of Christ. The Senate, because it had not given the approval itself, rejected the proposal. Tiberius held to his opinion, threatening wrath against all accusers of the Christians." (*Apologia* 5). This is akin in spirit to the forged reports of Pilatus, wherein the innocence of Jesus is proclaimed and the responsibility of his

death cast on the Jews. But Tertullian was too honest to invent it. Augustus had decided that no reports of sittings of the Senate should be published. Now, Suetonius (*Tib.* 31) mentions a case in which the emperor's opinion was defeated. This may have given rise, in Christian circles at Rome about 100 A.D., to the legend repeated by Tertullian, the more so as the punishment of Jesus had certainly been reported by Pilate to Tiberius and by the emperor to the Senate, according to the then established custom.

34. Bishop Ignatius of Antioch, in a very obscure phrase, wrote, about 110 A.D., against certain people who declared: "What we do not find in the [Roman?] archives, we cannot accept in the Gospel." This seems to be the first allusion to critical research, about which we regret to know nothing more.

35. A very old Christian sect, that of the Docetes, contended that Jesus had been but a phantom, that he had only assumed the semblance of a body—and this, exclaimed St. Jerome, when the blood of Jesus was not yet dry in Judæa! The great antiquity of the sect is confirmed by two letters attributed to St. John, which are partly directed against Docetism, and perhaps also by the passage in the fourth Gospel (xx, 24) concerning the unbelief of St. Thomas. Works by Docetes have not come down to us, and we have no adequate knowledge of their tenets. One thing, however, is ertain: the so-called extreme Docetes denied the Crucifixion. Irenæus (*c.* 180 A.D.) says that the heretic Basilides (*c.* 125) related the Crucifixion as follows: "Simon of Cyrene was crucified by mistake and Jesus himself took the form of Simon and stood by and laughed at the executioners." Foolish as that may be, the Manichæans maintained it, and the formula of abjuration which they were invited to sign ran thus: "I anathematize those who say that our Lord only suffered in appearance, and that there was a man on the cross and another one at a distance who laughed because the former suffered in his place." Indeed, several apocryphal writings of early Christianity are tainted with the same belief, which may have not been unknown to the author of the second Gospel (xv, 21): "And they compel

one Simon a Cyrenian, who passed by, coming out of the country, *the father of Alexander and Rufus*, to bear his cross." This seems to be an appeal to two witnesses who said (in Rome?) that Simon had carried the cross, but not that he had been crucified instead of Jesus, as maintained by Basilides and no doubt others before him.

36. The uncertainty and legendary character of the Christian tradition concerning Jesus does not warrant, however, an expression of radical disbelief. The first trace of such extreme criticism appeared in Lord Bolingbroke's free-thinking circle (*c.* 1730). Voltaire censured it, but not so Volney and Dupuis, two French scholars of the latter part of the eighteenth century, who considered the Christ of history as a solar myth. This explains why Napoleon, meeting Wieland in 1808, asked him if he believed in the existence of Jesus. The same scepticism was put forward, but on so-called historical grounds, by the German critic Bruno Bauer (1842), who attributed the Gospel story to *one* forger, and later on, as a result of comparative mythology and folklore, by many writers, Robertson, Benj. Smith, Drews, Couchoud, etc. However, the best liberal theologians of our age never consented to go so far, though admitting that, except the death of Jesus, there was much more legend than history in the Gospel narrative.

The rediscovery (1906, 1925) of what I believe to be part of the authentic testimony of Josephus about Jesus, at once saves in part the traditional story and discards it as a whole. Here I must enter into some detail.

37. Flavius Josephus, a Hellenised Jew, born in Jerusalem (*c.* 37-97 A.D.), first a foe, later a friend and flatterer of the Romans, was the author of two great works in Greek which have come down to us: the *History of the Jewish War* (73 A.D.) and the *Jewish Antiquities* (93 A.D.). In the former, though it begins with the capture of Jerusalem in 170 B.C., there is no mention of Jesus; in the latter (xviii, 3, 3) occur the following lines, also quoted by Eusebius (*Eccl. Hist.*, i, 11):

"At this time appeared Jesus, a wise man, if indeed he is to be called a man. For he accomplished marvellous things, was the master of men who accept truth gladly, and drew many Jews and also many Greeks after him. This man was the Christ. He was denounced by the elders of our nation to Pilatus, who condemned him to be crucified; but those who had loved him from the beginning did not cease to revere him; for he appeared on the third day, risen from the dead, as the holy prophets and a thousand other marvels connected with him had foretold. And the sect which received the name of Christians from him still exists."

If the Jew Josephus had written this, he would have been a Christian; the apocryphal character of those lines is obvious. But are they a complete forgery, or has the original text only been abridged and much tampered with? The latter opinion is the safer one, and that for the following reasons.

38. Josephus says himself that he began by writing the *History of the Jewish War* in his native language and sent it to the Jews living further north, in Parthia, Adiabene and Mesopotamia. That work is lost. Now, in 1906, attention was directed to a Slavonic (Old Russian) translation of the *War*, very different from the Greek work and *not* a translation of the same. An Austrian scholar, Robert Eisler, speaking before a congress of historians in 1925, suggested the following hypothesis on that subject:

a) We possess, in Slavonic, the equivalent of a first edition of Josephus' work, written for Jews, not for Romans, translated into Slavonic about the thirteenth century.

b) The Slavonic translators and copyists, who were Christians, added to the original many phrases taken from the Gospels and the Apocrypha, and deleted a great many others. The latter cannot be restored, but the former may easily be brushed aside.

c) If we neglect those obvious interpolations, there remain several passages of high import, in which Jesus appears as a worker of miracles, surrounded by a devoted mass of Jews who oblige him, as the long expected Messiah, to take their lead against the Romans. The revolt is put down by Pilatus and the leader crucified. No Christian interpolator of Josephus could have presented the facts in that light, but the Jew Josephus may well have done so. His father had held high priestly office and may have been an eye-witness; but Josephus himself, an intimate of Vespasian and Titus, had access to the Roman archives and may have borrowed his story, of which we only possess a small part, from the report of Pilatus to Tiberius.

39. I now give a free translation of the more important lines, omitting, of course, the interpolations. The reader will remember that they occur in the Slavonic text of the *War*, while the parallel and much altered passage about Jesus, as quoted above, belongs to the later work on *Jewish Antiquities*.

Jew. War, II, 9, 3: "At this time appeared a man, if indeed I may call him so, because, though human in form, he accomplished things more than human, thanks to some invisible power [Jesus not named; something must have been said about his parents and possibly his physical appearance, but that was erased]. Some thought that he was our first legislator [Moses] come to life again, others that he had been sent by God. For my part, knowing what I do, I would not say that, for he transgressed our Law on many points and did not observe the Sabbath according to the rules of our ancestors. But he did nothing shameful nor wicked, acting only through [magic] words. Many people followed him and accepted his teachings; many were moved by the hope that he would free the Jews from the Roman yoke. His usual abode was on the Mount of Olives, where he healed the sick. About 150 followers and a great many more poor people gathered around him. Seeing the power of his words, they exhorted him to enter the town, kill the Roman soldiers and Pilatus, and assume authority. But when the foremost Jews heard of that, they said to the High Priest: 'We are really too weak to fight the Romans. But as the danger is also one for us, we must inform Pilatus. If he learns what is going on from another source he will bespoil or kill us, and disperse our children.' Pilatus, warned by those Jews, sent soldiers who killed many of the mob and arrested the worker of cures. Pilatus had him tried and crucified according with [Roman] custom."

Jew. War, II, 11, 6: "At this time [about 46 A.D.] many people showed their allegiance to the miracle-monger mentioned above; they said that this rabbi was still alive, though he had died, and that he would free them from servitude. A number of people listened to them; they all belonged to the class of artisans, such as cobblers and the like. The governor consulted with the scribes and, fearing that the movement would spread, sent some of those people to the emperor, others to Antioch for judgement, others to the places they came from."

Jew. War, VI, 2, 3: "Above those three inscriptions [on a platform leading to the Temple] was a fourth one written in Hebrew, to the effect that: *Jesus has not been King, but was crucified, because he announced that the town and the Temple would be destroyed.*"[1]

Jew. War, VI, 5, 4: "[An oracle having foretold that a man in this country would rise to supreme power] some believed that it meant Herodes, others the crucified miracle-monger [Jesus], others Vespasian."[2]

40. The essential result to be gathered from those new texts is that Jesus was put (perhaps unwillingly) at the head of an insurrection against Roman rule, the details of which Josephus probably related, but were not allowed to stand. A stray mention of that has remained in the second Gospel (xv, 7): "One named Barabbas, bound with them *that had made insurrection,* who had committed murder in *the* insurrection." But our Gospels have studiously avoided any mention of a political disturbance, in order not to alienate Roman opinion. Jesus is made to say: "Render to Cæsar the things that are Cæsar's" (Mark xii, 17) and "My Kingdom is not of this world" (John xviii, 36). Such events as the triumphant entry of Jesus and his followers into Jerusalem, the casting out of the dealers and overthrowing the tables of the moneychangers, are not recorded as revolutionary, but as purely religious acts, which is obviously impossible; what Roman governor would have allowed such breaches of the peace? In fact, the rising was a matter of some consequence; a late writer, John of Antioch, who perhaps worked from an uncensored text of Josephus, speaks of a mob of Jews invading Jerusalem and shouting down the emperor. The upheaval could only be suppressed during the night.[3]

41. Those who believed—not, as we have seen, an undisputed belief—that Jesus had been crucified, must needs

[1] Compare Matthew, xxiv, 2: "There shall not be left here one stone upon another, that shall not be thrown down."

[2] See Thackeray's *Josephus,* in the *Loeb Classical Library,* vol. iii, p. 648 foll.

[3] *Fragmenta Historicorum græcorum,* vol. iv., p. 571, 81.

have remembered the passage in Scripture where that punishment, unknown to the Jews, but not so to the Persians and Phœnicians, is alluded to. I quote the following verses from Psalm 22; the first one was said, in the Gospel narrative, to have been uttered by Jesus himself on the cross:

"My God, my God, why hast thou forsaken me?

"All they that see me, laugh me to scorn, saying:

" 'He trusted to the Lord that he would deliver him; let Him deliver him!'

"The assembly of the wicked have compassed me; *they pierced my hands and my feet.*

"They part my garments among them and cast lots upon my vesture."

"Piercing the hands and the feet" means crucifying, as all the Fathers have agreed since Justin (*c.* 150 A.D.). What does that mean in the Psalm? Maybe a reference to some legend of which we are ignorant, but of which a sort of echo lingers in the strange words of Plato's *Republic* (ii, 362 A): "The just man will be scourged, tormented, fettered . . . and lastly, having suffered all manners of evils, will be crucified."

42. So it appears that Psalm 22 became the fountainhead of the Christian legend, the initial cause of the search for passages in the Jewish scriptures which might apply to, and more often complete, the little that was known about the life and teaching of Christ. Jesus having quoted the first verse of Psalm 22 on the cross, the parting of his vestments among the Roman soldiers became an essential feature of the tale. But the passages in Isaiah, describing the woes of the Righteous Servant, were also appealed to. The Righteous Servant (l, 6) gave his back to the smiters; he did not hide his face from shame and spitting; he is a man of sorrows (liii, 3-12), bearing our griefs, bruised for our iniquities, brought as a lamb to the slaughter, numbered with the transgressors, cut off out of the land of the living. "And he made his grave with the wicked and with the rich in his death."[1] All those sayings have been considered during long centuries, even by men of genius like Pascal, as "proph-

[1] *Cf.* Matthew xxvii, 57.

ecies fulfilled," till it occurred to critics that a supposed prophecy may sufficiently explain the invention of an episode and dispose of its historical character.

43. Indeed, many incidents in the life of Jesus are related in the Gospels with the more or less explicit comment that they were fulfilments of prophecy, every word in the Jewish Scriptures being considered as prophetic because emanating from God. The text quoted in the Gospels is the Greek version of the Old Testament, the mistakes of which are accepted. Jesus was born of a "virgin" because Isaiah was supposed to have said that a virgin would conceive; in the Hebrew text, he says "a woman," the wife of some Jewish king or prophet. Jesus is said to be "of Nazareth" because a prophet foretold that the Messiah should be a Nazarene (Matt. ii, 23) ; but Isaiah, who is invoked in this connection, said nothing of the sort. Jesus was born at Bethlehem because Micah (v, 2) had foretold that the Messiah would come from that place. He was taken by his parents into Egypt because Hosea wrote: "Out of Egypt have I called my son." The first preachers of Christianity did not carry about the bulky manuscripts of the Jewish Bible, but confided in extracts or *testimonies*, *i.e.*, reputed prophetic passages, which, as we now know, were full of blunders. All the coincidences which seemed at a time not only to attest the veracity of the Gospel narrative, but the superhuman character of the facts set forth in it, now furnish irrefragable proof of their uncertainty and the pious frauds underlying them.

44. A further interesting example of a legend thus concocted is the story of the traitor apostle. Judas of Karioth is said to have shown his Master to the soldiers who came to arrest him. After the death of Jesus, remorseful Judas would not keep the money he had received for his black deed and hurled it into the sanctuary; the priests used it to purchase the potter's field, henceforth called *Acedama*, the field of blood. According to Acts, Judas bought that field himself and died there a miserable death. Now, there are verses in the Psalms (xli, 9; lv, 12) mentioning the ill-treatment of the Righteous One by a "familiar friend"; there is a passage in Zechariah (xi, 12, 13): "So they weighed for my

price thirty pieces of silver, and the Lord said to me: Cast it unto the potter. . . . And I took the thirty pieces of silver and cast them to the potter in the house of the Lord." Whatever that may mean, it is the origin of the legend, as proved by Acts i, 16: "This Scripture must needs have been fulfilled, which the Holy Ghost by the mouth of David spake before concerning Judas, which was guide to them that took Jesus." So the story of Judas is founded on the interpretation of obscure texts, not on tradition.

45. A tale in the formation of which such elements have been at play, where the only fact known from another source —the anti-Roman rebellion—has been purposely concealed, is *not* history, though some historical details, very difficult to disentangle, may have survived from an earlier narrative, and though the general character of Jesus' sermons may have been preserved in the preaching of his followers. The founder of Gospel criticism, the German Reimarus (*d.* 1768) was quite right to assert that the essence of the Christian movement was the political ideal of Messianism: "Away with the Romans! Judæa to God and to the Jews!" After Jesus' death, his triumphant return was expected from day to day to fulfil his promises. But as the Lord did not return and the Roman power, even before the fall of Jerusalem, seemed invincible, the hope of a political redemption was abandoned: Jesus had come and had suffered to redeem mankind not from the Roman yoke, but from sin. That idea had been anticipated by Greek and Asiatic mysteries; it was already familiar to the Gentiles. It now assumed a quite different aspect, taking as a basis the Jewish Scriptures, considered as the very words of God, and preaching a moral favorable to the poor and oppressed, very different in spirit from that of the Roman law.

46. Numerous passages in the Gospels, culled from the parables and sayings attributed to the Lord, impress a quite different lesson from that of kindness, charity, non-resistance to evil and freedom from narrow ritualism; there are indeed many contradictory statements. But, as a whole, the teaching of benevolence, patience, justice, chastity and other virtues is the more conspicuous, in harmony with the

beauty, now idyllic, now tragic of the legend. It is true that Christian morality is no more original than is any other morality, religious or secular; it is that of the contemporary Jewish schoolmen, of a Hillel or a Gamaliel; but in the Gospels it appears divested of all scholasticism and ritualistic pedantry, robust and simple as befits a doctrine setting forth to conquer the world. It is the morality of the school without a school, purified and distilled in ardent souls, with all the charm and all the persuasive force of popular conceptions. It is not *social*, it neglects the duties of man to the city, because it invites to perfection, to individual purity; but it prepares man to carry out his social duties by condemning hatred and violence, and enjoining fraternity. It is absurd to say that this morality is against nature; so is kindness. But Christian morality was only the ideal rule of conduct of Christendom, a rule always imperfectly observed indeed. It was reserved for St. Paul to superimpose on these mild ethics the harsh doctrine of original sin, redemption and grace, which gave birth to eighteen centuries of arid disputation and still weighs like a nightmare on humanity.

. . .

47. The so-called Apocryphal Gospels are of two kinds; the one class, described as dogmatic, relates the whole life of Jesus, after the manner of the Synoptists; the others, known as legendary, deal only with episodes. The former, which the Fathers of the Church in the third century frequently quote as if they were of equal authority with the canonical writings, were destroyed, no doubt deliberately, because they belonged to schismatic sects. But in 1886 a portion of the Gospel of St. Peter, comprising the Passion and Resurrection, was found in a tomb in Egypt. This Gospel was probably identical with that of the Egyptians, which the Fathers quoted, and of which they have preserved extracts; it was no doubt written in Egypt, probably at Babylon (ancient Cairo). We have also some fragments of the Gospel according to the Hebrews, the loss of which is especially to be regretted, because it was written for the Judæo-Christian communities of Palestine. The episode of Jesus

and the woman taken in adultery, which was inserted in St. John's Gospel in the fourth century, was originally in this Gospel. This Gospel should be distinguished from that of the Ebionites (*Ebionim*, the poor), a Jewish sect anterior to Christianity, which developed a gnostic doctrine. A contemporary of St. John, Cerinthus, of whom unfortunately we know hardly anything, was supposed to be the author of this Gospel; from a very early period the Gospel of St. John was attributed to him; it was supposed to be a revised version of the Cerinthian Gospel.

48. The legendary Gospels which have come down to us are expurgated gnostic writings; all that has been left in them are absurdities which are inoffensive to dogma, though singularly repugnant to taste. In the Gospel of the Childhood, or of St. Thomas, Jesus is a malicious and vindictive little demon; the miracles of the apocryphal Gospels are worthy of the *Arabian Nights*. The result of the toleration shown by the Church for these legends was that they were widely circulated and translated into every language; literature and art found inspiration in them. Many popular incidents of Gospel history have no authority but that of the apocryphal writers; such are the story of Joachim and Anna, the parents of the Virgin, that of her marriage, of the birth of Jesus in a cave, where he was worshipped by an ox and an ass, of the descent of Jesus into hell,[1] and of the death or trance of the Virgin.

49. In addition to these texts we have a considerable collection of *sayings* (in Greek *logia*) attributed to Jesus, some reported by writers of the first century, others forming little collections which have been discovered in Egypt in our own days. The grains of gold in this Gospel dust are rare; there is indeed one very long sentence attributed to Jesus and recorded by Papias, which is nothing but an absurdity from beginning to end. Our Evangelists made a very happy choice among the confused elements of tradition; to appreciate their taste, we have only to read the apocryphal Gospels.

[1] The descent into hell has been one of the articles of Christian dogma since the Council of Nicæa (A.D. 325).

50. The Acts of the Apostles are by the same author as our third Gospel; they must have been written about 95 A.D. This compilation contains some precious information concerning a portion of St. Paul's journeys, taken apparently from an authentic journal of Luke's; these elements are distinguished from the rest by the use of the word "we" in the narrative. The remainder is very unequal in value, and cannot be attributed to a disciple of Paul's, whose Epistles and whose individual doctrine it completely ignores. The rivalry of Peter and Paul is intentionally modified, in a spirit of conciliation; but this was not the only aim of the writer. Christianity having then divorced from Judaism which, according to Roman law, was a *religio licita*, a tolerated creed, the Acts try to show that Christianity is nothing but a purer form of Judaism and record the benevolence with which the Roman authorities, in spite of Jewish hostility, treated the early Christians. The story circulated about Tiberius (§ 33) answered the same object, an essential requisite to the progress of Christian propaganda.

51. We have further a whole collection of apocryphal Acts of various Apostles, Peter, Paul, Thomas, John, Andrew, and Philip. They are romances full of marvels, amusing enough to read, in which certain precise details attest a good knowledge of history and geography. These texts, which have come down to us in different languages, seem to have been derived from expurgated editions of gnostic works. The Church permitted them to be read on the same terms as the apocryphal Gospels, but merely as a matter of curiosity.

The most attractive of these stories is that of Thekla. This young girl, a member of a good family at Iconium, was converted by the teaching of Paul, left her family, braved all sorts of dangers, and ended by successfully preaching Christianity at Iconium and Seleucia. Tertullian tells us (*c.* 200) that this story was fabricated by an elder of Asia Minor, who, when convicted of the fraud, confessed that he had perpetrated it "for love of St. Paul."[1] However, that confession of a pious fraud is rather suspicious; maybe

[1] Tertullian, *De Baptismo,* 17.

it was invented to discredit a little work embodying very ancient elements, but where the Church was scandalized by the story of a girl who freely preached and baptized.

52. The Canon of the Church accepts fourteen Epistles of St. Paul, one to the Romans, two to the Corinthians, one to the Galatians, the Ephesians, the Philippians, the Colossians, two to the Thessalonians and Timothy, one to Titus, one to Philemon, one to the Hebrews. A school of criticism which sprang up in Holland about 1885 denies the authenticity of these writings *en bloc*. Its principal argument is that in the communities Paul is supposed to address, a complexity and intensity of religious life is implied which is inadmissible at the period. But what do we know of the primitive history of these communities? All that can be conceded as probable is that the whole of St. Paul's Epistles have not come down to us in their original form. A recent theory admits that they all contain Pauline passages, much enlarged by the first collector of the Epistles, the heretic Marcion (*c.* 150), who was anti-Jewish, and modified in a later revision by an orthodox writer.

53. The Epistle to the Hebrews is a theological dissertation on the relations of the Law and the Gospels. Its attribution to St. Paul is purely hypothetical. Tertullian ascribed it to Barnabas, the friend of Paul, and Origen confessed that the author was not known. But it is an ancient composition, probably a little anterior to the year 70 A.D.

54. The Epistle to Titus and the two Epistles to Timothy are generally known by the name of Pastoral Epistles, because they are addressed to pastors of the Church. The attribution of the Pastorals to St. Paul has been strenuously contested, yet the spirit which animates them is certainly that of the Apostle; they are at least documents emanating from his school, if indeed they are not modified versions of authentic letters.

55. The Epistle to Philemon is unimportant. The second Epistle to the Thessalonians seems to have been recast. The Epistle to the Colossians cannot be separated from the Epistle to the Ephesians. At the time of Marcion, the latter

was superscribed "to the Laodiceans," who were no doubt the original recipients. There is no good reason for contesting its authenticity. On the other hand, the Epistle to the Philippians implies a state of organisation in the Church which is not borne out by St. Paul's authentic writings. It has therefore been looked upon with suspicion.

56. The four great Epistles, to the Romans, the Corinthians (1 and 2) and to the Galatians are the most important monuments of that Pauline doctrine which the Apostle himself, quoting the Greeks, called the "foolishness" of the Cross (1 Cor. i, 18-27). They are difficult texts, so rugged in style and capricious in composition, that they make us wonder how the recipients can have understood them. At one point Paul rises to great heights in an eloquent passage on charity (1 Cor. xiii) in the midst of an exhortation to purity of life; here and there his atrabilarious genius suggests to him observations of the profoundest psychology, verbal felicities worthy of the greatest writers. But generally speaking his thought seems to elude us just as we are about to grasp it; this Jew, though he wrote in Greek, had retained a purely Oriental method of expression. If we read the Epistles without a commentary, we are in peril of a good deal of lost labour and of ultimate bewilderment.

57. A vast literature has grown up round these Epistles. When minutely studied, they seem to yield up the secret of the evolution of St. Paul's thought, as it gradually diverged from Judaism under Greek influences not very easy to define. Broadly speaking, St. Paul teaches that sin and death came into the world by Adam's fall (which Jesus never mentioned), and that Christ came to redeem mankind by his voluntary oblation of himself. Jesus was the visible image of the invisible God; he was the Son of God, although of human birth (Paul knew nothing of the miraculous affiliation). The death of Jesus connoted that of sin; the new life, heralded by the resurrection of Jesus, was to be the reign of holiness. In due time the faithful would be caught up into heaven with the Lord; then the dead would arise and would be judged according to their deserts. Baptism and faith in Jesus Christ are essential to salvation; the works

prescribed by the Law of Moses are not enough, for Jesus has redeemed us from the curse of the Law. But faith is not within reach of every man. God chooses his elect as seems good to him. This is the doctrine of predestination by grace, which, however, St. Paul has not very clearly formulated (see Rom. ix, 11 and xi, 5).

58. Ever since St. Paul, the ruling idea of Christianity has been that of the redemption of man, guilty of a prehistoric fault, by the voluntary sacrifice of a *superman.* This doctrine is founded upon that of expiation—a guilty person must suffer to atone for his fault—and that of the substitution of victims—the efficacious suffering of an innocent person for a guilty one. Both are at once pagan and Jewish ideas; they belong to the old fundamental errors of humanity. Yet Plato knew that the punishment inflicted on a guilty person is not, or should not be, a vengeance; it is a painful remedy imposed on him for his own benefit and that of society. At about the same period, Athenian law laid down the principle that punishment should be as personal as the fault. Thus St. Paul founded Christian theology on two archaic ideas which had already been condemned by enlightened Athenians of the fourth century before our era, ideas which no one would dream of upholding in these days, though the structure built upon them still subsists.

59. In practice, Paul did not forget that he was addressing Jewish communities which already included many baptized pagans. The faithful are enjoined not to hold aloof from the Gentiles, but only from their sacrifices and impurities; they may disregard the alimentary restrictions of the Law. "Give none offence, neither to the Jews, nor to the Gentiles, nor to the Church of God" (1 Cor. x, 32). The virtue he enjoins is, in the main, of no very exalted order; there is a Pauline opportunism. Such is his theory of marriage; it is better to remain celibate, but he who marries does well; a widow is even authorised to take a second husband, for a regular union is always preferable to disorderly life (1 Cor. vii, 27-40). For the rest, he reminds his flock that the end of the world is at hand, and they should behave as if it were imminent: "the time is short" (1 Cor. vii,

29). The theologians who quote and commentate St. Paul, like those who expound the Gospels, often forget that these documents were written by men to whom the second coming of Christ and the final catastrophe were matters of daily hope or fear. If the Church contrived to build a lasting edifice upon such foundations, it was because, with necessary illogicality, she transformed them rapidly and completely.

60. The chronology of Paul's life is very obscure; the following are probable dates:

A.D. 35. The Conversion of Paul. He goes to Arabia.
38. Paul at Jerusalem. He preaches in Syria and Cilicia.
49. The Conference at Jerusalem. Paul in Galatia and Troas.
51. Paul in Macedonia.
53. Paul at Corinth and in Achaia.
54. Paul at Jerusalem, Antioch, and Ephesus.
58. Paul in Macedonia, Achaia, Philippi and Jerusalem.
60. Paul in prison at Cæsaræa.
61-63. Paul at Rome, where he is put in prison.
64(?). Death of Paul at Rome.

61. The group of letters attributed to St. Peter, St. John, Jude and St. James are called the Catholic Epistles, because they are addressed to the Church at large. Not one of them is authentic. The First Epistle of Peter, dated from Babylon, is thoroughly Pauline in spirit; it was fabricated for the purpose of suggesting that Peter had lived at Babylon (ancient Cairo), and that this community was more ancient than that of Alexandria, which claimed to have been founded by St. Mark. The author has overshot the mark, and has helped to accredit the story of the coming of St. Peter to Rome, which is called Babylon in the Apocalypse. It need hardly be pointed out that this satirical designation, comprehensible enough in an invective, would be absurd in the heading of a letter. The second Epistle of Peter is also Græco-Egyptian, and very near in date to the apocryphal Gospel of St. Peter (so called). The three Epistles ascribed to St. John are probably by the same John as the Gospel, but not by the Apostle; in the last two, the author speaks of himself as the *elder* (presbyter). The Epistle of Jude

is a little homily against the heretics, written in Egypt after the year 100, in the same tone as the second Epistle of St. Peter; it could not possibly be by its reputed author, Judas, the brother of Jesus. The Epistle of James upholds the doctrine of salvation by works, in opposition to St. Paul's theory; this is why Luther characterised it disdainfully as the *epistle of straw*. St. Jerome knew that it was not by the brother of Jesus.

62. One of these forgeries was subjected to an interpolation of later date, probably by the Spaniard Priscillian (*c.* 380). In chap. v of the first Epistle of St. John are these words: "There are three that bear witness in heaven, the Father, and the Word and Holy Ghost, and these three are one." If these two verses were authentic, they would be an affirmation of the doctrine of the Trinity dating from the first century, at a time when the Gospels, the Acts and St. Paul ignore it. It was first pointed out in 1806 that these verses were an interpolation, for they do not appear in the best manuscripts, notably all the Greek manuscripts down to the fifteenth century. The Roman Church refused to bow to evidence. "How," she argued, "if these verses were an interpolation, could the Holy Spirit, who guides and directs the Church, have allowed her to regard this lofty affirmation of the Trinity as authentic, and permitted its insertion in the official edition of the sacred books?"[1] The Congregation of the Index, on January 13, 1897, with the approbation of Leo XIII., forbade any question as to the authenticity of the text relating to the "three heavenly witnesses." It showed in this connection a wilful ignorance to which the rebuke in Job (xiii, 7) is applicable: "God does not need our lies."

63. The Apocalypse or Revelation of St. John was written, according to tradition, in the Isle of Patmos, to which John had been banished by Domitian. It is a glorification of the Lamb (Jesus), and a prediction of the downfall of Rome, which is designated "Babylon the Great, the mother of abominations of the earth, drunken with the blood of the saints and martyrs of Jesus" (chap. xvii, 5, 6). At the end

[1] See Houtin, *La Question biblique au XIX siècle*, p. 220.

of one thousand years, after the triumph of the Church, the dead are to rise again. Satan will be released from his prison, and God will send down fire from heaven; this was the origin of the so-called millenarian beliefs, which have seduced a large number of visionaries. The Apocalypse cannot be the work of the Apostle John, but it is quite possible that it may be by the same hand as the fourth Gospel and the three Johannine Epistles. The author has also made use of more ancient documents. The basis is a Jewish diatribe against Nero, who seems to be designated by the "number of the Beast," 666, the sum of the letters of the Emperor's name, according to their numeral value in Hebrew (xiii, 18); but the Christian revision must certainly have been carried out under Domitian—who was called the *bald Nero*—in 93, for there is a reference to the great crisis in the wine industry owing to a glut (chap. vi, 6), which, according to the pagan texts, took place in A.D. 92.

64. The author of Revelation calls himself John the Apostle, and addresses the seven Churches of Asia; as he was not the Apostle John, who died perhaps in Palestine about 66, he was a forger. Among the absurdities and astrological speculations with which this book is filled, there are certain sublime passages which have become classic in all literatures; but as a whole it is a work of hatred and frenzy. The church hesitated to admit this book into the Canon; it was the name of John which decided the matter.

65. Since the year 1892, we have been in possession of a large portion of an Apocalypse attributed to St. Peter, discovered in Egypt six years before this date, together with the Gospel known as that of St. Peter. It is a vision of the rewards and punishments of the other world, dating from about the year 100, and interesting as the first Christian essay in eschatology (the science of the Last Things). It is derived from popular Jewish and Greek sources, and shows striking analogies with the Orphic doctrines. The author was an Egyptian Jew, of Hellenistic tendencies and some erudition. This Apocalypse was probably produced in the same literary factory as the two letters of St. Peter and his Gospel, which are also Græco-Egyptian forgeries.

66. Certain writings not included in the Canon have exercised so strong an influence that they demand a brief mention here.

They are in the first place letters. (1) A letter attributed to the Apostle Barnabas, the companion of St. Paul; it is posterior to the fall of Jerusalem, and very hostile to the Jews in tone; this again is a forgery, fabricated in Egypt. (2) The first Epistle of Clement, Bishop of Rome, to the Corinthians; this is perhaps the work of a Hellenistic Jew, a freeman of the Consul Flavius Clemens, who was a Christian or a Jew. It is interesting to note at this early period (*c.* 100 A.D.) the moral influence exercised by the Church of Rome upon a Greek Church. (3) The so-called second Epistle of Clement is a homily by another author. (4) The epistle of the disciple of John the Elder, Polycarp, Bishop of Smyrna, who was martyred in A.D. 155, at the age of eighty-six. This letter is addressed to the Philippians, and is probably authentic. (5) Seven very instructive letters attributed to Ignatius, Bishop of Antioch, who was martyred under Trajan. Ignatius is supposed to have written them during his journey from Antioch to Rome, to communities which had received him cordially; he warns them against schisms, Docetism and Judaism; these communities were governed by Bishops. The first mention of the Gospels, in the sense of a history of Jesus, occurs in one of these letters (that to the Smyrnans). The fraudulent character of these letters has been repeatedly asserted, but not proved; it is by no means impossible that the episcopate may have been instituted in Greek territory as early as the year 100.

67. The *Pastor of Hermas* is a long and very tedious work which Clement of Alexandria and Origen believed to be "inspired." The Pastor is the guardian angel of the writer, who has had visions, and reveals them to bring back the faithful from error. Hermas, born in Greece, and sometime a slave in Rome, had obtained his freedom, and was living in the city with his family. The *Pastor* was probably written not much later than the year 100 A.D.

68. It was believed in Rome in the third century, that after Pentecost the Apostles had drawn up a joint confes-

sion of faith or *Symbol*, which had to be recited by all adults before receiving the rite of baptism. This is obviously impossible, but the most ancient *Symbol* of this nature, known to Justin in 150, was a product of the Church of Rome before the year 100.

69. We possess certain fragments of a work called the Preaching or Doctrine of St. Peter, which purports to be addressed to the heathen by the Apostle; this is another Græco-Roman forgery dating from the end of the first century.

70. A fortunate discovery in a Greek library (1883) revealed to us the *Doctrine of the Apostles* or *Didache*, a manual of the Christian life both individual and social, a document of the first importance to the student of the primitive communities, their organisations and rites. The Apostles, of course, had nothing to do with it; but the *Didache*, a compilation from ancient catechisms, seems to have been drawn up in Syria before A.D. 150.

71. An important group of documents—called the pseudo-Clementine writings, because they were falsely attributed to Clement, Bishop of Rome—comprises twenty homilies and a didactic tale entitled *The Recognitions*. The ground-work of these compositions is almost identical. Clement, instituted Bishop of Rome by St. Peter, describes his conversion, on quitting the school of philosophy, to St. James, the head of the Church at Jerusalem. Having learnt that the Son of God was born in Judæa, he set out for that country, met Barnabas at Alexandria, and Peter at Cæsaræa; the latter caused him to witness his dispute with Simon Magus and initiated him into his doctrine. Simon, vanquished, was pursued by Peter and Clement, who overtook him at Laodicea, and reopened the debate with him. Finally, Peter departed to Antioch, and there founded a community. The title of Recognitions is based on an episode in the seventh book: Matidia, the mother of Clement, had quitted Rome for Athens; she is discovered there with her sons by her husband, who had set out in search of her. In all this farrago, Paul is not even mentioned; it is a frankly Judæo-Christian document. The *Homilies* and the *Recog-*

nitions have a common source dating probably from about A.D. 150; the compilation was made in the third century.

72. There is no more mysterious figure than that Simon, the magician of Samaria, whom we find opposing St. Peter in the Acts, and whom Justin, the Clementine writings and the apocryphal Acts represent as a very important personage at Rome. There, under Claudius or Nero, he rivals Peter in supernatural power, and ends by promising to fly through the air before the Emperor; but a prayer offered up by St. Peter deprives him of his power; he falls and breaks his neck. Justin (A.D. 150) asserts that he saw his tomb on the island in the Tiber, with this inscription: "To Simon, the holy god." This shows the ignorance and carelessness of Justin; the inscription in question has been found, and bears a dedication to *Semo Sancus*, an ancient Roman god whom a professor of rhetoric like Justin should certainly have known. But who was this Simon, the divine honours accorded to whom in Samaria are attested? The question has never been answered. In the nineteenth century, the school of Tübingen insisted a good deal on the traditions relative to the rivalry of Peter and Simon; it suggested that Simon represented St. Paul, and hence drew the somewhat exaggerated conclusion that the rivalry between the two Apostles went as far as the most ferocious hatred. Their theological hatred, evident in the epistles of Paul, went far enough. Not only did the Judaising group at Jerusalem organise a kind of mission against him, but false epistles were circulated under his name (2 Thess. ii, 2). Paul accordingly denounces his adversaries as dogs, liars, children of the devil and forgers. It is necessary to call attention to these passages at the close of a chapter in which, examining the sacred books of the Church, we have found forgeries on every hand.

73. I might consider many questions connected with the above, the first Apologies addressed by Christians to the pagan emperors, the Acts of the martyrs, very few of which are authentic, the Apostolic Constitutions; but this would be to trench on the domain of literary history. I will conclude with a few words concerning Antichrist (*i.e.*, the ad-

versary opposed to Christ). This famous name first appears in the Epistles of St. John, but the idea is much more ancient; it is that of the Babylonian Tiamat opposed to Marduk. The principle of evil is substituted for the dragon of the primitive myth, and between this and the principle of good a terrible conflict will be waged before the coming of the kingdom of God. Traces of this conception are to be found in Ezekiel, in Daniel, in Baruch, and in the Apocalypse. It is referred to in the second Epistle to the Thessalonians (ii, 3): "That day shall not come, except there come a falling away first, and that man of sin be revealed, the son of perdition." Good being personified in Christ, evil was personified in Antichrist: "For many shall come in my name," said Jesus, "saying, I am Christ; and shall deceive many. And ye shall hear of wars and rumours of wars; see that ye be not troubled; for all these things must come to pass, but the end is not yet. . . . All these are the beginning of sorrows. . . . And many false prophets shall arise. . . . Then shall be great tribulation, such as was not since the beginning of this world to this time. . . . Then shall appear the sign of the Son of Man in heaven; and then shall all the earth mourn, and they shall see the Son of Man coming in the clouds of heaven with power and great glory" (Matt. xxiv).

74. These terrifying words have borne terrible fruit. From Nero to the French minister Combes, there has been no conspicuous adversary of the Church who has not been assimilated to the Antichrist whose appearance is to inaugurate an era of catastrophe. Luther identified the Pope of Rome with Antichrist; millions of English people recognised him in Napoleon. We have already seen how in the Apocalypse the beast was Nero. After the death of this wretch there was a rumour that he had fled to the Parthians, and that he would come back. There is perhaps an allusion to this legend in the Apocalypse itself and in the first Epistle of St. John (iv, 3): "Every spirit that confesseth not that Jesus Christ is come in the flesh is not of God; and this is that spirit of Antichrist, whereof ye have heard that it should come; and even now already it is in the world." Here,

Antichrist is already assimilated to heresy. In the Sibylline oracles fabricated by the Jews of Alexandria, the name of Antichrist does not occur, but the Roman Empire, the object of a ferocious hatred, takes its place. Popular Jewish literature gave the name of *Romulus* to this enemy of God, and described him as a hideous giant, the offspring of a stone virgin. The Christians in general reserved the name of Antichrist for heretics and schismatics; but in the fourth century the idea still prevailed that the coming of Antichrist would be the awakening and return of Nero.

BIBLIOGRAPHY

The most trustworthy repertory is Hauck's *Real-Encyclop. für protestantische Theologie* (3rd ed., 24 vols.), to which may be added the dictionaries quoted in the bibliography of chapter vii. There are dictionaries of Christian biography (down to Charlemagne) by Smith, of Christian archæology by Martigny, Smith, and Dom Cabrol (in progress), a dictionary of Catholic theology by Vacant (in progress), &c. Among periodicals I may mention the *Expositor*, the *Revue biblique*, and the *Theologische Literaturzeitung* (bibliographical).

Renan, *Origines du Christianisme*, 8 vols., 1862-1883 (with a good index); Duchesne, *Histoire ancienne de l'Eglise*, vols. i and ii, 1906-1908 (Engl. transl.); Guignebert, *Manuel d'histoire ancienne du Christianisme*, 1906; Wendland, *Die hellenistisch-römische Kultur in ihren Beziehungen zu Judenthum und Christentum*, 1907; Conybeare, *Christian Origins*, 1909; Ed. Meyer, *Ursprung und Anfaenge des Christentums*, 3 vols., 1921-1923.

2. Loisy. *Hist. du canon du N. T.*, 1891; Th. Zahn, *Gesch. des N. T. Kanons*, 2nd ed., 1904; J. Leipoldt, same title, 2 vols., 1907-1908.

4. Harnack, *Marcion*, 2nd ed., 1924 (comp. *Rev. hist. Rel.*, 1925, p. 169).

5. Text of the *Fragmentum Muratorianum* (and of most of the other documents of the primitive church) in Rauschen, *Florilegium patristicum*, fasc. iii, 1905.

11. E. Preusschen, *Antilegomena*, 2nd ed., 1905 (fragments of the lost Gospels and quotations from the Fathers, with German translation).

14. Ad. Jülicher, *Einleitung in das N. T.*, 4th ed., 1901 (English transl.); M. Goguel, *Introduction au nouv. Test.*, 1923-1924; Loisy, *Les Evangiles synoptiques*, 2 vols., 1907; Wellhausen, *Einleitung in die 3 ersten Ev.*, 1905; Holtzmann, *Handcommentar zum N. T.*, 3rd ed., 1901 *et seq.;* Nicolardot, *Les procédés de rédaction des trois premiers Evangélistes*, 1908; R. Bultmann, *Synopt. Evangelien*, 1925; A. Réville, *Jésus*, 2nd ed., 1906; P. Wernle, *Quellen des Leben Jesu*, 1906; J. Klausner, *Jesus of Nazareth*, 1925; A. Schweitzer, *Gesch. der Leben-Jesu Forschung*, 1913; Schmiedel, art. *Gospels* in Cheyne; Goguel, *St. Jean Baptiste*, 1929.

17. Preusschen, *op. cit.* (11), in Greek and German; Loisy, *Evangiles synoptiques*, vol. i.

18. L. Vénard, *Les Ev. synoptiques* (in *Rev. du clergé*, July 15, 1908, p. 178).

18 *d.* A. Harnack, *Lukas der Arzt,* 1906; Burkitt, *The Gospel History,* 1906 (connection between St. Luke and Josephus; cf. Loisy, *Rev. crit.,* 1907, i, p. 243); P. G. Sense (pseudonym of Lyons), *Origin of the Third Gospel,* 1901 (the Luke of Marcion).

18. *f.* Loisy, *Le quatrième Evangile,* 1903 (1924); Wellhausen, *Das 4te Ev.,* 1908; J. H. Bernard, *St. John's Gospel,* 2 vols., 1929; Delafosse, *Le 4ème Ev.,* 1925.

21. Saintyves, *Le Vierges mères et les naissances miraculeuses,* 1908.

22. G. M. de La Garenne, *Le problème des frères du Seigneur,* 1929.

25. Saintyves, *Le miracle et la critique historique,* 1907.

29 *et seq.* R. Eisler, *Jèsous basileus,* 2 vols., 1929, now the standard work on early Christian chronology and the Slavonic Josephus; S. Reinach, *Jean Baptiste et Jésus suivant Josèphe,* 1929.—Jesus and John: S. R., *Cultes,* vol. iii, p. 22.

30. Laible, *J. C. im Talmud,* 2nd ed., 1900; H. Strack, *Jesus nach jüdischen Angaben,* 1910; W. Bauer, *Leben Jesu,* 1909.

32. Letter of Claudius: *Rev. hist. rel.,* 1924, p. 109; 1925, p. 3; *Journ. Rom. Stud.,* 1926, p. 17.

33. Text of Tertullian: S. Reinach, *Revue historique,* 1929.

34. S. R., *Cultes,* vol. iv, p. 200.

35. *Ibid.,* vol. iv, p. 182.

36. Goguel, *Jésus mythe ou histoire,* 1925; Ch. Guignebert, *Le problème de Jésus,* 1921 (with references to recent work).

37. Th. Reinach, *Josèphe sur Jésus,* in *Revue des Etudes juives,* 1897; Laqueur, *Josephus,* 1921.

38. See above, § 29.

39. Thackeray, *Josephus,* vol. iii, 1928, with translations of all the Slavonic additions.

41-42. S. R., *Cultes,* vol. ii, p. 437, and *Congrès Loisy,* vol. i, 1928.

43. Strauss, *Leben Jesu,* 1835, first insisted on the "fulfilled prophecies," from the critical standpoint.

46. A. Bayet, *Les morales de l'Evangile,* 1927.

47. M. Lepin, *Evang. canoniques et Evang. apocryphes,* 1907; A. Robinson, *The Gospel according to Peter and the Revelation of Peter,* 1892 (supposed identity of the Gospels of Peter and of the Egyptians: Volter, in *Zeitschrift für N. T. Wissenschaft,* 1905, p. 368).—Attribution of the Fourth Gospel to Cerinthus: P. C. Sense (Lyons), *The Fourth Gospel,* 1899.

48. Roberts, *Apocryphal Gospels and Revelations,* 1890 (English translation); E. Hennecke, *Neutestam. Apokryphen,* 1924; M. Rh. James, *The apocr. N. Test.,* 1924.

49. Griffinhoofe, *The Unwritten Sayings of Christ,* 1903.

50. A. Harnack, *Die Apostelgeschichte,* 1908; E. Jacquier, *Les Actes des apôtres,* 1908; Loisy, *Actes des apôtres,* 1920; Goguel, *Livre des actes,* 1922; E. Norden, *Agnostos Theos,* 1913.

51. Lipsius, *Die apokryphen Apostelgeschichten,* 3 vols., 1883-1890 (important).—Acts of Andrew and of Matthias: S. R., *Cultes,* vol. i, p. 395; J. Flamion, 1911.—Thekla: S. R., *Cultes,* vol. iv, p. 229.—L. Vouaux, *Actes de Paul,* 1913.

52. W. Ramsay, *S. Paul,* 1895; A. Sabatier, *L'apôtre Paul,* 1896; Goguel, *Epîtres pauliniennes,* 1925-1926; Delafosse, *S. Paul,* 1926; A. Deissmann, *Licht von Osten,* 1908 (style of the Epistles compared with pagan documents of the same period); A. Schweitzer, *Gesch. der Paulusforschung,* 1911; H. Mayer, *Pastoralbriefe,* 1913.—Influence of the pagan mysteries on Paul: Renan, *Etudes,* p. 58; Loisy, *Rev. d'hist. et de litt. relig.,* 1913, p. 1; 1914, p. 63.

58. Aug. Sabatier, *La doctrine de l'expiation et son évolution* (in *Etudes de théologie,* 1901, p. 1).—On the Greek idea of responsibility,

first collective and then individual, Glotz, *La solidarité de la famille dans le droit criminel,* 1904.

60. New data about Paul in Greece: *Rev. du clergé,* Oct. 15, 1913; *Rev. hist. et de litt. relig.,* 1913, p. 487.

61. T. Calmes, *Epîtres catholiques,* 1905; Reuss, *La Bible,* vol. xv. On the First Epistle of Peter: S. R., *Rev. archéol.,* 1908, i, p. 150.

63. Boll, *Aus der Offenbarung,* 1914, has shown the astrological elements in that book.—R. H. Charles, *The Apocalypse,* 1921; A. Loisy, *L'Apocalypse,* 1924.

64. Texts on the death of John: Cheyne, art. *John,* p. 2509.

65. S. R., *Cultes,* vol. iii, p. 284, and the ed. of Robinson, Lods, &c.

66. Arts. *Barnabas, Clemens, Polykarp, Ignatius,* in Hauck; P. Haeufer, *Der Barnabasbrief,* 1911—On the primitive hierarchy: J. Réville, *Orig. de l'épiscopat,* 1894; Batiffol, *Etudes d'histoire,* p. 223.—Renewed doubts about the Ignatian letters: *Rev. hist. et de litt. rel.,* 1922, p. 303; Delafosse, *Lettres d'Ignace,* 1927.

67. Renan, *l'Eglise chrétienne,* vol. vi, p. 402 *et seq.;* A. Lelong, *Le Pasteur d'Hermas,* 1912.

68. F. Kattenbusch, *Das apostol. Symbol,* 2 vols. 1894-1900; Vacandard, *Le symbole des apôtres* (in *Etudes de critique,* 1906, p. 1 *et seq.*).

70. Krüger, *Altchristliche Literatur,* 1895, p. 38, 40; Massebieau, *L'enseignement des apôtres,* 1884.

71. H. Waitz, *Die Pseudoklementinen,* 1904; art. *Clementinen* in Hauck.

72. Art. *Simon der Magier,* in Hauck; Eisler (§ 29); Alfaric, *Rev. hist.,* 1924, vol. 145.

73. Apologies: Krüger, *Altchristl. Literatur,* 1895, p. 60 *et seq.;* A. Puech, *Les apologistes grecs,* 1912.—Acts of the martyrs: Cabrol, art. *Actes;* Hauck, art. *Acta martyrum;* Dufourq, *Les "Gesta martyrum" romains,* 3 vols., 1900-1907; P. Monceaux, *La vraie légende dorée,* 1928.—Antichrist: Renan, *l'Antichrist,* 1873; art. *Antichrist,* in Hauck and the *Jewish Encycl.* (cf. *Zeitsch. f. neutest. Wiss.,* 1901, p. 169).

74. H. Preuss, *Die Vorstellungen vom Antichrist im späteren Mittelalter,* 1906.

CHAPTER IX

CHRISTIANITY: FROM ST. PAUL TO JUSTINIAN

First Christian communities. The Preaching of St. Paul. Particularism and universalism. The Gnostics. Organisation of communities. The gift of tongues or glossolaly. The function of the Jewish synagogues. Persecution of Christians at Rome. Pliny's letter to Trajan. Motives for the persecutions. The martyrs. Christian virtues. Heresies; the influence of heretics on the Church. The concentration of the spiritual power. Montanism. Persecutions under Decius and Diocletian. Constantine and the edict of toleration. Persecution of pagans by Christians. The Donatist schism. Christian Monachism. Gradual changes in the Church. Arius and Athanasius; the dogma of the Trinity. The first murder for error of opinion. Priscillian. Monophysite heresy. The Coptic Church. St. Augustine and the doctrine of Purgatory. St. Jerome. St. Gregory Nazianzen. St. Basil. St. John Chrysostom. St. Ambrose. The growth of luxury in the Church.

1. We are told that the Jewish sect which proclaimed Jesus its master developed mainly in two small groups, one in Galilee, the other in Judæa. It was in Judæa, at Jerusalem, that the Apostles lived. While waiting for the glorious return of the Messiah, they organised their body with a view to the Kingdom of Heaven. It soon appeared necessary not to allow the double burden of preaching and distributing alms to rest upon the same men. For the latter task, deacons were instituted, among them a Judæo-Christian named Stephen, who was accused of blasphemy by the Jews and stoned. He is called the *Proto-martyr* by the Church. This execution, which was followed by a persecution, accentuated the opposition between the Jews and Christians; it was favourable to the propaganda of the Christians, inasmuch as it caused their dispersal. One of their most active missionaries in Samaria was the deacon Philip, who is said to have converted the treasurer of an Ethiopian princess, thus opening up Abyssinia to Christian influences.

2. Saul, a native of Tarsus, a Jewish doctor and a pupil of the Pharisee Gamaliel, had shown great activity in the

persecution. He set out for Damascus, to stir up the zeal of the synagogue in that city. On the way he had a vision which converted him to the new sect. After preaching at Damascus, Saul retired for three years to Hauran. On returning to Jerusalem, he was favourably received by the Apostles, and went to Antioch with their delegate Barnabas. It was the Jews of Antioch, converted by Barnabas and Paul, who first took the name of Christians. This Greek town played a more important part than Jerusalem in the primitive history of Christianity.

3. From Antioch, Saul and Barnabas went to Cyprus, the birthplace of Barnabas. They were sympathetically received by the Roman proconsul, Sergius Paulus, and to mark his gratitude, it is said, Saul changed his name to Paul. After Cyprus they visited Asia Minor. Paul preached at Antioch in Pisidia, and at Lystra.

4. The question now arose as to whether, in order to enter the new communion, it was necessary to pass into it through the synagogue, undergo circumcision, and conform to all the Jewish rites. These obligations were very irksome to the pagans. In spite of the opposition of Peter and the other Apostles of Jerusalem, Paul abolished them, preached salvation for all, Jews and Greeks alike, and thus rendered the rapid extension of Christianity among the Gentiles possible. Hence the name "Apostle of the Gentiles" (Gentiles = heathen) applied to St. Paul, and so eminently characteristic of his mission.

5. This evolution of infant Christianity was laborious. The struggle between Jewish particularism and Christian universalism was a struggle between Peter and Paul, between Jerusalem and Antioch. A first conference, held at Jerusalem, brought about a compromise which was almost immediately violated by both parties. Paul pursued his universalist apostolate in Asia Minor, then at Philippi in Macedonia, at Thessalonica, at Athens, and at Corinth, whence he returned by way of Ephesus to Antioch. The evangelisation of Ephesus had been already begun by an Alexandrian Jew called Apollos; it soon made such progress that the vendors of little objects of piety for the worship of the Ephe-

HERESIES

sian Artemis were alarmed, and stirred up an insurrection, the prototype of many others which the Christians, and afterwards the reformers of Christianity, had to undergo.

6. Paul returned to Jerusalem in 58. A second conference, the echo of persistent dissensions, took place in the house of James, the reputed brother of Jesus. A Jewish riot then gave occasion for the intervention of the Roman Governor, who sent Paul to Cæsaræa. Paul, who was a Roman citizen, demanded to be tried in Rome; he was sent there after the year 60. He was already in touch with the little Christian community founded in the capital by Jewish merchants from Syria, having addressed an epistle to them from Corinth. We have no details of his trial at Rome, and his legendary journey to Spain or Great Britain is improbable. He is supposed to have been put to death in Rome in 64.

7. Mark, the cousin of Barnabas, had accompanied Paul to Italy; after the arrest of Paul, it is alleged that he became the secretary of Peter. Luke, a Greek physician at Antioch, was also converted by Paul, and laboured to propagate his doctrine. As to Peter, his travels belong to the domain of legend; it is probable that he died by violence in Palestine, and not in Rome, where tradition declares him to have been executed at the same time as Paul. It is true that before the end of the first century it was believed that Peter had been at Rome with Mark; but this belief was based on an apocryphal letter attributed to Peter, which was circulated about the year 90 (*cf.* above, p. 259).

8. Nothing definite is known of the history of the other Apostles, and the stories told of them are mere fables. James, a pious Jew who was hostile to Paul, continued as the head of the Church at Jerusalem, and was killed in a disturbance. Matthew is supposed to have gone to Arabia, Andrew to the Crimea, Thomas to India, Philip to Syria. John was believed to have settled at Ephesus and to have lived there to an advanced age, surrounded by disciples, one of whom, the Presbyter John, has been thought by some to be the author of the fourth Gospel, of the Apocalypse and of the letters attributed to the Apostle. The story of the sojourn and death of the Virgin Mary at Ephesus is an in-

vention; the discovery of her reputed house at Ephesus is an illusion born of pious credulity.

9. We have seen that an Alexandrian Jew, Apollos, first preached Christianity at Ephesus. The numerous writings of Philo, a contemporary of Jesus, and the fourth Gospel may all be referred to Alexandrian Judaism, impregnated with Platonic speculations. The Hellenistic Jews introduced into Christianity the conception of the *Logos* or *Word*, the intermediary between God and man, incorporated in Jesus. But before they connected it with Jesus, they had already incorporated the Word in a legion of angels, of immaterial beings or *Eons*, of allegories; they had combined their traditional monotheism with the popular animistic and polydemonistic beliefs of Syria and of Babylonia. When Christianity took the place of Judaism in these combinations, Gnosticism (from *Gnosis*, a knowledge of hidden things) grew in importance. Outside Palestine, Christianity itself was a Gnostic sect, and this is why at a very early period the fourth Gospel was attributed to the Gnostic Cerinthus, a contemporary of St. John at Ephesus. But Christianity was destined to triumph over the other Gnostic sects, because it was more reasonable, simpler, and less inclined to lose itself in divagations. Intent on well-doing, on moral purity, and essentially hostile to the depressing forms of asceticism, it found its adherents mainly among men of good sense and good-will, whereas Gnosticism appealed to visionaries and persons of ill-balanced minds. The final victory of the Church over the other Gnostics was that of disciplined over intemperate mysticism.

. . .

10. The Church about the year 80 A.D. was a very simple organisation. In addition to the deacons, there were deaconesses, generally widows, who busied themselves with works of charity and propaganda among women. Its assemblies, presided over by an elder (*presbyter*, whence the word *priest*) or superintendent (in Greek *episcopos*, whence *bishop*), were held in private houses, first on Saturdays, and later on Sundays, the day of Christ's resurrection. The

Old Testament, the Epistles, and the sayings attributed to Jesus were read at these assemblies. Baptism was chiefly administered to adults, in the form of total immersion. Sick and dying persons were rubbed with holy oil, in order to scare away evil spirits, which baptism was also supposed to drown. *Agapæ* (love-feasts) gathered together the faithful, who celebrated the Holy Communion in common in the dual form of bread and wine. It was called an "act of thanksgiving" in memory of the sacrifice of Jesus; this is the *Eucharist* (from the Greek *Eucharistia*, thanksgiving).

11. Among the faithful of the primitive churches there were, of course, a certain number of visionaries, and of idle and degraded persons. Many believed themselves to be gifted with prophetic powers and disturbed the meetings by fits of *glossolaly*, that is to say, an outburst of inarticulate sounds. It was this gift of "speaking with tongues" which the apostles were supposed to have received at Pentecost by the grace of the Holy Ghost; later, the double meaning of the word "tongue" was played upon, and it was maintained that the Apostles had been endowed with the power of speaking the idioms of all the people to whom they were to preach the gospel. The manifestations of glossolaly were checked at an early stage; St. Paul forbids it altogether for women. Although celibacy was not imposed on any one, Christianity demanded purity of life, and had much difficulty in enforcing it. On the other hand, visionaries preached asceticism and vegetarianism, and inclined more or less openly to Gnostic mysticism; the firmness and good sense of the Elders did not always succeed in neutralising these dangerous tendencies.

12. The destruction of Jerusalem by the Romans (A.D. 70) and the final dispersal of the Jews throughout the Empire weakened the hopes cherished by the Christians of the speedy return of Jesus in glory; for these they substituted the expectation of his spiritual reign. The dispersed Jews founded houses of prayer or synagogues on every hand, with butchers' shops which did not sell the "meat offered to idols," which was forbidden to Jews and Christians alike; these became so many new centres for the Christian propaganda,

which, although it was now hostile to Judaism, could only recruit its first adherents round the synagogues, where the words of Moses and the prophets found an echo.

13. The Christian propaganda soon alarmed the interests of those who lived upon the official pagan cult, and of those innumerable charlatans who exploited alien forms of worship; it also alarmed the Roman Government, which distrusted secret societies, with good reason, and saw in the Christians a party of Jews more active and energetic than the rest. When Nero was suspected of setting fire to Rome he turned the accusation upon the horde of Orientals who were always talking about the last judgment and the destruction of the world by fire. The Roman police forthwith inaugurated a series of wholesale arrests and executions; Jews and Christians perished together; this was what is known as the First Persecution (A.D. 65). It did not put a stop to the Christian propaganda, which was already carried on in some of the patrician households by slaves, natives of Syria. Under Domitian, the Consul Flavius Clemens and his wife Domitilla were condemned for "atheism"; they had no doubt become Christians, and their "atheism" consisted in denying the Roman gods. "Many others," says the historian Dion Cassius, "were punished for *atheism and for Jewish customs*," and afterwards he mentions Acilius Glabrio, a former consul, among the victims of Domitian. The fact that Christianity had penetrated among the upper classes of Rome before the year 100 was of vast importance to its ultimate development.

14. Pliny the younger, legate to Bithynia in A.D. 112, wrote to the Emperor Trajan asking how he was to treat the Christians. On this occasion he was primarily the spokesman of the cattle-dealers, who lamented that victims for sacrifice were no longer bought. "You must not seek out the Christians," replied Trajan, "but if they are denounced and convicted, they must be punished. If, however, any accused person should deny being a Christian, and should prove his innocence by invoking our gods, he may be pardoned." These few lines are of immense historical value; they formed

the rule of the Roman government until the persecution which began under Decius. The picture Pliny paints of the Christians is so greatly to their credit that the authenticity of his letter has been (quite groundlessly) suspected; unfortunately the unique manuscript from which it was transcribed at the beginning of the sixteenth century has disappeared, no one knows how, and doubts as to the completeness of the published version are permissible.

15. The attitude of the Roman officials depended, in the first instance, on that of the communities they governed, who denounced the Christians or not, as best suited their own interests; in the second place, on the attitude of the Christians and the degree of hostility they showed to official paganism; finally, on the easily roused ferocity of popular superstition, which attributed all natural calamities to the enemies of its gods. The lying rumours that were spread abroad concerning the Christians, on account of the mystery with which they surrounded certain acts of their worship, such as the Eucharist, and more particularly the accusation, by which the populace was always readily inflamed, that they offered human sacrifices, determined certain local persecutions. The most notorious was that at Lyons in A.D. 177. Here there was a little community of Greek origin, persons of some means, against whom the most odious calumnies were circulated. Young girls and old men were cruelly tortured. "It is you who are the cannibals!" cried one of the victims to the judges. To combat these recurrent accusations, a literature grew up, first in Greek, then in Latin, several specimens of which have come down to us. The most interesting, the *Apology*, written in Africa by Tertullian in 197 A.D., was shortly afterwards translated into Greek.

16. There was also a literature hostile to Christianity, but it has perished almost entirely. It has, however, been possible to reconstitute the *True Discourse* of the philosopher Celsus (*c.* 170) from the long refutation of it composed by Origen, and a portion of the Emperor Julian's treatise against the Christians, thanks to the diatribe of St. Cyril (*d.* 444) which it inspired.

17. The ten persecutions enumerated by historians of Christianity are a fiction,[1] and Dodwell in the eighteenth century already made short work of the legends which exaggerated the number of martyrs. This name, which means *witness* in Greek, was given to those who proclaimed their faith in the face of suffering. The choice of the term seems singular, for testimony does not, to us, imply the infliction of a penalty. But this was not the case among the Greeks and Romans, where the evidence of a *slave* was not admissible unless it had been obtained by torture. In the language of the slave then, "to bear witness" and "to suffer" were synonymous terms, and thus the use of the word martyr implies that the intermittent persecution was directed chiefly against persons of servile or very humble condition, among whom the early Christians were mainly recruited.

18. This also explains certain fine characteristics of Christianity before Constantine. It was the religion of poor people, who worked and suffered and helped one another. A Christian woman buried in the catacombs of Rome is called in her epitaph "a friend of the poor and a workwoman." This is a kind of affirmation of the dignity of work which was a much greater novelty in the antique world than charity. Triumphant Christianity forgot this truth, but recalled it at a later period, when it undertook the reform of its monastic orders in the sixth century.

* * *

19. The Church of the second and the third centuries suffered less from persecution than from heresies. I have already spoken of Gnosticism, which, as a fact, was more ancient than Christianity. Exaggerating the anti-Jewish tendencies of Paul, in opposition to the Judaising Christians known as Ebionites, certain Gnostic doctors renounced the Old Testament and represented the god of Israel as a demon, the creator but the enemy of mankind. This tendency is related to the Mazdæan dualism which had such a strong influence upon Gnosticism. Had the Church wandered into

[1] The persecutions to the time of Decius were local and intermittent; there were many more than ten.

fully invested with their powers? Was it not necessary to baptize afresh those whom they had baptized? In other words, does the efficacy of the sacerdotal ministry depend on the personal character of the minister? If the Church had replied in the affirmative, her ruin would have been assured, for every bishop would have had to justify himself against accusations directed not only against his own conduct, but against that of the bishop who had ordained him, and the whole array of his spiritual ancestors. The good sense of the Church, in conformity with its interests, preserved it from this pitfall; but this did not satisfy the Africans, who were naturally turbulent and often hostile to their bishops. A bishop of Carthage, Donatus, placed himself at the head of the movement (A.D. 313), which soon attracted not only the adversaries of the clergy, but the ruined farmers, the oppressed peasantry, and the vagabonds known as *Circoncelliones.* Donatism assumed the character of a *Jacquerie.* The Emperors first attempted to stem the torrent by pacific means; then they had recourse to the extremes of violence. Donatus died in exile and his followers were massacred. The agitation broke out afresh under Julian, and in thirty years had spread throughout the greater part of Roman Africa. In A.D. 393 St. Augustine embarked on a long literary campaign against the Donatists, which was interrupted in 403 by a new insurrection of the Circoncelliones. The authority of the illustrious Bishop of Hippo, seconded by very severe imperial edicts, finally overcame the schism (A.D. 418). But it reappeared under the Vandals, and a few groups of Donatists still existed at the time of the Musulman conquest.

26. During the Decian persecution, many Egyptian Christians had withdrawn to the desert, where they lived as hermits (from *eremos,* desert). Others followed, who formed themselves into communities (cenobites, from *koinos bios,* life in common). Thus arose Christian monachism, which, indeed, had precedents both among Jews and Christians. The Essenes of the time of Jesus and the Pythagoreans of Southern Italy about A.D. 600 had lived as veritable cenobites. About A.D. 340 St. Pachomius, or Pachonius, founded

recognised the futility of his efforts, and abdicated. His successors were weaker, if not more tolerant.

23. Christianity had now become such a power in the Empire that the ambitious Constantine sought its support. After vanquishing Maxentius at the bridge of Milvius, where he had displayed a standard in the form of a cross (the *labarum*), he promulgated an edict of toleration in 313, which practically gave Christianity a privileged position. Constantius removed the statue of Victory from the Senate-chamber (356), and began the overthrow of the images of the gods in the East. After his death in A.D. 361, a pagan reaction took place under Julian, but a reaction of a peaceful nature, for Julian, the mildest of men, was content merely to take the direction of education out of the hands of the Christians. He did justice to Christianity, nevertheless, and exhorted the pagans to imitate its charitable institutions. His premature death in 363 was the signal for the downfall of polytheism; it retained adherents only in the aristocracy, the great schools, and the conservative population of country districts (*pagani*).

24. Theodosius prohibited heathen sacrifices, and in spite of the eloquent protestations of Libanius, ordered the temples to be closed (A.D. 391). The zeal of the monks manifested itself against these buildings, notably in Egypt. In 408, Honorius forbade pagans to hold public office; under Theodosius II., the fanatic Cyril, whom the Church has canonised, relentlessly pursued the learned Hypatia, the daughter of the mathematician Theon; she was stoned and torn in pieces by the populace in the streets of Alexandria (A.D. 415). Victorious Christianity waged war upon science. Justinian took but one step in advance when he closed the school of Athens (A.D. 529). The world was ripe for the Middle Ages.

25. The end of the persecutions gave rise in Africa to an original schism, that of the Donatists, one of the first to attack, not the doctrine, but the discipline of the Church. It was a schism before being a heresy. Could the bishops who had given up the Scriptures to be burnt, and those who had received ordination from them, be considered as law-

fully invested with their powers? Was it not necessary to baptize afresh those whom they had baptized? In other words, does the efficacy of the sacerdotal ministry depend on the personal character of the minister? If the Church had replied in the affirmative, her ruin would have been assured, for every bishop would have had to justify himself against accusations directed not only against his own conduct, but against that of the bishop who had ordained him, and the whole array of his spiritual ancestors. The good sense of the Church, in conformity with its interests, preserved it from this pitfall; but this did not satisfy the Africans, who were naturally turbulent and often hostile to their bishops. A bishop of Carthage, Donatus, placed himself at the head of the movement (A.D. 313), which soon attracted not only the adversaries of the clergy, but the ruined farmers, the oppressed peasantry, and the vagabonds known as *Circoncelliones.* Donatism assumed the character of a *Jacquerie.* The Emperors first attempted to stem the torrent by pacific means; then they had recourse to the extremes of violence. Donatus died in exile and his followers were massacred. The agitation broke out afresh under Julian, and in thirty years had spread throughout the greater part of Roman Africa. In A.D. 393 St. Augustine embarked on a long literary campaign against the Donatists, which was interrupted in 403 by a new insurrection of the Circoncelliones. The authority of the illustrious Bishop of Hippo, seconded by very severe imperial edicts, finally overcame the schism (A.D. 418). But it reappeared under the Vandals, and a few groups of Donatists still existed at the time of the Musulman conquest.

26. During the Decian persecution, many Egyptian Christians had withdrawn to the desert, where they lived as hermits (from *eremos,* desert). Others followed, who formed themselves into communities (cenobites, from *koinos bios,* life in common). Thus arose Christian monachism, which, indeed, had precedents both among Jews and Christians. The Essenes of the time of Jesus and the Pythagoreans of Southern Italy about A.D. 600 had lived as veritable cenobites. About A.D. 340 St. Pachomius, or Pachonius, founded

recognised the futility of his efforts, and abdicated. His successors were weaker, if not more tolerant.

23. Christianity had now become such a power in the Empire that the ambitious Constantine sought its support. After vanquishing Maxentius at the bridge of Milvius, where he had displayed a standard in the form of a cross (the *labarum*), he promulgated an edict of toleration in 313, which practically gave Christianity a privileged position. Constantius removed the statue of Victory from the Senate-chamber (356), and began the overthrow of the images of the gods in the East. After his death in A.D. 361, a pagan reaction took place under Julian, but a reaction of a peaceful nature, for Julian, the mildest of men, was content merely to take the direction of education out of the hands of the Christians. He did justice to Christianity, nevertheless, and exhorted the pagans to imitate its charitable institutions. His premature death in 363 was the signal for the downfall of polytheism; it retained adherents only in the aristocracy, the great schools, and the conservative population of country districts (*pagani*).

24. Theodosius prohibited heathen sacrifices, and in spite of the eloquent protestations of Libanius, ordered the temples to be closed (A.D. 391). The zeal of the monks manifested itself against these buildings, notably in Egypt. In 408, Honorius forbade pagans to hold public office; under Theodosius II., the fanatic Cyril, whom the Church has canonised, relentlessly pursued the learned Hypatia, the daughter of the mathematician Theon; she was stoned and torn in pieces by the populace in the streets of Alexandria (A.D. 415). Victorious Christianity waged war upon science. Justinian took but one step in advance when he closed the school of Athens (A.D. 529). The world was ripe for the Middle Ages.

25. The end of the persecutions gave rise in Africa to an original schism, that of the Donatists, one of the first to attack, not the doctrine, but the discipline of the Church. It was a schism before being a heresy. Could the bishops who had given up the Scriptures to be burnt, and those who had received ordination from them, be considered as law-

most interesting. Its founder, the Phrygian Montanus, a converted priest of Cybele, began to prophesy, in the company of two women, and recruited many adherents in spite of his condemnation by the bishops of the country (172). The serious element in his doctrine, to which Tertullian subscribed towards the end of his career, and which persisted to the sixth century, was, that the era of divine revelation was not at an end, that the faith of the Church accepted the possibility of further fruition, that women might receive and communicate inspirations (in opposition to the theory of St. Paul, who ordered them to keep silence). The Montanist discipline was rigorous; it ordained two additional weeks of abstinence, forbade second marriage and denied the remission of certain sins after baptism. The polemics to which Montanism gave rise inspired the Church with a wholesome aversion from pronounced asceticism, in practice too often associated with moral laxity. "I say to every man," wrote St. Paul, "not to think more highly than he ought, but to think soberly" (Rom. xii, 3).

22. Christianity, encouraged by the imperial favourite Marcia under Commodus, and protected under the Syrian dynasty by the piety of the Empresses and the eclecticism of the Emperors, had presently to reckon with the brutality of the military Emperors, who were exasperated by the distaste of its adherents for a martial career, and their persistent refusal to render divine honours to the head of the State. The Emperor Decius (A.D. 250) organised a serious persecution, which made many martyrs and even more apostates, known as *Libellatici*, persons who had received a *libellus* or certificate for having given in their adhesion to paganism. Bishops of Rome, Jerusalem and Antioch were put to death. Origen, the great Christian scholar of Alexandria, narrowly escaped the executioner (A.D. 249). Cyprian, Bishop of Carthage, fell a victim to the persecution, which broke out afresh under Valerian (A.D. 258). The position of the Christians improved somewhat under Gallienus, who restored their churches to them, but this lull in the storm was of short duration. Diocletian began by following the example of Decius with a veritable frenzy (A.D. 303); but he soon

this road, her ruin would have been assured, for she would have lost the support of the Old Testament and of the pretended prophecies which all were then agreed in accepting. She resisted the Gnostics energetically, though not without making certain concessions to them, and profiting by their literary activity. Even the great Alexandrian doctors of A.D. 180 to 250, Clement and Origen, who created Christian exegesis and theology, drew inspiration, not without peril to the orthodoxy of their doctrine, from the Gnostics who had preceded them in these sciences. It was to Marcion (*c.* 150), that the Church owed the first idea of a Canon, an authorised collection of the writings relating to the New Law. It was in opposition to the Gnostics that she was led to formulate her dogmas, her profession of faith (incorrectly called the *Symbol of the Apostles*), and no doubt also to publish the definitive version of the four Gospels whose *divine inspiration* she affirmed. Modern Christianity, the proselytising force of which is by no means spent, was evolved during the long trial to which the Church was subjected by the assaults of Gnostics. The works of the Gnostics are mainly known to us through the refutations of which they were the object. In these polemical writings theological animus plays an important part, and the Gnostics are accused of crimes which were no doubt imaginary; but their doctrines were dangerous both to society and the individual, and the Church did well to discard them.

20. It was also in the course of this struggle that the Church became a governing body and that spiritual power was concentrated in her. The bishop was the head of his community, and Rome being the capital of the Empire, the Roman Church naturally tended to become the Empress of the Churches. This supremacy was not achieved without opposition. The widely spread conception of the original primacy of the Roman See, of the papacy founded by St. Peter and exercised by the Roman bishops who succeeded him, is not confirmed by the texts, which rather reveal the usual phenomenon of a slow evolution.

21. Among the sects of the second century, Montanism, which was quite distinct from Gnosticism, was one of the

convents for women, who were called nuns (*non nuptæ*, not married), on the same lines as the monasteries for men. Monasticism reached the West about the end of the fourth century. Here, conforming to the temperament of the people, it assumed a less contemplative and more practical character. St. Benedict of Nursia (480-543) has the credit of having imposed poverty and manual labour upon the cenobites, together with a severe discipline; the monastery founded by him on Monte Cassino became the model of Benedictine monasteries, where, according to a famous formula, "he who works, prays." Civilisation owes to the Western monks the cultivation of a part of Europe, and the preservation of Latin literature, the texts of which were copied in the monasteries. If idle and luxurious habits tended to appear there, in spite of perpetual efforts for their reform, this was an effect of human weakness for which the institution must not be held responsible. In the course of centuries it did much harm, but also, especially at the beginning, a great deal of good.

∴

27. The example of the monks, added to the influence of Manichæan, Gnostic, and Montanist doctrines, tended to exalt the old popular idea of the superiority of a celibate life. As early as A.D. 305, the Spanish Council of Elvira enjoined the celibacy of the priesthood. This doctrine did not gain a complete victory until the twelfth century, and even now ecclesiastical celibacy is a matter of discipline, not of dogma, in the Roman Church. Following the example of the Empire, she adopted a rigorous hierarchy; the bishops of the large towns became prefects, presiding over the councils or assemblies of the provincial clergy. Rome, Antioch, and Alexandria, but especially the first named, became as it were Christian capitals; by the end of the second century, a bishop of Rome was threatening to put the churches of Asia Minor "outside the catholic union" (that is to say, the *universal* union) because they differed from him as to the date of Easter. Christian rites were complicated by hardly disguised borrowings from paganism: baptism implied the

exorcism of devils; the worship of martyrs, the origin of the worship of saints, took the place of the worship of the Greek heroes, and sometimes adopted even their names and their legends. The festival of Christmas or of the birth of Jesus, the date of which is not indicated by the Evangelists, was fixed on December 25, the reputed date of the birth of Mithra, who was identified with the Sun. Finally, the Church forgot her Jewish origin more and more, and changed the character of the festivals she was obliged to retain. Pasch (*Pesach*), the Easter festival, became the anniversary of Christ's Resurrection, and the date was fixed to avoid coincidence with the Jewish Pasch; Pentecost, which among the Jews commemorated the giving of the Law to Moses upon Sinaï, was henceforth to recall the pouring out of the Holy Spirit upon the Apostles. The Church, though even more hostile to Hellenism than to Judaism, became Hellenised by force of circumstances, because, ever since its origin under St. Paul, it had appeared as a Greek sect of Judaism. The transference of the seat of the Empire to Constantinople, a Greek centre over-inclined to theological subtleties, where the disputes of the sophists still re-echoed, contributed a good deal to this development.

28. As soon as Christianity felt itself master of the Empire, it began to persecute not only the pagans, but dissident Christians. The disputes of the third and fourth centuries related more especially to the connection of Christ with God; were they of the same substance? Was Jesus equal to the Father? What place was to be assigned to the Holy Spirit in this system? A Bishop of Antioch, Paul of Samosata, a *protégé* of the learned Zenobia, Queen of Palmyra, who definitely subordinated Jesus to God, was condemned by a council and deposed (A.D. 270). Arius, a priest of Alexandria (A.D. 280-336), engaged in a long conflict with Athanasius, the bishop of that city (A.D. 328), because he maintained the essential superiority of God to Jesus. This doctrine, known as the Arian heresy, was condemned in 325 by the Council of Nicæa, which declared Jesus to be: "the Son of God, of the substance of the Father, consubstantial with him, begotten, not born, eternal like the Father, and immutable

by nature." In spite of this luminous definition, to which Constantine lent the support of the secular arm—Arius was exiled and his books were burnt—Arianism spread not only in the Empire, but beyond it; nearly all the barbarian peoples who invaded the frontiers in the fifth century became Arians, no doubt because they were evangelised by the Arians at a time when Arianism was dominant in the Empire. Several of the Roman Emperors of the fourth century were themselves favourable to Arianism, which was combated by St. Ambrose, Bishop of Milan. The Church of Rome had pronounced against Arianism at an early date; at the Council of Constantinople (A.D. 381), which completed the work of the Council of Nicæa by declaring the Holy Spirit the third person of the Trinity, equal to the Father and the Son, it gained a decisive victory. Thus a third God was created as it were, by the evolution of Plato's *Logos*, through Philo, the fourth Gospel, and the sophistical theology of Alexandria.

29. The doctrine of the Trinity was formulated by the *Symbol* or Creed, erroneously ascribed to Athanasius, and perhaps the work of the African bishop Vigilius (*c.* 490): "We worship one God in Trinity and Trinity in Unity, neither confounding the Persons nor dividing the substance. . . . And yet they are not three Eternals but one Eternal, not three Almighties but one Almighty. So the Father is God, the Son God, and the Holy Ghost God, and yet they are not three Gods but one God. . . . For like as we are compelled by the Christian verity to acknowledge every Person by himself to be God and Lord, so are we forbidden by the Catholic Religion to say: There be three Gods or three Lords. The Father is made of none: neither created nor begotten. The Son is of the Father alone: not made, nor created but begotten. The Holy Ghost is of the Father and of the Son: neither made, nor created, nor begotten, but proceeding. . . . And in this Trinity none is afore or after other: none is greater or less than another; but the whole three Persons are coeternal together and coequal." Such is the belief it is necessary to hold if we would be Catholics and not Arians. In these days there are no professed

Arians, perhaps because all Christians are Arians at heart. This is more especially true of the Protestants among whom the idea of God is still vital; for the Catholics habitually invoke Jesus, Mary and Joseph (JMJ, "the Jesuit Trinity"), and only name the Eternal Father mechanically. The ancient Trinity subsists merely as a theological formula.

30. Meanwhile, the long series of judicial murders for errors of opinion had begun. From 380 to 395 Theodosius published edicts threatening the heresiarchs with death; but it was reserved for his co-regent, Maximus, a Spaniard like himself, to apply them for the first time. The victim was Priscillian, a Spanish bishop, who was accused of Manicheeism and denounced by two Spanish bishops to the Emperor Maximus at Treves. Priscillian, condemned by a council at Bordeaux, was summoned to Treves with six of his principal partisans; they were there judged and put to death (A.D. 385). The excellent St. Martin of Tours was indignant, as was also St. Ambrose; but a few years later, St. Jerome, exasperated by Vigilantius, who attacked the worship of relics, declared that temporal chastisements are useful to save the guilty from eternal perdition. The Church of Africa and St. Augustine appealed to the secular arm against the Donatists; finally, in 447, Pope Leo I. not only justified the crime of Maximus, but declared that if the upholders of a damnable heresy were allowed to live there would be an end of all laws, human and divine. The Church, adopting this monstrous doctrine, caused torrents of blood to be shed by the secular power, down to the day when in its tardy enlightenment the latter refused to lend itself any longer to the fury of theological hate.

31. The Arian quarrel had not exhausted the difficulties suggested by the incarnation of Jesus. Was Mary the *Mother of God?* No, said Nestorius, the Patriarch of Constantinople; she was only the Mother of Christ. In 431, at the Council of Ephesus, Cyril procured the deposition of Nestorius; his partisans migrated to Persia, and there founded the Nestorian Church, which still exists. Another question which arose was this: were there two natures in Jesus, one divine and one human, or only one? The second

thesis, called Monophysism, upheld by the Egyptian monks, was submitted to the Council of Ephesus (A.D. 449); this time the Emperor Theodosius II. sent troops and the adversaries of Monophysism were treated with the utmost violence. The Patriarch of Constantinople died of his wounds. This Council is known in history as the *Brigandage of Ephesus.* Another council in A.D. 451 pronounced against Monophysism, but declared at the same time that the humanity of Jesus was not absorbed by his divinity. The struggle began afresh under Justinian, who had a taste for theology. A perfervid Monophysite, like his worthy consort, Theodora, he deposed Pope Vigilius, who resisted him, and caused his opinions to be confirmed by a whole series of councils. After his death, the Monophysites were again defeated; but their doctrine has survived in the Christian Church of Egypt, the Copts (a corruption of *Aigyptios,* Egyptian), which preserved its religious independence as a result of this schism.

∴

32. We have already seen St. Augustine in conflict with African Donatism, and with Manicheeism, which he had once professed himself. A quarrel no less serious arose over the doctrine of the Breton monk Pelagius, which attacked the theory of original sin. How could the whole human race have been condemned for the sin of Adam? How could the results of his fault still weigh upon innocent creatures? Augustine, now an old man, combated these reasonable objections by an exaggeration of St. Paul's cruel paradox. Man can do nothing of his own will; he is utterly powerless; the grace of God alone can save him, and those who are not chosen by God are lost. The logical consequence is not fatalism, but the imperative necessity of faith, prayer, and appeals to intercessory saints. The Council of Ephesus condemned Pelagius (A.D. 431), who had already been condemned at Carthage in 412. Nevertheless, his doctrine, somewhat modified, survived in semi-Pelagianism, notably in Gaul, and Rome ended by adopting in practice a conciliatory attitude founded upon subtle distinctions concerning

the efficacy of grace, and the equal necessity for faith and works in the individual working out of salvation.

33. St. Augustine had held that there was an intermediate state of probation between future felicity and damnation, that of the purification of souls by fire. This is the Orphic and Virgilian doctrine of Purgatory: there is not a word about it in the Gospels. But as the Last Judgment, with the final separation of the good and bad into the saved and the lost, was put off to a very remote period, it became necessary to invent something to define the condition of souls immediately after death. In imitation of the pagans, who represented them as appearing for judgment before Minos and his assessors, a provisional judgment was suggested, followed by the classification of the dead in two divisions, the good, who have to undergo the probation of Purgatory, and the wicked, who go straight to Hell. The Church had formed the habit of praying for the dead, and invoking the intercession of the saints in their favour. The implication was that the dead required the good offices of the living, and that their fate was not irrevocably sealed. The doctrine of Purgatory, the logic of which is undeniable, was formulated in the sixth century, and proclaimed a dogma of the Church by the Council of Florence (1439); the Christians who reject it (Protestants and members of the Greek Church) have evidently little curiosity about the hereafter.

34. St. Jerome, who was born in Dalmatia, revised the Latin translations of the Scriptures by order of Pope Damasus, and made use of his personal influence, which was as considerable as his talent, to win over the ladies of the Roman aristocracy to a conventual life. "Thou hast become the mother-in-law of God," he wrote to one of them, whose daughter had entered a nunnery, and was therefore the bride of God. Establishing himself at Bethlehem with his penitents (A.D. 385), he made it a centre of monasticism, and worked unceasingly till the age of ninety at commentaries on the sacred books. His relations with St. Augustine were courteous, but not without an undercurrent of bitterness, especially towards the end.

35. One of the adversaries of St. Jerome was a Pyre-

nean shepherd, Vigilantius, who returned from a journey in Italy and the Holy Land disgusted with official Christianity. He protested vehemently against the idolatrous worship of images, the legacy of paganism to the Church, a practice directly opposed to that Mosaic law which Jesus came not to destroy, but to fulfil. It was idle to reply that these images were the Scriptures of the illiterate, that they were not the object of, but the stimulus to, worship. Experience showed that the majority of the faithful confounded (as indeed they still do) the sign with the thing signified. Vigilantius was no less hostile to the worship of relics, which had become at once a disgrace to the Church and a source of revenue to the clergy. Asceticism, prayers for the dead, the celibacy of the clergy, which was exacted with increasing rigour, all seemed to him contrary to true religion. Violently attacked by St. Jerome, who invoked the severity of the civil authority against him, Vigilantius died in obscurity in 420; but his courageous words did not fail to bear fruit in due season.

36. Two Greeks, St. Gregory Nazianzen and St. Basil, shed lustre upon the Eastern Church in the fourth century. They were scholars, gentle and amiable in disposition, whose somewhat effeminate eloquence still has a certain charm. Basil, the Bishop of Cæsaræa, set an admirable example of charity, founding many hospitals and refuges. Gregory was the son of a bishop of Nazianzus in Cappadocia, who had three other children after his ordination. Gregory became Patriarch of Constantinople, but, disgusted with the intrigues surrounding him, he returned to end his days in his bishopric of Nazianzus. When he was begged to leave his retreat and assist at a new council, he replied: "I never knew of a Synod that did any good or prevented any evil."

37. St. John Chrysostom ("the golden-mouthed") was a fluent orator, but, like St. Augustine, above all things a man of action. Born at Antioch in 347, a pupil of the pagan Libanius, he preached for twelve years in his native town. The Emperor Arcadius appointed him Patriarch of Byzantium, where he engaged in a memorable campaign against the Empress Eudoxia, whose extravagance and profligacy

he publicly denounced. Eudoxia caused Chrysostom to be condemned by a council, but a popular insurrection reinstated him. He renewed his attacks on the Empress, whom he compared to Herodias. Hereupon there was another council, and another insurrection, followed by a great fire; Chrysostom was exiled to Cucusus in the Taurus, and afterwards to Pontus, where he died miserably at Comana.

38. At about the same period, St. Ambrose, Bishop of Milan, the friend of St. Augustine, combated Arianism in the person of the Empress Justina, the wife of Maximus (386), refused the communion to Theodosius and compelled the Emperor to do penance for having ordered a massacre at Thessalonica. The spiritual sword was drawn against the temporal sword, heralding that struggle between the priesthood and the Empire which was to fill the Middle Ages. How beneficent might the influence of the Church have been if, following the lead of St. Ambrose, she had used her power to restrain the violence of princes, instead of perpetually exciting it to serve her own ends!

39. Vigilantius and Chrysostom agreed in protesting against the advance of luxury in the life and habits of the Church. This was, indeed, one of the inevitable results of her triumph. Extolling humility in theory, she began to love splendour and adorned herself with the gorgeous trappings of paganism. Magnificent basilicas arose on every side, which were all eclipsed by the crowning glory of St. Sophia at Constantinople. The bishops and the majority of the monks lived in opulence, enriched by gifts from the State and the devout. Divine service lost its first simplicity; even in broad daylight the churches were resplendent with the radiance of innumerable candles; incense and holy water were borrowed from pagan forms of worship; the sacerdotal vestments became magnificent, festivals were multiplied. But these changes, by which art profited, did not impede the expansive force of Christianity; following upon the Empire, the barbarian world became its pupils, and Clovis, a Catholic in the midst of Arian peoples, made the cause of the Roman Church triumph by subjugating them.

BIBLIOGRAPHY

In addition to the great church histories (Neander, Rohrbacher), now somewhat antiquated, and the first two volumes of the *Histoire ancienne de l'Eglise* by Duchesne (1906-1908), consult Hauck's Encyclopædia, and Smith and Wace's Dict. of Christian Biography. The following are useful manuals: F. Naef, *Histoire de l'Eglise chrétienne,* 1892 (a good book which I have found very useful); W. Walker, *History of the Christ. Church,* 1918; X. Funk, *Lehrbuch der Kirchengeschichte,* 5th ed., 1907; Kurtz, *Abriss der Kirchengeschichte,* 16th ed., 1906 (short and clear).

Wellhausen (and others), *Die christliche Religion mit Einschluss der jüdischen,* 1906; A. Harnack, *Lehrbuch der Dogmengeschichte,* 4th ed., 1909 (there is an abridgment by the author, 4th ed., 1906); Fr. Loofs, *Leitfaden zur Dogmengeschichte,* 4th ed., 1906; L. Duchesne, *Origines du culte chrétien,* 2nd ed., 1898; O. Bardenhewer, *Gesch. der altchristl. Literatur,* 1903; A. Harnack, *Die Ueberlieferung und der Bestand der altchristl. Literatur bis Eusebius,* 1899; *Die Chronologie der altchristl. Literatur,* 2 vols. 1897-1904; P. de Labriolle, *Hist. de la littérature chrétienne* (latine), 1920; A. Puech, *Hist. de la litt. chrétienne* (grecque), 1928; A. Denzinger, *Enchiridion symbolorum et definitionum,* 9th ed., 1900 (in Latin); L. Coulange, *Catéchisme pour adultes,* 1929 (admirable summary). See also Bibl. of chap. viii.

2. Renan, *S. Paul,* 1869. See chap. viii, § 47.

7. Supposed death of Peter in Palestine: art. *Petrus,* in Hauck, p. 201, 43; Guignebert, *La primauté de Pierre,* 1909.

8. Harnack, *Mission und Ausbreitung des Christentums,* 2nd ed., 1906 (*cf.* Monceaux, *J. des Sav.,* 1904, p. 404).

, 9. Bréhier, *Philon,* 1908; E. de Faye, *Gnostiques,* 2nd ed., 1926.

10. E. von Dobschütz, *Die urchristlichen Gemeinden,* 1902; A. Réville, *l'Eucharistie,* 1908; Batiffol, *L'agape* (in *Hist. et théologie,* p. 227); art. *Agape* in Cabrol's *Dictionnaire de Liturgie.*

11. Glossolaly and the supposed gifts of prophecy: art. *Spiritual Gifts* in Cheyne.

12. Harnack, *op. cit.* under 8.—The synagogues as nurseries of Christianity: S. R., *Cultes,* vol. iii, p. 449.

13. Allard, *Hist. des persécutions pendant les trois premiers siècles,* 5 vols., 1894-1903; *Julien l'Apostat,* 3 vols., 1900-1903; *Le christianisme et l'empire de Néron à Théodose,* 5th ed., 1903; *Dix leçons sur le martyre,* 1906; B. Aubé, *Hist. des persécutions,* 4 vols., 1875-1885; G. Boissier, *La fin du paganisme,* 2 vols., 1891; *L'incendie de Rome et la première persécution* (in *Journ. des Sav.,* 1902, p. 158); E. Chénon, *Les rapports de l'Eglise et de l'Etat du Ier au XXe siècle,* 1905 (good summary); A. Harnack, *Der Vorwurf des Atheismus,* 1905; Le Blant, *Les persécuteurs et les martyrs,* 1893; Leclercq, *Les Martyrs,* 1902 *et seq.;* Ramsay, *The Church in the Roman Empire,* 6th ed., 1900.

14. Art. *Trajanus* in the *Dict. of Christian Biography.*—Glut in the cattle-market of Bithynia: S. R., *Cultes,* vol. i, p. 395 (after Ramsay).

15-17. Bouché-Leclercq, *L'intolérance religieuse et la politique,* 1911 (Rome and the Christians); art. *Accusations* in Cabrol's *Dictionnaire.*—The Jewish community and the martyrs of Lyons: S. R., *Cultes,* vol. iii, p. 449.—Celsus and his *Logos Alethes* (True Discourse): Aubé, *Hist. des Perséc.,* vol. ii, p. 118; L. Rougier, *Celse,* 1926.—For the lost book of Julian see Allard's work quoted above, § 13.

18. Allard, *Les esclaves chrétiens,* 1876.

19. O. Harnack, *Marcion,* 1924.—E. Buonaiuto, *Lo gnosticismo,* 1907. —E. de Faye, *Clément d'Alexandrie,* 1898.—*Origène,* 1927-8 (cf. *Journ. des Sav.,* 1884, p. 177).

20. Art. *Verfassung* (*urchristliche*) in Hauck.

21. Selwyn, *The Christian Prophets,* 1900; P. de Labriolle, *Le montanisme,* 1915.

22. Renegades and Libellatici: Aubé, *L'Eglise et l'Etat,* 1885, p. 199; Foucart, *J. des Sav.,* April 1908.—Art. *Decius* and *Diocletianus* in *Dict. of Christian Biography.*

23. Boissier, *La fin du paganisme,* 2 vols., 1893 (Constantine, Julian, &c.).

24. Chastel, *Hist. de la destruction du paganisme,* 1850; V. Schultze, *Gesch. des Untergangs des Heidentums,* 2 vols., 1887-1892.—Art. *Cyrillus* and *Hypatia* in *Dict. of Christian Biography.*

25. Monceaux, *Histoire littéraire de l'Afrique chrétienne,* 1901 *sq.;* H. Leclercq, *L'Afrique chrétienne,* 2 vols., 1904.—Art. *Afrique* in Cabrol, and *Donatismus* in Hauck.

26. A. Harnack, *Das Mönchtum,* 1901.—Art. *Mönchtum* in Hauck.

27. Lea, *History of Sacerdotal Celibacy,* 2nd ed., vol. i, 1907.—Saintyves, *Les saints successeurs des dieux,* 1908; Delehaye, *Origine du culte des Martyrs,* 1912; E. Lucius, *Anfaenge des Heiligen Kultes,* 1905. —Th. Reinach, *La fête de Pâques,* 1906; A. Meyer, *Entst. d. Weihnachtsfestes,* 1911.

28. A. Dupin, *Le dogme de la Trinité,* 1907; G. Bardy, *Paul de Samosate,* 1923; A. Réville, *La christologie de Paul de Samosate* (in *Etudes de critique,* 1896, p. 189); *Athanase et Arius* (Brussels), 1904.—Art. *Arianismus, Nicaenisches Konzil,* and *Trinitaet* in Hauck.

29. Art. *Athanasium,* in Hauck.

30. Ch. Babut, *Priscillien,* 1909; Lea, *Hist. of the Inquisition,* vol. i.

31. Art. *Nestorius* in Hauck, and R. Duval, *L'Eglise nestorienne* (in *Journ. des Sav.,* 1904, p. 109).—Art. *Monophysiten,* in Hauck.—Diehl, *Justinien,* 1901.—Art. *Koptische Kirche* in Hauck (vol. xii, p. 801).

32. E. Vacandard, *S. Bernard,* new ed., 1904.—Art. *Pelagius* and *Semipelagianismus* in Hauck.

33. Art. *Fegfeuer* (purgatory) in Hauck.—Prayers for the Dead: S. R., *Cultes,* vol. i, p. 313.

34. Am. Thierry, *S. Jérôme,* 1867; Cavallera, *S. Jérôme,* 1923.

35-36. Art. *Vigilantius* in *Dict. of Christ. Biogr.;* Art. *Gregorius* and *Basilius, ibid.,* 1902.—A. Réville, *Vigilance,* 1902; P. Monceaux, *S. Martin,* 1926; M. Guignet, *Grég. de Nazianze,* 1911.

37. Am. Thierry, *S. Jean Chrysostome et l'imperatrice Eudoxie,* 1872; Puech, *S. J. Chrysostome,* 1891.

38. R. Thamin, *Morale de S. Ambroise,* 1895.

CHAPTER X

CHRISTIANITY: FROM JUSTINIAN TO CHARLES V.

The services rendered by the Church to medieval society. The conversion of heathen nations. Charlemagne inaugurates the era of violent proselytism. Pilgrimages: the Crusades. The constitution of the temporal power of the Popes. False Decretals. Exactions of the Holy See. Excommunication. Simony. Quarrels of the Popes and Emperors: Gregory VII., the Emperor at Canossa. The Popes and England. Innocent III. The Emperor Frederick II. The Great Schism of the West. The decadence of the Papacy in the fifteenth century.

The monastic orders. Franciscans and Dominicans. Knights Hospitallers and Knights Templars.

The worship of the Virgin. The Immaculate Conception. The worship of saints, and the Golden Legend. Mass. The Eucharist. The feast of the Holy Sacrament. Confession, and the sale of indulgences. Jubilees. The celibacy of the priesthood.

The Church and heresies. The image-breakers or Iconoclasts. The Catharists or Albigenses. The devastation of the south of France. The Vaudois or Waldenses.

Anselm of Canterbury and Abélard: Scholasticism. Roger Bacon and St. Thomas Aquinas. The Imitation of Christ. Humanism: Reuchlin and Erasmus. Wyclif and John Huss. Girolamo Savonarola.

The organisation of the Inquisition. The crimes of the Inquisition. Tortures and the stake. The persecution of so-called witches.

The Christian Churches which seceded from Rome: the so-called Orthodox Church.

1. Medieval society owed a great deal to the Church. To deny this is to make a miracle of her duration.

2. In the first place, the Church propagated the Gospel. Not that she practised it, or commended the study of it. But its principles were on her lips, a germ of humanity, a check upon barbarism. She also acted upon the inspiration of the Gospel in her charitable works, which Julian had held up to the admiration of the heathen. True, her charity was not always judicious. She gave freely and indiscriminately, and so encouraged mendicity. But both in the East and the West she multiplied hospitals, orphanages and asylums.

When we remember that the Emperor Claudius had to issue a decree forbidding people to abandon their sick slaves and cast them out to starve by the roadside, we realise that the Church, though intent, not on a social duty, but on spiritual salvation, was more humane than lettered paganism.

3. The Church further gave or imposed upon Europe the external forms of Christianity. It is, relatively, a simple creed, not surcharged with festivals, and unencumbered by alimentary prohibitions; it does not demand overmuch of its adherents; it suits a laborious race. Activity was, indeed, generally enjoined as a duty by the Church, even to its monks; Christianity is not, or has only occasionally been, a religion of parasites and sluggards.

4. Although the Church of Christ perpetually had recourse to violence and shed more blood than all secular ambitions, she at least affirmed the superiority of the spirit to mere brute force, at a period when might was by no means at the service of right. The bishops were the protectors, somewhat capricious no doubt, but effectual, of the weak and oppressed. The Church taught kings mercy. As early as the tenth century she established truces (the Peace of God), intervals in private warfare; she was not, it is true, the first or the only power who did so; but we must give her the credit due for having revived this ancient custom, at a time of universal massacre and pillage.

5. Without any deliberate intention of preserving the literary masterpieces of antiquity, she had a great many of them copied in her monasteries, just as she saved many masterpieces of art in the treasuries of her churches. Her worship demanded magnificence; artists worked for her glory and our delight.

6. Finally, at a time when society was divided into castes, when there were nobles, villeins and serfs, she upheld the principle of the equality of all men before God, and urged the essential dignity of the most wretched, since Christ had shed his blood for their salvation. The Church was the refuge of talent. She placed at her head, supreme over kings, the son of a workman, the son of a beggar. It was not necessary to be of noble birth to become a bishop, a

THE CRUSADES

cardinal or a pope. Monarchical at its summit, the Church was democratic at its base; it was never aristocratic. This fact was clearly recognised by Voltaire: "The Roman Church has always enjoyed the advantage of being free to give to merit what was elsewhere reserved for birth; and it is even noteworthy that the haughtiest among the popes (Gregory VII. and Adrian IV.) were those of the most humble origin. In Germany, there are still convents which admit only persons of noble birth. The spirit of Rome is marked by more grandeur and less vanity."

∴

7. The prodigiously rapid establishment of the Arab Empire was the first blow struck at the power of the Church; Christianity retreated, for the first time, in Syria, Asia Minor, North Africa and Spain (710). In Spain alone, centres of resistance were soon formed, which became triumphant in the fifteenth century. But the Christian princes never invoked the aid of a Crusade; this is remarkable as showing that even in Spain the reckless behaviour of the Soldiers of the Cross was a matter of common knowledge.

8. Powerless against Islam, the Church was successful everywhere else in her great work of proselytism among the Gentiles. Her best missionaries were the monks of Ireland, which had been evangelised by St. Patrick, and was called the Isle of Saints; they were the first militia of the Church in Western Europe. After converting the Franks, who were baptized by St. Remigius (496), she christianised the Anglo-Saxons by means of the Roman monk Augustine (596), and the Germans by means of the Anglo-Saxon Winfrid, called St. Boniface, who was finally assassinated in Frisia (689-755). Many brilliant conversions were due to princesses such as Clotilde, the queen of Clovis; Voltaire justly remarked that half Europe owes its Christianity to women. The conversion of Wladimir (988) was preceded by that of his grandmother, the Russian duchess Olga, who came to Constantinople (957). As early as 868, the Patriarch of Constantinople had obtained permission to found a church at Kieff. The Russian mercenaries of the Imperial Guard,

who became Christians at Constantinople, laboured to evangelise Russia after their return to their homes.

9. The Byzantine monks Cyril and Methodius baptized a Bulgarian chief in 863; Cyril translated the Bible into the Slav tongue, making use of an alphabet derived from the Greek, which he had composed for the purpose. After Bulgaria, Methodius evangelised Bohemia, whence Christianity spread to Poland and Hungary (*c.* 1000). In the ninth century, the Church converted the Normans and the Danes of England, and then those of Denmark and Sweden. The influence of Christianity extended far towards the East; the Persian Nestorians sent missionaries of the Gospel into Central Asia and even into China (*c.* 600). In the thirteenth century, Rome took up the propaganda of the Nestorians; a church was founded at Pekin, but was soon destroyed, and the Mongolians, at first favourable to Christianity, were partially converted to Islamism. The Nestorian Churches were destroyed in this reaction.

10. Down to the end of the eighth century, the spiritual victories of the Church had entailed no bloodshed. The era of violent proselytism was inaugurated by Charlemagne, who gave the Saxons a choice between baptism and death (772-782) and massacred over four thousand of them at once. The bishops he instituted were called upon to take cognisance of acts of idolatry and to punish them as crimes; they were the ancestors of the Inquisitors. After the year 1000, conversion by force became general. The Wends of Pomerania were compelled by the Dukes of Poland to accept baptism; Pope Honorius decreed a crusade against the Prussians, against whom the Teutonic Knights waged a war of extermination (1236-1283). The Brethren of the Sword treated Livonia and Courland in the same manner. But the conversion of the Lithuanians was not completed till the end of the fourteenth century.

∴

11. The custom of pilgrimages to the scenes of the Scriptures was anterior even to the triumph of Christianity; thus Helena, the mother of Constantine, went to Jerusalem, where

later writers (but not the contemporary Eusebius) report that she discovered the "true cross." The conquest of Syria by the Musulmans made these pilgrimages more perilous; pilgrims returned to tell moving tales of the sad state of Palestine, and the evils endured by the Christians. "Amidst the extreme sufferings of the Middle Ages," says Michelet, "men still had tears for the misery of Jerusalem." The Papacy, in conjunction with the feudal nobles, whose very existence was due to war, accordingly organized those great military pilgrimages to the Holy Land known as the Crusades (1096-1291). Although these cost millions of lives, exhausted the resources of Christian Europe, aggravated fanaticism, exaggerated the worship of saints and relics to the point of mania, and encouraged the abuse of and traffic in indulgences, they must be credited with having kept back the rising flood of Islamism, re-established regular intercourse with the East, and introduced into Western chivalry ideas somewhat more liberal than those of Frankish barbarism. Even the disasters of the Crusades were not in vain, for they awoke doubts among the masses as to the efficacy of divine protection and the infallibility of the councils of Rome. Finally, "liberty, natural to man, was born again from the want of money among the princes." [1]

12. The Crusaders in general, in spite of their sacred cause, behaved like highway robbers.[2] The first host which set out in 1095, and was annihilated by the Turks at Nicæa, killed, burned and pillaged all they encountered. The army commanded by Godfrey de Bouillon massacred the entire population of Jerusalem (1098). The astuteness of Venice turned aside the fourth Crusade upon Constantinople, and the sack of this city is a dark blot on the history of Western Christendom (1204). It was abominably ravaged, and the very church of St. Sophia was the scene of bloody and sacrilegious orgies. "This was the first time that the city of Constantinople had been taken and sacked by strangers: it was done by Christians who had vowed to fight only against the infidel." [3]

[1] Voltaire. [2] *Ibid.* [3] *Ibid.*

The one consolatory element in the story is to be found in the unhappy crusades of St. Louis directed upon Egypt and Tunis, in which the king, though a very indifferent general, showed himself at least worthy of the name of Christian.

. . .

13. The instigators of the Crusades were always the Popes, seconded by monks. As early as 1074, Gregory VII. had dreamt of reconquering Anatolia, which had fallen into the hands of the Seljuk Turks. Pope Urban II. appeared at the Council of Clermont in 1094, accompanied by a monk of Picardy, Peter the Hermit, promising the indulgences of the Church to all who would go and fight the infidel. The second Crusade was preached by Eugenius III. and Bernard, Abbot of Clairvaux; the fourth by Innocent III. and Foulques of Neuilly. Even the frantic Children's Crusade (1212) was encouraged by Innocent III. It was naturally to the interest of the papacy to appear thus as the supreme power which set all the military forces of Europe in movement. As soon as a noble had taken the Cross, he belonged to the Church. The Crusader's vow was indissoluble save by the Pope's consent; from the beginning of the thirteenth century he began to grant remission for ready money. In the crusading armies the papal legates became delegates of a theocracy which consolidated rapidly and threatened to absorb civil society altogether. On the other hand, the Church fattened on the general misery; to obtain the money necessary for their enterprises, nobles and vassals were obliged to sell their lands, which the Church bought at prices far below their value. Thus Godfrey de Bouillon, Duke of Brabant, sold his estate of Bouillon to the Chapter of Liége, and Stenay to the Bishop of Verdun.[1]

In the twelfth century the Popes paid tithes on the church revenues to the princes; but after the Lateran Council in 1215 they laid claim, as directors of the Crusades, to all this money, thus creating a tax which was levied in their interest throughout Christendom.

14. The last Christian town in Syria, St. John d'Acre,

[1] Voltaire.

was retaken by the Musulmans in 1291. Rhodes held out till the beginning of the sixteenth century. It was the zeal of the Hungarians and Slavs, newly converted to Christianity, and not the hopelessly divided forces of Europe, which arrested the Turks on the road to Central Europe and Vienna. Broadly speaking, the Crusades were a failure; the political object of the papacy was not realised. The condition of Christians and pilgrims in the Holy Land was slightly bettered by various treaties; but the Christian kingdom of Jerusalem lasted only eighty-eight years, and the Latin Empire of Constantinople was no less ephemeral. When the Paleologi overthrew it in 1261, they had to reckon not only with Musulman ambition, but with the religious hatred of the West. The loss of the Greek Empire to Christianity (1453), a disaster to all European civilisation, was the final defeat, I might almost say the logical conclusion, of the Crusades.

15. The ruin of the Western Empire had plunged Rome into poverty. Her bishop (the Pope) and her parish priests (the Cardinals) staggered under the crushing burdens imposed upon them by their dignity and the calls upon their charity. The Roman Church received large gifts of land even outside Italy to meet these requirements. In the seventh century she was deprived of nearly all her possessions by the disasters of the times. Her lands in the neighbourhood of Rome constituted the patrimony of St. Peter, called in later days the Roman Province and Roman Duchy. Finally, as the price of its alliance with Pépin le Bref against the Lombards, the papacy obtained a guarantee of its property, to which something was added by Charlemagne. It is a mistake, however, to credit Pépin with the foundation of the temporal power of the Popes. They were at first his lieutenants and administrators. It was not until the ninth century that the papal suzerainty asserted itself, thanks partly to the decay of the Frankish kingdom, partly to the disorder which reigned in Italy, and, above all, to a false document, the pretended donation of Italy to Pope Sylvester by the Emperor Constantine, imposed by Pope Adrian upon Charlemagne. It was not until the days of the Renaissance

that the forgery was recognised, long after it had produced all the effects which could be expected from it.

16. The papal decisions, entitled *canons* or *decretals*, were collected about the year 630 by Bishop Isidore of Seville. To this first collection a second was added about 850. This second collection, also put forward in the name of Isidore, is a series of impudent forgeries, supporting the pretensions of the Pope and the bishops, in opposition to the councils, the synods, and the civil power. "The boldest and most magnificent forgery which has deceived the world for centuries," Voltaire calls it. The forger, who was probably a bishop, seems to have been living in the diocese of Tours about the year 850. Strong in the possession of this weapon, the Popes no longer had any competition to fear in the spiritual kingdom, and were hereby encouraged to encroach upon the temporal. From 852 onwards the False Decretals were cited as authorities, and many among them still figure in the authorised collections of Canon Law. Definitive proof of their falsity was only brought forward in 1628 by the French pastor Blondel, whose work was put on the Index. Never yet has the papacy acknowledged that for a thousand years it made use of forged documents to its own profit.

17. Down to the time of Julius II. the papal territories, continually encroached upon by feudal princes, produced scarcely anything. The papal revenues consisted of gifts from the Universal Church, of the tithes occasionally conceded by the clergy, and the income from dispensations and taxes. A continual want of funds was one cause of the gravest abuses of the Holy See—extortions, sale of indulgences, contributions exacted from those appointed to vacant benefices. John XXII. instituted a tariff for sin. By an unhappy imitation of the German penal code, which allowed criminals to make a money compensation, he valued theft, murder, and worse, at a price, "and the men who were wicked enough to commit these sins were fools enough to pay for them."[1] "Lists of these contributions have been printed several times since the fifteenth century, and have brought to light infamies at once more ridiculous and more

[1] Voltaire.

odious than anything we are told about the impudent deceptions of the priests of antiquity."[1]

18. An Anglo-Saxon king founded an ecclesiastical college at Rome, and to maintain it imposed on his subjects a tax known as "Peter's Pence" (725). The first certainly authentic document on the subject is a letter of Leo III. Gregory VII. relied upon this practice to justify the inclusion of England among the vassals of the Holy See. After England, other northern countries were subjected to the same tax, and paid it with more or less regularity down to the Reformation. France and Spain resisted. The *Denier de St. Pierre,* re-established in 1860, had nothing but the name in common with the ancient tribute. It used to bring in more than £80,000 a year to Leo XIII., but was much more prolific in the days of Pius IX.

19. The most formidable weapon in the hands of the Church was excommunication, which deprived its victims of the sacraments and of all legal authority. The major excommunication had the force of an interdict. No one could speak to or serve the person excommunicated without contamination, and becoming *anathema* himself. When a prince was excommunicated, all religious rites were suspended in his State. It was a strike declared by God! Then the credulous population became terror-stricken, and drove their political chiefs into submission. Thanks to this weapon of excommunication, the Popes of the Middle Ages were able to "give" to their favoured candidates the crowns of the Empire, of Portugal, Hungary, Denmark, England, Aragon, Sicily, and finally of France, which Boniface VIII., after having excommunicated Philippe le Bel, gave to Albert of Austria by a Bull: "We donate to you, in the plenitude of our power, the Kingdom of France, which belongs of right to the Emperors of the West." We know how Philip replied (1303).

20. The Popes established the universal use of Latin in divine service, and aimed at making the supremacy of Rome manifest by forcing the Roman liturgy upon all. From the year 400 onwards, the Latin service appears to have super-

[1] *Ibid.*

seded the more ancient Greek in the churches of Rome. The *Kyrie eleison* (*Lord, have mercy*) of the Latin service is a Greek survival.

.·.

21. In the ninth and tenth centuries the papacy passed through a period of shameful disorder. The Rome of John X. was a *cloaca* in which the Popes set the example of the worst misconduct. The priestly functions were openly sold, a proceeding to which the name of simony was given, from the story of Simon in the Acts of the Apostles (viii, 18). This sore in the Church remained open till the thirteenth century, in spite of the honest efforts of Gregory VII. to close it. The Emperor Henry III. intervened, deposed three Popes, who hurled mutual anathemas at each other, and set in their place the honest Clement, Bishop of Bamberg. Clement was the first pontiff nominated by the Emperor. The German rulers must soon have regretted their interference, for Rome, in its turn, wished to give laws to Germany in order to avoid having to take them from the Emperor.

22. "The fundamental fact in the whole history of the Middle Ages is the papal claim to the suzerainty of all States, in virtue of the pretension that the Pope, alone, was the successor of Jesus Christ; while the German Emperors, on the other hand, pretended to believe that the kingdoms of Europe were nothing but dismembered fragments of the empire they had inherited from the Roman Cæsars."[1] The doctrine of the universal suzerainty of the Popes was never affirmed with more insistence than by Hildebrand, called Gregory VII., whom legend makes the son of a carpenter. He was a restless, enterprising spirit, who sometimes mingled cunning with his zeal for the claims of the Church. Not only did he wish to withdraw the papacy from the guardianship of the Empire and concentrate in himself the power to nominate and invest bishops; he even dared to excommunicate the Emperor Henry IV., who resisted, and had caused him to be deposed by the Council of Worms (1076). "All

[1] Voltaire.

the world trembled," says a chronicler of the time, "when the people learned the excommunication of their King." "Seek," says Voltaire, "for the source of all these humiliations on the one hand, and audacity on the other; you will find their origin in the populace, which alone gives superstition its dynamic power."[1] The Emperor had no choice but to humble himself before the Pope at Canossa, after having been kept waiting, we are told, barefooted in the snow (1077). "Believing himself then, not unnaturally, master of the crowns of the earth, Gregory wrote, in more than one letter, that he considered it his duty to humble the might of kings."[2] The quarrel broke out again as hotly as ever after this lame reconciliation. The Emperor laid siege to Rome, which was saved by the Norman, Robert Guiscard. But the Pope had to fly, and died miserably at Salerno (1085). He had been the friend and director of Matilda, Countess of Tuscany, who left her great territorial possessions to the papacy after Gregory's death.

23. An understanding between the Empire and the Holy See—between Ghibellines and Guelfs—took long to establish and cost much bloodshed. The conflict ended at last in a concordat (1122). "The real cause of quarrel was that neither the Popes nor the Roman people wanted emperors in Rome; the pretext, which was put forward as holy, was that the Popes, depositories of the Church's rights, could not allow secular princes to invest her bishops with pastoral staff and ring. It was clear enough that bishops, who were the subjects of princes and enriched by them, owed homage for their lands. Kings and emperors did not pretend to endow them with the Holy Ghost, but they demanded homage for the temporalities they had given. The ring and the pastoral staff were but accessories to the main question. But, as almost invariably happens, the heart of the matter was neglected and battle joined over an irrelevant detail."[3]

24. The papacy showed itself no less aggressive towards Henry II. of England. For having instigated the assassination of Thomas â Becket, Archbishop of Canterbury, he was

[1] *Ibid.* [2] *Ibid.* [3] *Ibid.*

excommunicated by the Pope, and driven to purchase absolution by enormous concessions. Barefooted, the king had to do penance at the tomb of the murdered bishop. To this same Henry, Pope Adrian IV., an Englishman himself, wrote: "It is not doubted, and you know it, that Ireland and all those islands which have received the faith belong to the Church of Rome; if you wish to enter that island, to drive vice out of it, to cause law to be obeyed and St. Peter's Pence to be paid by every house, it will please us to assign it to you."

25. At the Thirteenth Council of Lyons the English ambassadors said to Innocent IV.: "Through an Italian, you draw more than 60,000 marks from the kingdom of England; you have lately sent us a legate who has given every benefice to Italians. He extorts excessive contributions from all the faithful, and he excommunicates every one who complains of these exactions." The Pope made no reply, but proceeded to excommunicate Frederick II. In 1255 Alexander IV. ordered a crusade to be preached in England against Manfred of Naples, and sent a legate to collect tithes. "Matthew Paris reports that the Nuncio collected 50,000 pounds sterling in England. Seeing the English of to-day, it is hard to believe that their ancestors could have been such fools!"[1]

26. Gregory VII. found a worthy successor in Innocent III. The son of a gentleman of Anagni, "he finally erected that edifice of the temporal power for which his predecessors had been amassing materials for some four hundred years. . . . The Roman pontiffs began to be kings in fact; and religion, aided by circumstances, made them the masters of kings."[2] Innocent III. undertook, in the first place, to withdraw Italy from the influence of Germany; and, secondly, to subject all the rest of Europe to his own jurisdiction. In 1199 he excommunicated Philip Augustus for repudiating Ingeborg; in 1210 he excommunicated Otho IV.; in 1213 he excommunicated John Lackland, King of Eng-

[1] Voltaire.
[2] *Ibid.*

land. At one moment he stood out, the uncontested master of Christendom. He preached the fourth Crusade, which threw the Greek Empire into Catholic hands (1204); he let loose all the furies of the crusade against the Albigenses (1207); from the fourth Lateran Council he obtained the terrible laws against heretics and Jews (1215). His successor, Honorius III., secured the help of a formidable army of monks, the Dominicans, for the papacy.

27. The death of Innocent III. marks a turning-point in the history of the Popes. From this date onward the temporal power shows a tendency to dwindle before the resistance of the secular authorities. Frederick II.'s Chancellor, Petrus de Vinea, wrote in support of the rights of the State. The Emperor himself replied to an excommunication by besieging Rome. Frederick II., who made atrocious laws against heresy, was himself a free-thinker. "We have proofs," wrote Gregory IX. in 1239, "that he declares publicly that the world has been deceived by three impostors, Moses, Jesus Christ, and Mahomet. Jesus Christ he places below the other two, because, he says, they were glorious in their lives, while he was nothing but a man sprung from the dregs of the people, who preached to others of the same condition." Sixty years later, Philip the Fair, intent on the posthumous condemnation of Boniface VIII., brought fourteen witnesses to declare that the Pope had been heard to ask: "What profits have we not derived from this fable of Christ!" Calumny or not, it showed a considerable advance towards intellectual emancipation when such blasphemies could be ascribed to an emperor by a Pope, and to a Pope by a king.

28. After the fall of the Hohenstaufens, the Hapsburgs showed themselves but little disposed to put up with the tutelage of the Popes. England was at first more docile. The interdicted John Lackland had to submit to Rome when Innocent III. threatened to award his kingdom to Philip Augustus. But, in France, St. Louis was the true founder of that doctrine of royal and national independence, suggested by the legists of the South, which has since then been

called Gallicanism (the *Pragmatic* ascribed to him is, however, a forgery [1]). Philip the Fair, having quarrelled with Boniface VIII., who declared that every living creature owed obedience to the Bishop of Rome, laughed at both interdict and excommunication, and caused the Pope to be insulted and arrested in his palace at Anagni (1303).

29. The great Western schism originated in 1378, as a result of the contest for the papacy between two rival competitors. Urban VI. established himself in Rome and Clement VII. at Avignon, where a French Pope, Clement V., an accomplice in the judicial murder of the Templars, had already lived under the haughty protection of Philip the Fair in 1305. For sixty years the Church had two Popes, and sometimes three. To put an end to the scandal, the cardinals summoned the two Councils of Pisa and Constance. The former (1409) set up a third Pope against the other two, but had no practical results. The latter (1414) ended in the deposition of both Popes, and the election of Martin V. (1417). "The Council declared itself above the Pope, which was incontestable, as it had arraigned him; but a council passes, whereas the papacy and its authority endures." [2] Unity was only re-established in 1429, by the renunciation of Clement VIII. Finally, the Council of Basle (1431), which elected an Anti-Pope to Eugenius IV. and was dissolved by him, tried in vain to bring about important reforms in the Church. The papacy, supported on this occasion by the Empire, held to its pretensions, and, strengthened by the end of the great schism, would only consent to insufficient changes for the better.

30. At the end of the fifteenth century the papal dignity sank very low in the person of the Borgia Pope, Alexander VI., a man of taste and a friend to the arts, but a debauchee who scandalised even his contemporaries. His successor, Julius II., was an old man of great energy, given to laying about him with his stick, and more occupied with war and politics than with the Church. Finally, the great Renais-

[1] A forgery due to some jurisconsult of the fifteenth century, put forward as a royal decree of 1268. *Pragmatic* is a word derived from the Greek, and means an ordinance regulating (religious) affairs.

[2] Voltaire.

sance Pope, Leo X., always surrounded by artists and men of letters, gave himself up to the joy of life. "Monks' quarrels!" he cried upon hearing of Luther's early outbursts. Rome in his time was so pagan, so in love with antiquity and with plastic beauty of every kind, that, without the rude shock of the Reformation, she might well have led the cultured world into the conditions it reached in the eighteenth century. Cardinal Bembo, the Pope's intimate friend, refused to read the Epistles of St. Paul, lest, he declared, they should contaminate his Ciceronian Latin. The Church's awakening was terrible. We may judge from what occurred during the second half of the sixteenth century, of the enormous force which lay concealed within her, in spite of her apparent senility and corruption.

.˙.

31. The privileges and relative independence of the monastic life attracted the best Christians. The order of Cluny was founded in France in the tenth century, that of the Camalduli in Italy in the eleventh. These orders soon became possessed of great properties, given and bequeathed by the faithful. The consequence of this wealth was the corruption of the monks. To bring about a reaction, orders were founded with very severe "rules": the Carthusians by St. Bruno, the Poor of Christ at the end of the eleventh century, and the Cistercians (monks of Citeaux) adorned by the eloquent St. Bernard (1091-1153). Other orders, such as the Premonstrants (1120) and the Carmelites (1105), continued to absorb the best elements of the population, thus condemning them to sterility. Some among them rendered great and signal services; the Mathurins, for instance, whose mission it was to redeem Christian prisoners from Turkish slavery. This order was founded by Jean de Matha, a doctor of Paris University, and encouraged by Pope Innocent III. But the literature of the Middle Ages sufficiently proves that both monks and nuns were unpopular, and that the morality of convents was subject to the gravest suspicions. The assertions of lay writers are confirmed by ecclesiastical writers, who never ceased to demand the reform

of the monasteries, and gave excellent reasons for their clamour.

32. The fame of the mendicant orders—Franciscans or Cordeliers, and Dominicans—finally eclipsed that of all the others. The mendicant orders formed a striking innovation on the old monastic conception. Monasticism was essentially the egotistic effort of the individual to ensure his own salvation while repudiating the duties and responsibilities of life. It is true that, at a certain period, monks had done good service to humanity by leaving their retreats and carrying Christian civilisation into regions still barbarous. St. Columba, St. Gall, St. Willibrod, and their companions were such pioneers. But that period had long passed away, and monasticism had declined for centuries into a state even worse than its primitive egotism. The mendicant orders were a revelation to Christendom. Men, it seemed, existed, who were ready to abandon all that made life sweet, and imitate the Apostles, doing for nothing what the Church failed to do with all its wealth and its privileges! Wandering on foot from one end of Europe to the other, under burning suns and icy winds, refusing alms in money, but accepting the coarsest food with gratitude, taking no thought for the morrow, but incessantly occupied in snatching souls from Hell, such was the aspect under which the early Dominicans and Franciscans presented themselves to men who had been accustomed to look upon a monk as a greedy, sensual worldling.[1]

33. The Franciscan order, created by Francis of Assisi (1182-1226), in spite of some resistance from the papacy, owed its early prestige to the virtues of its founder. This gentle mystic, who refused to be ordained a priest, forbade his disciples to hold, not only private, but even collective property. He died opportunely and was hastily canonised two years later. The Inquisition was not long in falling out with the *spiritual* Franciscans or *fraticelli*, as they were called in Italy; these followed the example of their master with a fidelity which was a standing reproach to the cupidity

[1] Lea, *History of the Inquisition*, vol. i.

of Rome, and not a few were burnt by the Church in the fifteenth century (1426-1449).

34. The short life of St. Francis left a deep impression on the spirit of the Middle Ages. One may say that to him Christianity owed a new lease of life, because in him the faithful found among themselves, and not in the mists of history, a man whom they could admire and even worship. "Never," says Voltaire, "have the eccentricities of the human intellect been pushed further than in the *Book of the Conformities of Christ and St. Francis*, written in his own time and afterwards augmented. In this book Christ is looked upon as the precursor of Francis. In its pages we find the tale of the snow woman made by the saint with his own hands: that of the rabid wolf, which he cured miraculously, making it promise to eat no more sheep; of the doctor whose death he brought about by prayer, that he might have the pleasure of resuscitating him by further prayers. A prodigious number of miracles were credited to St. Francis. And, in truth, it was a great miracle to establish his order and so to multiply it that he found himself surrounded by five thousand of his monks at a General Chapter held near Assisi during his own lifetime." Our age understands St. Francis better than did Voltaire. We see in him not so much the worker of miracles as the friend of the lowly, the mystic spouse of Poverty, the heart beating in sympathy with that of universal nature, even of animals, trees and flowers. That sentimental Christianity is so different from the high and dry religion of the Church before his day, and recalls Buddhism by so many traits, that an Oriental influence is here very probable. Such an influence may have been transmitted to Italy by the Manichæans called Albigenses (§ 62), among whom Francis seems to have spent his early life; indeed, the legend of Francis is not unlike that of Buddha, then known to Christianity by the novel of Barlaam and Joasaph. His respect for the hierarchy, which the Albigenses repudiated, saved him from persecution. Thanks to him, the Church assimilated the better part of the heretic teaching of that period, just as, ten centuries before, some of the Hellenic spirit of Gnosticism (p. 276).

35. The idea occurred to St. Francis of affiliating the laity to his order. This led to the powerful institution of the "third order" which was imitated by the Jesuits of the sixteenth century. St. Clara of Assisi, the friend of St. Francis, founded the order for women known as the *Poor Clares* (1224), whose rule was fixed by the saint herself. Thus the Franciscan army drew its recruits from Christian society as a whole, male and female, religious and secular.

36. The Dominicans, more practical than the Franciscans, though equally vowed to poverty, were founded in 1216 by the Spaniard, Domingo di Guzman (1170-1221). They were called punningly the Dogs of God, *Domini canes.* They formed a kind of militia of preachers and inquisitors, with affiliated laymen, who devoted an unbending fanaticism and an unlimited obedience to the service of the papacy. They were also known as the Preaching Friars, and in France as the *Jacobins.* Quarrels soon arose between Franciscans and Dominicans, and introduced a new element of disorder into times already troublous enough.

37. Another blossom sprang from the mystic spirit of Tuscany in the fourteenth century, in Catherine of Siena, a member of the lay order of St. Dominic. She flogged herself three times a day, once for her own sins, once for those of others still alive, and once for those of the dead. Betrothed in ecstasy to Jesus, she believed he had given her the nuptial ring; she also believed she had been nourished on milk from the bosom of Mary. She played a considerable part in politics, and, in her charity for the suffering and desire to bring about the reign of peace among men, she showed more common sense than is usually expected from mystics. Sent to Pope Gregory XI., a native of the Limousin, to persuade him to quit Avignon and return to Rome, she succeeded in her mission with the aid of a Swedish visionary, St. Bridget, to whom an angel dictated several letters for delivery to the Pope (1376). Raimondo da Capua, Catherine's confessor, witnessed the majority of her miracles. "I saw her," he declares, "transformed into a man, with a little beard on her chin. The face into which hers was suddenly changed was that of Jesus Christ himself." A credible witness, indeed!

But under all the puerility of this legend, as under that of St. Francis receiving the *stigmata* (that is, the nail-marks of the crucifixion on his hands and feet), we may recognise the general idea of the supernatural identification of the faithful with their God, which is to be traced in the most ancient forms of human religion. Catherine was one of the most popular saints of the Italian Renaissance. She was canonised in 1461. Her miracles and her ecstasies are celebrated in a hundred masterpieces of art.

38. The eleventh and twelfth centuries saw the birth of various orders which were at once religious and military. Consecrated in the first place to the service of the wounded in war, they vowed themselves, after 1118, to actual warfare against the infidel. Such were the Hospitallers, or Knights of St. John of Jerusalem, the Templars, the Teutonic Knights, the Knights of the Sword, of Santiago, of Calatrava, and of Alcantara, in Spain. Their common object was to fight with and incidentally to convert infidels and heretics. They were, so to speak, in a condition of perpetual crusade, and their activity well represents that spirit of proselytism by violence which, after the year 1000, superseded proselytism by persuasion. Moreover, Templars and Hospitallers were always fighting with each other: "in a certain combat between these military monks," says Voltaire, "no Templar was left alive."

The Templars were bankers as well as warriors and became rich, although never so rich as the Hospitallers. Princes and Popes were tempted by their property. They were accused of secret rites of idolatry, and of various infamous practices. In 1307, Philip the Fair, assisted after a short resistance by Pope Clement V., arrested all the Templars in France. He caused them to be examined by his agents, who used torture to extort confessions, and afterwards handed them over to the Inquisition, his docile instrument. The knights confessed a thousand crimes. Outside France, however, where torture was not applied, they protested their innocence, while even in France itself the following singular fact was observed: two Templars belonging to different commanderies, when tortured and questioned by the same judge, confessed the same crimes, while two Templars of the same commandery, tortured by different judges, confessed different crimes. The fraud is obvious. The confessions were extorted and dictated. There is not a shadow of proof that the Templars borrowed idolatrous rites and immoral practices from the Orientals with whom they had come in contact. Besides, at the last moment, those who could do so retracted their avowals, whereupon they were burnt alive for having relapsed (1310). The Grand Master, Jacques de Molay, who had confessed under the threat of torture, retracted his confession four years later and perished at the stake (1314). The persecution spread to the other nations of Europe. Even in England, where the employment of torture has always been repugnant to the free instincts of the people, it was brought into play at the express demand of the Pope. When the order was suppressed (1312), the princes confiscated its property, giving a part to other orders and not a little to the papacy. This was one of the most detestable affairs of a period in history which ignorant and fanatical people are still apt to admire. But if the Pope's responsibility was great, that of Philip the Fair was still heavier: for the pontiff, weak and domesticated, was the accomplice, not the instigator of the king. Philip acted with no less cruelty and cynicism when he turned his attention to getting rid of Jews and lepers.

∴

39. The dogma of the Incarnation was a stumbling-block for the more intelligent. As early as the fourth century they attempted to meet the difficulty by the theory of adoption. God had adopted Jesus Christ at the time of his baptism in the Jordan. This theory, not far removed from Arianism, was upheld chiefly in Spain, in the time of Charlemagne, condemned by the Council of Ratisbon (792), and refuted by Alcuin (799). Traces of it are to be found, however, in the teaching of Abélard.

40. Vain attempts have been made to impute the worship of the Virgin Mary to the Christians of the fourth century. It was not until the fifth and sixth centuries that Mariolatry

declared itself in the East. Men were taught that Mary was carried up to Heaven by angels, and the Emperor Maurice instituted the Feast of the Assumption in her honour (582). This feast was adopted in the West about the year 750. From the twelfth century Mary has been adored, especially in France, as the Mother of God, almost as a goddess. It was to this epoch that a singular miracle was ascribed in documents concocted some three centuries later. It was said that the house (*Casa*) of the Virgin in Nazareth had been transported (1291) by angels, first into Dalmatia and thence to Loretto, where it became the object of a lucrative pilgrimage, attracting even now more than a hundred thousand faithful annually. In order that nothing may be wanting to these pagan rites, many pilgrims get a figure of the Madonna of Loretto tattooed in blue on their arms. Many other still existing sanctuaries owe their foundation and prosperity to Mariolatry. Two facts contributed very powerfully to the formation of this cult: the honour in which celibacy was held, and the necessity for a feminine ideal in the Christian pantheon. Monasticism found satisfaction here for starved affections, as also did chivalry for its romantic gallantry. Mary became the mediator between suffering humanity and the glorified Christ, who yielded up his *rôle* of intercessor to her more and more, being in his turn moved to pardon by her prayers.

41. But did Mary, at her birth, receive the infection of original sin? If so, why did she not hand it on to Jesus? This difficulty was met, in the twelfth century, by the doctrine of the Immaculate Conception, which means, not what the less instructed public supposes, but that at the moment when the body of Mary received its soul, a particular act of grace preserved it from the contagion of sin. This doctrine was upheld by Duns Scotus against St. Thomas, by the Franciscans against the Dominicans, by the Jesuits against the Jansenists. In 1854 it became an article of faith in the Roman Church. The Greek Church, Mariolatrous as it is, does not admit it. As for the Reformed Churches, they all, with the exception of the English Ritualists, hold the adoration of Mary in horror.

42. In order to combat the new opinion, the Dominicans of Berne, at the beginning of the sixteenth century, chose a young man of weak intellect, a tailor's apprentice, and caused Mary herself to appear before his eyes to protest against the doctrine of the Immaculate Conception. The fraud was discovered, and four Dominicans were burnt at the stake (1509). Long before this, however, the Dominicans had made use of St. Catherine of Siena, to whom the Virgin revealed that she had been born in sin; unfortunately, the Franciscans had a contemporary saint of their own, St. Bridget, to whom Mary declared, with equal confidence, that she had been born free from sin (1375).

43. It became necessary to put limits to the cult of saints, and the Church reserved to herself the right of naming them (tenth century). Ever since the twelfth century, the papacy alone has had the right to beatify or canonise individuals, after a regular process of trial in which the *devil's advocate* has to be heard. This advocate did not prevent the canonisation of blood-thirsty Inquisitors, like the Italian Peter Martyr of Verona (*d.* 1365), and the Spaniard, Pedro Arbues (*d.* 1485), the latter enrolled among the saints by Pius IX., in defiance of all modern and humane ideas. The Roman Church, moreover, honours a number of saints—such as René, Philomena, Reine, Corona—whose only fault is that they never existed.

44. In order to feed the piety of the populace, which delighted in tales of miracles, a monk called Jacobus de Voragine published, in 1298, the *Golden Legend*, which still exercises a certain influence on literature and art. It is a regular Christian mythology, taken from the most doubtful sources, charming to the sceptical dilettante, exasperating to a reverent believer. If the first result is the more usual one in these days, it is easy to guess the reason.

45. In Catholic countries a man is still said to fulfil his religious duties when he "goes to Mass." The word *Mass* comes, perhaps, from the concluding formula of the service in the course of which the bread and the wine are consecrated and absorbed by the officiating priest: *ite missa est*. Doubts, however, attach to this derivation. It is possible that *missa*

was a popular Latin word meaning function, or ceremony. As early as the end of the first century traces of a religious ceremony connected with the offering of bread and wine are to be found in Rome: this was the origin of the modern Mass.

46. If we examine the texts relating to the Eucharist in their chronological order, it appears that at first this repast was merely the commemoration of the Last Supper of Christ by the consumption of bread and wine in common by the faithful. As time passed the supper in common disappeared, the consumption of bread and wine took on a magic character, until finally it was believed that the actual body and blood of Jesus were present in the host and the chalice. That is the case as put by the Protestants. But to those who know how great a part theophagy played in the more or less secret rites of many non-Christian religions it is difficult to deny that as early as the time of St. Paul, and in his thoughts, the Holy Supper tended to put on a similar character, hidden, of course, from the non-believer by a discreet and even compulsory silence (as were the arcana of the mystic rites of paganism). The dogma of the Real Presence was distinctly formulated by the monk Paschasius Radbertus (844), but it had existed, as a pious belief, long before his time. Berengarius of Tours, by whom this materialistic conception was attacked, had to retract in 1059, and twenty years later the dogma of transubstantiation was adopted by a Council at Rome.

47. About the year 1150 a discussion arose in Paris as to whether the bread was changed into the body of Christ as soon as the words "This is my body" were pronounced, or whether it awaited the transformation of the wine. It was in order to assert the former opinion that, about 1200, the priests of Paris were instructed to elevate the host in full view of the congregation, immediately after having pronounced the formula. By the thirteenth century this custom had become general.

48. It was at this period that the privilege of sharing the wine was withdrawn from the laity, who thenceforth had the right only to the host, the priest drinking the wine on behalf of all. The change was brought about by accidents

which had become so frequent as to be a scandal, especially the spilling of the sacred wine. Those who persisted in claiming participation in the chalice were called *Calixtines;* in Bohemia, where they were connected with the heresy of John Huss, they were treated with great rigour.

49. The Eucharist gave occasion for a new festival. "No ceremony of the Church, perhaps, is nobler, more magnificent, more capable of filling beholders with piety, than the feast of the Holy Sacrament. Antiquity itself had no ceremony more august. And yet who was the real cause of its establishment? A nun of the Convent of Moncornillon (near Liége) who fancied every night she saw a hole in the moon! This was duly followed by a revelation from which she learnt that the moon meant the Church and the hole a festival which was yet wanting. A monk called John collaborated with her in composing the office of the Holy Sacrament. The festival was first established at Liége; Urban IV. adopted it for the Church at large (1264). This festival was long a source of trouble. In Paris, in the sixteenth century, the Catholics forced the Protestants to decorate their houses and kneel in the streets as the Communion procession went by. One of the crimes which brought the Chevalier de la Barre to the scaffold, in 1766, was that of having kept on his hat one rainy day as he passed a procession of the Sacrament."[1]

50. The Church's tendency after the year 1000 was towards domination both in spiritual and temporal matters. The clergy had to think and act for every one. The laity was forbidden to read the Scriptures (1229). "It was an insult to humanity to say: we wish you to cherish a certain belief, but we do not wish you to read the book on which that belief is founded."[2] Prayer became little more than a mechanical exercise, aided, after the twelfth century (perhaps from Mahometan example), by the use of chaplet and rosary. Hundreds, thousands of *Ave Marias* had to be recited as penance for the slightest fault. Excluded thus from religious life, which was the only life for the simple

[1] Voltaire.
[2] *Ibid.*

thought of the age, the crowd attached all the more importance to those rites in which they were allowed, and even compelled, to participate. The Church adjudicated on these points also. Following Peter Lombard, she decided in the twelfth century that there were seven sacraments, neither more nor less: Baptism, the Eucharist, Marriage, Confirmation, Ordination, Penance, and Extreme Unction. Needless to say, no foundation for such a doctrine could be discovered in the Gospels.

51. "Confess your faults one to another," says the writer of the epistle ascribed to St. James. The primitive Church had practised confession in public, which had its obvious drawbacks. The victorious Church saw in confession a powerful means of influencing souls, and substituted private confession to a priest for confession in public. Confession implied penance, which was usually some good work, such as a gift to the Church. But the Church, the custodian of the infinite virtues of Christ and the Saints, could draw upon this inexhaustible treasure to exempt the penitent, either wholly or in part, from the consequences his acts would otherwise have brought upon him in the other life. Thus the practice of confession led inevitably to that traffic in the chastisements of Purgatory and in ecclesiastical indulgences which was one of the determining causes of the Reformation.

52. In 1215, under Innocent III., auricular confession at least once a year was made obligatory. A priest alone could hear confession. An abbess, even of the most important convent of women, had no such right—a curious indignity put by the Church on the sex to which the Mother of God belonged.

53. "A custom which began to be introduced in the eleventh century must not be forgotten, the custom of buying off the dead and delivering their souls from Purgatory by the alms and prayers of the living. A solemn festival consecrated to this form of piety was established. The Cardinal Pierre Damien relates that a pilgrim, on his way back from Jerusalem, was cast upon an island, where he found a pious hermit, from whom he learnt that the island was inhabited by devils, that the country in his neighbourhood was cov-

ered with flames, into which the devils threw the souls of the newly dead, that these same devils never ceased to cry out and howl against Odilon, Abbot of Cluny, whom they called their mortal enemy. 'The prayers of Odilon,' they declared, 'and his monks, were always robbing them of some soul.' This being reported to Odilon, he established the *Fête des Morts* (Festival of the Dead) at his Abbey of Cluny. The Church soon followed his example. If matters had stopped there it would have been but a form of devotion the more; but abuses were not long in creeping in. The mendicant friars, especially, required payment for delivering souls from Purgatory. They talked of apparitions of the dead, of piteous souls who came to beg for rescue, and of the sudden deaths and eternal tortures of those who refused their help. Pure brigandage succeeded to pious credulity, and was one of the causes which lost half Europe to the Church."[1]

54. The traffic in indulgences became more shameless than ever after the institution of the jubilees by Boniface VIII (1300). It was not long before jubilees at intervals of twenty-five years were established, in order that every one might have a chance of participating in the indulgence promised by the Church to all who made the pilgrimage to Rome. At the same time monks travelled about selling indulgences, both plenary and partial. One Franciscan declared that the Pope, if he chose, could empty Purgatory at a single stroke. Why, then, did he hesitate to do so? That Franciscan was embarrassing, but his statement was logical; the Sorbonne condemned him on both counts.

55. The marriage of priests seemed intolerable to Gregory VII., who sought to have it forbidden by the secular power. In spite of the Church's efforts, the principle of ecclesiastical celibacy did not triumph, however, until the thirteenth century; and even now certain compromises with the full rigour of the law are admitted—in South America, for instance. Celibacy did not make the priests any better, but it exposed them to taunts which were often justified; this provided the Reformers with one of their arguments. On the other hand, a priest, having no family to feed, is

[1] Voltaire.

more likely to devote himself entirely to the Church and to become, as has been said, one of its janissaries; that advantage outweighs the drawbacks.

∴

56. When we examine the attitude of the Church toward heresies we are at first struck with admiration. She has always known how to preserve the just mean between mysticism and rationalism. Obliged by her very origin to impose upon the world a certain number of beliefs the truth of which she cannot demonstrate, she allows nothing to be either subtracted from or added to them. Dogma is a province administered by herself, in which intruders are treated as enemies. This good sense of the Church was nothing but a comprehension of her temporal interests. Mystics and infidels alike claim to do without her, without her priests, her images, her relics, her magic. They are "unprofitable servants." But the Church is a vast and very expensive organisation. She requires a great deal of money. Now, I defy any one to name a single opinion persecuted by the Church in the Middle Ages, the adoption of which would not have brought about a diminution in her revenues. Voltaire misses the point when he writes: "In all the disputes which have excited Christians against each other, Rome has invariably decided in favour of that opinion which tended most towards the suppression of the human intellect and the annihilation of the reasoning powers." The Church was not tyrannical for the mere pleasure of being so; she had to think of her finances.

57. Whenever her authority and material interests were not involved the Church was tolerant enough. People might amuse themselves, even at the expense of the decencies of worship, so long as they made no pretence of doing without it. "The most august features of religion were disfigured in the West by the most ridiculous customs. The Feast of Fools, and that of the Ass, were established festivals in the majority of churches. On certain solemn days a Bishop of Fools was elected; an ass was introduced into the nave dressed up in cope and biretta. The ass was honoured in

memory of the animal which carried Jesus Christ. At the end of the Mass the priest set himself to bray three times with all his might, and the people echoed him. Dancing in the churches and indecent fooleries formed part of the ceremonies at these commemorations, a practice which lasted for some seven centuries in many a diocese. Rome could not put an end to these barbarous usages, any more than to the duel and the trial by ordeal. In the rites of the Roman Church, however, there was always more decency and gravity than elsewhere; we feel that, on the whole, when she was free and well governed, she existed to set a good example to other communions." [1]

58. The *Iconoclasts*, or image-breakers, were those Eastern Christians who attempted, in the eighth century, to strip the churches of works of art, which had come to be venerated like idols. Many causes have been named for this movement —memories of the Mosaic legislation, so hostile to idolatry; fear of Musulman satire. The true reason seems to have been hostility to the monks, whom the manufacture of images enriched. Leo the Isaurian was a violent Iconoclast; his son, Constantine Copronymus, obtained the condemnation of images by the Council of 754. But the Empress Irene, wife of Leo IV., Constantine's successor, was won over by the monks when she became regent, and caused the condemnation to be reversed by a later council (786). To worship images was not permitted, but to kiss them, to prostrate oneself before them, to burn candles and incense at their feet, was legitimate. Charlemagne, or rather Alcuin, director of the Palace School, who had iconoclastic tendencies, protested against the adoration at least, if not against the existence, of the images themselves, in the West. His protest was upheld by two French councils; but the pagan current in the Church was too strong, and too many material interests were involved. Down to the time of the Reformation the advocates of images triumphed all over Europe.

59. "A heretic," says Bossuet, "is a man with an opinion" (*hairesis*, in Greek, "choice"). In the darker centuries of the Middle Ages few men had intellect enough to think for

[1] Voltaire.

themselves. Gottschalk, a monk of Fulda, exaggerated Augustinism and the doctrine of predestination. He was condemned by two synods and thrown into prison (849). The other heresies of the time need not be recorded here. It is only after the year 1000 that they become interesting.

60. The great heresies of the twelfth and thirteenth centuries may be divided into two classes. The first were the revolts of honest people, who dreamt of the purity of apostolic times and wished profoundly to reform the hierarchy, or even to suppress it. These were the *anti-sacerdotal* heretics, whom the Church persecuted with most severity because they threatened both her organisation and her property. The other class were the *dogmatic* heretics, affiliated to Oriental Manicheeism, who had their own tenets and their own clergy. The Church, which is a government, always anxious to enforce obedience, could not tolerate them either.

61. Arnold of Brescia, a pupil of Abélard, took the field in Italy, Switzerland, and France against the wealth and corruption of the clergy. By his eloquence he gained over the citizens of Rome, who established the simulacrum of a republic. The Pope summoned the Emperor Frederick I. to his assistance. Frederick besieged Rome, and took it through the treachery of the nobles. Arnold was strangled and his body burnt (1155).

62. A sect of Eastern Manichees, or Manichæans, the Paulicians (referring not to Paul the Apostle, but to Paul of Samosata),[1] had spread over Bulgaria, and thence up the valley of the Danube towards Italy and France. Its members called themselves *Cathari;* that is, *The Pure.* The name was corrupted in Italy into *Patarini,* and in Germany into *Ketzer,* which became the German term for heretics in general. They taught that the God of the Old Testament was the Devil, that Jesus was the good God, and that the Devil was to be fought against in the form of sensuality. An inner ring, the *Perfect,* vowed themselves to celibacy, and all renounced the eating of flesh, except that of fishes. They had no baptism, only a laying on of hands, which they called

[1] That opinion of a great scholar, Fred. Conybeare, is not accepted by others.

Consolation. It was equivalent to initiation. The members confessed to each other. The *Cathari* were strictly moral, although they were calumniated by the public. In the comparatively advanced civilisation of the south of France they gathered numerous recruits, and had bishops both at Toulouse and at Albi. It was from the latter city that they took their name of Albigenses.

63. The Church waged a relentless war against these inoffensive sectaries. As St. Bernard failed to convince them of their errors, Innocent III., in 1208, preached a crusade against them. Raymond VI., Count of Toulouse, was obliged to take the field against his own subjects. He saw his lands invaded by 300,000 adventurers, who for some twenty years murdered, burnt, and pillaged under the orders of the Pope's legate (1209-1229).[1] Flourishing cities, like Béziers and Carcassonne, were treated as the Crusaders treated Byzantium. At the siege of Lavaur "the *Seigneur* and eighty knights were taken prisoners and condemned to be hanged. But the gallows being broken, they were handed over to the 'Crusaders,' who massacred them all. Three hundred of the inhabitants, who refused to recant their opinions, were burnt round a well down which the heart of their *Seigneur* had been previously thrown (1211)."[2] And besides the thousands of wretched people who died by the sword and at the stake, how many rotted to death in obscure dungeons! The Inquisition, established in 1232 in order to stamp out the remains of this particular heresy, set the faggots blazing all over the country and completed its ruin. Provençal civilisation received such a blow that it took three centuries to recover. We are still waiting, both at Béziers and at Carcassonne, for expiatory memorials to the Albigensian martyrs. The Church, the sole instigator of so much violence, has found writers to glorify her action even in our day.

64. As early as the ninth century, when Claude, Bishop of Turin, combated the worship of images and other pagan practices, Piedmont formed a school of honest clerics who turned their attention to the reform of the Church. Towards

[1] Lea, *History of the Inquisition,* vol. i.
[2] Voltaire.

1100 we find Pierre de Brueys, burnt in 1124, insisting that the Bible afforded the only rule of faith and worship. After him Henry, a Lombard, preached at Lausanne, in Burgundy, and at Le Mans. He was condemned in 1148. Finally a rich citizen of Lyons, Pierre Waldo, having read the Bible and admired it, caused it to be translated into the vernacular, divided his property among the people, and founded a church for the poor, the *Pauvres de Lyon*, or *Humiliés*. Of course these "Poor Men" were persecuted. The remains of their community withdrew into the valleys of the Alps, and there founded the Church of the Waldenses, the principles of which are very similar to those of the Reformation. Like the Reformers, the Waldenses endeavoured to spread the knowledge of those sacred writings which Pope Innocent III. had forbidden the faithful to read.

65. The persecution of the Waldenses was revived under Clement XII., an Avignon Pope. Hundreds were burnt by the Inquisition at Grenoble and in Dauphiné. Towards the end of the fifteenth century a papal legate undertook their extermination, and conducted a ferocious crusade against them. Whole bands were smoked to death by him in caves in which they had taken refuge. Those of the Piedmontese valleys only escaped similar treatment through the protection of one of the Dukes of Savoy. In 1663, and again in 1686, these hateful persecutions were revived at the instigation of Louis XIV., and entire valleys were depopulated. The executioners were Irish mercenaries, retained for the purpose by the then Duke of Savoy. The survivors found asylum in Switzerland and Germany. Acting from that base, a few hundred brave men, led by their pastor, Henri Arnaud, undertook to reconquer their country. They were on the point of failure, when the Duke of Savoy, who was by that time at war with France, made peace with them and put the defence of their valleys into their own hands. An edict of toleration, obtained in 1694, allowed them to live in peace thenceforward.

66. Other less extensive heresies were suppressed with equal vigour by the Church. Nicholas of Basle, founder of the Friends of God (*Gottesfreunde*), was burnt by the Inqui-

sition in 1383. The Flagellants, who were at first encouraged in their silly forms of penance, had to undergo the lot of all those mystics who fell short of entire submission to the Church. We have seen that the Inquisition raged against the spiritual Franciscans; it also persecuted the *Béguins* and *Béguines* of Flanders, whose semi-secular associations had a tendency to disregard the hierarchy.

67. With the exception of the Waldenses, the sects persecuted by the Church somewhat lacked moderation and good sense. Even the Albigenses, with their extravagant asceticism, would eventually have become a danger to civil society. It does not appear, however, that in its struggle against the sectaries the Church was moved by any such wise consideration as this. Those historians who uphold the opposite view are not arguing in good faith. The Church fought for her own authority, for her privileges and wealth; and she did so with an unexampled ferocity, which was all the more culpable in that she pretended to be inspired by the Gospel, by a religion of kindness and humility.

. . .

68. During the second half of the twelfth century Paris was the centre of theological studies. Pope Innocent III. and John of Salisbury, the one Italian, the other English, came there for instruction. Speculative thinking had been revived in the schools, about the end of the eleventh century, by the influence of Aristotle, whose works had been translated first into Arabic, and afterwards into Latin. Thence arose what was called the Scholastic Philosophy, a sort of Aristotelian Christianity. Among its teachers, who sought to found Christianity upon logic and metaphysics, were some men of great ability, such as Anselm, Archbishop of Canterbury (1033-1109). Not only did he conceive what is called the ontological proof of God's existence ("I conceive God as perfect; being perfect He must exist, because reality is an attribute of perfection"—the sophistry of this was only fully demonstrated by Kant); he also formulated, with the full approbation of the Church, the ingenious theory of Atonement. Man has sinned against God, he has accumulated an

infinity of misdeeds; to counterbalance such a mass of indebtedness all good works are insufficient; hence the necessity for the sacrifice of God made man, for the Incarnation and the Redemption. It was by the example of Anselm that people were taught to find arguments for the faith in reason, and not only in the opinions of the Fathers of the Church. So far we may say he opened the door to rationalism. Progress in this direction was helped by the long quarrel of the Nominalists, who denied the real existence of general ideas; of the Realists, who (like Anselm) affirmed it; and of the Conceptualists (like Abélard), who declared that conceptions were the only realities. This discussion, which has seemed so idle since the days of Kant, helped to withdraw educated men from the tyranny of ready-made opinions, to induce them to seek truth outside tradition and to reason freely. "You may discuss," said St. Bernard, "provided that your faith is impregnable." In his eyes philosophy was the servant of faith. It was a servant, however, who from the very beginning sometimes assumed the attitude of a mistress. This the Church perceived, and Scholastic Philosophy soon created plenty of trouble for her.

69. The learned and subtle Abélard (1079-1143), surrounded by hundreds of disciples, both in Paris and Champagne, transformed the sacraments into symbols and denied the power of indulgences. Condemned by a Council of 1121, and combated by St. Bernard, he ended his days in a Clunisian cloister, almost as a captive. Albertus Magnus, or Albert the Great, the Dominican, was chiefly occupied with science, and, while gaining for himself the reputation of a sorcerer, contrived to turn minds towards the study of bodies (1205-1280). Another learned monk, the English Franciscan Roger Bacon (1214-1294), was charged with being a magician. If his scientific importance has been much overrated, his presentments of modern discoveries were flashes of genius. At the same epoch the Catholicism of the Middle Ages found its most complete expression in the vast *Summa Theologiæ* of St. Thomas Aquinas. This Italian Dominican, who died in 1274, aged only forty-nine, was a superior man in his way. In spite of its crabbed and essentially scholastic

character, his work betrays an intellect that was almost liberal. The papacy of our day recommends the study of St. Thomas as the foundation of all sound Theology.

70. To St. Thomas Aquinas the Franciscans opposed a member of their own order in Duns Scotus (*d.* 1308), who would now be completely forgotten but for the long rivalry of the *Scotists* and the *Thomists.* No less neglected are the mystics Bonaventura, Eckart, and Tauler, on whom, moreover, the Church looks askance. But the chief mystical work of these dreary times is still read with emotion. This is the *Imitation of Christ*, sometimes attributed to Jean Gerson, a Paris doctor, but in reality the work of the canon Thomas à Kempis, of Deventer (*d.* 1471). Disgusted with the world, and even with the Church, the soul of the monastic writer turns wholly towards God, and finds happiness in solitude.

· · ·

71. The dawn of the Renaissance at once brought new tendencies into the world of thought. The exodus of Greek scholars from Byzantium introduced the works of Plato to Western Europe, and initiated a change which was greatly hastened by the invention of printing. In Italy the *Humanists* were inclined towards a sort of pagan pantheism; in Germany they became passionately absorbed in the study of texts, both Greek and Hebrew, and inaugurated historical criticism. Hans Reuchlin, of Basle (1455-1522), a Hebraist of great merit, saved the Jewish books of the Middle Ages which the Cologne Inquisition wished to burn. Erasmus of Rotterdam, prince of the scholars of his age, established himself in 1521 at Basle, which he made a focus of light. In his elegant Latin he laughs at the superstitions, abuses, and ignorance of the monks with an irony worthy of Voltaire. He published the Greek text of the New Testament for the first time, with a really exact translation into Latin, and recommended knowledge of the Scriptures as the pious work *par excellence.* The philological study of the sacred texts, which was destined to destroy the pretensions of the Church, recognises Erasmus and Reuchlin as its founders.

72. Even more than these keen-minded scholars, two men

of action, John Wyclif and John Huss, deserved to be called reformers before the Reformation. Wyclif, a native of England (*b.* 1320), led a strong party against the tyranny and greed of the monastic orders, against the encroachments of the Roman Curia and the idolatrous beliefs it propagated. "What the Waldenses taught in secret he preached in public; and, with but slight modifications, his doctrine was that of the Protestants who appeared more than a century after his death."[1] In 1380 he translated the Bible into English, which gave him great *prestige* with the people. But his advanced opinions disquieted the ruling classes, who obliged him to resign his chair at Oxford and retire into a country parish, where he died in 1384. His disciples, who were called *Lollards*, or "mutterers," were persecuted after his death.

73. John Huss was born in Bohemia in 1373. He was rector of the University of Prague, and in conjunction with his friend Jerome of Prague, who had read Wyclif's books, undertook a war against the papacy in the name of the Bible. Driven out of the university, and a wanderer, but always commanding an audience, he was summoned by the Emperor Sigismund before the Council of Constance. Arming himself with a safe-conduct, he obeyed the summons; but his safe-conduct was outrageously set at naught by the Dominicans. In spite of the protests of the Bohemian deputies, he was kept in prison for six months, and afterwards brought before the Council, by which he was ordered to retract his opinions. On his refusal they burnt him. He met his death like a hero. Shortly afterwards they burnt his friend Jerome also. Sigismund had behaved like a coward, and the fathers of the Council like rascals. There was an explosion of fury in Bohemia, where the sect of the *Calixtines*, who demanded the Eucharist in both sorts (chalice and host), had already found many adherents. Calixtines and Hussites united to call for the reform of the clergy and the suppression of abuses. The mountain of Tabor became their fortress, whence they defied the armies of Sigismund, and replied to the massacres of Hussites by massacres of friars. In the end the Council of Basle re-established peace; but

[1] Voltaire.

Hussite communities survived in both Moravia and Bohemia. The so-called Moravian Brothers, who have distinguished themselves as missionaries, were recruited from what was left of the Hussites (1457). Reconstituted after the persecutions of 1722, the Moravians settled at Herrnhut, in Lusatia. They are the *Quakers* of Germany. These Herrnhutians exercised a strong influence over the English Methodists in the eighteenth century. They enlisted many recruits even in America, and still number more than a hundred thousand souls.

74. Even in Italy, at the very gates of Rome, the militant spirit of reform was blowing up for tempest. The eloquence of the Dominican monk Savonarola, directed in the main against immorality and luxury, aroused extraordinary enthusiasm at Florence. Bonfires were made of pictures, books, women's ornaments. It was not long, however, before this wild sect (*Arrabiati*) had to count with the ill-will of the Medici and of all those who depended on luxury and depravity for their living. Florence was by no means ripe for a Calvin; and yet she bore with the Dominican for eight years. The flight of the Medici and the invasion of Italy by Charles VIII. seemed at first to confirm his forecasts. But as soon as the French king left the country Rome excommunicated Savonarola, and Alexander VI. (Borgia) determined to make short work of him. As Alexander was a voluptuary himself, the Dominican attacked him openly, and was foolish enough to offer to prove his own innocence by undergoing the ordeal of fire. At the last moment he shrank from the test, and the Franciscans, his sworn enemies, took the offensive against him. Condemned as a heretic by the Inquisition, he expiated his reforming ardour at the stake (1498).

Voltaire thus concludes his account of these events: "You follow these scenes of absurdity and horror with pity; you find nothing like them among the Romans, the Greeks, or the old barbarians. They were the fruit of the most infamous superstition which has ever degraded man. . . . But you know that we have not long emerged from such darkness, and that not even yet is the light complete."

75. The repression of unacceptable opinions, considered to be offences against God, was at first left to the bishops and the secular priests. But the progress of the Albigensian heresy convinced the Holy See that a special organisation, entirely dependent on Rome, was required to make head against such formidable dangers. The bishops were too much occupied, too indulgent, too accessible to local considerations. From 1215 to 1229, between the fourth Lateran Council and the Synod of Toulouse, the nascent Inquisition felt its way. In 1232 Gregory IX. created the tribunals of the Inquisition to deal with heretical perversity (*hæretica pravitas*), and put the Dominicans in charge of them. The term "Inquisition" was borrowed from the juridical language of ancient Rome. Inquisition is an inquiry, set afoot by denunciations or merely on suspicion, having for its object to compel those suspected to prove the orthodoxy of their beliefs. The tribunals of the Inquisition were empowered to condemn their victims to be imprisoned, to be flogged, to go on distant pilgrimages, to wear disgraceful badges which prevented them from earning their bread; but they could not inflict the punishment of death: this would have violated the axiom "The Church has a horror of blood," a principle which forbade, for instance, a priest to practise surgery. It was in obedience to this principle that a bishop of Beauvais, in the time of Philip Augustus, used a mace in battle instead of a lance, saying it would be irregular for him to shed human blood.[1] The Inquisition, however, concocted a device which allowed it to be sanguinary without "irregularity." When it considered one of its prisoners to be worthy of death, it announced that the Church could do nothing more for him, that he was cut off from her and abandoned to the secular arm—that is, to the civil magistrates. These latter were directed to burn him alive. If they hesitated, the Church threatened them with excommunication. Thus she combined hypocrisy with cruelty. All this did not prevent sophists like Joseph de Maistre from affirming, in the nineteenth century, that blood had never been shed by the Church; she had contented herself with forcing the civil

[1] Voltaire.

power to shed it for her! Not only was the papacy responsible for the Inquisition; it actively encouraged and excited its ferocity. The horrible punishment of death by fire was formally prescribed by Rome (1231), and indulgences were promised to those who provided faggots for the purpose. As a well-meaning old woman at Constance deposited a faggot at the feet of John Huss, "Oh! sacred simplicity," said the martyr, with a smile.

76. Frightful as were the punishments inflicted by the Inquisition—and imprisonment for life in pestilential gaols was perhaps worse than death at the stake—its methods of procedure were still more abominable. The accused, who was generally some poor wretch without education, had to do without counsel, for an advocate would have been accused of impeding the Inquisition, and prosecuted in his turn. He did not know of what he was accused; he knew neither the names of the witnesses against him nor the nature of their depositions. Captious questions were put to him; traps were laid for him; he was induced to accuse himself. If he proved obdurate he was tortured. To torture more than once was forbidden, but the torture was "continued," even after a long interval, if at first it had not produced the desired effect. Manuals for the use of inquisitors are still extant, with their schemes of interrogatories. They are monuments of astute trickery. The chief object of "the question"—as torture was called—was to oblige the accused to denounce his accomplices, or those who shared his opinions. One can imagine how many innocent victims must have been dragged before such tribunals, which, as a consummation of their infamy, took possession of the property they confiscated and handed it over to the Holy See. They had the power to put a man who had been dead for forty years on his trial for heresy, and, if he were convicted, to dig up and burn his body, strip his heirs of their property, and reduce his family to misery and despair. Such was the *régime* established by the Dominican Inquisition in the south of France, and extended so far as possible to the other nations of Christendom.

77. We are speaking here of the Inquisition of the Middle Ages, called the *Papal* or *Holy Inquisition*, and the *Holy*

Office, because it depended on the Holy See. Further on we shall discuss the *Royal Inquisition* of Spain, the only one of which the general public has some knowledge. The former was the more atrocious and pitiless of the two. It burnt Albigenses, Waldenses, Franciscans, Hussites, and witches by the thousand. It meanly placed itself at the service of the political authorities, satisfying their cupidity and their revenge, as when it burnt the innocent Knights of the Temple and the innocent Joan of Arc. It covered the world with desolation and terror, until kings and rulers, disgusted by its arbitrary proceedings, had gradually proscribed its entrance into their States. It is difficult to understand how such horrors could have been submitted to by one part of Europe for century after century. Such toleration is only to be explained by the idea the Church had implanted in the hearts of the people, who thought heresy, the crime against God, to be the worst of crimes, one which exposed a city, a province, or a nation to the divine anger, and to such punishments as floods, pestilence, and famine, if it were not promptly and sternly suppressed. The heretic had to be treated like one stricken by the plague, or rather like his garments, which are thrown into the fire without hesitation. Again, the sight of these solemn executions, to which people flocked as if to a *fête*, hardened hearts, awakened hereditary instincts of ferocity, and made the populace indifferent to the sufferings of others. Indeed, the long duration of the Inquisition is not so surprising as the fact that means were found to put an end to it.

78. Except in Spain, where its flourishing period was just setting in, the Inquisition was greatly discredited at the opening of the sixteenth century. This was one cause of the comparative success of the Reformation. If they had found themselves in presence of the formidable Inquisitors of the thirteenth century, the Reformers would have met the same fate as the Albigenses.

79. Satan was all-pervading in the Middle Ages, both as God of Evil and as dispenser of worldly wealth. This belief was not created by the Church, any more than the idea that certain women, having made a bargain with the devil, be-

took themselves to the "Sabbath" on grotesque steeds, and there acquired redoubtable powers for evil. These tenacious superstitions had an ancient pagan and Germanic foundation. But the better instructed Church ought not to have shared them. Not only did she do so, but her theologians, pointing to the verse of Exodus, "Thou shalt not suffer a witch to live," organised witch hunts with the help of the Inquisition, and stirred up the civil power to do likewise. Denounced by gossips and subjected to frightful tortures, the unhappy women avowed that they had joined in a "Sabbath," and gave details of imaginary orgies. They were burnt in crowds, and their punishments both inflamed imaginations and loosened tongues. Every inquisitor who received a mandate to suppress witchcraft became an active missionary in spreading it. People's minds grew familiar with the idea that they were surrounded by sorceries, and that the least misfortune was the result of some witch's malignity. Wherever an inquisitor came, he found himself overwhelmed with denunciations, accusing every one who might be supposed guilty, from young people to very old women. The epidemic was greatly increased by the publication of the Bull *Summis desiderantes*, launched by Innocent VIII. on December 5, 1484. In it the Pope affirms with sorrow that all the Germanic territories are filled with men and women who put the maleficent power of sorcery in action against the faithful. He describes the results with a terrifying wealth of detail. . . . To contest the reality of witchcraft was, therefore, to throw doubt on the authority of Christ's vicar on earth.[1]

Under the sceptical Pope Leo X., the friend of Bembo and Raphael, hundreds of witches were burnt in the Lombard and Venetian valleys. It was in Germany, however, that the fury of the Dominican inquisitors piled up the greatest heaps of victims. Two of these inquisitors published an absurd book, "The Hammer of Witches," in which they pointed out the signs by which such women might be recognised and the means by which avowals might be extorted from them. The witch hunts lasted throughout the sixteenth and seventeenth

[1] Lea, *History of the Inquisition*, vol. iii.

centuries. It has been calculated that 100,000 were burnt in Germany alone. It may be undeniable that in this business the civil tribunals showed themselves even more savage and credulous than those of the Church; that—even in America, in the eighteenth century—the Protestant communities were no less so; it is none the less true that the Roman Church, in giving its official sanction to prosecutions for witchcraft and in appointing inquisitors for its suppression, must bear the chief responsibility for a murderous frenzy which confounds and humiliates human reason.[1]

∴

80. Before the Reformation, the only great schism which succeeded was that of the Eastern Empire.

Since the time of Theodosius, Byzantium had become the "New Rome"; so it was but natural that she should claim supremacy over the other Oriental Churches, especially that of Alexandria. About the year 500, the Bishop of Constantinople received from the Emperor the title of Œcumenical Patriarch; that is to say, Patriarch of the Empire (not of the Universe, as they pretended to interpret it in Rome). The Western Church rendered good service to the Eastern in the quarrel over images, when the seventh and last council before the schism, that of Nicæa, put an end to the Iconoclastic feud (787). But the pretensions of Rome to the government of all Christendom soon became intolerable in the city of Constantine. As early as the ninth century the Patriarch Photios protested against the innovations of Rome. The dispute was envenomed by the disagreement over the so-called "procession" of the Holy Ghost. Did the Holy Ghost proceed from both the Father and the Son? No, said the Eastern Church, from the Father alone. This was

1 The most celebrated case of sorcery in the seventeenth century was that of Urbain Grandier, a parish priest. He was accused of having bewitched the Ursulines of Loudun by throwing a branch of laurel into their convent. Prosecuted with atrocious virulence by the Counsellor Laubardemont, a creature of Richelieu, he was convicted of black magic and burnt alive (1634). The most extraordinary part of the business is that Cardinal Richelieu, by whom the prosecution was inspired, seems to have believed in all good faith that a priest could bewitch nuns. Writing but fifty years later, Bossuet never alludes to witchcraft, though he was too prudent to deny its existence.

the substance of the *Filioque* quarrel. The two churches failed to come to an agreement. The causes, however, of their antagonism were in reality more profound, and were of a political nature. The divorce, which still endures, was completed about the middle of the eleventh century by the mutual anathemas of the Pope and the Patriarch. The Maronites of the Lebanon and, to some extent, the Armenians, alone remained faithful to their Roman allegiance.

81. Attempts at reunion were not lacking. It was thought that success had crowned these efforts at the Council of Florence in 1439, when the Byzantines, in fear of the Turks, made all the concessions demanded. But the people, who had not forgotten the horrors worked by the Latins in 1204, refused to confirm the agreement. Constantinople fell to the infidels, sent by God to punish heretics. The latest attempt was due to Leo XIII. (July 1894), who addressed a most conciliatory letter to the Patriarch of Constantinople. The latter replied with some violence (August 1895), recalling all the innovations of the Roman Church: the Holy Ghost proceeding from the Son, Purgatory, the Immaculate Conception, Papal Infallibility; and there the matter rests. Other differences between the two Churches have to do with the baptismal rite—the Greeks practising total immersion, like the Primitive Church—and the Eucharist, in which they give leavened bread, dipped in wine, to the communicant, instead of a dry, unleavened wafer.

82. The Eastern Church, which calls itself the Orthodox or Greek Church, embraces 120 millions of adherents. It is subdivided into fifteen Churches, each with its own head and its own hierarchy. The Patriarch of Constantinople, great personage though he be, has no real authority. He has for a long time been on bad terms with the Churches of Bulgaria and Roumania. The Russian Church was not governed by the Czar, but by the Holy Synod, whose procurator, however, was nominated by the Czar. The priests of the Greek Church marry, but do not remarry. Bishops are chosen from among the unmarried monks. Nuns are not much esteemed and live quite apart from the community. In the pomp of its ceremonial and its borrowings from pagan-

ism, notably its use of incense and wax candles and its adoration of images, the Orthodox Church stands closer to Romanism than to the Reformed Churches. These dallied with her, nevertheless, at the end of the sixteenth century, and the Anglican Church has not abandoned the game even now. The Russian *moujik*, or peasant, has remained more pagan than Christian. His real religion belongs to the domain of folk-lore. The Hellene is profoundly sceptical, but clings to his Church as the safeguard of his nationality. It has been said that the Greek awaited the restoration of his independence for four centuries, in the shadow of his Church. This is true. Enslaved Greece was nourished by her Church as an infant in swaddling-clothes is nourished by milk. But this is no reason why the adolescent should continue to live on milk. If the Greeks of to-day, like the Byzantine Greeks of the Middle Ages, are inferior to their glorious ancestors, their inferiority seems to be in some degree imputable to their Church. It familiarises them, from their earliest youth, with horrible colour-daubs which it calls *Icons*, with drawling and nasal voices, with stories of the saints which are an outrage on reason. The modern Greeks are no artists, they cannot sing in tune, and they have not yet given a man of genius to the world.

83. Their long struggles with the Mongols, the Musulmans, and the Latins have kept the Eastern Churches conservative and nationalist. For the people, forms of worship are more important than creeds. Divine service is performed in the national languages, but archaic forms no longer understood by the commonalty are employed. The sacred books play a great part in worship, but they are not generally used in the vernacular. In March 1903, the publication of a translation of the Gospels caused a popular outbreak in Athens. Festivals do not coincide with those of the Roman Church, because the Greek Church is faithful to the Julian Calendar, which is now thirteen days behind ours. There is no regular process for the canonisation of saints, who consequently swarm, and work miracles through their images. Pilgrimages, especially to Jerusalem, are held in great honour, and the adoration of relics is no less flourish-

ing than in the Roman Church. The clergy and the monks are held in slight consideration. "You are good for nothing," says a Greek song, "become a pope [*pappas*]!" Perhaps the terrible upheavals which marked the second decade of the twentieth century may exercise a sort of reflex influence for good on the antiquated and formalist religions of the Eastern Christians.

BIBLIOGRAPHY

The most abundant source of information is the *Real-Encyclopädie* of Hauck. Reference may also be made to the *Biographie Universelle* of Michaud, to the *Grande Encyclopédie,* to the *Dictionary of National Biography* (Stephen and Lee), and to Pastor's *Geschichte der Päpste,* 12 vols., 1899-1927 (Engl. transl.).

1. P. Viollet, *Histoire des Institutions politiques de la France,* 3 vols., 1890 (on the beneficent part played by the Church, vol. i, p. 380).

2. Art. *Armenflege* (Charity) in Hauck.

4. The Truce of God is found among the Germans, Arabs, and other nations. See art. *Gottesfriede* in Hauck.—Sémichon, *La Paix de Dieu,* 2nd ed., 1869.

5. Em. Mâle, *L'art religieux du XIIIe siècle,* 1902.

8. Art. *Augustinus, Bonifatius* (*Winfrid*) *Gregorius, Keltische Kirche, Russland* in Hauck; Dom Cabrol, *L'Angleterre chrétienne avant les Normands,* 1908; S. Czarnowski, *Saint Patrick,* 1922.

9. Art. *Cyrillus und Methodius, Tschechen* (Bohemians), *Anglikanische Kirche, Mongolen, Nestorianer,* in Hauck.—J. Labourt, *Le Christianisme dans l'Empire Perse,* 1904.

10. Art. *Sachsen, Wenden, Albert von Riga* (Livonia) in Hauck.

11. Art. *Kreuzauffindung,* in Hauck.—A. Luchaire, *Le Culte des reliques* (in *Revue de Paris,* July, 1900).—L. Bréhier, *Les Croisades,* 5th ed., 1928.

13. Art. *Legaten* in Hauck.

15. Lea, *Rise of the Temporal Power* (in *Studies,* Phil., 1883, p. 1 *et seq.*); Duchesne, *Les Premiers Temps de l'Etat Pontifical,* 1904.—Th. Hodgkin, *Italy and her Invaders,* vol. viii, p. 135 (1899); M. Moresco, *Il patrimonio di S. Pietro,* 1916; A. Gaudenzi, *Il Constituto di Costantino,* 1920; art. *Konstantinische Schenkung* in Hauck.

16. Lea, *Studies,* 1883, p. 46 (forged decretals); art. *Kanonen und Decreten-Sammlungen* and *Pseudoisidor* in Hauck; P. Fournier, *Etude sur les fausses décrétales,* 1907 (decides in favour of Touraine rather than the neighbourhood of Reims); Lot, *Rev. historique,* xciv, p. 290.

17. Lea, *Auricular Confession and Indulgences,* 3 vols., 1896.

18. Art. *Peterspfennig* (Peter's Pence) in Hauck.

19. Lea, *Studies,* 1883, p. 235 (excommunication).

20. Duchesne, *Origines du Culte chrétien,* 1899; art. *Liturgie* in Hauck.

21. Art. *Simonie* in Hauck.

22. The sources are given in F. X. Funk, *Lehrbuch der Kirchengeschichte,* 5th ed., p. 281; A. Fliche, *Grégoire VII.,* 1920. See also art. *Gregorius VII.* in Hauck, with a copious bibliography.

24. Art. *Becket* in Hauck.

26. A. Luchaire, *Innocent III.,* 4 vols., 1904-1908.

27. Frederick II., the heretics and free thought: Lea, *History of the Inquisition*, vol. i; Ch. V. Langlois, *Philippe le Bel et Boniface VIII.* (in Lavisse, *Histoire de France*, iii, 2, 1901); H. Koehler, *Die Ketzerpolitik der Kaiser*, 1913. The legend of the three impostors is of Islamic origin (*Rev. hist. litt. rel.*, May 1920).

29. N. Valois, *Histoire du grand schisme d'Occident*, 4 vols., 1896-1902.—Valois, *Journal des Savants*, 1905, p. 345 (on the Council of Basle); G. Mollat, *Les papes d'Avignon*, 1912.

30. Burckhardt, *Cultur der Renaissance*, 5th ed., 1906.

31. O. Zoeckler, *Askese und Mönchtum* (Western), 2nd ed., 1897; Montalembert, *Les Moines d'Occident*, 2 vols., 1860 (Engl. transl.). Vacandard, *Saint Bernard*, 2 vols., 1895 (abridged in 1904). See also under the names of the different religious orders in Hauck.

33. P. Sabatier, *Vie de St. François*, 1894 (numerous editions and translations); F. van der Borne, *Die Franziskusforschung*, 1917; S. R., *Cultes*, vol. v, pp. 343, 368 (Oriental influences); Lea, *History of the Inquisition*, vol. ii (persecution of the *fraticelli*).

36. Dominicans: S. R. Galbraith, *The Dominican Order*, 1925.

37. Gebhart, *Sainte Catherine de Sienne* (in *Revue des Deux Mondes*, 1890, vol. xcv, p. 133, reprinted in *L'Italie Mystique*); Fautier, same subject, 1912.—Art. *Stigmatisation* in Hauck.

38. Templars: Lea, *Hist. of the Inquisition*, vol. iii; H. Finke, *Papstum und Templerorden*, 1907 (*cf.* Langlois, *Journal des Savants*, 1908, p. 417).

39. Art. *Adoptianismus* in Hauck; Conybeare, *Key of Truth*, 1898, p. 87 *et seq.*

40. L. Coulange, *La Vierge Marie*, 1925.—Holy House of Loretto: U. Chevalier, *N. D. de Lorette*, 1906 (*cf.* Delaborde, *Journal des Savants*, 1907, p. 367; *Rev. Arch.*, 1906, ii, p. 460).

41. Art. *Maria* in Hauck.—Lea, *Hist. of the Inquisition*, vol. iii, p. 596.

43. H. Delehaye, *Les Légendes hagiographiques*, 1905; P. Saintyves, *Les Saints successeurs des dieux*, 1907; Boudinhon, *Proces de béatification et canonisation*, 1905.—Pedro Arbues: Lea, *Inquisition of Spain*, vol. i, p. 252; Peter Martyr: Lea, *Inquisition of the Middle Ages*, vol. ii.

44. T. de Wyzewa, *La Légende Dorée*, 1902.

45. L. Coulange, *La Messe*, 1927.

46. Art. *Transubstantiation* in Hauck; Pres. Smith, *Christian theophagy*, 1922; A. Boudinhon, *Les Origines de l'élévation* (in the *Rev. du clergé*, June-July 1908, p. 535, 158).—*Arcani disciplina:* Batiffol, *Etudes d'Histoire*, p. 1 *et seq.;* art. *Arcani disciplina* in Hastings' *Encyclop.*, vol. i.

48. Lea, *Hist. of the Inquisition*, vol. ii.

49. Art. *Fronleichnamsfest* (Feast of Corpus Christi) in Hauck.

50. Prohibition to read or translate the Bible: Lea, *Hist. of the Inquisition*, vols. i, iii.—Art. *Gebet, Rosenkranz* (rosary), and *Sakrament* in Hauck.

51. Lea, *Auricular Confession and Indulgences*, 3 vols., 1896; A. Boudinhon, *Histoire de la Pénitence*, 1897 (criticism on Lea); Batiffol, *Les Origines de la Pénitence* (in *Etudes d'Histoire*, p. 43); V. Normand, *La confession*, 1926.

52. Upon the question of Woman and Christianity, see an acute note by Lejay, *Rev. Critique*, 1908, i, p. 79.

53. *Allerseelentag* (*Commemoratio fidelium defunctorum*) in Hauck; Saintyves, *Les Saints*, &c., p. 83.

54. Art. *Indulgenzen* in Hauck.

55. Lea, *Hist. of Sacerdotal Celibacy*, 2 vols., 1907.

56. J. Havet, *L'hérésie et le bras séculier jusqu'au XIIIe siècle* (re-

printed in his *Œuvres,* vol. ii, 1896); H. Ch. Lea, *Hist. of the Inquisition in the Middle Ages,* 1900-2; E. Jordan, *La responsabilité de l'Eglise dans la rèpression,* 1915.

57. Art. *Narrenfest* (Feast of Fools) in Hauck.

58. L. Bréhier, *La Querelle des Images,* 1904.

59 *et seq.*—All the details will be found in Lea's work (§ 56), which has an excellent index.

62. Paulicians inspired by Paul of Samosata: Conybeare, *Key of Truth,* 1898, p. 105 *et seq.*—Albigenses: A. Luchaire, *Innocent III et la Croisade des Albigeois,* 1905 (*cf. Journal des Savants,* 1905, p. 528; 1908, p. 17); H. J. Warner, *The Albigensian heresy,* 2 vols., 1922-1926; E. Broekx, *Le catharisme,* 1916.

63. The Inquisition glorified: *Rev. Arch.,* 1907, ii, p. 184; *Rev. Crit.,* 1907, i, p. 211; S. R., *Cultes,* vol. iv, p. 323.

64. Lea, *History of the Inquisition,* vol. i.

65. Art. *Waldenser* (Vaudois, or Waldenses) in Hauck; J. Marx, *L'Inquisition en Dauphiné,* 1914.

66. Flagellants: Lea, *Hist. of Inquisition,* vols. i and ii.

67. See Fredericq's preface to the French translation of Lea's *Hist. of the Inquisition.*

68. M. Grabmann, *Gesch. der scholast. Methode,* 2 vols., 1909; H. de Wulf, *Philosophie Médiévale,* 5th ed., 1925 (Engl. transl.); Gilson, *Philosophie du Moyen âge,* 2 vols., 1922; K. Werner, *Die Scholastik,* 4 vols., 1881-1887; Prantl, *Gesch. der Logik im Abendlande,* 4 vols., 1855-1870; F. Picavet, *Histoire générale des Philosophies médiévales,* 1906; Ch. de Rémusat, *S. Anselme,* 2nd ed., 1868; Vacandard, *Abélard et S. Bernard,* 1881; V. Cousin, *Introd. aux œuvres d'Abélard,* 1836; S. Reinach, *Lettres à Zoé,* 1926, vol. ii (a convenient summary, based on research).

Hauck adds a long bibliography to his article *Scholastik.*

69. R. Carton, *L'expérience chez Roger Bacon,* 1924; L. Thorndyke, *History of Magic and Experimental Science,* 2 vols., 1923; Ch. H. Haskins, *Hist. of Medieval Science,* 1924; E. Perrin, *La Somme théologique de St. Thomas,* 1927, 1929.

70. Preger, *Gesch. der deutschen Mystik im Mittelalter,* 3 vols., 1879-1893. On the *Imitatio,* see art. *Thomas à Kempis* in Hauck (vol. xix, p. 719); Vacandard, *Rev. du clergé,* December 1908, p. 633; A. Hyma, *The Christian Renaissance,* 1925.

71. J. Burckhardt, *Die Kultur der Renaissance,* 5th ed., 2 vols., 1896; art., *Erasmus* and *Reuchlin* in Hauck; J. P. Pineau, *Erasme,* 1924.

72. Wyclif: Lea, *Hist. of the Inquisition,* vol. ii; Huss: *Ibid.*—Lollards: *Ibid.*—H. B. Workman, *John Wyclif,* 1926.

73. Moravians and Herrnhutians: Art. *Brüder* (*böhmische*) and *Zinzendorf* (re-founder of the Herrnhutians) in Hauck.

74. J. Schnitzer, *Savonarola,* 2 vols., 1924.

75. Art. *Inquisition* in Hauck. Recent works: E. Vacandard, *The Inquisition,* 1908; G. J. Coulton, *same title,* 1929. On the scruple touching the shedding of blood, see Lea, *Hist. of the Inquisition,* vol. i.

76. Torture: Lea, *Superstition and Force,* Phil., 1892, pp. 429 *et seq.*

79. An English translation of the *Malleus maleficarum* by Montague Summers appeared in 1929. (On the sources of that book, see the *Rev. Crit.,* 1905, ii, p. 458); J. Hansen, *Zauberwahn, Inquisition und Hexenprozesse,* 1900; Hoensbroech, *Das Papstum, Inquisition, Hexenwahn,* 1901.—See also the art. *Hexen* in Hauck, and Lea's *Hist. of the Inquisition,* vol. iii.

80. Art. *Orientalische Kirche,* in Hauck; Pargoire, *L'Eglise Byzantine de 527 à 847,* 1905; Pisani, *A travers l'Orient,* 1897.

81. Art. *Ferrara-Florenz,* in Hauck. On the Encyclical of Leo XIII. and the Patriarch's slighting reply, see the *Rev. Anglo-Romaine,* 1895, p. 108 *et seq.*—On the flirtation of the Anglicans with the Greek Church: *Rev. du clergé français,* March 1908, p. 550.

CHAPTER XI

CHRISTIANITY: FROM LUTHER TO THE ENCYCLOPÆDIA

Causes of the Reformation. Martin Luther. Diet of Worms. The Anabaptists and the Peasants' War. Zwingli. Calvin at Geneva. Miguel Servetus. Henry VIII. and the Anglican Church. Mary Tudor. Elizabeth. The Reformation in France. Massacre of the Waldenses.

The Counter-Reformation. New Policy of the Church. The Council of Trent. Progress of Catholicism. The Jesuits. Protestant Sects. Philip II. and William the Silent.

Charles I. and the English Rebellion. James II. and William of Orange. The Persecutions in Ireland. The Pilgrim Fathers. The Quakers. The Thirty Years' War. German Pietism. Socinus.

France under the last Valois. Massacre of St. Bartholomew. Edict of Nantes. Revocation of the Edict of Nantes. The Dragonnades. The Camisards. Responsibility of the Roman Church. The Earliest Ideas of Toleration. New Religious Orders. The Liberties of the Gallican Church. The Four Articles of 1682. Jansenism and Port Royal. The Bull Unigenitus. Quietism: Fénelon and Bossuet.

The Inquisition in Spain: Torquemada. Expulsion of the Jews and Moors. Conquest and Christianisation of America.

Condemnation of Giordano Bruno. Retractation imposed on Galileo by the Inquisition.

1. If the Reformation had been the effect of a single cause, it would not have succeeded, even partially. Its comparative success was due to the variety of its origins—religious, political, and social.

2. The religious cause was the corruption of Catholicism, which appeared to Luther on his visit to Rome in 1511 to be a caricature of Christianity. Paganised by her rites and by the traffic in indulgences, the Church had also lost her salutary contact with Scripture. The Reformation wished to lead her back to the Bible, and succeeded with its own adherents at least.

3. One political cause was impatience of the spiritual domination of Rome, and of her interference in temporal

THE REFORMATION

affairs; another was the necessity of resistance to the Emperors, who called themselves Roman Emperors and were making long strides towards despotic power.[1] The definitive successes of the Reformation were won in those countries into which the influence of Rome, from the first to the fourth centuries, had not penetrated very deeply. In this connection, the Reformation was only a continuation of the movement which had withdrawn the ancient provinces of the Eastern Empire from obedience to Rome; it was, in short, a reaction of Germanism against Romanism.

4. The social and economical causes were numerous. Both prince and peasant coveted the riches of the Church. The Knights with nothing—*conti di Allemagna poveri*, as the legate wrote to the Pope—were jealous of the wealthy abbots. The people resented being squeezed by monks and priests. The secular clergy rebelled against the exactions of the Roman Curia and the competition of the monastic orders. These abuses were not new, but the invention of printing (1447), by spreading the taste for reading, had stimulated thought and enabled one man to speak for many.

5. The transition from despotism to liberty must be slow. Wherever it was successful, the Reformation adopted the authoritative principles of the Roman Church. Instead of individual freedom of faith and thought, it produced a kind of attenuated Catholicism. The seeds of religious liberty were there, but it was only after two centuries that they blossomed and bore fruit, thanks to the breach made by Luther in the ancient edifice of Rome. The Reformation miscarried in those quarters where habit was stronger than the desire for an even partial emancipation. Face to face with the uncompromising theologians of Wittenberg and Geneva, many confessed that "all they had was a choice of fetters, and that it would be better to keep those to which they had been born."[2] Again, rulers such as Charles V. and Francis I. were alarmed at the effect so profound a revolution threatened to have upon the principle of authority. Monarchists

[1] Voltaire.
[2] *Ibid.*

by trade—as Joseph II. was to say at a later date—they fought against a movement which menaced all authority and pointed to the triumph of the democratic idea as its natural conclusion. Even Luther himself, during the Peasants' Revolt, took fright and recoiled before the social consequences of his own doctrines. After ten centuries of Catholicism, Europe was unripe for liberty, all the more unripe because no criticism of the Scriptures yet existed. Luther's work had to be completed by that of a pious French Catholic, Richard Simon.

* * *

6. The final exciting cause of the Reformation was an extravagant sale of indulgences conceded to the German Dominicans, under pretext of a war against the Turks, but in reality to provide funds for the construction of St. Peter's at Rome. In the sixteenth century it was asserted, but not proved, that the Augustinians envied the Dominicans this privilege. An Augustinian monk, Martin Luther, a native of Eisleben, where he was born in 1483, on the approach of Tetzel, the indulgence broker, affixed to the Cathedral door at Wittenberg ninety-five arguments against the abuses of such a commerce (October 31, 1517). These flew over Germany like a train of gunpowder. Luther had penned what thousands of the faithful had been thinking in silence. A war of words began between Dominican and Augustinian. Others struck in and embittered it. Leo X., impatient at this "monks' quarrel," began by trying to make terms, but ended by launching his anathema. Luther treated him very roughly in his *Captivity of Babylon*, in which he fulminated against private masses and against transubstantiation, "a word not to be found in the Scriptures." The gravest difference of opinion had to do with the Communion. "Luther retained one-half of the mystery and rejected the other. He confesses that the body of Jesus Christ is in the consecrated elements, but it is, he says, as fire is in red-hot iron: the fire and the iron subsist together. This is what they called *impanation*, *invination*, *consubstantiation*. Thus, while those they called Papists ate God without bread, the

Lutherans ate God and bread; soon afterwards came the Calvinists, who ate bread and did not eat God."[1]

7. In order to make the schism complete, Luther burnt Leo's Bull of excommunication on the public place of Wittenberg (December 1520), and hurled insults at the Holy Father: "Little Pope," he wrote, "little Popelet, you are an ass, a little ass." German grossness found such an address amusing. "Luther, rough and uncouth, triumphed in his own country over all the urbanity of Rome."[2]

8. "He demanded the abolition of monastic vows, because they were not of primitive institution; permission for priests to marry, because several of the apostles were married men; the Communion in both kinds, because Jesus said *Drink ye of it;* the cessation of image worship, because Jesus had no image; in short, he was in harmony with the Roman Church in nothing but the doctrines of the Trinity, Baptism, the Incarnation, and the Resurrection."[3]

Under the influence of St. Augustine, the patron of his order, Luther also rejected free-will, which was afterwards admitted by his followers; and, to the great scandal of the Faculty of Paris, he denied that the study of Aristotle was any help to the comprehension of the Scriptures. Reacting against the Roman doctrine of salvation by works, the origin of the abuse of indulgences, he proclaimed that faith alone was efficacious, and that faith was the fruit of grace. This was to reject as superfluous all those ideas on which the Church lived, all those things by which her wealth and power were secured.

9. Charles V., who had been Emperor since February 1519, summoned the reformer to appear before the Diet at Worms (January 1521). He obeyed the summons with a safe-conduct which was respected, supported by popular sympathy, and protected by Frederick the Wise and the German Knights. Before the Diet, he pleaded his conscience and refused to retract. Charles placed him under the ban of the Empire, but the sentence could not be put in force. Frederick the Wise, Elector of Saxony, a convert to the new

[1] Voltaire. [2] *Ibid.* [3] *Ibid.*

ideas, carried him off in the night and hid him in the Saxon fortress of the Wartburg, where he lived under the name of "Junker Georg." It was in this Patmos, as he called it, that he began his translation of the Bible, an admirable version, which became the Reformer's most efficient weapon.

10. "The aged Frederick hoped for the extirpation of the Roman Church. Luther thought it was time to abolish private mass. He pretended the devil had appeared to him and reproached him for saying mass and consecrating the elements. The devil had proved to him, he said, that it was idolatry. Luther declared that the devil was right and must be believed. The mass was abolished in Wittenberg, and soon afterwards throughout Saxony. The images were thrown down, monks and nuns left their cloisters, and, a few years later, Luther married a nun called Catherine von Bora (1525)."[1] This is why when a priest quits the Roman Church in order to marry, he is said "to go out through Luther's door."

11. After having taken the devil's advice as to the abolition of the mass, Luther restricted or abolished the use of exorcisms intended to keep the fiend at a distance. "It was afterwards noticed that wherever exorcism was abandoned, the number of those possessed or bewitched greatly diminished."[2]

12. Luther's activity was seconded by that of a gentle and amiable scholar, Melanchthon. It was embarrassed rather than helped by the fanatical Carlstadt, who declared the marriage of priests not only permissible, but obligatory, and, in his hatred of Catholicism, handled the monks roughly and destroyed works of art. In 1522, Luther quitted his retreat in order to combat the violent adherents of Carlstadt at Wittenberg itself. These were known as the Sacramentarians, because they refused to recognise more than one sacrament, that of Baptism. Luther denounced them as "supporters of Satan," and drove them out of the town.

13. Denmark and Sweden, where the archbishops of Upsala had wielded despotic power, also rallied to the Refor-

[1] Voltaire.
[2] *Ibid.*

mation. "Luther found himself the apostle of the north, and enjoyed his glory in peace. As early as 1525 the States of Saxony, Brunswick and Hesse, and the cities of Strasburg and Frankfort embraced his doctrine. . . . This Anti-Pope imitated the Pope by authorising Philip Landgrave of Hesse to marry a second wife while his first was still alive. This permission was accorded at a little Synod gathered at Wittenberg. It is true that Gregory II., in a decretal of 726, had allowed that in certain cases a man might marry a second wife. But neither times nor circumstances were the same. . . . What no pontiff since Gregory had ventured to do, Luther, who attacked the excessive power of the Popes, did without any power at all. His dispensation was secret, but time reveals all secrets of this nature." [1]

.

. .

14. A new burst of fanaticism came to trouble these "pacific scandals." A pair of Saxon enthusiasts, pretending to be inspired, demanded that children should be rebaptized, on the ground that Jesus was baptized after he was grown up. They founded the violent sect of the Anabaptists, who preached a sort of holy war against both Romans and Lutherans. This sect attracted the peasantry, which then suffered from the most outrageous oppression that ever existed, and stirred up a *Jacquerie.* "They made the most of the dangerous truth that all men are born equal, and that if the Popes had treated princes as their subjects, peasants had been treated like brute beasts by their lords. . . . They claimed the rights of humanity; but they sustained their claim like wild beasts." [2]

15. The peasants rose, from Saxony to Lorraine (1525), and, after committing horrible excesses, were exterminated by the regular troops. The number of victims has been put at 150,000. They got no sympathy from Luther. Alarmed at this menace to social order, the doctrinaire turned his back on the fanatics created by his own teaching.

When the second Diet of Spires (1529) attempted a Cath-

[1] Voltaire. See also, for the decretals of Gregory II., Bossuet, *Œuvres,* ed. Gaume, vol. vii, p. 540.

[2] Voltaire.

olic reaction, fourteen cities and several princes protested, from which action the enemies of Rome took their name of *Protestants*. At Augsburg, the Lutherans presented a confession of faith, to which a third of Germany subscribed. The princes of this party combined against the Emperor, Charles V., as well as against Rome (1530).

16. The Anabaptists, however, seized Münster and drove out the bishop (1536). "At first they wanted to re-establish the Jewish theocracy, and be governed by God alone. But a tailor, named John of Leyden, declared that God had appeared to him and appointed him king. His assertion was believed."[1] John, monarch and prophet, polygamous in the fashion of the Kings of Israel, was crowned with pomp and sent his apostles into Germany. He was afterwards taken with arms in his hands, and tortured, by the Bishop of Münster's orders, with red-hot pincers. All the Anabaptists caught in Westphalia and the Low Countries were drowned, strangled, or burnt. The sect survived, however, but in a quiescent state, and amalgamated with the *Unitarians*, that is, with those "who recognise only one God, and, while venerating Christ, live without much dogma and with no disputations. . . . The Anabaptists began with barbarism, but have ended with mildness and good sense."[2]

17. The embarrassments of Charles V., who was being threatened by the Turks, had prevented him from acting with energy against the Reformation. After the Diet of Augsburg (1530) the Lutherans came to an understanding with each other at Smalkalde (1532), and Charles concluded an agreement with them which held good for twelve years (1534).

18. Luther died in 1546. The Emperor, at peace with France and Turkey, then summoned the Protestants to dissolve their league, and, on their refusal, crushed them at the battle of Mühlberg (1547). But this victory did not end the war. At last, in 1552, religious liberty was conceded to the Protestants by the treaty of Passau. Not long afterwards Charles, discouraged as Diocletian had been before him,

1 Voltaire.
2 *Ibid.*

abdicated and retired to the monastery of Yuste, leaving the Empire to his brother Ferdinand and Spain to his son Philip II.

∴

19. Switzerland had taken fire at the same time as Germany. "Zwingli, parish priest of Zurich, had gone even further than Luther: he refused to admit that the Deity entered into the bread and wine."[1] The senate of Zurich agreed with him, Berne followed Zurich (1528), and soon afterward Œcolampadius brought about the triumph of the Reformation at Basle. But Lucerne and four other cantons remained faithful to Rome. They declared war, and Zwingli was defeated and killed at Keppel (1531). The Catholics quartered his body and burnt it. "Zwingli's religion was called Calvinism. Calvin gave it his name, just as Amerigo Vespucci gave his to the continent discovered by Columbus."[2]

20. The magistrates of Geneva, following the example set by Zurich and Berne, undertook a patient examination of the conflicting doctrines. They ended by proscribing popery, and the bishop had to fly. The Genevese, in their alliance with Fribourg and Berne against the Duke of Savoy, called themselves *Eidgenossen* (allied by oath), whence, perhaps, the French word *Huguenots*. Their reformation was characterised by a moral severity amounting to austerity. It found a sort of Pope in Calvin (born at Noyon in 1509), a man of irreproachable morals and as hard as Luther was violent. He was, moreover, a good writer, as his *Institution Chrétienne* proves, and a man of power in the bitterness of his convictions. Games and shows were forbidden. For more than a hundred years no musical instrument was allowed in Geneva. The practice of public confession was restored to favour. Calvin established synods, consistories, and deacons; he even instituted a consistorial jurisdiction with the right of excommunication. The Reformation had good reason, no doubt, for shutting up the convents; but Calvin

[1] *Ibid.*
[2] *Ibid.*

tended to re-establish them in a lay form, and even to transform a whole canton into a convent!

21. A Spanish doctor, Miguel Servetus, who had a premonition of the circulation of the blood even before Harvey, and had distinguished himself by his courage during an epidemic at Vienne (Dauphiné), addressed a letter to Calvin on the Trinity. They held different opinions on the question. Beginning with discussion, they ended by invective. A theological work which Servetus had printed secretly appeared anonymously, but was denounced to the Inquisition at Lyons by a friend of Calvin's. To reinforce his denunciation, this man followed it up by a number of letters written by Servetus, which Calvin gave him for this base purpose. What a part for an apostle to play! Servetus, who well knew that in France they sent all innovators to the stake, took flight while his cause was pending. Unhappily he passed through Geneva, where Calvin denounced him. And yet Calvin was not the monster of intolerance he has been called. Shortly before the prosecution of Servetus, he wrote: "In a case where a man is simply heterodox, we do not consider that a sufficient reason for rejecting him; we must tolerate him and not drive him from the Church or expose him to censure as a heretic." Servetus was tried by the Council of Geneva, an elected body, quite independent of Calvin, and, indeed, hostile to his ideas: the indictment was drawn up by a member of the Anti-Calvinist party. On August 26, 1553, Calvin wrote to his friend Farel, who had endeavoured to get Servetus to retract: "I hope he will be condemned, but I desire that he should be spared the atrocities of the penalty." And on October 26: "To-morrow he will be executed: we did our best to change the manner of his death, but in vain." The Council had, in fact, decided the day before that he should be burnt alive at Champel. He bore his punishment like a stoic. On November 1, 1903, the Calvinists of Geneva inaugurated a monument to his memory. The crime of his burning must be judged like those of the Terror. It was a fruit of the education in intolerance given to Europe by the Roman Church.

22. Voltaire remarks that certain letters of Luther

breathe a spirit no more pacific than those of Calvin, to which the Protestants answer that "they believe it their duty to follow the doctrines of the primitive Church, not to canonise the passions of either Luther or Calvin." To which Voltaire: "A wise reason! The spirit of philosophy has at last blunted the sword. But was it necessary to pass through two centuries of lunacy to arrive at these peaceful years?" When Voltaire wrote, the days of a new frenzy were not very far off.

∴

23. The elements of the Reformation had existed in England since the days of Wyclif; it only wanted the caprice of a prince to bring them to maturity.

24. "It is well known that England severed her connection with the Pope because Henry VIII. fell in love. What neither Peter's Pence, nor the sale of indulgences, nor five hundred years of extortions, always resisted by parliament and people, could effect, was effected, or, at least, determined, by a passing love affair."[1] Henry VIII. wished to exchange Catherine of Aragon for Anne Boleyn, and Clement VII. refused to annul his marriage with Charles V.'s aunt. Henry accordingly had it annulled by Cranmer, Archbishop of Canterbury. The Pope excommunicated him; so he proclaimed himself supreme head of the Church and his parliament abolished the papal authority. Being in want of money, the king confiscated the property of the religious bodies, and displayed the most impudent cynicism in stripping the rich abbeys of their wealth. A Pope himself, in his own way and to his own advantage, he took good care not to declare himself a Lutheran. "The invocation of saints was only restricted, not abolished. He caused the Bible to be read in English, but wished to go no further. It was a capital offence to believe in the Pope; and also to be a Protestant." The Lord Chancellor, Sir Thomas More, and Fisher, Bishop of Rochester, were condemned to death by Parliament for refusing to acknowledge the king as head of the Church. Henry, after the fashion of the sixteenth century,

[1] Voltaire.

was completely unaffected by moral scruples, but he was a king! After his death England had Lutherans, Zwinglians, and even Anabaptists, "the fathers of those peace-loving Quakers whose religion was so often laughed at while their morals enforced respect. . . . Believing themselves to be Christians and in nowise priding themselves on their philosophy, they were in reality deists, for in Christ they only recognised a man to whom God had given purer lights than to his contemporaries. The people called them Anabaptists, because they did not acknowledge the validity of baptism for infants, requiring adults to be baptized even when they had already undergone the rite." [1]

25. Mary Tudor, the daughter of Henry VIII. and wife of Philip II., was passionately Catholic. While she was on the throne, over two hundred Protestants were burnt, including Archbishop Cranmer; her successor, Elizabeth (1558-1603), was a Protestant. "Parliament was Protestant; the whole nation became Protestant and is so still. Its religion was now fixed and its liturgy established. The Roman form of hierarchy, with a greatly diminished ceremonial, although with more than the Lutherans allowed; confession, permitted but not ordained; the belief that God is in the Eucharist without transubstantiation: broadly speaking, these are the elements of the Anglican religion." [2] During the short reign of Edward VI., the son of Henry VIII. (1547-1553), a Confession of Faith in forty-two articles and an official prayer-book had been promulgated. Elizabeth retained thirty-nine of the forty-two articles in her *Act of Uniformity*, which also imposed the Creed (1562). The Edwardian prayer-book, proscribed under Mary, was re-established, with a few alterations, and became the foundation of Anglican worship.

26. Elizabeth, though very hostile to Popery, was no more of a fanatic than her father. She hanged two Jesuits and beheaded Mary of Scotland (1587), but these cruelties were inspired by political considerations. By excommunicating Elizabeth during Mary's captivity, Pope Pius V. only

[1] Voltaire.
[2] *Ibid.*

made her more implacable. Scotland was agitated by the wars between Catholics and Protestants. A preacher, John Knox, who had at one time been a refugee with Calvin (1554), propagated Calvinism in Scotland. He led it to victory after the flight of Mary, for whose head he clamoured as early as 1570. Ireland remained faithful to Rome in spite of Elizabeth, who showed her despotic temper by forcing an Anglican priesthood on the Irish parishes. That unhappy island was still more harshly treated in the sequel, but remained faithful to her Church; that she has remained to this day.

.˙.

27. In 1516, Francis I. and Leo X. had concluded a Concordat which gave the king the nominations to benefices and the Pope their first year's revenue. The University and the Parliament of Paris judged these terms too favourable to Rome. The king's sister, Marguerite d'Alençon, afterwards Queen of Navarre, encouraged the propaganda of Jacques Lefèvre of Etaples (born in 1435), in support of Augustinian doctrines which resembled those of Luther. Among the disciples of Lefèvre was Guillaume Farel, afterwards a friend of Calvin, who preached the Reformation at Neuchâtel and invited Calvin to Geneva. Calvin himself could not stay in France; his *Institution chrétienne* was first published at Basle. In spite of Marguerite's influence, the reformers were horribly persecuted in France. Jean le Clerc was torn to pieces with pincers for having spoken against images and relics: twenty reformers were burnt at the stake. At the same time Francis I. was allying himself with the German Protestants and even with the Turks against Charles V. Profoundly indifferent in religious matters, he let his parliaments and his monks do as they liked. The close of his reign was disgraced by an infamous crime. The Parliament of Provence condemned to the stake nineteen Waldenses of Mérindol, who had adopted the reformed doctrines. Francis offered to pardon them on condition that they recanted. On their refusal the First President of the Parliament, one Oppède, called in troops, who burnt and massacred

them all. "A company of sixty men and thirty women had taken refuge in the walled village of Cabrières. They surrendered on a promise of their lives; no sooner was the surrender complete than they were massacred. A few women escaped to a neighbouring church; they were dragged out by Oppède's orders, shut up in a barn, and there burnt. Twenty-two small townships were burnt to the ground. Francis I. was horrified. The warrant he had signed was for the execution of nineteen heretics only. Oppède and Guérin, the *Avocat Général*, had caused the massacre of thousands."[1] On his death-bed the king requested his son to punish this barbarity. The Parliament of Paris condemned Guérin to death, but acquitted Oppède, the more criminal of the pair.

28. "The progress of Calvinism was not stemmed by these executions. On one side the faggots were ablaze, on the other the psalms of Clément Marot were sung laughingly, true to that genius of the French nation which is always light and sometimes very cruel. Marguerite's whole Court was thoroughly Calvinist; that of her brother, the king, more than half so. What the people had begun, the nobles were carrying on. More than one member of the Parliament of Paris itself was attached to the Reformation."[2] Henry II. arrested five counsellors, among them Anne du Bourg, who was hanged and burnt under Francis II.

The success of the Reformation among the French nobles was not solely due to the Renaissance and the intellectual illumination which followed it; they saw the German knights growing rich on the spoils of the abbeys, and hoped for similar good fortune. In all the religious wars which disgraced the second half of the sixteenth century, both sides were eager for rapine and pillage. At that sinister epoch honest and kindly men like the Chancellor de l'Hôpital and Admiral de Coligny were rare and admirable exceptions.

*
* *

29. The so-called Counter-Reformation was the movement towards reform within the Roman Church brought

[1] Voltaire. [2] *Ibid.*

about by the threat of a Protestant revolution. It was, in a sense, a Protestant infiltration into Romanism, not, of course, in rites and dogmas, but in the discipline of the clergy. Not only did the Popes become, for the most part, respectable men, whose only weakness was the appointment to lucrative posts of their own nephews (*nipoti*, whence the term *nepotism*); but priests and monks were better controlled and their duties more clearly defined. The sale of indulgences came to an end; and, in confession, the use of a little box known as a confessional was made obligatory, which minimised certain dangerous opportunities.

30. Profiting by its trials, the Church, without ceasing to urge violence upon the "civil arm," now sought to gain, or regain, souls by softer methods. In this task she was admirably seconded by the Jesuits, who gradually acquired the control of education, and, through the confessional, of the consciences of the ruling classes. Lay societies, more or less affiliated to the Jesuits, were formed in many centres to work "for the greater glory of God." Recent publications have made us well acquainted with one of these, which wielded a great and mysterious influence in France between 1627 and 1666. This was the Brotherhood of the Holy Sacrament (*Confrérie du Saint Sacrement*), which was known as the *Cabale des Dévots*.[1] The secrecy with which this Brotherhood carried on its works of charity is to be explained by the fundamental object of its activity: An elaborate system of espionage, directed against the reputation and property of all heretics and unbelievers. To deprive them of their functions or their customers, and reduce them to poverty became the ambition of opponents who were no longer permitted to burn them.

31. While Protestantism, inspired by Saint Paul and Saint Augustine, narrowed the way of salvation and frightened the sinner by insisting on his sin, Jesuitical Catholicism adopted a more skilful policy: it made religion gentle and almost indulgent to human frailty. The Jesuits were not in-

[1] It was perhaps in opposition to this cabal, fallen into discredit with the powers, that Molière wrote *Tartufe,* which was represented at Versailles in 1664, by command of Louis XIV.

deed the inventors of casuistry, which was familiar to classic Greece, and of which many examples are to be found in Cicero's *De Officiis;* but they developed the useful science which takes note of the shades and degrees of acts no less than of thoughts, and judges them chiefly by their motives. The Jesuits never taught the crude doctrine that the end justifies the means, but their main preoccupation was, very rightly, with intentions. Those Jesuits whom the Jansenists were never weary of vilifying, writers on practical morals like Sanchez and Suarez, were, in their way, profound psychologists, liberal and liberating moralists, to whom humanity would have owed a deep debt of gratitude had they not used liberty itself in a domineering spirit, and lightened the chains of the human race in order to subdue it the better.

32. The new course of the Church was fixed by the Council of Trent, which lasted for seventeen years (1546-1563), with considerable intervals. In its early days, the Primate of Portugal facetiously announced that "these most illustrious cardinals will have to be most illustriously reformed." The necessity of a firm discipline was universally acknowledged, but it was by no means the only necessity. The Council of Trent dealt a good deal in scholastic theology; it codified Catholicism; it defined original sin; it decreed the perpetuity of the marriage tie; it pronounced anathema against those who rejected the invocation of saints or the adoration of relics, who denied the existence of Purgatory or the validity of indulgences. "The theologians, who had no votes, explained the dogmas; the prelates voted under the directions of the papal legates, who quieted the grumblers, softened the acrimonious, parried everything that might offend the Court of Rome, and were from first to last the masters." [1]

33. Thanks to the Counter-Reformation and to the Jesuits, the Church regained part of the ground she had lost in Europe, Southern Germany, France, some of the Swiss Cantons, Savoy, and Poland. In Italy, Protestantism was almost completely crushed by the Inquisition established in

[1] Voltaire

1542. It was the same in Spain. The propaganda of the Polish Jesuits spread into Western Russia and into Lithuania. Catholicism conquered America, several of the cities of India, and won a footing in Japan and China. This development in the Far East was chiefly the work of the zealous Jesuit François Xavier (1542-1552). But while the Jesuits kept their place in Pekin, thanks chiefly to concessions to the native faith which brought suspicion upon their own, they were driven out of Japan and their religion proscribed (1637) as soon as the intelligent population of its islands awoke to the fact that their liberty was in danger.

34. In the war against the Reformation the Jesuits played a part no less considerable than that of the Dominicans in the less dangerous struggle with the Albigenses. Taking their share in every political and religious conflict, they have, down to our own days, excited violent hatred and equally fervent admiration. History, moreover, has to show some reserve in discussing them, for no one outside the Order knows exactly where its archives are kept, and no independent layman has ever been allowed to explore them.

35. The founder of this illustrious company was Ignatius Loyola, a noble from Guipuscoa (1491-1556). Wounded at the siege of Pampeluna, he was attracted to mysticism by a perusal of the *Lives of the Saints*. After certain pilgrimages to the East, he came, at the age of thirty-three, to study first at Salamanca and afterwards at Paris. In Paris he founded an association which at first devoted itself to teaching. In 1540, Paul III. promulgated the Bull by which the Order of Jesuits was instituted. The fourth vow it imposed was that of absolute obedience to the Pope. Loyola edited, or rather compiled, a work in Spanish, *Spiritual Exercises*, which has been translated into all modern languages. It puts forth a programme for the society, in which God is represented as a general and the Jesuits as his officers. An old soldier himself, he understood how to bring his order under that quasi-military discipline which has counted for so much in its success. In this respect, perhaps, it was in some measure inspired by those brotherhoods of Islam, at once religious and military, which

had already been imitated in the Middle Ages by the Templars and the Hospitallers.

36. Loyola found very efficient lieutenants in Lainez and Salmeron, and since his time the Society has never lacked men of talent. "It has controlled several European Courts and won a great name for itself by the education of youth [Voltaire was one of its pupils]; it reformed science in China, Christianised Japan—for a time!—and gave laws to the people of Paraguay. At the time of its expulsion from Portugal, it numbered about 18,000 individuals, all subject to a permanent and absolute ruler in their General, and bound to each other by this obedience sworn to a single person. . . . The Order had great difficulty in establishing itself in France. It was born and reared under the House of Austria, France's sometime enemy, and was protected by her. In the days of the League, the Jesuits were the pensioners of Philip II. The other religious bodies, who all belonged to this faction except the Benedictines and the Carthusians, fanned the flame only in France; the Jesuits did so in Rome, Madrid and Brussels, as well as in Paris itself."[1]

37. Whereas the forces of the Roman Church are centralised for the struggle, the reformed Churches are divided. Closely allied to the civil power, they are national and not universal. If Rome tends to dominate the secular authorities, her rivals too often and too willingly became their instruments. Another characteristic these latter have in common is the large share in ecclesiastical matters given to the laity, which is not differentiated from the clergy by marriage. In England and in the Scandinavian countries a hierarchy analogous to that of Rome was preserved. Those countries are *episcopalian*. The Calvinists of Switzerland, France, Holland and Scotland preferred the *Synodal* or *Presbyterian* system, so called because the synods or councils of elders (*Presbyteroi* in Greek) had the direction of spiritual affairs, as in the primitive Church. The Lu-

[1] Voltaire.

therans, in default of bishops, had superintendents. Finally, the sects called *Independents* and *Congregationalists* had no hierarchy at all, but governed themselves. These flourished chiefly in England. As for their methods of worship, the Reformed Churches agreed in banishing images, relics, and the invocation of saints; but in detail they varied, according to the severity of their principles. The Anglican Church remained very close to Roman Catholicism, and, in the nineteenth century, part of it, known as the High Church, approached it more closely still. The Lutheran Church gave an important place to music and singing; the Calvinist Churches no more tolerated instrumental music than images, and permitted nothing but psalms and hymns. The national languages everywhere ousted Latin in the liturgies, and preaching encroached upon ritual.

∴

38. The spirit of the Inquisition was incarnate in Philip II. He swore before a crucifix to exterminate the scanty Protestants of Spain and had them burnt under his palace windows. Hearing that heretics existed in a certain valley of Piedmont, he wrote to the Governor of Milan: *Send them all to the gallows!* They told him of reformers in Calabria: he directed that they should be put to the sword, reserving thirty for the gallows and thirty for the stake. It is not to be wondered that such a monster should have employed a hangman like Alva in the subjection of the Protestant Netherlands, where he had established the Inquisition in 1565.

39. "William the Silent had neither the men nor the money to resist such a monarch as Philip II. The persecutions gave him both. The new tribunal set up in Brussels threw the people into despair. Counts Egmont and Horn, with eighteen others of gentle birth, were beheaded and their blood was the first cement for the Republic of the United Netherlands."[1] When the Duke of Alva was at last recalled, he boasted of having put eighteen thousand people to death. A vain boast; for the *Union of Utrecht* brought

[1] Voltaire.

about the birth of the political liberties of Holland in the seven united provinces (1579). But religious liberty only comes after a long education, and the Dutch Reformation was far from being always liberal. In its turn, it was guilty of murdering men for their opinions.

40. Calvin had uncompromisingly upheld the Augustinian theory of predestination, which makes God either the benefactor or the capricious foe of individuals. This doctrine, a logical deduction from premises which are an outrage upon reason, was contested by Harmensen, called Arminius, a pastor of Leyden (1603), against Gomar, a fanatical Calvinist. As the Arminians were Liberals in politics, they were opposed by the Stadtholder, Maurice of Nassau. At the Synod of Dort (1618), they were insulted, maltreated, and condemned. One of their number, the old patriot Barnevelt, was beheaded. Arminian pastors and professors were stripped of their offices. Many took refuge in Schleswig, whence they returned in 1625, the death of Maurice having caused a certain reaction in favour of toleration. We must add, for the credit of Holland, that the Dutch neither proscribed nor persecuted the Roman Catholic worship.

41. The Catholics did not abandon the idea of regaining England, even after the dispersal of Philip's "Invincible Armada." Elizabeth's successor, James I., the son of Mary Stuart, was driven by the Protestant party in the direction of persecution. For this a pretext was found in the Gunpowder Plot, a conspiracy to blow up the Houses of Parliament, the inception of which was ascribed to the Jesuits (1605). Their complicity has never been established. The Jesuit Garnet, executed for a share in the plot, was most probably innocent. Charles I., son of James I., married Henrietta Maria, the Catholic daughter of Henri Quatre. He was reproached with favouring *ritualism*, those ceremonies of the Anglican Church which brought it nearest to Rome. This tendency was fostered by Laud, Bishop of London, and afterwards Archbishop of Canterbury. Charles was imprudent enough to attempt the imposition of the Anglican liturgy on Presbyterian Scotland, which revolted.

Passing through various stages of a struggle with his Parliament, he was finally arrested, tried, and beheaded (1649). Parliament was dominated by the spirit of the Scottish Puritans, an austere and sectarian form of Protestantism. Sensible men as they were, they were drunk with the wine of the Bible, and believed themselves prophets of Israel because they could quote their sayings. One of the most energetic members of Parliament, who soon became its leader, Oliver Cromwell, conqueror of Charles I. at Marston Moor (1644) and Naseby (1645), had passed from the *Presbyterians* to the *Independents*, that is, to a democratic form of religion, in which full autonomy was left to local communities (1640). But when he became Lord Protector (1653), he gave a Presbyterian form to the English Church, modified by a large toleration, which was not, however, extended to the Catholics.

Charles II., restored by General Monk after the death of Cromwell, reverted to the Anglican forms and tried to impose them in his turn. The main point was to compel every ecclesiastic to receive ordination from a bishop. Thousands preferred destitution to such an appearance of concession to Catholicism. The truth was that Charles, a dissolute prince and pensioner of France, sought to re-establish the ancient faith. His brother and successor, James II., threw off the mask, and imprisoned seven Anglican bishops who refused to lend themselves to an understanding with Rome. The bishops were tried and acquitted. The king's unpopularity went on increasing until at last his son-in-law, William of Orange, Stadtholder of the Netherlands, deprived him of his crown, with the help and consent of Parliament (1689). Thenceforward English policy took *No Popery!* for its motto: a principle which became all the dearer to the English people through the attempts made by Louis XIV. to restore James II.

42. Ireland rose in 1641. The Catholics massacred thousands of Protestants, but were punished with equal cruelty by Cromwell (1650). A second rising took place in favour of James II. (1690); after the rebels had been defeated, the oppression of Catholic Ireland became atro-

cious. And yet it must be confessed that England never behaved towards her Catholic subjects as Louis XIV. did towards the French Protestants. Their lives were made insupportable, but their priests were not condemned to death, nor were those who wished to emigrate sent to the galleys.

A Swiss follower of Zwingli, Thomas Lieber, called *Erastus* (*d.* 1583) claimed that the Church should be subordinate to the State. His doctrine, by no means a new one, is known in Great Britain as *Erastianism;* it has been that of Henry II., Edward III., Henry VIII., Elizabeth and later statesmen, but was opposed, ever since 1560, by the Church of Scotland.

43. At the time when, under James I., Presbyterians and Independents refused to accept the Anglican liturgy, a certain number of these austere Puritans, known as the *Pilgrim Fathers,* embarked for North America on a ship called the *Mayflower* (September 1620). They landed in Massachusetts and there founded the colonies which also afforded asylum to the persecuted French Protestants. It is now a kind of title to *noblesse* in the United States to count one of the Pilgrim Fathers among one's ancestors.

44. Reformed England has never lacked reformers. One of these—George Fox, the founder of the *Society of Friends*—was imprisoned under Charles II. He taught that the divine spirit acted directly upon individuals, occasionally inspiring them with a sort of convulsive shaking. People took advantage of this doctrine to call the Friends *Quakers,* although their worship is remarkably free from fuss or affectation. The Quakers are honest folk, who know neither sacraments nor rites, whose lives are simple to austerity, who neither swear nor play, nor carry arms, nor dance, nor drink strong liquors. Their religious exaltation, inoffensive enough, declares itself at their "meetings," when, amid a profound silence, one of the congregation may begin to hold forth in the name of the Holy Spirit. The most intelligent of the Quakers, William Penn, the son of an admiral, was a creditor of Charles II.'s government, which paid its debt with a gift of land in America. Penn betook himself thither with a body of Friends in 1681. The flourishing state of

Pennsylvania preserves his name, and its capital, Philadelphia, reveres his memory. The Friends have always exercised a certain influence in England and in the United States, where they co-operated with effect in the movement for negro emancipation. Quite recently, they have had the honour of being the first to rebuild houses in the devastated regions of France (1915), and they have played a merciful part in combating the famine in Russia (1922).

.
. .

45. One of the first results of the Catholic reaction was the Thirty Years' War. It ruined Germany for two hundred years, but with the help of Catholic France under Richelieu, Protestant Sweden under Gustavus Adolphus, and the Low Countries, the Reformed Princes of Germany were upheld against the House of Austria. In the end this frightful havoc and bloodshed left things much as it found them. Catholics and Protestants retained their position. France alone profited by the long conflict in the weakening of the Empire. The Treaty of Westphalia (1648) made her the first Power in Europe. Dreadful cruelties were committed on both sides, but the Catholic leaders showed themselves much more savage than their opponents. Few more disgusting acts of barbarity are on record than the sack and burning of Magdeburg by Tilly. Not only was the torch of war lighted by the Jesuit Councillors of Ferdinand II., but after all its ravages the Pope refused to recognise the peace of 1648. In 1631 Urban VIII. had congratulated Ferdinand on the destruction of Magdeburg, and had expressed the hope that other rebel cities would soon meet with the same fate.

46. The Lutherans of Germany had a reformer of their own in the Alsatian, Philip Jacob Spener (1635-1705). Distressed by the external and formalistic character of the religion he saw about him, he founded what he called *Collegia pietatis*, from which his followers were called *Pietists*. It was in Berlin that he wielded most influence, the upper middle classes receiving an impression from his teaching which they preserved down to the middle of the nineteenth cen-

tury. A *Pietist* is not a theologian. His preoccupations are with the practical side of the Christian life. Here he approaches the rationalist and the simple deist. From these, however, he is separated by a certain air of superiority and by a slight pretension to asceticism. A religious movement in its origin, Pietism became an attitude, and a tiresome one. However, the tendency breathed by the writings and preachings of Spener evolved very differently in various parts of Germany, so that we cannot speak of Pietism in general, but only of Pietists in particular places and times.

47. Towards the end of the sixteenth century, Poland seemed almost lost to the Roman Church. The nobility were either Lutherans or Calvinists; there were more than 2000 reformed communities in the country. Then a singular thing took place. Two natives of Siena, Lælius Socinus (Lelio Sozzini) and his nephew Faustus, or Fausto, taught in Switzerland the doctrine known as Unitarianism, a kind of deism hostile to the dogma of the Trinity and still more to that of salvation by faith. Faustus came to Poland and founded a Socinian Church there, which Jesuits and Reformers united to attack. The Socinians had to take refuge in Transylvania, and the Polish reformers, weakened by the struggle and their loss in numbers, were soon reduced to impotence. The Roman Church profited by these events to regain all the ground she had lost.

∴

48. In spite of all the violence that darkened the reign of Henri II., violence in which the populace, excited by the monks, began to participate, the French Protestants were a fairly powerful body when François II. mounted the throne; he was a sickly and timid child, dominated by the faction of the Guise family. The struggle soon took on a political complexion, the Huguenots recognising Prince Louis de Condé for their chief, the Catholics the Duc François de Guise. Desiring to withdraw the young king from the influence of François de Guise and his brother, the Cardinal de Lorraine, certain Protestants organised what

is known as the Conspiracy of Amboise. This failed and was followed by numerous executions. At the beginning of Charles IX.'s reign, the States-General demanded liberty of worship (1561). As a result of this a congress of theologians was held at Poissy, in which the Reformation was defended by Théodore de Bèze, a pupil of Calvin and afterwards his successor at Geneva. Like all religious conferences it was quite useless.

In January 1562, an important concession was made to the Protestants by an edict which gave them permission to have conventicles in cities. But almost immediately afterwards François de Guise attacked a group of Huguenots who were at worship near Vassy, and basely massacred women and children. A civil war followed which lasted with a few intervals for some eight years. It terminated through the influence of Admiral de Coligny, by a treaty favourable to liberty of worship, signed at St. Germain.

Shortly afterwards, Henri de Bourbon, King of Navarre, was betrothed to the sister of Charles IX. As it appeared unlikely that either Charles or his brother Henri would have children, the Crown of France threatened to pass to a Prince of the Reformation; an alarming prospect for Rome, for having lost England, she was all the more tenacious of her footing in France. As early as March 28, 1569, Pius V. wrote to Charles IX.: "Pursue and crush all the enemies who remain. Unless you pull up the last roots of the evil, they will shoot again as they have already done so often." This was preaching the policy of extermination, which had already been put in force against the Albigenses. It led directly to the Massacre of St. Bartholomew.

49. Catherine de' Medici and her son Charles prepared the trap. They chose a moment when all the Huguenot chiefs were in Paris for the marriage of the King of Navarre. On the night of August 24, 1572, the Eve of St. Bartholomew, the mob, warned by the tocsin, flung themselves upon the Huguenots and began a massacre which lasted for several days. Admiral de Coligny, who "only breathed for the good of the State,"[1] was the first victim. Ten thousand men were

[1] Montesquieu.

slaughtered in Paris, and in spite of the resistance of a few governors and military commandants, who were willing to be soldiers but not murderers, the same horrors were enacted in all the provinces. Henry of Navarre abjured his faith to save his life, and for some four years gave himself up to shameful pleasures. He even did his best to harry his former co-religionaries. One day, however, he disappeared from Paris, and again joined the Reformers.

"The throats of thirty thousand of their comrades had been cut at a time of peace; about two millions were left to make war." [1] After the death of the wretched Charles IX., which followed the massacre at no long interval, his brother and successor, Henri III., fearing the ambition of the Duc de Guise, began by making overtures to the Protestants and disavowing the Massacre of St. Bartholomew. Henri de Guise, encouraged by the Pope and helped by Philip II., created the Holy League, the object of which was to exterminate the Reformers and to prevent the Crown of France from passing to a Huguenot king. They avowedly preferred the daughter of Philip II. to the King of Navarre, secretly hoping to substitute the House of Lorraine [2] for that of Valois. The League was recruited among the ignorant rabble, directed and paid by the monks, who took care to feed their fanaticism. It was an army of crime and disorder in the service of the Church. Henri III., a feeble and abject creature, was driven by fear to declare himself head of the League. Under the impulse of the same passion, he ended by allying himself with the King of Navarre, and besieging Paris in his company (1589). He was assassinated by Jacques Clément, a Dominican friar. Henri de Bourbon then became legitimate King of France. He knew well enough, however, that in spite of his repeated successes he was not accepted by the Catholic majority in the country. So once more he abjured, made the dangerous leap (*saut périlleux*), in the conviction that "Paris was well worth a mass," and obtained the submission of the League (1593) chiefly by gifts of money and pensions.

[1] Voltaire. Two millions seems an overstatement of their number.

[2] The first Duc de Guise, who received the title from François I., was Claude de Lorraine, father of François de Guise.

50. Pius V.'s successor, Gregory XIII., struck a medal in memory of the St. Bartholomew with the legend *Ugonotorum strages* (the carnage of the Huguenots), and commissioned Vasari to paint those frescoes representing the massacre which still dishonour the walls of a saloon in the Vatican. Vain attempts have been made to absolve the Pope and his Legate of all responsibility for this inexpiable crime. The Church found it quite a natural proceeding to get rid of the Huguenots, as it had of the sectaries of the Middle Ages, by collective murder. We have already quoted the message of Pius V. to Charles IX. On the fatal 24th of August, while the massacre was going on, the Nuncio Salviati wrote to Gregory XIII.: "With your Holiness I rejoice from my heart that the King and the Queen Mother have been able to exterminate these infected people with so much prudence and at a moment so opportune, when the rebels were all locked up in their cage." Gregory XIII. celebrated "the most happy tidings of the destruction of the Huguenot sect" with a religious ceremony. He sent to the French Court the Legate Orsini, who, on his way through Lyons, publicly distributed indulgences to those who had taken part in the massacres. Finally he presented the golden rose, instituted to reward ardent zeal for the Church, to Charles IX., the crowned assassin of his own subjects.

51. The Edict of Nantes (1598), a decree confirmatory of previous treaties, though with certain restrictions, gave religious peace to France for a time. This "perpetual and irrevocable" edict authorised the reformed worship and the teaching of Protestant theology; also, by the institution of mixed tribunals (*Chambres mi-parties*), it secured equality for the Huguenots in the administration of justice. Several cities, called Cities of Refuge (*Villes de sûreté*), were awarded to the Protestants. One of these, La Rochelle, became a sort of French Geneva. This was repeating the mistake already committed in the Edict of St. Germain, and setting up a State within the State for the benefit of the Reformers.

⁂

52. After the assassination (1610) of Henri Quatre by Ravaillac, the "blind instrument of the spirit of the age,"[1] the condition of the Huguenots remained a favourable one during the early years of Louis XIII.'s minority. But Richelieu, although allied with the Protestant princes against the House of Austria, was too eager for the grandeur and unity of France to tolerate such an institution as the *Villes de sûreté*. After an heroic defence by her mayor, Guiton, La Rochelle had to yield to famine (1628). The Edict of Nantes was confirmed by that of Nîmes (1629), but the Huguenots were deprived of their strongholds.

53. From this time onward it was no longer policy but fanaticism and cupidity which controlled events. Taking advantage of every rivalry in interests or commerce, the Church never ceased to demand from the Crown the withdrawal of all concessions granted to the Protestants. Her chief supporters in this campaign were the Chancellor Le Tellier and his son Louvois. The Edict of Nantes was never accepted by the Catholic clergy, and its history is that of its revocation.[2]

The learned Oratorian, Richard Simon, wrote: "If Cardinal Richelieu had not died so early, we should long ago have had no Huguenots in the kingdom." The Crown needed the gratuities it received from the clergy. These were always accompanied by demands for measures against the Protestants. "Where are the laws," said an orator before the child Louis XIV., at an assembly of the clergy in 1651—"where are the laws which banish heretics from intercourse with their fellow-men?" "We hope, at least," said another speaker, "that if your authority cannot put a summary end to this evil, it may cause it to languish and die through the gradual retrenchment and diminution of its forces." This programme was faithfully carried out. Protestant advocates were excluded from the tribunals (1664), Protestant notaries were forbidden to practise (1682). Protestants were shut out from all sorts of trades. They could not be apothecaries, or surgeons, or midwives;

1 Voltaire.
2 Puaux, *Les précurseurs français de la tolérance,* Paris, 1881, p. 2.

they could be employed in no public office. Their places of worship were next attacked and demolished, their pastors were driven out, their schoolmasters restricted to teaching their pupils to read, while children were allowed to become Catholics at the age of seven, whether their parents sanctioned their conversion or not (1684). The condition of the Protestants became intolerable. Many of the rich and able apostatised in order to obtain posts at Court. Thousands of the poor were bought by the gold of Pellisson, himself a converted Calvinist, who had the administration of the secret largesses of the Church. Many more of the poor and of the learned classes emigrated, and formed, especially in Holland, those communities of refugees from whom the world learnt the truth about Louis XIV.'s government, and among which, under the lash of persecution, the notion of religious toleration took definite shape.

54. Louis XIV. seems to have been led to believe that most of the Protestants had been converted or had quitted France. So he revoked the presumably useless Edict of Nantes, "in order to efface the memory of the past troubles" (October 18, 1685). Protestant places of worship were to be demolished, Protestant worship itself suppressed, schools closed, pastors banished on pain of death. But the Protestant laity were forbidden to leave France on pain of the galleys. They were allowed to remain on condition that they practised no form of worship. Their children, being inscribed on no parish registers, were all accounted illegitimate. The family was outraged as well as the conscience.

55. Those Protestants who succeeded in evading or corrupting the King's police, passed the frontier (fifty thousand families in three years), taking their energies and what was left of their property to Holland, Prussia, England, and Switzerland. In order to crush those who stayed behind, the authorities imposed garrisons of dragoons upon them (1685). These soldiers behaved like drunken savages, hanging, smoking out, and flogging men and women, dragging them half dead to the churches, "where their mere enforced presence," writes Pastor Claude in 1686, "was reckoned as a recantation." Houses were destroyed, trees cut down,

women and children thrown into convents. Even the dead were not spared. As in the days of the Inquisition in Languedoc, the corpses of those who had died without confession were tried and dragged off on hurdles to be thrown into the common sewer. "At Caen, as in many other towns, unhappy parents might be seen following the hurdles on which the bodies of their children were being drawn, to be hacked in pieces by the pupils of the Jesuits." [1] The Huguenots made the country ring with their lamentations, but they did not rebel. "Must they make all these efforts," asks Jurieu, "to tear out those French hearts which God and our birth have given us?" [2]

56. At last, after seventeen years of atrocious persecution, an insurrection did break out (1702). Deprived of their pastors, the Protestants of the Cévennes used to celebrate their worship in the solitude of the mountains. Every meeting surprised by the authorities was treated with frightful severity, chiefly on the instigation of the *Intendant* Lamoignon de Bâville, a *protégé* of Madame de Maintenon. The unhappy people, who were called Camisards, exasperated and fired by mystic delirium, revolted, and for three years kept at bay three marshals of France, of whom Villars was one. Their leaders were Roland and Jean Cavalier.[3] It was a horrible war, in which the vanquished were put to death or sent to the galleys, and in which neither age nor sex was a protection from the violence of the soldiers. The memory of all this still lingers in the Cévennes. It should be kept alive everywhere. But during the whole of the nineteenth century public education, severely controlled by the Roman Church, threw a veil over these crimes as it did over so many others. French historical manuals gave them at most a few lines, while one generation after another has learnt from these same books to pity the victims of the Terror.

[1] F. Puaux, *Précurseurs de la tolérance,* p. 23 (after Legendre, *Vie de Du Bosc,* p. 150).

[2] *Ibid.*

[3] Cavalier afterwards escaped to England, where he was well received by Queen Anne, and ended his days as Governor of Jersey. Voltaire met him in England, and formed a high opinion of him.

57. Everywhere and always, in this long catalogue of outrages on human right, when kings and ministers proscribe and soldiers strike, it is the implacable Roman Church which directs sword or pen. This has to be shown, in answer to the falsehoods of those apologists who pretend, for example, that the Pope disapproved of the Revocation. After the disaster of Ramillies, Louis XIV. cried: "Has God then forgotten all I have done for him?" As God did not address himself directly to the *Roi Soleil*, Louis here implies that he had followed the advice of his clergy, of those Jesuit directors who were for him the sole interpreters of the Divine Will. In January 1685, the French Ambassador to the Vatican transmitted the following words of Pope Innocent XI. to Versailles: "Truly, we give all praise to the king [Louis XIV.], who has destroyed so great a number of heretics, and wishes to exterminate that unhappy sect entirely in his kingdom." On May 8, 1685, d'Estrées wrote to the king: "The Pope praised not only the continual care and application of your Majesty for the extirpation of heresy, but also the methods of which your Majesty has made use, winning some by kindness, driving others from their charges and employments, striking terror into those who could not be otherwise reduced." After the Revocation, the Pope declared to the ambassador "that nothing could be finer, and that no other instance of such an action could be found." He also decided "that he would bear public witness to his joy and satisfaction with all possible splendour." On April 28, 1686, he celebrated the Revocation by giving plenary indulgence to all those who visited the French Church of St. Louis in Rome. St. Peter's and the Vatican were illuminated. Father Coronelli published an account of these celebrations under the significant title, "Rome triumphant on the occasion of the extirpation of heresy, by an edict given at Fontainebleau in October 1685." The Jesuit Sémery gave a discourse from which we learn that Pope Innocent XI. had requested the Cardinal d'Estrées to use all his influence with Louis XIV. to get him "to destroy the plague and contagion of Calvinism." Finally, it must not be forgotten that on November 13, 1685, Innocent addressed

a brief to Louis, in which he declared the Revocation to be "the finest thing his Majesty had ever done, the best fitted to immortalise his memory and to draw upon him the rarest blessings of Heaven."

58. If God forgot what Louis XIV. had done for him, there were also a few Catholics who preached a somewhat tardy toleration after the military and economical disasters by which the Revocation was followed. Thus Fénelon said in 1707: "Can violence persuade? Can it oblige men to will what they do not will? No human power can break open the impervious intrenchment of a free heart!"[1] But the same Fénelon had been during several years director of the convent of the so-called New Catholics, Protestant girls who were torn away from their families and subjected to the most cruel intolerance. As for his great rival, Bossuet, he argued against the Protestant ministers, calling attention, in his own magnificent periods, to the variations of their creeds, but, so far as we know, he had no word of pity for their sufferings. Indeed, he glorified the Revocation: "You have," he said to Louis XIV., "strengthened the faith; you have exterminated the heretics; that is an exploit worthy of your reign." What is true of Bossuet is true of most of his contemporaries. When the Church's glory is at stake, hearts are hardened. "Our one preoccupation is the destruction of heresy," cried Daniel de Cosnac, Bishop of Valence, on July 2, 1685.

∴

59. Louis XIV., who came near to extirpating Protestantism in France, deserves credit for introducing order and decency (*la règle et la décence* is Voltaire's phrase) into the religion of Rome. Great disorders had existed under Louis XIII. "Nearly all the benefices were in the hands of laymen, who employed poor clergy at small salaries to carry on the services. Every prince of the blood owned rich abbeys. More than one benefice of the Church was looked upon as

[1] Fénelon, *Œuvres* (Gaume ed., vol. v, p. 612). Another often quoted passage (*ibid.*, vol. vii, p. 162) is in the same vein, but not of undisputed authenticity.

family property. An abbey would be given as part of a dowry, and a colonel would use the income of a priory to equip his regiment. Churchmen about the Court often wore swords, and ecclesiastics were engaged in not a few of the duels which at that time brought such sorrow to France."[1] These abuses ceased, at least in great part, and the French clergy became what they have remained to our own day, the most respected and respectable in Catholic Europe.

60. Those religious orders which were founded in France in the seventeenth century were nearly all of a charitable and practical character. Cardinal de Bérulle established the Oratorians, an association of teaching priests on the model of the Italian foundation of St. Philip Neri. The Benedictines of Saint-Maur were distinguished for their works of erudition. J. B. de la Salle founded the *Frères des Ecoles Chrétiennes* (Christian Brothers) in 1680. St. Vincent de Paul, an active apostle, of untiring zeal, founded the Lazarists, or priests of the Mission, and inspired the association of Sisters of Charity, who devoted themselves to the help of the poor and suffering without being bound by any perpetual vows (1634). The whole world has done homage to the virtues of these young women, whose starched caps have served religion better than many a tiara. Among the contemplative orders only one has become famous, that of La Trappe, founded in 1671 by a penitent libertine, Armand de Rancé.

∴

61. The "liberties of the Gallican Church" had nothing to do with the consciences of the faithful, but were connected chiefly with the royal authority and with financial interests. It was not a question of religious liberty, but, in the first place, of the right, called the *Régale*, claimed by the crown to absorb the revenues of vacant bishoprics and abbacies, and to nominate to benefices in any vacant see. It was asserted that these rights had been exercised by the two first French dynasties; after being neglected for a time to the advantage of the bishops, they were energetically reclaimed by Louis XIV (1673). Certain bishops resisted; the Pope

[1] Voltaire.

protested. An assembly of clergy, convoked in 1682, adopted the following resolutions, as reprisals against Rome: (1) God gave no power in temporal concerns to either Peter or his successors. (2) The Gallican Church approves the Council of Constance, which declared Councils-general superior to the Pope in spiritual matters. (3) The rules, usages, and practices accepted in the Gallican Church and kingdom are immutable. (4) The Pope's decisions in questions of faith are only valid after they have been adopted by the Church.—These propositions, which were ratified by the tribunals and theological faculties, appeared, with good reason, so intolerable to Innocent XI. that he at once refused Bulls to any bishops or abbots appointed by the king. At his death, in 1689, twenty-nine French dioceses had no bishops. His successors were no less uncompromising. Louis XIV., importuned by the Jesuits, ended by permitting the bishops to send letters to Rome expressing their regret at the decisions the assembly had adopted. He himself wrote to the Pope to the same effect. Innocent XII. accepted these excuses. Later, Cardinal de Fleury caused the four articles to be partly disavowed by a second congress of clergy, and the struggle relaxed. The vital point was never decided, however. It was turned by various expedients which need not here be detailed.

* * *

62. From the *fabliaux* of the fourteenth century down to the Encyclopædia, through Rabelais, Montaigne, Molière and Bayle, runs a vein of criticism, of thought hostile to Christian dogma, to unproved assertions, to the intolerance of Popes and priests. In private conversation, this free-thought went as far as atheism. This was suspected in the seventeenth century; it was believed, according to Père Mersenne, who wrote under Louis XIII., that there were as many as 40,000 atheists in Paris. Among the forces by which these were controlled, the most important, no doubt, were the clergy and the monarchy. But two others existed which, in spite of being condemned by the Church, did good service in repressing what was then called libertinage. These

were the Protestant Reformation, which was a renaissance of the religious spirit; and Jansenism, which a Jesuit described as a bungled Calvinism (*Calvinisme barbouillé*).

63. The famous quarrel between Jesuits and Jansenists in France corresponds to the fight between Arminians and Gomarists in Holland. Cornelius Jansen (Jansenius), Bishop of Ypres, had written three great folio volumes upon St. Augustine which appeared after his death and found a certain number of readers in France. In this book Jansen adopted St. Augustine's opinions on Grace, whittling away, like Calvin, the part played by the human will in the work of salvation. The Jesuits, with their practical good sense, could not admit such a doctrine; not that it was logically false, but because it tended, like Calvinism, towards the neglect of those good works which benefited the Church and, it must be allowed, society at large. In France, certain theologians grouped about the Abbey of Port Royal—Duvergier, Abbot of St. Cyran, the Arnaulds, Nicole and Pascal—adopted Jansenism in their antagonism to the Jesuits, to whom some of the Port Royalists, the Arnaulds, for instance, were also opposed for personal motives. They made a difference of opinion on an insoluble question a pretext for discrediting their enemies. These latter, supported by Rome and with the strength given by the confessional and by their wealth, ended by getting the upper hand. But a whole century was disturbed by the dispute. The details of the long controversy are so absurd that it would be folly to load one's memory with them. But the men who set themselves against the facile religion of the Jesuits, and the saintly women, such as Angélique Arnauld, Abbess of Port Royal, who were associated with them, still retain their influence on men's minds by the intensity of their moral life, the gravity of their mode of thought, and their tranquil courage. "Ces Messieurs de Port Royal" are imposing doctrinaires, great figures towering above the baseness and corruption of their times.

64. In 1641, the Jesuits obtained the condemnation of Jansen's book by Rome. The Paris Faculty of Theology denounced five of its propositions. The sense of these propo-

sitions was taken from the book, but not their text. Hence an interminable quarrel. Were the five propositions in Jansen or were they not? Innocent X., in his turn, condemned the five propositions, but again without quoting the pages from which they professed to be taken. Antoine Arnauld, a prolific and lucid writer, took up the struggle; the propositions, he said, were in St. Augustine, so it was that great Father of the Church they were condemning! Here Arnauld was quite right. "The Jansenists affirmed that their system, the doctrine of St. Augustine, was the veritable tradition of the Church. In this they were not altogether wrong, but their mistake lay in wishing to impose St. Augustine on a Church which had to some extent outgrown him."[1] In 1654 the Sorbonne expelled Arnauld, but it could not silence him. Under persecution he had more friends than ever. The French bishops wished to compel the nuns of Port Royal to endorse the condemnation of the five propositions. They refused. Rigorous measures were about to be taken, when Pascal's niece, a *pensionnaire* of Port Royal, was cured of a lachrymal fistula by kissing a thorn from the Crown of Jesus. The Jesuits denied the miracle. Racine and Pascal believed it, the latter to the extent of accepting it as proof that the five propositions were true! Fanned by a passion of credulity, the campaign against the Jesuits grew more furious than ever. "Every means of making them odious was tried. Pascal went further: he made them ridiculous. His *Provincial Letters*, which appeared at this time, were models of eloquence and judicious mockery. The best comedies of Molière are not richer in humour than the earlier *Letters:* Bossuet has left us nothing more sublime than the later."[2] No doubt. But if we look a little closer, we see that what Pascal denounces in the Jesuits is modernism in the moral law, preference of the spirit to the letter, and at least a tendency to progress.[3]

65. The subtle Italian, Clement X., re-established a semblance of peace. Jansenism, under the protection of the

[1] Loisy, *Quelques Lettres,* p. 175.
[2] Voltaire.
[3] We must, of course, except certain intolerable theories advanced by a few Jesuit writers, which Pascal very justly condemns.

Duchesse de Longueville, sister of the great Condé, took advantage of this to extend its influence. The king and the Jesuits resumed the struggle. Arnauld had to fly, and died at Brussels in 1694, at a great age. A new Bull from Clement XI. (1705) was presented for signature to the nuns of Port Royal. On their refusal they were again driven out of their convent. Worse still, this was demolished in 1709 by order of the lieutenant of police. In 1711 the bodies interred in the churchyard were dug up. Boileau himself shuddered at this. His fine epitaph on the "Great Arnauld," whose corpse in its Belgian grave was beyond the reach of Jesuit vengeance, concludes with the following quatrain:

> Et même par sa mort leur fureur mal éteinte
> N'aurait jamais laissé ses cendres en repos,
> Si Dieu lui-même, ici, de son ouaille sainte
> A ces loups dévorants n'avait caché les os.[1]

66. An Oratorian, Père Quesnel, a friend and companion of Arnauld, had written a pious book which at first won the approval of Clement XI. It was dedicated to Cardinal de Noailles, Archbishop of Paris, an honest prelate who was hated by the Jesuits. These latter, who had become all-powerful when Père de la Chaise had been chosen to direct the conscience of Louis XIV., denounced Quesnel, who retired to Amsterdam, where he died. The condemnation of his book was demanded from Rome, and obtained from the same Pope who had previously blessed it. After the death of La Chaise, the king's Jesuit confessor was Le Tellier, a malevolent monk, bent on the ruin of Cardinal de Noailles. He reached his end through the weakness of Louis, who obtained the famous Bull *Unigenitus* from the Pope. This Bull condemned a hundred and one more or less Jansenist propositions put forward by Quesnel. Most of these were entirely inoffensive. The cardinal refused to accept the Bull, and appealed to the Pope. The king forbade the car-

[1] "Their fury, hardly cooled down even by his death, would never have left his ashes in peace if God himself had not hidden here the bones of his saintly sheep from the teeth of those ravenous wolves." Those verses were not published during Boileau's life. See Sainte-Beauve, *Port-Royal*, vol. v, p. 476.

dinal to appear at Court. Le Tellier was all-powerful, and the prisons were filled with Jansenists. The king's death alone prevented the deposition of the cardinal. As the latter was very popular, the Regent made him president of the *Conseil de Conscience*, and banished Le Tellier. But the affair of the Bull was by no means at an end. "The Church in France remained divided into two camps, the *Acceptans* and the *Refusans*. The acceptors were the hundred bishops who had given in their adhesion under Louis XIV., together with the Jesuits and the Capuchins. The refusers were fifteen bishops and the nation at large."[1]

67. Thanks to the amiable scepticism of the Regent, who wanted peace, and the tact of Archbishop, afterwards Cardinal, Dubois, the Bull was at last registered, and Cardinal de Noailles retracted (1720). But the Jansenists did not disarm. A deacon called Pâris, who had died in the odour of sanctity, had been buried in the cemetery of St. Médard. The Jansenists announced that miracles were being worked at his tomb; that tremblings and upheavals were felt there, which cured the deaf, the blind, and the lame. "These prodigies were attested in due form of law by a crowd of witnesses, who had almost seen them, because they had come in hopes of seeing them!" As the cemetery was invaded day and night by a crowd of sick and idle people, it was shut up and a guard set at the gate on which some wit wrote the famous distich:

> De par le roi, défense à Dieu
> De faire miracle en ce lieu![2]

68. The Jansenists survived in France throughout the eighteenth century, especially in the parliaments. When Christophe de Beaumont, Archbishop of Paris, attempted, in 1752, to refuse absolution to those who had not subscribed to the Bull *Unigenitus*, the parliaments rose against the foolish pretension, and it required the intervention of the Pope to prevent the quarrel between the parliament and the arch-

[1] Voltaire.

[2] "In the name of the King, God is forbidden to work miracles in this place."

bishop from becoming one between the parliament and the monarchy.

69. There are Jansenists still in Paris and in Holland. They are quiet people, of excellent morals, who no longer work miracles.

∴

70. The *Quietist* movement was of no less import, for it set Bossuet and Fénelon in opposition to each other. This extravagance was of Spanish origin. Thanks to the protection of Philip II., St. Theresa had escaped the rigours of the Inquisition, which did not tolerate mystics. But the Spaniard, Miguel Molinos, who taught in Rome the doctrine of the *perfect contemplation,* of direct communication with God, without the intervention of a priest, was condemned by the Inquisition (1685) and died in prison (1696). A young and fascinating widow, Madame Guyon, aspired to be the St. Theresa of France. Under the direction of a Barnabite called La Combe, she succeeded in gathering recruits in Paris, among others Madame de Maintenon and the Duchesses de Chevreuse and de Beauvilliers. Fénelon, at that time tutor to the royal children, set himself to love God in company with Madame Guyon. "It is strange that he should have been seduced by a woman given over to prophecies, revelations, and other absurdities, who was choked by internal grace, and had to have her stays loosened to give it room, pouring out the overflow of her own grace on the elect who sat beside her."[1] When Madame Guyon propagated her illusions at Saint-Cyr, Madame de Maintenon, warned by the bishops, withdrew her countenance and forbade the lady to enter the house. Fénelon advised Madame Guyon to submit her writings to Bossuet, Bishop of Meaux. Bossuet condemned them, and the lady promised to dogmatise no more. Meanwhile Fénelon had become Bishop of Cambrai (1695). In spite of her promise, Madame Guyon failed to keep silence, so the King shut her up in Vincennes. Bossuet required Fénelon to associate himself with the condemnation of Madame Guyon. Fénelon refused, and pub-

[1] Voltaire.

lished his *Maximes des Saints,* which is tainted with Quietism. Bossuet hated the Quietists and no longer loved Fénelon. He wrote in opposition to his quondam friend, and both submitted their works to Innocent XII. The Pope hesitated for eighteen months, but under pressure of the King and of Bossuet, he ultimately condemned Fénelon in mild terms. The bishop submitted nobly, and disavowed his own book from his pulpit at Cambrai. He spent the rest of his life in "honourable and philosophical" retreat, as Voltaire called it, at Cambrai, and gave up his time to good works. His charming *Télémaque,* which is still read, suffices to class him among the Utopians; those who see in him an intellectual ancestor of Rousseau are not altogether wrong.

71. Madame Guyon died in obscurity, in 1717, after fifteen years of retirement in the neighbourhood of Blois. Age and solitude calmed the nerves of this honest but hysterical woman, "who had espoused Jesus Christ in one of her ecstasies and, from that time onward, had prayed no more to the saints, explaining that the mistress of a house does not petition her servants." [1]

∴

72. In Spain, political supremacy had been reconquered by the Christians after long years of war (1492). The population was divided into three groups, the Christians, the Musulmans or Moors, and the Jews. The first were chiefly warriors, the second agriculturists, and the third scholars and traders. All these people asked for nothing but to live in peace and keep up friendly relations. It was the Church which worked hard, as early as the eleventh century, to set them at each other's throats. She succeeded only too well. The Inquisition, legally subject to the royal power, which, however, it threatened to usurp, was instituted in 1480. It set about harrying and burning Musulmans and Jews. Many of these had been forcibly converted in the fourteenth century, but were suspected of secretly practising their ancient rites, which was the crime of relapse. Infidels, as infidels, escaped the Inquisition, but if a man had been baptized, even

[1] Voltaire.

by force or fraud, it claimed power over his body and conscience. As the smallest offence in the direction of relapse (such, for example, as abstaining from pork) was punishable by the confiscation of the offender's property and its division between the Crown and the Inquisition, the cupidity of her princes joined to the fanaticism of her monks soon turned Spain into a hell lighted only by the flames of the stake.

73. The first Grand Inquisitor, who was also the King's confessor, the Dominican Torquemada, received the congratulations of the Pope. He himself had caused six thousand victims to be burnt. These infamous ceremonies were called acts of faith, *autos de fé*. The king was present at them, bareheaded, and on a seat lower than that of the Grand Inquisitor. Thus began a long drama of misery and oppression. All scientific activities were suppressed, and the Middle Ages were prolonged in Spain down to our own days. "Thence it is that silence has become one of the characteristics of the Spanish people, though they are born with all the vivacity given by a warm and fertile climate." [1]

But the most outrageous prosecutions were not enough. The authorities believed, or pretended to believe, that national unity could only be secured by the expulsion of the Jews (1492) and Moors (1609) *en masse*. Hundreds of thousands of these unhappy people had to go into exile; tens of thousands died on the way. Spain was stripped of its best workers, of its ablest traders, of its most skilful doctors. The papacy found all these severities quite natural. If, sometimes, it seems to have sought a quarrel with the all-powerful Spanish Inquisition, this was not because the latter roasted or slaughtered too many unbelievers, but because it failed to show sufficient respect for the rights or financial interests of the Church.

74. The eighteenth century saw the Inquisition discredited in the Spanish peninsula, but it was still formidable for mischief in the colonies, both Spanish and Portuguese. It was suppressed by Napoleon when he entered Madrid (December 1808). It was re-established at the Restoration and

[1] *Ibid.*

still tried to bite; but, even in Spain, the days of the *auto de fé* were over by then. The Inquisition was finally abolished by Queen Christina in 1834. It had put to death at least 100,000 persons in Spain alone; it had expelled 1,500,000, and had ruined the civilisation of that noble country.

. . .

75. At the very moment when the capture of Granada had assured the triumph of Christendom in Spain, a native of Genoa discovered a new world and opened it to Christianity. The Spanish conquerors of the American continent behaved like bandits. Peaceable and confiding populations were exterminated, root and branch. Those who were forcibly "converted," vegetated in a condition often more cruel than slavery. The Inquisition was installed and brought about a reign of terror. In the East Indies, especially at Goa, it was no less murderous. In Rome, warned by a popular outbreak at the death of Paul IV., it showed itself more prudent. Nevertheless, on February 17, 1600, it sent to the stake the philosopher Giordano Bruno, the opponent of Aristotle and partisan of Copernicus, who had been handed over to the Holy Office by the Inquisitors of Venice.

76. The Roman Inquisition made itself both odious and ridiculous by its prosecution of Galileo. As early as 1616 the opinion of Copernicus on the movement of the earth, revived and demonstrated by Galileo, was denounced by the Dominicans as inconsistent with the story of Joshua, who, according to the Bible, caused the sun to stand still. The Inquisition declared Galileo's assertion to be "not only heretical in faith, but absurd as philosophy." Galileo bowed to this decision, but went on with his researches. His great work, the *Dialogo di Galileo Galilei*, appeared in 1632, under licence from the Inquisition of Florence. Extremely prudent in form, it was substantially a new demonstration of the system of Copernicus. The upholder of the opposite system was made to talk learnedly enough, but like an imbecile: a trick which had escaped detection by the good Florentine inquisitor. Urban VIII. referred the *Dialogo* to a commis-

sion, and Galileo, nearly seventy years old and weak in health, had to travel from Florence to Rome to appear before the Inquisition. At a sitting of the Congregation of the Holy Office (June 16, 1633), the Pope decided that he should be interrogated "even under threat of torture." Galileo was a scholar of genius, but no hero. When thrown into prison he retracted humbly, on his knees. The famous saying, "E pur si muove" (And yet it does move!) was invented for him by a wit, 130 years later (in 1761). The system of Galileo was universally admitted in the eighteenth century; but it was not until September 11, 1822, that the Congregation of the Inquisition gave a licence to print books teaching the true movement of the earth, a decision approved fourteen days later by Pope Pius VII. "It is wrong to nurse an eternal suspicion of the well-known prudence of the Roman congregations on account of a single blunder. But those men of little faith mentioned by the Evangelist are very numerous, and they still instinctively believe that what has happened once can happen again. And this dread, this proneness to voluntary or involuntary distrust, is a lingering consequence of the condemnation of Galileo." [1] So writes an honest apologist, and he is right: but are the men of little faith to blame?

BIBLIOGRAPHY

L. Ranke, *Deutsche Geschichte im Zeitalter der Reformation,* 6 vols., 1867-1868; J. Janssen, *Geschichte des deutschen Volks seit dem Ausgang des Mittelalters,* 8 vols., 1876-1894 (several editions); Ward, Prothero and others, *Cambridge Modern History,* vol. iii, 1905; Imbart de la Tour, *Les Origines de la Réforme* (1476-1520), 1905; Lavisse and others, *Histoire de France,* vols. v, vi, 1904-1905 (the Reformation in France).

6. H. Strohl, *Luther,* 1922-1924; J. Köstlin, *Luther,* 1883; James Mackinnon, *Luther,* 1929; L. Febvre, *Luther,* 1928.

11. Art. *Exorcismus* in Hauck.

12. Art. *Karlstadt* and *Melancthon* in Hauck.

13. J. Martin, *Gustave Vasa et la Réforme en Suède,* 1906.

14-16. Art. *Anabaptisten, Augsburger Bekentniss* and *Bauernkrieg* in Hauck.

18. Art. *Augsburger Religionsfriede* in Hauck.

19-21. Arts. *Zwingli* and *Calvin* in Hauck; A. Bossert, *Calvin,* 1906; P. Paulsen, *Calvin,* 1909; E. Doumergue, *J. Calvin* (7th vol., 1927).

24-25. G. G. Perry, *A History of the English Church,* 3 vols., 1861-

[1] Vacandard, *Etudes de Critique,* 1906, p. 386.

1864; Gasquet, *Edward VI. and the Book of Common Prayer,* 1890; H. N. Birt, *The Elizabethan Religious Settlement,* 1908; J. Hungerford Pollen, *The English Catholics in the reign of Elizabeth,* 1920; art. *Anglikanische Kirche* and *Cranmer* in Hauck.

26. Skelton, *Mary Stuart,* 1893; Edwin Muir, *John Knox,* 1929; Hassenkamp, *Geschichte Irlands,* 1886.

27. Aguesse, *Histoire de l'Etablissement du protestantisme en France,* 2 vols., 1891; F. Buisson, *Sébastien Castellion,* 2 vols., 1893; J. Viénot, *Hist. de la Réforme française,* 1926; *Le Paris des Martyrs,* 1914; art. *Waldenser* (Vaudois) in Hauck.

29. M. Philippson, *La Contre-Révolution religieuse au XVIème siècle,* 1884; L. Ranke, *Die Römische Päpste im 16ten und 17ten Jahrhundert,* 9th ed., 1889 (Engl. transl.); Ugo Balzani, *Rome under Sixtus V.* (in *Cambridge Modern History,* vol. iii, 1905).—On the Confessional: Lea, *Inquisition of Spain,* vol. iv, p. 96.

30. R. Allier, *La Cabale des Dévots* (1627-1666), 1902 (*cf.* Rébelliau, *Rev. des deux Mondes,* 1903).

31. *See* the prefaces by H. Michel, Brunetière, &c., to the classic editions of the *Provinciales.*—Art. *Kasuistik* in Hauck; Lejay, *Le rôle théologique de Saint-Césaire d'Arles,* 1906.

32. Art. *Trienter Konzil,* in Hauck.

33. The reconquest of Poland: art. *Hosius* and *Polen* in Hauck.—The Inquisition in Spanish America: Lea, *The Inquisition in the Spanish Dependencies,* 1908.—Missions to India, Japan and China: Funck, *Kirchengeschichte,* p. 500.

34. Boehmer, *Les Jésuites,* 1910; E. Boyd Barrett, *The Jesuit Enigma,* 1928; A. Michel, *Les Jésuites,* 1879; Peyrat, *La Compagnie de Jésus* (in *Histoire et Religion,* p. 86 *et seq.*).

36. M. Fassbinder, *Der Jesuitenstaat in Paraguay,* 1921.

38-39. Forneron, *Histoire de Philippe II.,* 4 vols., 1880-1882; Namèche, *Philippe II. et les Pays-Bas,* 4 vols., 1886.

40. Art. *Arminius* and *Remonstranten* in Hauck.

41-42. In addition to the great histories of England (Hume, Gardiner, Green), consult Th. Firth, *Oliver Cromwell,* 1900; R. Gardiner, *The Gunpowder Plot,* 1897; Peyrat, *La révolution et la restauration anglaise* (in *Histoire et Religion,* p. 207); Eth. Taunton, *Hist. of the Jesuits in England,* 1901; Duncan-Jones, *Archbishop Laud,* 1927.

43. Walker, *A History of the Congregational Churches in the United States,* 1894; R. G. Usher, *The Pilgrims,* 1918; art. *Kongregationalisten* in Hauck (p. 684).

44. Cunningham, *The Quakers,* 1868; Lester M. Jones, *Quakers in Action,* 1929.

45. Art. *Urban VIII.* in Hauck. The Pope's brief to Ferdinand II. was published in 1884.

46. *Pietismus* and *Spener* in Hauck; A. Ritschl, *Geschichte des Pietismus,* 3 vols., 1880-1886.

47. Art. *Hosius, Polen,* and *Socin* in Hauck.

48. Lavisse and others, *Histoire de France,* vols. v and vi; art. *Coligny* in *La France Protestante* and in Hauck; A. Maury, *La Saint-Barthélemy* (in *Journ. des Savants,* 1880, p. 154); Vacandard, *Les Papes et la Saint-Barthélemy* (in *Etudes,* 1906, p. 217).

50. The medal, of which there is an example in the Bibliothèque Nationale, was engraved in the *Numismata romanorum pontificum* by Bonanni (vol. i, p. 323). On the face is a portrait of Gregory XIII; on the reverse, the destroying angel smiting the Huguenots, and the inscription *Ugonotorum strages,* 1572. Vasari's paintings are described in Lafenestre and Richtenberger, *Le Vatican,* p. 136. (Royal Room. Admiral Coligny, wounded by an arquebuse, is carried into his house; murder of the Admiral, of his son-in-law, Teligny, and his servants;

King Charles IX. manifests his joy at the deed.) "Thus," wrote Stendhal, "there is still one place in Europe where murder is publicly honoured." That room is not open to the public.

51. Peyrat, *Henri IV.* (in *Histoire et Religion,* p. 374), a learned and original memoir; art. *Nîmes* in Hauck.

53-58. F. Puaux, *Les précurseurs français de la tolérance,* 1884; Lavisse and others, *Histoire de France,* vol. vii, 1905 *et seq.* (Louis XIV.); P. Gachon, *Préliminaires de la Révocation en Languedoc,* 1899; Rébelliau, *Bossuet, historien du protestantisme,* 1891; Crouslé, *Bossuet et le protestantisme,* 2 vols., 1894-1895; *Fénelon et Bossuet,* 2 vols., 1894-1895; Peyrat, *Bossuet* (in *Histoire et Religion,* p. 1-44); J. Viénot, *A propos de Fénelon,* 1910.

55. Orders issued by the minister Louvois: "Let there be as much disorder as possible . . . allow the soldiers to live as licentiously as they choose" (1685). "Make very few prisoners, but shoot down a great many people; and do not spare the women any more than the men" (1687). Concerning the Camisards, see *Revue hist.,* cxxix; cxxxvi; cxxxvii (new material).

59. Voltaire, *Siècle de Louis XIV.,* edition with notes by E. Bourgeois, 1898.

60-61. Langénieux and Baudrillart, *La France chrétienne dans l'Histoire,* 1896; Gérin, *Louis XIV. et le Saint-Siège,* 2 vols., 1894.—The practical character of religious Orders in the seventeenth century: R. Allier, *La Cabale des Dévots,* 1902, p. 17.—On Rancé: Sainte-Beuve, *Derniers Portraits,* p. 414; H. Brémond, *L'Abbé Tempête* (Rancé's nickname), 1929; on St. Vincent de Paule: E. de Broglie, *Saint Vincent de Paule,* 5th ed., 1899.

62. Sainte-Beuve, *Port Royal,* 6 vols., 1840-1862; A. Gazier, *Une Suite à l'histoire de Port Royal,* 1908; A. Hallays, *Le Pèlerinage de Port Royal,* 1909; Strowski, *Le Sentiment religieux en France au XVIIème siècle* (St. François de Sales, Pascal, &c.), 3 vols., 1906-8; H. Brémond, *Hist. du sentim. religieux en France,* 1917 *et seq.;* Séché, *Les derniers Jansénistes,* 2 vols., 1891; G. Hardy, *Le Cardinal Fleury et le mouvement janséniste,* 1925.—On the French free-thinkers of the seventeenth century: F. T. Perrens, *Les Libertins,* 1887; Brunetière, *La Philosophie de Molière* (in *Etudes critiques,* 4th series).

63-69. A. Le Roy, *Le gallicanisme et la bulle Unigenitus,* 1892.—J. Turmel, *Histoire de la théologie positive du Concile de Trente au Concile du Vatican,* 1906 (learned and lucid).

68. Napoleon, hearing that there were Jansenists in the Lyonnais in 1803, ordered them to be evicted and even imprisoned; he had no liking, he wrote, "for lunatics allied to the sect of convulsionaries" (*Revue d'Histoire de Lyon,* 1905, p. 431).

70. J. Galzy, *Ste. Thérèse d'Avila,* 1927.—E. de Broglie, *Fénelon à Cambrai,* 1884.

71. C. T. Upham, *Madame Guyon,* 1905; M. Masson, *Fénelon et Madame Guyon,* 1907; E. Seillière, *same title,* 1920.—On Fénelon: Sainte-Beuve, *Lundis,* vol. ii, p. 5 and vol. x, p. 16; J. Lemaître, *Fénelon,* 1910.

72-74. Lea, *History of the Inquisition in Spain,* 4 vols., 1906-1907; see also *Edinburgh Review,* April 1908.—The Inquisition and the Jews: S. Reinach, *Cultes,* vol. ii, p. 401; E. Adler, *Auto de fé and Jew,* 1908; Vacandard, *The Inquisition,* 1908; art. *Inquisition* in the *Jewish Encyclopædia;* Lea, *The Moriscos in Spain,* 1901 (*cf.* Morel-Fatio, *Rev. Hist. Relig.,* 1902, vol. xlv, p. 113, an apology for the Inquisition).

75. Lea, *The Inquisition in the Spanish Dependencies,* 1908.—Bartholomès, *G. Bruno,* 2 vols., 1847; Plumptree and Boulting, *same title,* 2 vols., 1884, 1917.

76. Vacandard, *Galilée* (in *Etudes,* 1906, p. 292).

CHAPTER XII

CHRISTIANITY: FROM THE ENCYCLOPÆDIA TO THE CONDEMNATION OF MODERNISM

From the sixteenth to the twentieth century: Emancipation of thought and reaction. Persistence of religious feeling in France in the eighteenth century. The Encyclopædia. The Philosophers. Voltaire's hostility to Christianity. *"Écrasons l'infâme."* Calas. Expulsion of the Jesuits from France and Portugal: Suppression of the Order. Secularisation of Church property by the National Assembly. The Civil Constitution of the clergy. Public worship impeded by the Convention. The Goddess of Reason. The Theophilanthropists.

Revivals in Protestant countries: Sects. Sects in Scotland. Baptists. Methodists. Darbyites and Irvingites. Christian Scientists. The British Israelites. Tractarianism, Puseyism, Ritualism. The Unitarians.

Liberty of worship in the United States. The Mormons.

Joseph II. and the Catholic reaction in Austria. Protestantism in Austria. Sects in Russia: persecution of the Poles and the Uniates. Mme. de Krüdener.

Catholic renaissance under the Directory. The Concordat and its results. Reaction begun by Pius VII. continued by Pius IX. The Syllabus and the Vatican Council. End of the temporal power. The reaction in French literature: Chateaubriand, Bonald, J. de Maistre and their successors. Liberal Catholicism: Lamennais, Lacordaire, Montalembert. The political reaction in France: the White Terror, the *Congrégation,* the Law of Sacrilege. Religious indifference. Freedom of teaching and the *loi Falloux.* Religious affairs under Napoleon III. The clerical reactions after 1871. Boulangism. Anti-Semitism. The Dreyfus affair. Separation of Church and State. French Protestantism. Switzerland: War of the *Sonderbund.* The Jesuits since 1814; their influence in France and the Catholic world generally. The German "Old Catholics." H. Loyson. Politics of Leo XIII. Pius X. The Sacré Cœur, La Salette, Lourdes. The Church and mysticism. Swedenborg. Mediums. Condemnation of spiritualism. The Neo-Buddhists. The Freemasons. The Church and socialism.

Religious philosophy: Schleiermacher, Vinet. Evolutionary Catholicism. Americanism. Modernism. Foreign Missions. The Church and Slavery. The Church and the upper classes. Conclusion.

1. The sixteenth century saw the development of the critical spirit and the breaking down of Roman despotism in Europe. The seventeenth century was almost universally a

period of reaction towards the principle of authority. The eighteenth century took up the work of the sixteenth, and freed the human intellect from its shackles. Kings philosophised and philosophers reigned. The Order of Jesus was abolished by the papacy itself. The Inquisition became absurd, and hid itself to die. Under the stimulus of progressive science, liberty of thought made definitive conquests among the enlightened classes. Unhappily it was not realised that these classes were not very numerous. In default of a sufficient provision for lay teaching, the great majority of men remained ignorant and superstitious. The French Revolution put influence and power in the hands of a class unprepared for their use. The result, both in France and elsewhere, was the reaction of the nineteenth century, a reaction which was Catholic in one place, Calvinist or Pietist in another, Greek Orthodox in a third. To twentieth-century France belongs the honour of renewing the march towards liberty, in her attempts to laicise society by the separation of Church and State.

∴

2. Eighteenth-century France was not to be looked for only in the *salons* of Paris and Versailles, in the Courts of Frederick the Great and Voltaire. The country as a whole remained profoundly Catholic, with a tendency towards Jansenism in the upper classes, especially among the so-called *noblesse* of the *robe* (judges and barristers). Atheistic cardinals were to be found at Versailles, frivolous and sceptical *abbés* abounded. But the clergy, the magistracy, and the *tiers état* included even then a mass of austere Catholics intent upon working out their salvation, and a still greater mass of the intellectually deficient, in whom the religion of the Middle Ages survived. The latter formed, so to speak, the reserves of the nation. When these were called to political and social action, medieval ideas reappeared on the surface, and brought about a reaction which still endures.

3. The Encyclopædia began to appear in 1751. Voltaire was its soul, from his retreat, Les Délices, and afterwards at Ferney. But Diderot, the most universal of all men of let-

ters, was its mainspring for twenty years, in spite of all the thunders of the clergy and the severities of the Parliament. The manifesto of the Encyclopædia was d'Alembert's excellent preface on the classification of our knowledge. The articles on theology, from the pen of a liberal priest, are irreproachable in tone, although hostile enough to the pretensions of the papacy. But the irreligious tendency of the compilation as a whole is clearly shown by the articles on philosophy. These are chiefly from the pen of Diderot himself, a materialist and atheist.

4. All the philosophers of the eighteenth century were not men of the highest refinement. D'Alembert was the best and most trustworthy. Voltaire, with all his genius, was a buffoon, not over-delicate in money matters, sycophantic to the great, and contemptuous to the masses. Montesquieu had some of the pettinesses of a provincial lawyer and shows an over-weening conceit in his writings; Diderot inclined both to declamation and foul language; Rousseau was set against the philosophers by jealousy and against reason by vanity. But all these men had one admirable quality—their love of humanity. They wished rather to serve than to shine. Their intellectual activity had a practical object, to destroy prejudices and better man's lot; so we must forgive them much.

5. To understand the spirit in which the Encyclopædists really worked, we should read Voltaire's correspondence with d'Alembert. The latter had to be prudent. He lived by his pen, in Paris, where he had been a member of the Académie des Sciences ever since he was twenty-three. "Fear of the stake," he wrote to Voltaire, "is cooling to the blood!" (July 31, 1762.) But Voltaire was rich; he was a member of the King's household; he reigned both at Ferney and to some extent in every capital in Europe; he never ceased to spur into the fight those who were to feel the blows he himself had earned. His letters breathe an anti-Christian rage which d'Alembert did nothing to combat in his replies, because as a fact he shared it. Voltaire writes: "It is a good tree, say the devout rascals, which has produced bad fruit. But as it has produced so much, doesn't it deserve to be

thrown into the fire? Light one then, you and your friends, and make it as hot as you can" (November 28, 1762). Clearly, here he is concerned with Christianity, not with fanaticism. D'Alembert answers: "Yet a little time and I daresay all these books will not be wanted; the human race may have sense enough to understand of itself that three do not make one, and that a piece of bread is not God. Even now the enemies of reason cut a silly figure enough" (March 31, 1762). "I can see from here the Jansenists dying a natural death twelve months hence, after killing the Jesuits this year; I can see toleration established, the Protestants recalled, priests married, the confession abolished, and fanaticism crushed as a matter of course" (May 4, 1762). And Voltaire: "Many a fanatical group may kick against it, but reason will triumph, at least among the better sort; as for the rabble, reason is not for them" (February 4, 1757). "Our business is not to prevent our lackeys from going to mass or preachings; it is to snatch fathers of families from the tyranny of impostors" (December 6, 1757).

6. Such quotations might be multiplied almost indefinitely; they show how much we restrict the *rôle* of Voltaire in making him an apostle of toleration, a term which implies the compliance of truth towards error. Voltaire demanded legal toleration because that represented progress at a time when Calas and the Chevalier de la Barre died, the victims of religious bigotry. But his ambition went much further. He dreamt of the abolition, even by violence, of positive religions as impostures, at least in those well-to-do and enlightened classes which alone excited his interest. In his hatred of fanaticism he became intolerant himself.

7. Many of Voltaire's letters end with "*Ecr. l'inf.*" (*Ecrasons l'infâme:* Crush the infamous thing!) A comparison of texts leaves no doubt that by *l'infâme* Voltaire meant not only fanaticism and superstition, but Christianity. He was, or called himself, a deist. But the God of Voltaire was a prop of the social system. He was a *Dieu-gendarme*—a policeman-God!—like that of the right-think-

ing middle classes of the nineteenth century, a God to be imposed on the lower orders, without any thought of loving or pleasing Him oneself. There is more honesty and frankness in the atheism, otherwise dull enough, of Diderot or even of the Baron d'Holbach. As for the God of Rousseau, he was in the main a mere text for declamation. But Rousseau's God, who identifies himself alternately with the beneficence of Nature and the rigour of the moral laws, is thoroughly impregnated with the spirit of the Bible. If no longer Christian, he might become so again. Rousseau's eloquent and sentimental deism leads to the eloquent and sentimental Catholicism of Chateaubriand. The Calvinistic Jean-Jacques thus prepared the way for the Catholic reaction of the nineteenth century, after corrupting the Revolution with his sophistry. For it was in his name that the Revolution was made, and ill made. Voltaire, who was little read between 1789 and 1815, would have inspired it better.

. . .

8. The Revocation of the Edict of Nantes was never repealed under the *ancien régime*. As late as 1762 a pastor was condemned to death for having preached. It was only in 1787, two years before the Revolution, that Protestants were admitted to civil rights (*état civil*) and that their children ceased to be considered illegitimate. Philosophy had something to do with this change for the better. It had undertaken, through the mouth of Voltaire, the posthumous defence of Calas, the Protestant who had been broken on the wheel at Toulouse, 1762, for having, it was asserted, killed a son who wished to abjure Calvinism. In reality the young man had committed suicide. Voltaire demanded the rehabilitation of the innocent victim, and was seconded in his honourable task by the "intellectuals" of his time, as well as by the upper classes of society. In 1765, three years after Calas had suffered, his efforts were crowned with success. A century later, it took ten years to bring about the rehabilitation of Alfred Dreyfus.

9. Although the Jesuits had shown themselves tyrannical, seditious, and greedy ever since the middle of the sixteenth

century, it cannot be denied that the suppression of the Order in the eighteenth century was brought about by the basest intrigues and calumny. Having taken to trade, like the Templars of old, they had become very rich. The trade with South America and with India was partly in their hands. Their wealth awoke the cupidity of Sebastian Pombal, Prime Minister and more or less Viceroy of Portugal. He accused them of conspiring against the State (1757), confiscated their property, and burnt one of them alive. This was the old visionary, Malagrida, whose trial was conducted by the docile Inquisition.

10. In France a great many families were ruined by the failure of a commercial house intimately connected with the Jesuits. In this the Parliament saw an opportunity for indulging its Jansenist rancour. Strong in the support of Choiseul and of Madame de Pompadour, whom one of the king's Jesuit confessors had offended, it instituted an inquiry into the affairs of the Order and obtained its suppression. This, however, Pope Clement XIII. was not inclined to ratify. The example of France was soon followed by Spain, where the Order had fallen under suspicion with the king and the Inquisition. A new Pope, Clement XIV. accepted the inevitable and declared that the Order no longer met the needs of the time. He suppressed it in 1773.

11. Some of the fugitive Jesuits were welcomed at Ferney. Educated by the Jesuits, Voltaire had kindly feelings towards his masters, and displayed them in his own fashion. But he disgraced his pen by scandalous jests at the hapless Malagrida, the innocent victim of Pombal's tyranny.

∴

12. During the second half of the eighteenth century the philosophers frequently demanded the secularisation, in other words, the confiscation, of Church property, which was valued at several milliards.[1] This the National Assembly decreed (November 2, 1789), but at the same time it voted an annual contribution in return for what the nation received. This was the origin of the *Budget des Cultes* (Pub-

[1] A milliard of francs equals forty million pounds sterling.

lic Worship Budget). On July 12, 1790, the Assembly went still further, imposing on the clergy the *Constitution Civile*, inspired by all the most radical ideas of Gallicanism. This Constitution absolutely ignored the Pope's authority, taking from him the right to institute bishops and making all the functions of the clergy elective. This was the end of the Concordat of 1516. The Assembly required that all ecclesiastics should pledge themselves by oath to accept the Civil Constitution. This the Pope, Pius VI., forbade (March-April 1791), and from that time the clergy were divided into *assermentés* or *jureurs* (jurors) on the one hand, and *insermentés* or *refractaires* (non-jurors) on the other. The latter were soon compelled to celebrate mass in secret, in barns or lonely farm-houses. Although less molested than the Protestants after the Revocation, they were persecuted in the same spirit; so true is it that toleration is not to be learnt in a school of intolerance.

13. The Convention took a great stride in advance. Though it did not actually suppress Catholic worship and did proclaim religious freedom, it gave no pecuniary aid to the Church, and failed to protect the priests in the discharge of their duties. Many were put to death; churches were looted and art-treasures wantonly destroyed. For the space of about two years, Catholicism was almost abolished in a great part of the country. The Abbé Grégoire, one of the bishops who had taken the oath, and had distinguished himself by his noble efforts for the emancipation of the Jews and the abolition of negro slavery in the colonies, protested in the name of Christian tradition and liberty, but in vain. The Bishop of Paris, who had also taken the oath, came to the bar of the Convention to lay down his insignia. Inverted fanatics, who could not live without some form of worship, founded in Paris that of the Goddess of Reason (November 10, 1793). The new goddess was impersonated by an actress from the Opera. She was received with great pomp at the Convention, the members joining the people in escorting her to the Temple of Reason (Notre-Dame), and in singing the hymn to Liberty. These buffooneries were imitated in other sections of the capital, where Temples of Reason multiplied.

Robespierre, bitten by Rousseau's deism and intolerance, caused the Convention to decree the existence of a Supreme Being and the immortality of the soul. The terms of this decree were affixed to the Temples of Reason (May 1794).

14. The sect of *Theophilanthropists* was not long in making its appearance. "Friends of God and Man," they pretended to supersede all religions by a belief founded upon morality alone. Protected by the Director, Larevellière-Lépeaux, in 1797, they had many churches in Paris at their disposal. Their services were carried on by the members in turn: they consisted of moral sermons and French chants and hymns. The sect made a certain headway in Paris, but as it came under suspicion of Jacobinism, the Consuls deprived it of the churches in October 1801, and the Theophilanthropists disappeared after a somewhat ridiculous existence of about five years.

∴

15. The strides made by free-thought, materialism, and atheism in the eighteenth century excited, in Protestant countries, those reactions which are called *revivals*. They are generally characterised by mysticism, and by fantastic interpretations of the Holy Scriptures. These movements have taken place chiefly in England and the United States, where they occurred as late as the nineteenth century. But Germany, Switzerland, and Holland have had them too, especially after the political reaction of 1815. In England and America, *revivals* have led to the creation of new sects, for which the struggles of parties and the continuous encroachment of the temporal domain on the spiritual have also furnished occasions.

16. Although the Presbyterian system implies the election of clergy by the congregations, a *right of patronage*, or nomination of parochial clergy by the Crown or overlord, existed in Scotland as an abuse, and was confirmed by an Act of the British Parliament in 1715. This brought about a first disruption in 1733, when a minister at Stirling, one Ebenezer Erskine, founded a body known as the *Reformed Presbyterians.* In 1847 the greater *Disruption* took

place. The reformed communities, which had much increased, took the name of the *United Presbyterian Church*, to distinguish them from the *Established Church of Scotland.* In 1874 Parliament finally abolished patronage, and, in 1900, the Free Church and the United Presbyterians amalgamated to form the *United Free Church.* A small minority of the Free Church ministers were hostile to this fusion, and contested its legality. They established their claims to the whole property of their Church, bringing about new difficulties which were, however, happily arranged. The Scottish Churches do not differ in doctrine. They have a creed in common, known as the *Westminster Confession* (1647), the Calvinistic rigours of which have been softened by the Declaratory Acts of 1879 and 1892.

17. Baptist sects, which have been erroneously supposed to have their roots in the Christianity of Roman Britain, appeared in England at the beginning of the seventeenth century. Like the *Mennonites,* disciples of the Dutchman Simonis Menno (*d.* 1559), who were scarcely distinguishable from the *Anabaptists,* the early *Baptists* condemned the baptism of infants, the taking of oaths, and military service. Their distinctive rite is baptism by total immersion, which is received by adults only. The poet Milton has been claimed by this sect, to which John Bunyan, author of *The Pilgrim's Progress,* who spent ten years in prison under Charles II., certainly belonged.[1] The Baptists have enjoyed toleration ever since 1689, and have greatly increased in numbers in Germany, the United States, and elsewhere. They number 350,000 in England, four millions in the United States. They keep up important foreign missions, especially in Africa and Asia. The Baptists have no bishops. Their officers are *elders* elected by the communities, *doctors* entrusted with preaching, and *servitors* or *deacons.* The Baptists are perhaps the only Christian sect in which a Christian of the first century would not find himself out of place.

18. More than thirty millions of Protestants call them-

[1] Milton was an "irregular and defective Baptist." Like Bunyan and many other devout spirits of his time he belonged rather to that independent group of Nonconformists who were neither Presbyterians nor Anglicans. See R. Hofmann's article, *Baptisten,* in Hauck, p. 387.

selves *Methodists* to-day. This great sect was founded in England about the year 1740 by an eloquent and energetic Puritan, John Wesley (*d.* 1791), with the help of his brother Charles and his friend Whitefield (*d.* 1770), who preached more than 18,000 sermons. At first their one aim was to bring about a revival in the Anglican Church by the reading of the Bible, by regularity of religious observance, and by the purification of the moral life. The name *Methodists*, which occurs as early as 1639, designated a school of preachers who taught a *method* of reaching happiness through virtue. While directing most of its attention to preaching, practised by laymen as well as ministers, the Methodists fostered the creation of religious societies, which became the centres of propaganda. Methodism offers certain analogies with German Pietism, but, unlike the latter, it addresses itself to the masses, which it desires to educate religiously and morally. The great meetings of the sect have been occasionally discredited by a touch of convulsionary charlatanism, but, on the whole, they have been powerful instruments of evangelisation and conversion. The Methodist missions have now spread themselves all over the globe and have done much good.

19. Since 1797 the Methodists have been divided into various sects—the *Wesleyans*, the *Bible Christians*, &c.—which are separated by but slight shades of difference in opinions. The rupture with the Anglican Church, which John Wesley did his best to avoid, was gradually brought about towards the end of the eighteenth century. The Methodists of to-day form a dissenting Church, which governs itself through its *Conference*, and possesses a hierarchy composed of both clerics and laymen.

20. Introduced into New York in 1768, Methodism was rapidly extended by the missionary vigour of Whitefield. It attracted most of the negroes, who constituted independent communities. It is to the honour of the American Methodists that they protested against negro slavery as early as 1784. The sect multiplied even more rapidly in America than in England, but its principles everywhere remained the same: it is above all a revivalist and missionary Church.

21. The dry formalism into which the Anglican Church had sunk in the early years of the nineteenth century provoked the formation of yet another sect in the *Plymouth Brethren.* These were joined in 1831 by the Anglican priest, John Darby, from whom the Plymouthists are generally known as *Darbystes,* or *Darbyites,* on the Continent. The sect was really an association of *brothers,* because the Holy Spirit, they said, was "essentially the Spirit of Unity." This opened the way to prophesying at large, and to all the evils of individualism in religion. The *Plymouth Brethren,* in their various subdivisions, have spread all over Western Europe and North America.

22. Darby, about the year 1826, encountered some of the disciples of Edward Irving (*d.* 1834), a Scottish minister who prophesied the end of the world, and the Second Coming of Christ in glory. In 1832, after all kinds of absurdities, Irving founded a Church, and in order to preserve the prophetic enthusiasm of his followers, instituted a hierarchy inspired by St. Paul, which alone had authority to talk the official nonsense. The most extraordinary thing about this particular mystification is that its effects have been permanent. There are from seven to eight thousand members of the Catholic Apostolic Church (as the Irvingites call their community) in the British Empire, twenty-five thousand in Prussia and Bavaria, with many more in Holland and even in Java. They have tacitly abandoned some of the follies which attended their foundation, but they still cultivate prophecy and await in joyous confidence the Second Coming of their Lord.

23. England and the United States contain more than 200,000 members,[1] divided among 1800 churches, of a sect first established in Boston (1879), which calls itself the *Church of Christ, Scientist.* Its founder was a certain Mary Baker Eddy, of New Hampshire (died 1910), and its chief propagators have been Bible-reading women. It pretends to cure all sorts of illnesses and sins with no remedies but meditation and suggestion. The suggestion is not hypnotic;

[1] No exact statistics concerning present membership in the Church of Christ, Scientist are available. (1929.)

neither occultism nor spiritualism are allowed. It is simply the assertion, reproduced until conviction is produced, that, matter and evil being contrary to the nature of God, are "unreal" and imaginary. *Christian Scientists* are found also in France and in Germany where, as well as in England, they have been prosecuted for illegally acting as doctors, or preventing men of real science from interfering with disease. Though they pretend to derive their wisdom from the Bible only—the Bible read without any touch of criticism—their belief in a practical efficiency of curative formulæ obliges us to give them a place, which they by no means solicit, in the modern history of magic.

24. The idea that America was colonised by Jewish refugees, in very ancient times, is an illusion older than Mormonism. A large number of people still exist, both in England and the United States, who believe the Anglo-Saxons to be identical with the lost tribes of Israel, the ten tribes who never returned to Judæa after their Babylonian captivity. An itinerary has even been traced for them! According to this they moved along the valley of the *Danube* to *Denmark* (countries of the tribe of *Dan*). God promised Israel that she should reign over the nations. God cannot lie. The Anglo-Saxons are the strongest race in the world: therefore the Anglo-Saxons are the descendants of Israel! I myself heard this doctrine preached at Brighton in the open air, by a man of venerable appearance who seemed to believe what he said.

∴

25. The established Anglican Church, with the king for its head, is Calvinist in spirit, Romanist in form. Putting Rome aside in matters dogmatic, she has preserved, or at least imitated, the Roman hierarchy. Her declaration of faith is contained in the Thirty-Nine Articles promulgated by Elizabeth. At the beginning of the nineteenth century she had all the faults of a rich and powerful institution. She was governed by formalism, and all warmth of piety was smothered under external correctness. The other Protestant sects—Presbyterians, Methodists, Baptists—made up the

great body of *Nonconformists* or *Dissenters.* With them the Calvinistic traditions were undiluted by borrowings from the Catholic hierarchy.

26. In 1661 and again in 1673, fear of Catholicism and hatred of the Dissenters led to the imposition of a *test* on all public functionaries. They were called upon to reject on oath the doctrine of *Transubstantiation* on the one hand, and, on the other, all connection with the *Solemn League and Covenant,* the Scottish pact concluded in 1588 and renewed in 1637, for the defence of the National Presbyterianism against Anglicanism and Popery. The *Corporation* and *Test Acts* remained in force until 1828, when they were abolished, and public functions opened to both Catholics and Nonconformists.

27. The Dissenters, who included a large part of the middle and lower classes, were no less hostile to Popery than to the Established Church. The latter, deprived of the protection of the *Test Acts,* not unreasonably felt itself threatened. One of its intellectual centres was the University of Oxford, whose Christianity, it used to be said, was "high and dry." There a movement towards reform took place, which has been called the *Oxford* or *Tractarian Movement.* This second title commemorates the publication of a series of ninety tracts, which issued from Oxford between 1833 and 1841 to spread all over England.

28. Among the writers of these tracts the two most notable were Newman (1801-1890) and Pusey (1800-1882). They proposed to breathe new life into the Anglican Church by removing its Calvinistic elements, and bringing it nearer to pre-Reformation Christianity while purifying the latter. Here the influence of Schleiermacher, whom Pusey had known, came in and also that of the Romantic movement, with its uncritical admiration for the Middle Ages. This admiration had been raised in England almost to the point of intoxication by the popularity of Sir Walter Scott's novels.

29. It soon became apparent that, in his search for a *via media* between Anglicanism and Romanism, Newman was taking on a strong bias towards the latter. The Bishop of Oxford condemned *Tract No. 90,* and forbade the continua-

tion of the series (1841). Newman obeyed, but four years later was received into the Roman Church (1845). For a time he was Rector of the Catholic University in Dublin (1851-1858), was made a cardinal by Leo XIII. in 1879, and died in 1890, in a religious house founded by himself (the Birmingham Oratory). Pusey, who wished to stop short of Rome, became the head of a new group in the Church, which, while professing fidelity, dreamt of reconciliation with the Papacy down to the time of the Vatican Council (1869-1870). Personally, he was always against the adoption of medieval ceremonies in Anglican worship. His disciples, however, were not so wise. They were carried away by the spirit which produced the great æsthetic movements of the time, and *Puseyism* degenerated into *Ritualism* (about 1850). This *High Church* sect, forming the extreme Right of Anglicanism, borrows the crucifix, candles, incense and sacerdotal ornaments of Rome, to whom it also makes important concession in matters of dogma, admitting the Real Presence, auricular confession, and the cult of the Virgin. Gregory XVI. said of the Tractarians: "They are Papists without a Pope, Catholics without unity, and Protestants without liberty." His dictum was truer still of the Ritualists.

30. Orthodox Anglicans and Dissenters united against the new tendencies. The London mob sacked a Ritualist church (1860). The national sentiments were wounded by what was called the *Papal Aggression,* when in 1850 Pio Nono nominated a Roman hierarchy for Great Britain, appointing the vicar apostolic, Wiseman, a cardinal and Archbishop of Westminster. The cry of *No Popery!* was raised as in the days of Anne. In reply to the creation of the *English Church Union* (1860) by the Ritualists, the *Church Association* was formed (1865) to combat the Romanising of English worship. Parliament and the Courts of Justice interposed more than once in favour of Anglicanism. But they failed to arrest the growth of Ritualism, which denies the right of the State to meddle with religious matters, and clamours, like the Nonconformists, for disestablishment. Any union with Rome is prevented—in spite of the renewal,

by Leo XIII. (1896), of attempts at an understanding—by the opposition, even of the Ritualists, to the primacy and infallibility claimed by the "Bishop of Rome." The internal conflict has died down within the last ten years, not because the Ritualists have modified their practices, but because the differences between them and the orthodox High Churchmen are gradually vanishing.

31. The Ritualists not only have schools, hospitals, and missions: they have imitated Rome in founding congregations, like those of the *Holy Cross* (1853) and the *Holy Sacrament* (1862). They have even formed a congregation of *Sisters of Mercy*, the first idea of which came from Pusey. These *Sisters* are now established in most of the great London Hospitals.

32. The good sense of the English soon taught them that Ritualism was disguised Catholicism. Many Tractarians and Ritualists—Newman, for instance, and Manning, who both became cardinals—went over to Rome. Romanism is *integral* Ritualism. At first Ritualism gained most of its recruits among the upper classes, to whom religious dilettantism and love of art made the severity of Calvinistic worship repulsive. But thanks to its organisation of work among the poor, which every one can appreciate, it has now conquered a great following among the labouring and necessitous population.

33. The accession to Catholicism of a scholar like Newman, trained in Anglican Oxford, had grave results for the religion he embraced. One of his works, an *Essay on the Development of Christian Doctrine* (1845), introduced the idea of religious progress and the evolution of dogmas among educated Catholics and made its author, against his will, one of the parents of *Modernism.* Down to 1854 the Catholic doctrine was reputed to be unchangeable. St. Vincent de Lérins had given as its formula: "What all men have believed, everywhere and always." Bossuet had contrasted the stable and definite character of the Roman Church with the variations of the Reformed Churches. But in 1854, Pius IX. promulgated the dogma of the Immaculate Conception, without summoning a council, converting what had previ-

ously been a free opinion into a dogma of the Church. This was to break with tradition, to affirm, according to Newman's ideas, the dogmatic evolution of Catholicism. Where was this to stop? The dogma of Papal Infallibility, promulgated in 1870, was the answer: it would stop where the Pope chose! This solution, which satisfied Newman, was only valid in dogmatic questions. Historical matters remained where they were. The idea of evolution in dogmas, and the resulting necessity for the study of their genesis and development, opened the door to free exegesis, which had previously been out of the reach of Catholics. The Abbé Loisy, in France, passed through the door thus flung wide.

34. The nineteenth century saw the development, in England and the United States, of the rationalistic Christian sect of the *Unitarians*. As early as the sixteenth century people had been burnt in England for professing the principles of Arianism and denying the Trinity. The adherents of this doctrine coalesced with the *Socinians* in the seventeenth century, and with the *Deists* in the eighteenth. Theophilus Lindsay (*d.* 1808) and Joseph Priestley, the great chemist (*d.* 1804), were the prophets of British Unitarianism. The latter was obliged to leave England (1794) on account of his sympathies with the French Revolution. He introduced Unitarianism into Pennsylvania. Christianity thus purified found a favourable soil in Boston, the American Athens. Channing, who was to become so famous for his opposition to slavery (1835) and for his championship of the rights of justice and reason, became a Unitarian in 1819, although he was opposed to the foundation of a new Church. "An Established Church," he declared, "is the tomb of intelligence." After Channing, the poet and moralist, Ralph Waldo Emerson, advocated Unitarianism, the religion of intellectual people, a Christianity without dogma, and with no temple but men's hearts. In England, its chief representative was James Martineau (*d.* 1900), the author of works on Unitarianism which have now become classics. In their pantheistic tendency they have much in common with Spinoza, and no dogmatic difficulties stand in the way of their acceptance by the liberal Judaism of our own day.

35. The United States was the first great country to separate Church and State completely, leaving the field entirely open to the free rivalry of religions. The result has been to give a certain advantage to Catholicism, which has the centralisation of power for one of its principles, over Protestantism, which splits naturally into sects. Among the numerous Protestant sects, selection will do its work and will develop, as elsewhere, a form of religion without any exacting theology, but preoccupied rather with social and moral questions. At the present moment the fifteen millions of Catholics form a larger group than any one of the Protestant sects of America.

36. Spiritualism, which is really a cult, had its origin in the United States. There, too, arose one of the strangest phenomena of the nineteenth century, in *Mormonism*. Mormonism is one of those religious epidemics, or *revivals*, to which the Anglo-Saxon peoples seem more prone than others, on account of their free reading, often practised in common, of the sacred writings. In 1830, Joseph Smith, a visionary pedlar, announced to credulous people that he had had a revelation referring the American people to the family of the patriarch Joseph, and foretelling the early appearance of a Messiah. An angel had brought him this revelation, engraved on gold plates in Egyptian characters. The imposture succeeded in spite of its grossness. After several migrations, the new sect established itself in the State of Illinois, where it built a great temple (1841). It called itself *The Church of Latter Day Saints*. They were also called *Mormons*, because one of the pretended descendants of Joseph, who had emigrated to America some six hundred years B.C., bore the name of Mormon, and had compiled the holy book of the sect, a translation of the pretended golden tablets. This holy book is a clumsy plagiarism from the Bible and from a romance published in 1812. It is devoid of both talent and originality; but religious enthusiasm does not reason. Formed into an agricultural and industrial republic, rapidly increased by immigrants from various other countries, the Mormons gave themselves up with docility to the guidance of their "prophet." Smith, wishing to restore patri-

archal manners, authorised polygamy (1843). This scandalised the population of Illinois, who first imprisoned the prophet and then put him to death (1844). Upon that the Mormons, led by Smith's favourite disciple, Brigham Young, a carpenter, went on trek once more. They settled in Utah, near the Great Salt Lake, and there built a new capital in Salt Lake City (1847). When Brigham Young died in his turn (1877), he left seventeen wives, fifty-six children, and a fortune of two million dollars. The head of the Mormons in 1901 was Joseph F. Smith, a nephew of the prophet. The number of his followers was estimated at 300,000, exclusive of some 15,000 dispersed about Europe. Their religion requires the baptism of adults only by total immersion. They also baptize "for the dead," after the example of certain primitive Christians. Franklin and Lincoln were thus rescued from the fires of hell.

37. In 1884 the United States Congress forbade polygamy in any part of the Union, and instituted prosecutions against those who practised it; so the Mormons renounced part of their inheritance from the patriarchs of Israel. The 2000 missionaries they support have been better received in consequence. The still incomplete history of the *Latter Day Saints* is that of an initial fraud from which certain energetic organisers, helped by many willing dupes, have won great results in the interest of their whole community.

∴

38. Frederick the Great and Catherine II. were philosophic sovereigns, so far as laughing at sacred things in company with Voltaire, Diderot, and others went; but they had no idea of weakening in their States that Christianity which, personally, they despised. The German Emperor, Joseph II., was the true crowned philosopher of his time, in spite of his mediocre abilities. He wished to realise in law the secular ideas with which his mind was imbued. In 1781 he established toleration in his Empire, closed nearly all the convents and sequestrated their property, forbade the publication of papal briefs without his own authority, and stopped those appeals to Rome which kept up a want of discipline in

his clergy. He was compared to Julian the Apostate and became most unpopular, in spite of the useful reforms by which his reign was distinguished. The French Revolution frightened him. By the time he died, in 1790, he could foresee that philosophy would soon attack the occupants of thrones themselves. Nevertheless, it was not until 1855 that Austria disavowed Joseph II. In that year a Concordat (repealed in 1870) was concluded with Pius IX., restoring their prerogatives to the clergy and rescinding all the laws by which the Church was deprived of its power over education. The Roman Church again took up its control of schools, of marriage, and of literature. This treaty was one of the last triumphs of theocracy in Europe.

39. In the eighteenth century Protestantism was no more allowed in Austria than in France. The province of Salzburg, which had been governed by a prince-bishop ever since 1278, drove the Protestants out in 1731, after inflicting outrages upon them which drew protests from the Prussian king. The exiles went to Holland and North America, where refugees are always welcome. The nineteenth century recognised toleration, at least in principle. During the last twenty years Protestantism even gained some ground in Austria. A movement which took *Los von Rom* (Away from Rome!) for its motto detached several thousand families from Catholicism—but soon came to a stop.

40. The revision of the Russian liturgical books by the patriarch Nikon (1605-1681) provoked the secession of the *Raskolniks* from the State Church. These fanatical conservatives are known as "Old believers," and still number several millions in Russia. Among Russian heretics there are certain wild mystics, called *Skoptsy*, who aim, not at the amelioration, but at the extinction, of the human race. There is also the rationalistic sect of the *Dukhobortsy*, who reject all ceremonial and veneration of images. As Orthodox Christianity was before 1917 the State religion, all these sectaries were more or less persecuted.

41. We have already touched on the fate of the Jews. The Polish Catholics and those Ruthenians who remained in communion with the Roman Church, although their rites were

Oriental, have not had less to suffer. If the Polish martyrs were immolated for political rather than fanatical reasons, the Uniates were persecuted solely because they refused to enter the State Church. "They have undergone trials and punishments of every kind, exile from their homes, Siberia. They numbered eight millions in the seventeenth century; had shrunk to 800,000 at the beginning of the nineteenth; to-day (1897) not more than 100,000 Ruthenians are left to groan. . . . The others have disappeared: exile, prison, death, and apostasy have accounted for what was once an important Church."[1]

42. A curious episode in the reaction of 1815 was the influence wielded over the Czar Alexander I. by the Baroness von Krüdener, who, after a most dissipated youth, became a mystic at the age of forty. Still beautiful, and believing herself inspired, she gained such ascendancy over the Pietist Emperor that he accepted from her (and from the mesmerist Bergasse) the curious idea of the *Holy Alliance*, concluded on September 26, 1815, in the name of the Trinity, between Russia, Prussia, and Austria. Alexander ended by finding that she lacked discretion, and broke with her. But she continued to rush about the world, preaching, giving alms, dragging people as crazy as herself into her own track. The *missions* undertaken by her and her friends were a sort of foretaste of the *Salvation Army*. Madame de Krüdener's adventurous existence came to an end in the Crimea, in 1824. In one of her last letters she wrote: "Very often have I taken for the voice of God what was nothing but the fruit of my own pride and imagination." She might have recognised this a little sooner.

∴

43. The period of the Directory in France witnessed a revival of Catholicism, under the new *régime* of Disestablishment. In 1796 public worship had been resumed in more than 30,000 French parishes. Parisian society again found its way to church, ecclesiastics again donned their vestments. Five hundred priests were ordained in a single year. Madame

[1] Pisani, *A travers l'Orient*, p. 177.

de Staël, Lafayette, and other moderate spirits wished this state of things to continue, as favourable to the free exchange of opinions. But the First Consul had need of the Pope, and thought he could secure the support of the Roman Church by intimidation, that he could turn bishops and priests into gendarmes without again subjecting France to the demands of the Holy See. He made up his mind to conclude a new Concordat with Pius VII., to replace that of 1516, which had been torn up by the National Assembly.

44. The essential aim of every Concordat between a Pope and a temporal sovereign is to secure the latter in his right of nominating bishops, and to preserve for the former the right of *canonical institution*, permitting him to reject unworthy candidates or those whom Rome has reason to mistrust. The Parliament of Paris, looking with favour on the old Gallic custom by which bishops were elected by the cathedral chapters, long resisted the Concordat between Leo X. and Francis I. (1516). The French monarchs, who owed their spiritual investiture to the papacy, never ceased to busy themselves with whittling away the rights of Rome over the Church of France, not because they wished to make that Church independent, but because, from fiscal motives among others, they wished to keep it well in hand. In that, as in many other things, Bonaparte simply took up the traditions of the monarchy.

45. After rapid though difficult negotiations, in which Bonaparte recoiled neither before threats of violence nor attempts at fraud, the Concordat was signed in 1801 and promulgated in 1802. Catholicism was recognised not as the State religion, but as the religion "of the great majority of French citizens." The clergy were to receive salaries from the State, the bishops were to be nominated by the State, with the reserve that their investiture lay with the Pope. Resorting to trickery, Bonaparte promulgated at the same time as the Concordat (April 8, 1802), certain so-called *Organic Articles*, forming a sort of religious police code. Among other things these articles had to do with the regulation of Protestant worship (Jewish worship was not recognised and regulated until 1808). But the essential arti-

cles were aimed at Rome, paralysing all direct interference by Rome in the affairs of the French Church. Pius VII., who had received no warning, protested (1803). "The Organic Articles," said Montalembert in 1844, "were in our opinion a violation of the Concordat. They were never recognised by the Church." The contrary has been asserted. The whole question is one of shades of meaning. It is certain that Pius VII., although he was obliged to crown Bonaparte at Notre-Dame, believed that he had been duped, and never ceased to show his resentment. He refused investiture to the new bishops, and replied to the brutalities of Napoleon by excommunication (1809). Deprived of his dominions, he became the Emperor's prisoner, first at Savona and then at Fontainebleau, where in 1813 he was driven almost by force to sign a new Concordat, which was never recognised. By it the Pope agreed thenceforward to live at Avignon! Very soon afterwards this treaty was disavowed by Pius VII., who regained the States of the Church after the successes of the Allies in 1814. If Pius VII. had died at this juncture he would have left the reputation of a saint and hero behind him, for he had faced the insults and injustice of Napoleon with a steadfastness which was truly admirable. Unhappily for his memory, he lived long enough to unchain the reaction.

46. The definitive restoration of temporal power to the Popes (1815) marked the beginning of a long period of bad government. In their own States, where the oppression of the papal agents brought about poverty, and poverty brigandage, the Popes had to reckon with ever-increasing opposition; outside, in Italy, aspirations towards unity threatened the very foundations of their power; in Europe generally those liberal ideas which had survived the collapse of the Encyclopædia were enemies against which it was difficult to make head, now that the scourge, the dungeon and the stake were no longer at the service of the Church.

47. Pius VII. re-established the Society of Jesus (August 1814), which, indeed, had managed to survive in Prussia and Poland, in spite of the condemnation of Clement XIV. Their wealth, intelligence, and influence over women and young peo-

ple made the Jesuits very powerful auxiliaries to the papacy. The Pope condemned the Freemasons and the *Carbonari* (a secret society which had the liberation of Italy for its aim), excited the Congregation of the Index to renewed activity, restricted the translation of the Bible into the vulgar tongue, and fought against that liberal evolution in Spain and Portugal which was presently to be arrested by French intervention. His successors were scarcely more happily inspired. But the supreme perils and difficulties were reserved for Pius IX. (Mastaï Ferretti, 1846-1878). At the beginning of his reign he showed a disposition to grant the reforms demanded by the wretched economical condition of his States. But after a popular outbreak, which obliged him to take refuge in Gaeta (November 1848), his attitude changed completely. The French Republic declared war against the Roman: Rome was taken, and Pius IX. replaced on his throne (April 1850). He abused his power like a tyrant. Between 1850 and 1855 more than ninety people were condemned to death in Rome for political offences. Between 1849 and 1856, no fewer than 276 executions took place in Bologna. The Papal Government was for years in the hands of the unworthy Cardinal Antonelli, who scandalised Europe with the reign of terror he established. A Jewish child, Mortara, baptized by a servant, was taken by force from its parents at Bologna and kept in a convent, in spite of the energetic protests of Napoleon III., of the English Government, and of liberal Europe generally (1858). Four years earlier Pius IX. had promulgated the doctrine of the *Immaculate Conception.* In 1864 he published, or allowed to be published, what was called *The Syllabus.* This was a summary of all the opinions condemned in his previous Bulls and allocutions. Every one of the condemned propositions is such as any sensible man and liberal Christian would accept without hesitation. It was a defiance to secular Europe, to science, to the very idea of progress. Napoleon III. forbade its official publication in France, and would, indeed, have abandoned Pio Nono's government to its fate but for the influence of the Spanish empress which hindered an advance in this direction. The States of the Church had been greatly diminished in 1860, to the gain of the new kingdom of Italy. Ever since 1850 a French garrison had occupied Rome, upholding Antonelli's oppressive *régime*. In 1864 it was withdrawn at the instance of the Italian Government. In 1867 Garibaldi marched against the Papal States. A French division was landed to oppose him; it added the pitiful name of Mentana to the list of French victories, and renewed that occupation of Rome which lasted until 1870.

48. It occurred to the Jesuits to have a new council, in order that the doctrine of Papal Infallibility might be erected into a dogma. This meant, of course, that the Pope should be declared infallible when proclaiming a religious proposition from his throne (*ex cathedra*). But even when so restricted, infallibility wounded the reason not less than the obsolete teachings of the past. It was an outcome of that *Ultramontanism* which the pious Dominican Lacordaire once declared to be "the greatest piece of insolence yet put forward in the name of Jesus Christ." The first result was, contrary to the general opinion of theologians, to put the Pope's authority in dogmatic questions above that of a council. The second was to give the lie to undeniable historical facts, such as the condemnation of the heresy of Pope Honorius I. by the Œcumenical Council of 681 and a whole series of its successors. Enlightened prelates, in France, Germany and Austria, were hostile to the doctrine of Infallibility; but the Jesuits, relying on the support of the credulous masses, pushed on to their goal, and the dogma was proclaimed on July 18, 1870, on the eve of the declaration of war between France and Prussia. At that moment, Napoleon III. might have saved his crown and secured the military co-operation of Victor Emmanuel by abandoning Rome to Italy. The Catholic coterie at the Tuileries prevented him. But he had eventually to withdraw the French troops from Rome. After a slight bombardment, the Italian troops marched in through the breach on September 20, and put an end to the temporal power of the Popes. Pius IX. refused to accept the *law of guarantees*, which left him, with certain other privileges, the sovereignty of the Vatican and the Lateran. Until his death in 1878 he never ceased to

protest against the Italian usurpation, and his successors, Leo XIII. and Pius X., have done the same. The Italian Government has shown the greatest deference towards the Popes. It has scrupulously refrained from pushing its authority over the thresholds of the pontifical palaces. But that has not prevented the Roman clergy from talking of the "prisoner of the Vatican," or from describing to emotional peasants "the damp straw of the Pope's dungeon."

· ·
·

49. As early as the end of the eighteenth century, the Catholic reaction began to show itself in France in the domain of ideas. La Harpe, the *protégé* and servile admirer of Voltaire, chanted a palinode after the Terror and posed as an enemy of the philosophers. A Breton noble, more highly gifted than La Harpe, published in 1802 a brilliant and superficial work which foreshadowed Romanticism and had an extraordinary success. This was Chateaubriand's *Génie du Christianisme*. The Catholicism of Chateaubriand was mainly sentimental and æsthetic; that of Bonald, also proclaimed in 1802, was simply theological, and even theocratical. Joseph de Maistre, a Savoyard by birth, went still further in his hatred of revolutionary principles, in his exaltation of the papacy of the Middle Ages, in his impudent denials of, and apologies for, the misdeeds of the Church. This gifted fanatic was the founder of the *Ultramontane* School, so called because it looks for its inspiration to Rome, "beyond the Alps." Throughout the nineteenth century Jesuit intolerance of the Gallican tendencies shown by many of the French clergy, and of the liberal trend of opinion generally, found its spokesmen among the publicists of this school. Of these men the most noisy and aggressive was Louis Veuillot (1813-1883). Most of the present members of the Royalist party known as the *Action française* are followers of Joseph de Maistre and Veuillot, although personally they may be avowed sceptics. One of the worst features of Ultramontane polemics is their scurrility. Once enrolled in the party, even cultivated laymen talk like monks of the League, lying and insulting *ad libitum*. Writing in

1850, Victor Hugo thus castigated Veuillot and his organ, *L'Univers:*

> Regardez: le voilà! Son journal frénétique
> Plaît aux dévots et semble écrit par des bandits.
> Il fait des fausses clefs dans l'arrière-boutique
> Pour la porte du Paradis. . . .
>
> C'est ainsi qu'outrageant gloires, vertus, génies,
> Charmant par tant d'horreurs quelques niais fougueux,
> Il vit tranquillement dans les ignominies,
> Simple jésuite et triple gueux.[1]

50. Of a higher order than these men whose pens were steeped in gall and mire were the Liberal Catholics, who endeavoured to reconcile Catholicism not only with the principles of 1789, but even with more recent aspirations towards fraternity and social justice. The first organ of this party in France was *L'Avenir* (1830), a journal edited by the Abbé de Lamennais (1782-1854), Père Lacordaire (1802-1861), and Montalembert (1810-1870). It exhorted the Church to accept democracy, and was denounced as subversive to Gregory XVI. Lamennais made his submission in 1832, but shortly afterwards published his *Paroles d'un Croyant*, in which he aggravated what were called his errors. A bishop stigmatised it as an "Apocalypse of the devil." He was excommunicated, and passed over to the revolutionary party. Lacordaire submitted without reserve in 1832, after which he devoted his great powers to preaching. He became a Dominican in 1840, and did much to revive the glory of the order in France. No less docile under the censures of the Church, the Comte de Montalembert took refuge in politics, and became a brilliant defender of oppressed nationalities—the Poles, the Irish—but nevertheless did his best to stem the flowing tide of democratic ideas, which terrified him. Men like the Duc Victor de Broglie, and the two Cochins, Augustin and Denys, followed the same route down

[1] "Behold, here he is! His frantic paper pleases the devout and seems to be written by bandits. He makes false keys in the back-shop for the door of Paradise . . . thus insulting glory, virtue and genius, delighting by so many horrors some impetuous simpletons, he lives quietly in his ignominy, simple Jesuit and treble scoundrel."

to our own time, a route midway between Ultramontanism on the one hand, and aristocratic Liberalism on the other.

51. Catholic democracy was later represented by the priest Murri, in Italy, and in France by the lay society of the *Sillon,* founded by Marc Sangnier. The *Sillon* was censured by the bishops on account of its independence, while Murri was ordered by Pius X. to cease his publications, and excommunicated (March 1909) for having disobeyed the injunction.

52. The political reaction which followed the Hundred Days was marked, in Southern France, by a sanguinary persecution of Protestants and Liberals. This was called the *Terreur blanche*, or *White Terror*. In Paris, and in spite of the moderation of the Voltairian Louis XVIII., the so-called *introuvable* Chamber seemed desirous of bringing back the Middle Ages. It was dissolved by the king on the advice of his minister Richelieu (September 1816). Thereupon a society of priests and laymen, known as the *Congrégation* (originally founded under the Directory) rose to considerable importance in politics. Its leaders were the Comte d'Artois (Charles X.), the Vicomte de Montmorency, and Prince Jules de Polignac. It opposed Liberal ideas with all its force, especially in matters of education. In its solicitude for the *throne and the altar*, it imposed upon Louis XVIII. the shameful Spanish expedition which restored despotism in that unhappy country. Under Charles X. the *Congrégation* was powerful enough to secure the passing of the *Loi du sacrilège* (1825), which, among other severities, put the profanation of the host on the same level as parricide. It must be allowed that this medieval law was never put in force.

53. The extravagances of the *Congrégation* should not mislead us, however. Its members were inspired more by politics than by religious fanaticism. These survivors from the eighteenth century put the throne before the altar, and what the throne had to give before the throne itself. While the *Chambre introuvable* was still in existence, Lamennais was writing his *Essai sur l'Indifférence*, in which he reproached the upper classes of his time with infidelity, and

with giving all their aspirations to temporal matters. One only has to read the *Mémoires* of the Comtesse de Boigne and of the Duchesse de Dino to be convinced that the aristocracy of those days looked upon religion mainly as a guarantee of the social order which safeguarded their interests.

54. Louis Philippe, who had ousted the legitimate monarchy, thought a great deal more about the throne than about the altar. The University, founded by Napoleon, possessed the monopoly of instruction. She clung to it jealously, and the struggles in favour of what was called *liberty of teaching*—that is, the teaching of the Jesuits—did not succeed. There was a change after the revolution of 1848. In their hatred of the Orleanists, the clergy made common cause with the Republicans, especially after those sanguinary days of June which terrified the Conservative middle classes. "Let us throw ourselves at the feet of the bishops!" cried the philosopher Victor Cousin. The Jesuits at once reappeared in France. Louis Napoleon Bonaparte, elected President in December, had need of the clergy in his meditated usurpation. He gave them a pledge of his good intentions by the expedition to Rome which restored the government of Pius IX. But the chief aim of the Jesuits was to lay their hands once more on the machinery of secondary education. Thanks to the interested complaisance of the President and the unscrupulous skill of the Comte de Falloux, an apologist for the Inquisition, they succeeded in their aim (1850). From that time forward, French youth was divided into two camps. The most numerous, and, in consequence of the desire of the *bourgeois* to rub shoulders with the noble, the most rapidly increasing was that which grew up in the hatred of Liberalism, and in the worship of an intolerant and despotic past. In twenty years this *régime* bore fruit; the Third Republic, long captive to the "*parti noir*," tasted all its bitterness.

55. The insatiable pretensions of the Roman Church were a cause of weakness to the Second Empire. Napoleon III., liberal enough himself, but married to a devout Spanish wife, was gradually driven, by the pressure of cardinals, bishops, and Jesuits, to sacrifice his throne and country to

the cause of Pius IX. In home affairs his most liberal and best-liked minister, Victor Duruy, was continually called upon to defend the teaching of the University against the calumnies and chicaneries of the Clericals. The Emperor was the captive of his past. The Church had sung the *Te Deum* after the *Coup d'état;* so he was compelled to put up with its encroachments.

56. The disasters of 1870-1871 brought about a religious and political reaction. In 1871 France fell into the grip of Clericalism. While awaiting the restoration of the monarchy and the temporal power of the papacy, the clergy developed their educational machinery in every direction and founded Catholic universities. Two reactions, baffled by universal suffrage, those of May 24, 1873, and May 16, 1877, were the scarcely masked work of the clerical party, which had found a discreet but safe protector in Marshal MacMahon, who had succeeded Thiers as President of the Republic. Under a third President, Jules Grévy, the Republican party became the majority, and, awakening at last to the source of its peril, obtained the dissolution of all non-legalised congregations (1880). This dissolution was a farce, very discreetly combined, of which we do not yet understand the details. A few years afterwards the Jesuit schools were even more numerous and flourishing. It was within their walls, especially within those of the *Ecole de la Rue des Postes*, that the future officers of the army and navy were prepared. The Congregations supported General Boulanger in his attempt at a dictatorship (1887), and imprudently threw in their lot with those Anti-Semitic, Anti-Protestant, and Anti-Liberal movements which declared themselves after 1885. Pope Leo XIII. advised Catholics to rally to Republican institutions (1891). Their chiefs obeyed, without enthusiasm, and set themselves to prepare a clerical republic.

57. The condemnation for treason of a Jewish officer, Alfred Dreyfus (December 1894), was a triumph for the Anti-Semites. Unhappily for them, Dreyfus was innocent. He had been saddled with the crime of a quondam papal officer, Esterhazy, who had passed into the service of France. As soon as Scheurer-Kestner, Vice-President of the Senate,

had convinced himself of the prisoner's innocence, he formed a party to demand the revision of his trial. The one document on which Dreyfus had been condemned and sent to the Ile du Diable (Guiana), was a letter in which all the expert paleographers recognised the writing of Esterhazy, as soon as they had had an opportunity of comparison (1897). The evidence was decisive, and the whole business might have been settled in a fortnight. It took nearly ten years. In spite of all the proofs of his felony, Esterhazy was acquitted. Colonel Picquart, who had discovered and asserted the innocence of Dreyfus even before Scheurer-Kestner, was thrown into prison. Those who cried for justice were accused of forming a "syndicate of treason," and the whole Church, priests and monks, with a few honourable exceptions, cast its influence into the scales on the side of injustice, flooding the entire country with calumnies and lies. The Assumptionists especially distinguished themselves in the disgraceful campaign. Their organ, *La Croix*, rivalled that of the declared Anti-Semites in preaching a new St. Bartholomew. The head of the General Staff of the army, General Boisdeffre, was an intimate friend of Father du Lac, the most influential of the Jesuits. The Jesuits had in their hands the supply of officers and their promotion. Every Republican and Liberal officer had a bad mark against him. The President himself, Félix Faure, had been captured by the Clericals, who had their creatures and accomplices in all the public offices. For two years a real terror hung over France. Encouraged by practically the whole of external Europe, the *Intellectuels* fought for the honour of their country under a flood of insults at home. Their final success, modest though it was, was due to the help of the Socialists, who, indifferent at first to what they looked upon as a *bourgeois* quarrel, understood at last that they would be the first victims of any political reaction. Condemned a second time at Rennes (1899), but afterwards pardoned by the new President, Loubet, Dreyfus did not regain his rank until 1906, when his rehabilitation followed upon an inquiry which enabled the *Cour de Cassation* to quash the Rennes conviction. Picquart became Minister of War after being promoted General, but the Amnesty voted by the Chambers in 1900 prevented the prosecution of the scoundrels who had brought about the whole affair.

58. Waldeck-Rousseau, who was Prime Minister in 1899, had been greatly stirred by the scenes of disorder which had marked the election of President Loubet at the beginning of the year. He determined to make an end of those whom he called *moines ligueurs* and *moines d'affaires* (Leaguers and commercial monks). Various circumstances led to an increase in the rigour of his early proposals. Emile Combes, who succeeded him as minister, was not a man to be content with appearances. This time the non-authorised congregations were really dispersed. No exception was made in favour of certain inoffensive, and even useful, congregations, which was against the interest of the country and religious peace. In 1905 the Chambers passed a law for the separation of the Churches from the State, which put an end to the Concordat of 1801. But the *loi Falloux* of 1850 was not abrogated and the monopoly of teaching was not restored to the State.

59. In the bosom of French Protestantism the two opposite tendencies, obscurantist and liberal, were represented by the rival faculties of Montauban and Strasburg. After 1871 the latter was transferred to Paris. This rivalry gave rise to a wretched occurrence in 1864, when Coquerel, a pastor in the capital and an adherent of the *Union Protestante Libérale*, was deprived by the *Conseil Presbytéral* at the instance of Guizot. This historian, who pretended to believe in miracles, brought about a general synod at which an obligatory confession of faith was drawn up. Orthodox Protestantism, which is a caricature of Romanism, has again sown dissension in the attempt, made at the Synod of Orleans in 1906, to impose a creed on the active members of the Protestant Associations formed after the separation of the Churches from the State (1905).

∴

60. At the beginning of the eighteenth century, Switzerland had engaged in a civil war, which ended in the triumph

of the Reformers (1712), although the numerical proportion of Catholics and Protestants remained practically unchanged; but in Switzerland, as elsewhere, the Reformed cantons were the richest and the most industrious. The recall of the Jesuits to Fribourg (1818) was the signal for intrigues and disturbances throughout the Catholic cantons. To put an end to these, the Helvetic Diet suppressed the convents; upon which the Catholic cantons formed a league, the *Sonderbund,* in open preparation for civil war. General Dufour, at the head of 30,000 men, averted this calamity by his energy; he took possession of Fribourg, which the Jesuits evacuated, not, however, without a sanguinary encounter in which the Catholics were defeated; the *Sonderbund* was dissolved, and the disaffected cantons submitted. The new Swiss Constitution of 1848, while it proclaimed liberty of association and of worship, forbade the Jesuits to settle in the territory of the Confederation. Nevertheless, they returned to the Catholic cantons after 1858; the University of Fribourg belongs ostensibly to the Dominicans, but the theology taught there is that of the Jesuits.

61. Thus, as we have seen, the Catholicism of the nineteenth century was dominated by the Pope and the Jesuits, always closely united "for the greater glory of God." Of the 20,000 Jesuits struck at by the sentence of Clement XIV., the greater part, secretly favoured by Pius VI., took refuge in the Confraternities of the Heart of Jesus, and in those of the Fathers of the Faith, or Paccanarists, founded by Father Paccanari in 1797.[1] Russia was the only country where they subsisted openly. Catherine II., who wanted them in Poland, even allowed them to affiliate foreign Jesuits to their body. Pius VII. formally re-established the order in Rome (1801) and in Sicily (1804). He restored it in its entirety on August 7, 1814; but at first the Jesuits were only received in Spain, Naples, Sardinia and Modena; even Austria and France would not have them.

62. In 1820, the Jesuits were banished from Russia,

[1] Napoleon to Fouché (Dec. 17, 1807): "I won't have any Fathers of the Faith, I won't allow them to meddle with education, and poison the mind of youth by their ridiculous Ultramontane principles" (Lecestre, *Lettres inédites de Napoléon,* i, p. 129).

where their propaganda had alarmed Greek Orthodoxy. Leo XII. consoled them for this check by entrusting the Roman College to them (1824), thus placing the entire education of the clergy in their hands. In 1836, Gregory XVI. also confided the direction of the College of the Propaganda to them, and delighted them by the canonisation of Alfonso of Liguori, not a Jesuit himself, but one of their favourite theologians. The General of the Order, living either at Fiesole or Rome, became known in popular speech as the Black Pope.

63. In Spain, the Jesuits were the mainstay of despotism until their banishment in 1834 by the Queen Regent, Maria Christina; they returned shortly afterwards, notwithstanding this measure. In 1838 they established themselves in Austria, and still dominate all the education of the country. They have also regained their power in Belgium since the revolution of 1830, which was rather clerical than liberal; but here, in spite of the extraordinary multiplication of convents, the secular clergy remained strong enough to counterbalance the influence of the Congregations.

64. Louis XVIII. would not admit the Jesuits; but by an ordinance of October 5, 1814, he left the direction of the smaller seminaries in the hands of the bishops, who appointed Jesuit professors. Soon their colleges at Saint-Acheul and Montrouge, and also a propagandist society founded by them at Lyons, gave the government a good deal of anxiety, and provoked the ordinance of 1828. The colleges were closed. The Revolution of 1830 expelled the Jesuits again, not without some outbreaks of popular violence. As usual, they returned quietly, and began to be talked of again in 1838; the eloquence of one of their number, Père de Ravignan, contributed greatly to their growing credit, which Eugène Sue denounced as a danger in a famous novel, *The Wandering Jew*. In 1845, an action at law made it evident that the Jesuits were very numerous in France, in spite of a law which threatened them with imprisonment. The Chamber of Peers was alarmed, and Guizot, then Prime Minister, took certain ineffectual measures against them; the Second Republic was soon to make them reparation.

65. In spite of the defeat of their party in Switzerland, the Jesuits profited by the Revolution of 1848; they became the directors of the reactionary policy of Pius IX.; they acquired or regained a preponderating influence in Prussia and Austria; they laid hands on education in France (1850). The events of 1870-71 were unfavourable to them in Prussia, where they were forbidden by a law of 1872 to establish themselves; but in all Catholic countries, the close alliance of the Papacy, the Episcopacy and Jesuitism, uniting to suppress free thought, made the Jesuits the true masters of the faithful, while the Anglo-Saxon countries were once more open to their propaganda. In the United States and in England, the Jesuits, now numerous and very active, constitute a growing power which has aroused some uneasiness from time to time.

66. One of the great sources of strength of the Jesuit Order, setting aside its admirable recruiting system, is the absence of any rivalry between it and the other religious orders. The reconciliation between Dominicans and Jesuits has long been an accomplished fact. Assumptionists, Redemptorists or Liguorists are mere instruments, sometimes mere aliases, of the Jesuits. These have no charitable organisations; their activities are all lucrative, and even very lucrative ones, notably schools for the well-to-do classes; thus the Jesuits are richer than all the other orders put together, and can command support among the laity when they require it. Nearly the whole of the Catholic press in both hemispheres is controlled by them, and they have affiliated members even in the Liberal press. In spite of the measures taken against them in France, the Jesuits rival the bureaucracy (in which their influence has long been and still remains powerful) in the strength and perfection of their organisation in that country.

∴

67. The Vatican Council ended in the triumph of the Jesuits. After the proclamation of Papal Infallibility (July 18, 1870), in spite of the opposition or abstention of many bishops, Pius IX. embarked upon reprisals against the dis-

sentient German bishops; abandoned by their governments, which were absorbed in the war, they submitted. The learned Canon Döllinger (1799-1890) then organised the opposition of Old Catholics at Munich (April 1871); they formed themselves into associations for worship, choosing for their bishop, Reinkens, professor of theology at Breslau (1873), who was consecrated by a Dutch Jansenist bishop. The Old Catholics were recognised by several of the German States, and penetrated into Switzerland; but the celebration of worship in the orthodox Catholic churches set up grave difficulties, which were further increased by Germany's reaction in favour of Leo XIII.'s policy, after the check administered to Bismarck's attempt to humiliate Catholicism (*Kulturkampf*, 1872-1879). There is no longer faith enough in Western Europe to make the creation of a new religion possible; the Old Catholics subsist, but with difficulty, and in small numbers. Reinkens' successor, Bishop Weber (1896), was recognised only by Prussia, Hesse and the Grand Duchy of Baden; there was also an Old Catholic Bishop at Berne, Herzog.

68. The French bishops of the opposition, Darboy and Dupanloup, had submitted in 1870, when men's minds were oppressed by other and more cruel preoccupations. In 1869, a former Barefooted Carmelite, Hyacinthe Loyson, after a brilliant career as a preacher, was censured on several occasions for the freedom of his opinions. In 1871 he went to see Döllinger at Munich, and tried to create a Church in France analogous to the Anglican Church. Loyson, who married in 1872, remained to an advanced old age the disciple of truth and justice, those consolations of the disillusioned theologian; but his attempt at schism was even less successful than that of the German Old Catholics.

69. Leo XIII. (1878-1903) was a skilful diplomatist, and showed that the *prestige* of the Holy See had as a fact gained by abolition of a temporal power in which its spiritual dignity was often compromised. His successes in the United States, in England, in France, in Germany, and even in Italy itself, belong more especially to political history; it will be sufficient to allude to them here. Not only did the

Kulturkampf directed against Catholicism by Bismarck end in the victory of Leo XIII., but the German Catholic party, known as the *Centre,* became the pivot of the policy of the Empire. In France the Pope enjoined the Catholics to rally to the Republic, a measure which put a great number of the highest posts in the State into the hands of Clericals calling themselves Republicans; the success of this "turning movement" was so complete that but for the Dreyfus affair, in which the French Church embarked on a fatal course, France would have become a Clerical Republic. In the domain of religion, Leo XIII. did not favour Modernism, but he was careful not to adopt a bellicose attitude towards it. His successor, Pius X. (August 1903), was the antithesis of a clever politician; he was simply an honest parish priest. Bossuet said of Pope Innocent XI.: "Good intentions combined with a limited intelligence are fatal in high places." Guided by fanatical and ill-informed Spanish cardinals, Pius harshly condemned the Modernists in France and Italy, as well as in Germany; he refused the conciliatory offers of the French Government, prohibited the formation of Catholic associations for worship, which were readily admitted by French Protestants, and thus caused the partial ruin of the Church of France; separated from the State since 1905, she had great difficulty in finding sufficient means of subsistence. Beneath this crisis, the gravity of which may still increase, it is easy to distinguish the determining cause, the old hatred of the international congregations for the Gallican clergy. Their sufferings are a matter of indifference to the monks, who have managed to place their own possessions in safety, and have preserved all their influence over the faithful. If the French bishops will not act in concert with the Pope, he will depose them, and replace them by more docile prelates, chosen from among the monks. Thus, since 1905 a silent terror has been hanging over the Church of France, not by the action of the secular government, but by that of the Pope. Piux X. subjected it to a more than military discipline, threatening the daily bread of the recalcitrant, and organising a system of espionage which transformed even the moderates into suspects. Catholic France, at once superstitious and sceptical, bows to the authority of the Roman pontiff; and liberal France, which cares only for the maintenance of a ritual—if, indeed, it cares for anything of the sort—holds aloof from the government of the Church no less than from its theology.

* * *

70. The influence of the Order of Jesus is not only exercised upon dogma, upon politics, and upon social life; it penetrates and corrupts all the religious manifestations of Catholicism. The sentimental or puerile aberrations of the worship of the Virgin and the saints (as, for instance, of St. Anthony of Padua, who causes lost objects to be found), the exploitation of relics, amulets, and miraculous springs, have been established or developed under its protection. Even in the sixteenth century people said with good reason:

O vos qui cum Jesu itis
Ne eatis cum Jesuitis![1]

71. The worship of St. Joseph, which was non-existent in the Middle Ages and during the Renaissance, has grown up under the Jesuit influences of the nineteenth century. Pius IX. raised St. Joseph to the rank of a patron of the Catholic Church, above the Apostles Peter and Paul (1870); this promotion was confirmed by Leo XIII. (1889). To the Christian conception of the Trinity, the Jesuits have added one which is expressed by the formula JMJ—that is to say, Jesus, Mary, Joseph. It has practically superseded the other. God is too lofty, and the Holy Spirit too immaterial; the people must have white idols, with plenty of gold, pink, and blue. An aristocratic contempt for the devout masses is a ruling sentiment among the Jesuits, one they share with their pupil Voltaire.

72. The Jesuits also instituted the worship of the Sacred Heart of Jesus, beside which that of the Pure Heart of Mary holds but a secondary place. A girl-mystic, Marguerite or Marie Alacoque, had a vision of the bleeding heart of Jesus

[1] "O you who walk with Jesus,
walk not with the Jesuits!"

Christ (1675); she gave Him hers, and received His in exchange. Her Jesuit confessor, Père La Colombière, exploited the utterances of this mad woman, and founded a new form of idolatry, which Rome at first energetically condemned. But special confraternities propagated *Cordicolism* under the protection of the Jesuits, mainly in France, Germany, and Poland, in spite of the attacks of the Jansenists. Pius VI. yielded to the popular idolatry, and sanctioned the worship. Pius IX. went still further; he instituted the Feast of the Sacred Heart for the whole Church, and proclaimed the beatification of Marie Alacoque (1864). The Church had originally insisted on the symbolic character of the heart, but the mystic materialism of the Jesuits, harmonising with the spirit of the nineteenth century, proposed the adoration of the actual heart of the Saviour. This conception, a survival from very primitive religion, was approved by Pius IX. Painted images of the Sacred Heart have found their way into all the churches. The National Assembly of 1871 pronounced the construction of a basilica at Montmartre, dedicated to the Sacred Heart, to be a work of public utility. It was begun in 1875, and the white mass of its buildings now towers over Paris from the height. It will stand to future ages as a monument of Jesuit theology, and of the illimitable credulity of the human mind.

73. The increased facilities of communication in the nineteenth century multiplied pilgrimages and brought increasing crowds to privileged altars, to the relics of the saints, and to healing springs. Commercial exploitation of faith has kept pace with the mystic exaltation which has been stimulated by every possible means. Those who wish for information on this score should read Paul Parfait's *Dossier des Pèlerinages*. The Jesuits have been foremost among the religious orders which have encouraged these practices; the learned and pacific orders, such as the Benedictines and the Oratorians, have held significantly aloof. In France the mania for pilgrimages developed chiefly under the Third Republic; a special newspaper, *Le Pèlerin* (*The Pilgrim*), with a circulation of hundreds of thousands, fans the ardour of

the ignorant by tales of miracles; and wealthy society—Voltairian at the beginning of the eighteenth century, and Jesuitical at the dawn of the twentieth—adopts these debased forms of piety in fear of the political and social consequences of liberty.

74. In 1846 a fanatic, one Mdlle. de la Merlière, dressed herself in yellow robes and a sugar-loaf hat, and "appeared" on the mountain of La Salette (Isère) to two little shepherds, revealing herself to them as the Blessed Virgin. A subsequent legal inquiry exposed the fraud, against which the Cardinal Archbishop of Lyons had protested from the first. Nevertheless, the canonical examination resulted in the confirmation of the miracle by the Bishop of Grenoble in 1847. A congregation was founded to exploit it. Pilgrimages began, and still continue, to La Salette, where a certain spring was supposed to work miraculous cures.

75. "Three years after the day on which, by a solemn act of Pius IX., the Virgin was declared free from the taint of original sin, she appeared in a little town of the French Pyrenees to a child of the people. When asked her name, she replied: '*I am the Immaculate Conception.*' This was the definition of heaven following on that of earth! A doctrine had been taught to the world by the Church: God put his sign manual upon it!"[1] Bernadette Soubirous, the little girl to whom the Virgin Mary declared that her name was that of a dogma, an obvious absurdity,[2] *saw* the Virgin several times from February to July, 1858; she lived twenty years after this, supported, or rather sequestrated, by the nuns "as a destitute sick person," but the celestial vision "never again appeared to dazzle and delight her eyes."[3]

[1] G. Bertrin, *Histoire critique* (sic) *des événements de Lourdes,* new ed., Paris, 1908.

[2] The error may be explained by a confusion arising out of the inscription on a devotional print. Coloured pictures of the Virgin inscribed *The Immaculate Conception* have been widely circulated, especially since the year 1852, when the Louvre acquired Murillo's famous picture of this name for the then enormous sum of 615,000 fr. A confusion of the same sort arose of old at Athens (Acts xvii, 18): the philosophers thought Paul was preaching a new deity, *Anastasis,* when he announced the *Resurrection.*

[3] Bernadette was severely forbidden to mention her visions, excepting to visiting bishops, for fear the whole fraud might be revealed.

Ecclesiastical authority did not neglect this striking miracle. It was, indeed, forced to take action by popular credulity, which made the grotto a place of pilgrimage. Very soon a report that the water of the spring cured all sorts of diseases found credence, and religious commerce took the matter in hand. The grotto became a sanctuary over which an imposing church was built. The little town was covered with hotels and boarding-houses; hundreds of thousands of pilgrims flocked to it, and a great number of miraculous cures after immersion in the piscina were certified. Cures equally wonderful had been recorded twenty centuries before of sufferers issuing from the dormitories of Asklepios at Epidaurus and Cos; whether they were due to suggestion or to the radio-active qualities of the water is a scientific, not a religious, question. The "Fathers of the Grotto" have become very wealthy, and the Government is indulgent to their traffic, in order not to ruin the town of Lourdes. Official consecration of this worship was given by Leo XIII., who had a model of the grotto and the church put up in the Vatican gardens. But as the Council of Trent decided at its twenty-fifth session that all new miracles should be recognised and approved by the bishops before being published to the world, cases of healing are always submitted to the Church. On June 14, 1908, the Parisian *Semaine religieuse* published an ordinance of the Archbishop of Paris, Mgr. Amette, declaring that the cures of five young girls at Lourdes, from 1891 to 1899, which had been studied with the utmost attention by the commissioners, were to be attributed to a special intervention of God, brought about by the intercession of the Virgin, and consequently were to be accounted miracles.[1]

76. Those whose piety takes them to Lourdes are not seeking their salvation in the world to come, or preparing a blessed eternity for themselves; their most pressing preoccupations are purely secular and terrestrial; they ask for health and long life. The Church of the sixteenth century sold indulgences; she abused this traffic, and the merchandise

[1] From 1905 to October 1908, a score of episcopal ordinances of this kind were promulgated; a certain number of "cures" are always under canonical consideration.

lost its value. In the twentieth century, at Lourdes and elsewhere, she no longer claims to give dispensation from Purgatory, but to put off the day of reckoning; she opposes sacerdotal to secular medicine, and thus, consciously or unconsciously, returns to the errors of pagan materialism.

. . .

77. Mysticism, a supposed communion with God in ecstasy, is a chronic delusion of the human heart. The Church has beatified or canonised certain mystics, but she has silenced many more. The Spanish Inquisition showed a good deal of sense in this connection; it treated mystics as impostors rather than as persons possessed. One of the benefits of Christianity as organised into Churches has been to regulate mysticism and the superstitions to which it gives rise; wherever official religion has lost its power, individual magic and charlatanism have become rampant. This phenomenon was noticeable in France towards the close of the eighteenth century, when clairvoyants and swindlers like the Comte de St. Germain (*d.* 1784), Cagliostro (*d.* 1795), St. Martin (*d.* 1803), and Mesmer (*d.* 1815), acquired an amazing ascendency in a society which was reading Voltaire, but was not content with that.

78. The most influential of eighteenth century mystics was the learned Swede Emmanuel Swedenborg, the son of a clergyman (1688-1722). His followers still exist as members of the *Church of New Jerusalem.* After having done good service in many branches of natural sciences, where he sometimes showed the way to Buffon, Laplace and Goethe, Swedenborg had his first vision in 1743. From 1745 onwards he gave himself up entirely to theosophy, which means individual theology, in contrast with that of the accepted creeds. In 1749 he wrote as follows: "It has been granted to me, now for several years, to be constantly and uninterruptedly in company with spirits and angels. I have thus been instructed concerning the state of souls after death." Later on, he conversed with Jesus, the Apostle Paul, Luther and others. His diary for 1744, discovered in 1858, shows clearly that he was deranged; but there was little of a mira-

cle-monger or of a charlatan about him. His theology, founded not only on revelation, but on allegorical interpretation of Scripture, may even be called reasonable and humane when compared with the orthodox teaching on salvation, damnation and the like. Swedenborg believed himself to be the herald of the Second Coming. Jesus had, in fact, returned, having paid a visit to Swedenborg. "All religion," he said, "has relation to life, and the life of religion is to do good." That warm desire to benefit humanity associates him, in spite of his vagaries and dreams, with the more temperate philosophers of his age.

79. Territory gained by science is always lost to dogmatic religion. Nevertheless, certain writers have tried to add lustre to the latter by the, as yet, very obscure phenomena which belong, broadly speaking, to the domain of *spiritualism,* because they are attributed to the intervention of spirits. The Roman Church has wisely opposed this tendency. She only admits the marvels that are under her own control. All the rest are the work of the devil, or of human rascality. Magic, be it white or black, cannot be the handmaid of religion. Every one has heard of table-turning, spirit-rapping, crystal gazing, evocations of the dead, who appear as phantoms or dictate answers and revelations to *mediums.* These *mediums,* several of whom have become famous in our times—the Englishman, Daniel Douglas Home, for instance, who deceived the famous scientist Crookes, and the Italian, Eusapia Paladino, who cheated many others—were charlatans who had resource to subtle methods of fraud, and always refused to operate in daylight and in the presence of learned bodies; but the progress of science, and more especially the study of nervous phenomena, have brought to light physiological or psychological facts which must necessarily have seemed miraculous in the eighteenth century, and even later. Thus, it has been shown that nervous persons may be thrown into a hypnotic sleep; some even assert that, receiving orders in this state, they will carry them out on waking. It has also been said that persons of this temperament are amenable to suggestions made at a distance. The power of suggestion of some persons is unde-

niable, and has already effected cures which resemble those obtained by pilgrimages and relics. The facts of *telepathy*—that is to say, of communications from a distance, such as a sudden vision, sometimes confirmed by the event, of the death of a friend—are not yet scientifically established; but, after all, they do not seem any more extraordinary than the experiments of wireless telegraphy, though the former cannot be repeated at will.

80. When the spirits dogmatise, they show a disposition to amalgamate existing religions, in order to rise to forms they hold to be superior. The most striking instance of this syncretism is furnished by the so-called *Theosophists* or *Occultists*, founded at New York about 1875 by Colonel Olcott (*d.* 1906), and Helena Blavatsky (*d.* 1891). This sect, which has met with increasing favour, claims to combine Buddhism, Platonism, Christianity, and certain mysterious doctrines, such as the Jewish Kabbala. The Russian lady pretended to derive her knowledge from two Thibetan sages, with whom she enjoyed communication at a distance; but her works are full of unacknowledged extracts from printed books. Truly, Indian and other philosophies had better be studied at first hand; but whatever their scholarly attainments, theosophists are quiet and kind people who do no harm.

81. In the Middle Ages there were, in addition to the stationary guilds of masons, a number of *free-masons*, who travelled from town to town; they constituted, it is said, a confraternity whose headquarters were at Strasburg. These associations existed in England longer than elsewhere, and the Great Fire of London (1666), which necessitated the rebuilding of the city, increased their activity. After the completion of St. Paul's Cathedral (1717), the last four groups of masons founded a Grand Lodge in London, designed, not for the furtherance of their calling, but for the amelioration of the moral and material condition of man. Side by side with, and above temples of stone, was to rise the spiritual temple of humanity. From the end of the sixteenth century, members who were not masons had been admitted to these conventicles—a modification of the primitive character of

the institutions. But certain features were preserved with a jealous and, indeed, pedantic care; such were the distinctions between masters, associates, and apprentices, the exclusion of non-members, and the oath never to reveal the proceedings in the lodges. The constitution of the Freemasons was the work of the preacher James Anderson. It binds its adherents to respect for morality, humanity, and the fatherland; each member may continue to practise his special religion, but the community is further to hold collectively the religious principles of all mankind, the rest being accounted merely individual opinion. The religion of English Freemasonry is, accordingly, a sort of humanitarian deism, which found, and still finds, many adherents in Great Britain.

82. A few English noblemen founded the first Lodge in Paris in 1725; in spite of the interdict of Louis XV. (1737), it made numerous recruits. In 1733 a Lodge was established at Florence and at Boston, and in 1737 at Hamburg. The Hamburg Lodge included the Crown Prince of Prussia, afterwards Frederick the Great, among its members. After his accession, he founded a Lodge at Berlin, and became its Grand Master. Since this period, all the Kings of Prussia down to William II. have presided over this Lodge. William II. declined the office, but nominated Prince Frederick Leopold of Prussia as his substitute. In the course of the eighteenth century, Freemasonry took root in all European countries and also in North America. Catholicism naturally could not tolerate a society of religious tendencies which ignored it; the Pope condemned Freemasonry as early as 1738. An edict of the Cardinal Secretary of State of January 14, 1739, pronounced sentence of *death* not only against Freemasons, but against all who should seek admittance to the order, and all who should let premises to the association.[1] The papacy has never ceased the renewal of these prohibitions. Leo XIII. solemnly reiterated them in his Encyclical of April 20, 1884.

83. Shortly after this, a Frenchman who had written some scurrilous pamphlets against the Church, under the

[1] Lea, *History of the Inquisition in Spain,* vol. iv.

pseudonym of Leo Taxil, declared himself a convert to Catholicism, and offered to reveal the secrets of Freemasonry. He had his information, he declared, from a young American, Miss Diana Vaughan, who had been initiated into all the details of the Satanic rites performed at the Lodges. Taxil published several absurd books, full of horrors and divagations borrowed from ancient trials for witchcraft; they had an immense success in Catholic circles. Cardinal Parocchi sent the Papal benediction to Miss Vaughan. In 1896, an international Anti-Masonic Congress was held at Trent. As doubts were here cast upon Leo Taxil's statements, the rascal thought it better to unmask himself. He summoned a large meeting at Paris, and there, to the great scandal of the assembled priests and clericals, he declared that the Satanic Diana Vaughan was his typewriter, and that he had been deceiving the Roman Church for ten years (April 19, 1897). The laugh was hardly on the side of the Jesuits and their friends, the protectors or dupes of Leo Taxil.

84. Freemasonry was complicated and perverted by all kinds of affectations and impostures in the course of the eighteenth century. Superior grades were created, such as the Templars, the Rosicrucians and the Egyptian Masons; absurd pretensions were formulated, connecting these with the Knights Templars, the medieval Rosicrucians, and the mystic teachings of the Egyptian priesthood. The Egyptian or Coptic Order was founded by Joseph Balsamo (*d.* 1795), the *soi-disant* Count Cagliostro. Spiritualism, the search for the philosopher's stone, and innumerable other chimeras were grafted on to Masonic Deism and its principles of tolerant philanthropy. Fortunately, most of the Lodges held aloof from these follies.

85. English Freemasonry separated from French Freemasonry in 1877, when the latter pronounced a belief in God to be non-essential. In England, Scotland and Northern Germany, the Masonic Lodges have remained merely centres of humanitarian philosophy; in France, from the Revolution onwards, they have played a certain political part, which has, however, been greatly exaggerated by their

enemies. In 1903, General André, Minister of War, a freethinker, but not himself a Freemason, was imprudent enough to ask the provincial Lodges to furnish reports on the religious opinions of officers in the army. This system of denunciation was betrayed to the Clericals by a defaulting clerk of the Grand Orient of Paris; the result was the so-called Scandal of the *Fiches* (*i.e.*, dockets), which showed that it is easier to combat Jesuitism than to break with the tradition it has instilled.

⁂

86. A similar mania (intelligible enough, indeed) for imitating Catholicism while claiming complete emancipation from its influence, appears throughout the nineteenth century in rationalist sects with a practical philosophy, tending to the material and spiritual amelioration of man. The Comte de St. Simon, the founder of Saint-Simonism, was something of a prophet; but his disciples, Bazard and Enfantin, behaved like pontiffs. Auguste Comte, the founder of Positivism, in his *Système de Politique positive*, sets forth a social programme almost identical with the conventual *régime* established by the Jesuits in Paraguay. He even sought to enrich Positivism with the worship of the Virgin and the saints; his Virgin, however, was to be his dead friend, Clotilde de Vaux, his "St. Clotilde," and his saints the illustrious men, or men he considered illustrious, whose grotesque nomenclature enlivens the Positivist calendar.[1] The basis of Fourierism (Fourier, *d.* 1837) also rests upon medieval Catholicism; its phalansteries are closely akin to monasteries. Even the Socialism of Karl Marx' disciples betrays sometimes the same intellectual habits, the fruits of a long apprenticeship to servitude; modern Socialists have pontiffs, councils which excommunicate, *credos* they claim to impose, a discipline no less tyrannical than that of the Jesuits. Among them there are persons who think them-

[1] I deal here with Comte as a mystic, and am not concerned with his philosophy, which has exercised a great and beneficent influence on the modern mind. But I may recall Huxley's saying "Positivism is the incongruous mixture of bad science with eviscerated papistry." (*Collected Essays*, vol. v, p. 255.)

selves revolutionaries when they preach paradoxes twenty centuries old. Thus the anti-militarist crotchet called Hervéism (once dear to Professor G. Hervé in France) is a doctrine of the second century, aggravated by a menace of civil war. It is the mystic doctrine of non-resistance, of abhorrence of all service but that of God, which the philosopher Celsus made a reproach to the Christians when he exhorted them to unite with the pagans to defend the threatened Empire against the barbarians.[1]

87. The Roman Church, which cannot afford to alienate the middle classes, has hitherto shown no disposition to ally itself with Socialism; but it has insisted on its solicitude for the working classes. Leo XIII. even published an Encyclical "on the condition of workmen," in which he suggests as a remedy for the social evil "equitable payment," without saying how this is to be fixed. Both in France and Austria, indeed, Catholics who call themselves Socialists are not uncommon, and taking into account the fondness of clerical strategy for "turning movements," there may be some reason to distrust these more extreme Socialists, whose extravagances may occasionally be suggested by the party which openly combats their views.

In Protestant countries, Socialist doctrines have found numerous adherents among the clergy. "Christianity is the theory of which Socialism is the practice," said a minister at the Pan-Anglican Conference in London (1908). The same doctrine was taught by the *Avant-Garde*, the organ of the French pastors who professed modern Socialism. This is a novel example of the old anti-historical illusion of Concordism; it consists in harmonising, by means of a partisan exegesis, the mystic conceptions of two thousand years ago, with the realistic and practical ideas of reform which have sprung up in our industrial societies.[2]

[1] "We Christians," replied Origen (*Contra Celsum,* viii, 73), "fight for the Emperor even more than do the others; it is true that we do not follow him into the field when he orders us, but we form an army of piety for him, and support him by our prayers." This could not satisfy a military emperor like Decius.

[2] "There is no more absurd error than to represent Jesus as an apostle of Socialism. The exhortation to voluntary abnegation in the Gospel bore upon the idea of the approaching *Parousia,* or second coming of

88. Together with German Pietism, the influence of which is even perceptible in the philosophy of Kant, Voltairian free-thought had grown up, especially at Berlin. The reaction was not Pietist, but poetic and scientific. Schleiermacher (1768-1834) pointed out a new path for the Reformation, that of religious Romanticism, in which sentiment plays a greater part than dogma, and allies itself with the critical study of history. "Religion," he said, "should float about human life like a sweet and pleasant melody, a vague but beneficent presentiment of a life of dreams in which the human soul can find felicity." This was at once to exalt religion and to make it inoffensive to science, by assigning it a separate sphere. Schleiermacher, the translator of Plato, the admirer of Spinoza and of Kant, encouraged the critical exegesis of the New Testament. His pupil Neander, a converted Jew (1789-1850), built up the history of primitive Christianity on a solid basis. But the great German school of exegesis, that of Tübingen, was formed more especially under the influence of the "doctrine of development" due to Hegel, who introduced the idea of evolution into science before Darwin. Anything I could say of it here would be insufficient, and therefore obscure; but it is well to remember that the scientific liberty of German criticism was mainly effected by the teaching of two philosophers, Schleiermacher and Hegel.

89. One of the noblest thinkers of the nineteenth century, Alexandre Vinet (of Ouchy, 1797-1847), holds a place in French Protestantism analogous to that of Schleiermacher in Germany. Less a reformer than a religious initiator, he combated all forms of official intolerance, claimed the independence of Churches in relation to the State, and preached a pacific Christ, reconciled to modern civilisation, and still living in the conscience of humanity. This ideal has been shared by many superior minds. But one may reasonably ask which Christ they mean—the Christ of Mark or the Christ of John? They must choose, for the two are his-

Christ in glory; it was purely mystical, or rather at once mystical and utilitarian, without any economical or social application." (Dide [a former pastor], *La Fin des Religions,* p. 130.)

torically irreconcilable. Jesus as he may actually have lived and taught is almost inaccessible to us; the only concrete reality we have before us is Christianity, which is divided into many hostile sects. Is it not therefore simpler to seek a moral law in our consciences, the depositories of all the experiences and teachings of the past, including those of Christianity?

.
. .

90. The name *Americanism* has been given by theologians to an attenuated form of Catholicism which was propagated mainly in the United States by Father Isaac Hecker, of the Paulist Order (*d.* 1888). The papacy has always shown indulgence to the Catholicism of America, both North and South, on condition of its making no attempt to extend beyond the continent. About 1890, Americanism, of which Archbishop Ireland (of St. Paul, Minnesota) was the accepted high priest, began to penetrate into Europe. Its distinguishing doctrine was the characteristically American exaltation of good works over faith. Leo XIII. nipped it in the bud by a letter addressed to Cardinal Gibbons of Baltimore, which brought about the submission of Archbishop Ireland (1899). A curious incident in this connection was the publication in the United States in 1896 of a book by a monk, Father Zahm, purporting to reconcile Darwinism and the Book of Genesis. Its author was congratulated by Leo XIII., but the work was at once "withdrawn from circulation" after its translation into Italian (1899).

The *Pragmatism* of the American psychologist, William James, responds to some extent to the practical tendency of Americanism. Doctrines are not, he says, solutions of problems, but principles of action. They must, therefore, be judged by their fruits, and according to their moral efficacy. This conception, applied to religious dogmatism, would sanction the sophism of "beneficent errors," and contempt of the historical criticism which seeks to combat them.

91. The last years of the nineteenth century witnessed the rise, especially in France, of the momentous Catholic movement commonly called Modernism. In its general out-

look it is related to Newman and his doctrine of development; but Modernism is something more and something better than a religious philosophy. It is the assimilation of criticism by orthodox Catholicism. As such, it is essentially French, for it may claim descent from Richard Simon, the real founder, together with Spinoza, of critical exegesis of the Scriptures. This science, which was received with suspicion in France, passed into Germany, and flourished there in the Protestant Universities from the middle of the eighteenth century onwards. The most famous, if not the most readable book it has produced, is David Strauss' celebrated *Life of Jesus*, translated into English by "George Eliot," and into French by Littré. An Alsatian Protestant, Edouard Reuss, a scholar of the highest rank, and Michel Nicolas, a pastor of Nîmes, who held a professorship at Montauban, made an attempt to popularise these studies in France; but the general public and the Catholic seminaries remained impenetrable, in spite of the sensation created by Ernest Renan's *Life of Jesus*. The author's lectureship at the Collège de France was suppressed because he contested the divinity of Christ (1862). Religious teaching continued to be very antiquated in the seminaries, dwelling complacently on the puerilities of Concordism. Strange to say, reform has come, not from the laity, but from the Church herself. The Catholic Institute of Paris was founded in 1875, and the Abbé Duchesne, still a young man, was appointed professor of sacred history. Duchesne, prudent and discreet, wrote in general on non-Scriptural subjects, but he nevertheless inculcated a severe scientific method among his pupils. He himself applied it, exciting the acrimonious disapproval of the orthodox, in refuting the absurd legends of the Apostolic origin of the French Churches. These had been condemned as puerile even by the pious Tillemont (1637-1698), but they had found favour again as a result of the debasement of theological study, local interests, and the ingenuous credulity of hagiographers.

92. One of Duchesne's pupils, the Abbé Loisy (*b.* 1857), a Hebrew scholar and an Assyriologist, made a very brilliant *début*, and was soon himself nominated a professor of

exegesis at the Catholic Institute. About the year 1890 this young priest was the pride of the Gallican Church; a splendid future seemed assured to him. But the orthodox, and more especially the Jesuits, soon detected in his lectures and writings what they called "Protestant infiltrations" (1892). When Mgr. d'Hulst, the Rector of the Catholic University, published a liberal article in the *Correspondant*, in which he proposed to abandon the thesis of the infallibility of the Old Testament in scientific and historical matters, this daring attempt was attributed to the influence of Loisy. As a fact, he had nothing to do with it, but Mgr. d'Hulst had supposed himself inspired by Loisy's ideas. Leo XIII. responded by an Encyclical on Scriptural studies (called *Providentissimus*), in which the infallibility of the Sacred Books was reaffirmed, in accordance with the teaching of the Council of Trent, but discounted by so many linguistic niceties that the question was left very much as before (1893). This Pope was patient and prudent; he knew that Loisy was greatly respected by the French clergy, and he dreaded a revolt. Loisy, though continually denounced by the monks and canons, published in 1902 his *L'Evangile et l'Eglise*, in which he formulated his doctrine in reply to the *Essence of Christianity* of Harnack, a Protestant theologian of Berlin; this was followed in 1903 by his commentary on the fourth Gospel, the historic character of which he denied. At the same time, the *enfant terrible* of the clergy, the Abbé Houtin, gave the history of Biblical study in France with much grace and a spice of malice. An English Jesuit, Tyrrell, several German professors, and even a learned Jesuit, Father Hummelauer, manifested tendencies that were disquieting to the orthodox exegesis of the Sacred Books. Pius X., after hesitating for a while, felt called upon to act; in 1907 he published in rapid succession a decree of the Inquisition (*Lamentabili*) and an Encyclical (*Pascendi*), which were aimed at the very heart of Modernism. Loisy, whose books had already been put upon the Index, was excommunicated outright; Tyrrell was deprived of the Sacraments, and left, as it were, on the threshold of the Church; Hummelauer was reduced to silence.

93. "The Pope has spoken—Modernism is no more!" wrote the novelist Paul Bourget with naïve fervour. What greater insult could he have offered to the thousands of honest and intelligent priests of the Catholic clergy, who cannot change their opinions as they change their cassocks, or, following the example of the snobs M. Bourget knows so well, accept without conviction the *credo* of the houses where they are invited to dine! Modernism is an irresistible movement, for it is founded on Catholic science. Orthodoxy has defended itself successfully against the libels of laymen and the aggressive erudition of Protestants; the originality and the menace of Modernism lie herein, that it was born in the Church herself, at the foot of the altar; that it is a product of the learning of clerics, who, by study of the texts, have arrived at conclusions even more radical than those of Protestants and liberal historians.

94. The accepted thesis of the Roman Church is that the authority of the Sacred Books is guaranteed by the Church, and that the authority of the Church is founded on that of the Sacred Books. Is not this to argue in a vicious circle? Protestantism was content with the authority of the Sacred Books, as demonstrated by a study of these books themselves. But Modernism—or, to be more precise, the Modernist Left—maintains that neither the existence of God, nor the redeeming mission, nor the divinity, nor the miracles of Jesus, nor a single dogma, nor a single sacrament, can be founded on the fragile historical basis of the Scriptures. This leaves us face to face with a great fact, indisputably historical: this is the Church, inspired by the Scriptures, in the shadow of which hundreds of millions of souls have lived, which is the realisation of the Scriptures throughout the ages, whatever the authority of these may be. The Church has been able to promulgate dogmas, which have evolved like herself, but not historical truths, which belong to the domain of criticism alone. Thus the whole edifice is without an ontological foundation; and yet it is an edifice, one of the most magnificent the world has seen, and this is enough for those who seek shelter in it. Thus enlarged, it may receive not only Protestants and Jews, but all "men of

good-will." The evolution of the Christian temple makes it a house of refuge for all humanity. Such, at any rate, are the conclusions that may be drawn from the thesis of Modernism; it is obvious that the Roman Church cannot accept them, and no less obvious that her narrow orthodoxy is doomed to founder, sooner or later, in utter discredit.

95. The Church has not only to reckon with erudite Modernism, but with parallel philosophical tendencies. In 1834, Gregory XVI. condemned the so-called *Fideist* thesis of a Strasburg *abbé*, Bautain, according to which reason is powerless to establish truths, the benefit of which must be sought in the traditional faith. This doctrine was resuscitated from Pascal; it is also to be found in the writings of Bonald and Lamennais. But Rome maintains that there can be no conflict between faith and reason, and that the use of reason, the gift of God, *precedes* the act of faith. In spite of the condemnation reiterated by the Vatican Council in 1870, *Fideism* made numerous recruits in the Catholic world, especially in France, where Brunetière, Blondel, Laberthonnière, and Le Roy showed themselves to be more or less imbued with it. In its principles, as in its conclusions, it is akin to Modernism, to Pragmatism, and to the Symbolism of the Alexandrians of the third century. It has even been said that Loisy's Modernism was the historic form of Fideism, as Brunetière's Catholicism was the social form. Fideism had its uses when historical criticism was as yet nonexistent. Now that this has become a positive science, any system which tends to dispense with it is open to the suspicion of ignoring it.

*
* *

96. Conversions of cultured unbelievers to Protestantism are rather rare; but in the latter decades of the past century and the two first of this numerous distinguished men of letters and artists, especially in France and in Italy, have returned, with some ostentation, to Catholicism: one of these was Psichari, Ernest Renan's grandson, who fell a victim to the war; others were the novelist Huysmans and the poet Verlaine. Such conversions are usually sentimental, æsthetic,

and quite independent of theological knowledge. Even a scholar like Brunetière, when asked what he really believed in (he had been an agnostic from the age of thirteen) answered: "Go and inquire from Rome!" hinting thereby that he accepted a discipline, not a creed. Many conversions savour of dilettantism and drawing-room devoutness. The religion of such converts is a kind of modernised Franciscanism with no small mixture of sensuousness, snobbishness and frivolity. The real and enduring power of the Roman Church rests not on such brilliant and self-advertising recruits, but on the great and silent mass of the faithful who strain every nerve and faculty to support a Church now abandoned to her own resources by the State.

97. Down to the beginning of the eighteenth century, the missionaries of the Gospel were, for the most part, Catholics; since this period the Protestant sects, more particularly those of England and the United States, have shown even greater activity. The sums now spent by Protestants and Catholics in non-Christian countries must be counted by tens of millions. They are applied to the construction and maintenance of churches, schools, training colleges and hospitals, and to the distribution of Bibles and catechisms in all tongues. It cannot be said that this money is always well spent. No praise can be too great for the courage and self-denial of certain missionaries, the labours of a Livingstone or a Huc, which have benefited both the cause of civilisation and that of science; thousands of obscure heroes have fallen in like manner on the field of honour, victims of disease and often of cruel tortures. But in too many cases the indiscreet zeal of missionaries, their interference in the home affairs of States, their national and denominational rivalries, have brought some discredit upon their work.

98. The centre of the Catholic missions is the Roman Congregation of the Propaganda (*De Propagandâ fide*); its most important branch was, up to our time (1922), the Société de Saint-Xavier at Lyons, which dispensed an annual budget of 7,000,000 francs (£280,000). That branch has since been transferred to Rome. A French society, called the Sainte-Enfance (1843), has spent nearly 80,000,000

francs (£3,200,000) in a half-century to ensure the baptism of heathen children at the point of death; China has been the chief beneficiary of this extravagance. The Protestant missions, English and American, spend about £2,400,000 a year; Protestant Germany contributes about £240,000 to the same cause, France and Switzerland together about £40,000. The Russian Church had missionaries in Siberia; Buddhism sends its emissaries into the Far East, and Islamism proselytises mainly among the negroes of Africa, where it has made rapid progress within the last seventy years.

99. Following the example of Jesus in Israel, the Church has also organised missions to convert the "heathen at home," criminals, infidels, and ignorant persons. This was one of the favourite ideas of St. Vincent de Paule. As the temporal sword was blunted in the nineteenth century, these missions have become civilising and charitable undertakings, especially in Protestant countries, where the religious orders which carry on the work in other lands are lacking. Germany reveres the pastor Bodelschwingh (*b.* 1831), who founded a great many charities for the sick, labour colonies, asylums and workmen's dwellings. But no efforts in this direction have equalled those of the *Salvation Army* (the name dates from 1878 only), founded in London in 1872 by the Reverend William Booth. This charity, which is organised on a purely military model, and is not afraid of advertisement even of the noisiest kind, has done an immense amount of good, both in England and abroad. "General" Booth and his wife were popular figures throughout the world. To procure the funds necessary for its far-reaching benevolence, the Salvation Army has become a manufacturing, commercial and agricultural enterprise; it undertakes banking and insurance, and extends its influence and its relations everywhere. Originally an off-shoot of Methodism, it has gradually lost its sectarian character, to concentrate its efforts upon the elevation of the masses; the spirit which now inspires it is essentially philanthropical. Some critics have found fault with its Socialist tendencies, others with its abuse of advertisement and its buffoonery; but the work it has done in the slums of London and New York, and more

recently in the war-stricken countries, is enough to command gratitude and respect.

. . .

100. It may be asked whether moral progress or the influence of Christianity was the determining factor in the abolition of slavery, that blot upon antiquity which had been transmitted to the nineteenth century. No doubt the two influences were at work side by side; but in justice we must not forget that the Book of Deuteronomy (xv, 14; xxiii, 16) bears witness to a touching solicitude for slaves, that the Jewish Essenes and the Therapeutists alone in the civilised world of antiquity refused to keep slaves, and that the Primitive Church looked upon slaves as brothers—*spiritu fratres, religione conservi,* as Lactantius says in imitation of Seneca.[1] She facilitated enfranchisement and reckoned it among good works. Although she made no direct attempt to abolish slavery, and even herself owned slaves in the Middle Ages, she made great efforts to redeem the Christian slaves of the Musulmans, and when the conquest of America introduced negro slaves into the Continent, she did her utmost to improve their condition. "The Christian principle," as Viollet truly says, "slowly struck at the heart of slavery."

101. In the twelfth century, slavery tended to disappear in the North-West of Europe, but serfdom survived in France until the eighteenth. In the South and the East, slavery persisted much longer, as a result of contact with Islamism; the Crusaders even had Greek Christians as slaves. The restoration of Roman law, and the sanction of Aristotle—who considered slave-holding a natural right—were obstacles to the reform for which Eastern monks had prepared the way in the fifth century. There were Saracen slaves at the Papal Court in the fifteenth century, and in 1548 Paul III. confirmed the rights of laity and clergy to own them. The importation of negro slaves to Portugal began in 1442; in 1454, this traffic was endorsed by Nicholas V. In the New World, the Spaniards and the Portuguese reduced the natives to a state more terrible than slavery; as

[1] Lactantius, *Inst.*, v, 15, 3 (written about A.D. 300).

they were dying by hundreds as a result of forced labour in the mines, the Dominican, Bartolomeo de Las Casas, sought to save them by advising the importation of negroes. His counsel was followed, and at the end of his life, he repented it, realising too late that the negroes were men as well as the Indians. The traffic in negroes became a very profitable trade, entailing horrible cruelty, in both Africa and America. By the year 1790, there were 200,000 negroes in Virginia alone. The economic rivalry between North and South played a part in the Abolitionist campaign, which began in the North; but the Quakers of Pennsylvania, who had prohibited the slave-trade in their State as early as 1696, were actuated by religious motives. In 1776, the House of Commons rejected a motion of David Hartley's "that the slave-trade is contrary to the laws of God and the rights of man." Undaunted by this, the English Quakers formed an Anti-Slavery Association in 1783; others sprang up in America. Wilberforce (1759-1833), a member of the House of Commons, has the honour of having effected the repudiation of the traffic by England (1807), following the example of Denmark, who had led the way in 1792. In France, the Convention decreed the enfranchisement of slaves (1794), a measure which was repealed under the Consulate (1802). Slavery did not disappear from the English colonies till 1833, and from the French colonies till 1848. Its abolition in the United States was only brought about by a long civil war (1860-1865). The wisdom of Dom Pedro gradually delivered Brazil from the evil (1871 and onwards); finally, a French prelate, Lavigerie, threw himself with great fervour into a campaign against the traffic in negro slaves for the Musulmans. The Anti-Slavery Congress held at Brussels in 1889 also took measures in this connection, which have proved more or less futile. We must unfortunately add that certain forms of slavery, notably the forced labour of the blacks, still obtain in the European colonies of Africa, and that the Chinese *coolies* are often treated like slaves where they are employed in mines or on public works. In this long struggle against an execrable custom, the part played by the Catholic clergy has been, on the whole, less prominent than that of the Protestant Churches.

⁂

102. It was not generally recognised by the society of the eighteenth century that religions, and even superstitions, are conservative forces. The French Revolution opened its eyes. Society did not become religious, but it pretended to do so; it desired that women, children, and the poor should be disciplined and tempered by faith. This is the hypocrisy denounced afresh by Leo Tolstoy on the day of his Jubilee (July 1908): "The infamous lie of a religion in which we do not believe ourselves, but which we forcibly impose on others." This lie filled the nineteenth century, and has survived it. The French University, by nature liberal, was long obliged to pay homage to it, notably in the teaching of the so-called spiritualist philosophy, a Christianity without dogmas, but not without theological prejudices. Sainte-Beuve wittily remarked that whereas the bishops spoke of the *Holy Scriptures*, Professor Victor Cousin said the *most Holy Scriptures*. What is known as "Society" has been the greatest offender in this respect; seconded by the middle-class infirmity of snobbery, it has constrained its members either to adopt the conventional falsehood, or to keep silence. Throughout the reign of Queen Victoria, England set the example of this insincerity; free-thought was considered *disreputable*. But nowhere has the tyrannical power of the so-called upper classes, coalescing to stifle truth in favour of a clerical faction, manifested itself more painfully than in France, at the time of the Dreyfus affair, when the revision of a trial in which all the evidence was in favour of the right was resisted by the Jesuits and nearly all the French clergy at their commands, and divided all France into two hostile camps. No one could belong to "Society" and retain his place in it if he would not voluntarily shut his eyes to the truth, and take the part of Jesuitism against justice. Even in the literary world there were examples of lamentable weakness which had not even the excuse of religious conviction. The Esau of the Scriptures sold his birth-

right for a mess of pottage; our *fin-de-siècle* Trissotins bartered their right of judgment for truffles.

103. Amidst all these shades of hypocrisy, and all the honourable bonds of tradition and habit, it is impossible to determine, even after long investigation, how far dogmatic religion still retains its hold upon the souls of our contemporaries. How are we to distinguish among those who conform without believing, those who believe even without professing conformity?[1] But a general fact, which was already perceptible towards the middle of the nineteenth century, becomes more and more apparent in our days. In the time of Voltaire, free-thought lighted up the summits only; it did not descend into the depths. In the nineteenth century, the leisured classes professed without believing; the workers, in the towns at least, ceased to believe and dared to say so. The working classes are everywhere escaping from the authority of the Churches; even the peasants are emancipating themselves. Musset's apostrophe to Voltaire is being verified:

> Ton siècle était, dit-on, trop jeune pour te lire:
> Le nôtre doit te plaire, et tes hommes sont nés. . . .[2]

But as free-thought, without the support of solid knowledge, is only an inverted dogmatism, leaving the field open to other attacks upon the reason, one of the most pressing duties of the twentieth century is to fortify the reason by study, with a view to the calm and deliberate exercise of free-thought.

104. Religious instruction, which exists in almost every country in Europe, has been suppressed in French schools, those "schools without God," as their detractors call them. And further, it has been impressed upon the teachers in the name of "scholastic neutrality" that they are never to speak of religion to their pupils. This silence is sensible enough in the elementary schools, where the minds of children are not sufficiently cultivated to receive scientific knowledge.

[1] "In many a town society people who disbelieve think they are the table cloth while they are only the fringe" (Galsworthy).

[2] "Your century was, it is said, too young to read you; our century must please you, and your men are now there." Musset was an unbeliever, but with a sentimental longing for Christianity. So was Lamartine. Victor Hugo was a pantheist.

But the adolescent pupils of the colleges and higher schools know nothing of the Pentateuch, the Prophets and the Gospels, the origin and the evolution of dogmas, save the historical errors taught in the catechisms, or the equally pernicious absurdities dear to the free-thinking orator of the wine-shop. In Protestant countries the Scriptural texts are better known, but those who read do not, as a rule, understand them, and criticism of them is reserved for scholars. Thus practised, "scholastic neutrality" is at once a neglect of duty on the part of the State as instructor, and an abdication of its powers in favour of those who propagate error. Not only in France, but throughout the world, the salvation of thinking humanity must be sought in education, and if there is one duty more imperative than another laid upon secondary education, it is to teach young men, the future fathers of families, wherein religions consist, when and how they have met a universal want, what indisputable services they have rendered, but also how past generations have suffered from ignorance and fanaticism, on what literary frauds the domination of the Church was established in the Middle Ages, and finally, what a consoling prospect the reign of reason and the enfranchisement of thought opens out before the human mind.

BIBLIOGRAPHY

General sources the same as for Chapter X.

1. A. Lorand, *L'Etat et les Eglises* (constitutional texts regulating their relations in the different countries), Brussels, 1904.

2. H. Brémond, *Hist. litt. du sentiment religieux en France,* vol. iv, 1920; P. Mornet, *La pensée française au XVIIIe siècle,* 1926.

3-4. In general, see Lanson, *Histoire de la littérature française,* 1894. —On Voltaire: Lanson, *Voltaire,* 1906; Nourrisson, *Voltaire et le Voltairianisme,* 1896; on J. J. Rousseau, L. Ducros, 3 vols., 1918.

6. On the Chevalier de La Barre, a silly libertine: Marc Chassaigne, *Le procès du chevalier d. L. B.,* 1921.

7. R. Hubert, *Holbach et ses amis,* 1928.

8. R. Allier, *Voltaire et Calas,* 1898; F. H. Morgan, *The case of Calas,* 1928.

10. A. Theiner, *Geschichte des Pontifikats Klemens XIV.,* 2 vols., 1852.

12. E. Chénon, *L'Eglise et la Révolution, L'Eglise sous le Consulat et l'Empire,* in Lavisse and Rambaud's *Histoire générale,* vols. viii and ix (1906); Pisani, *La Constitution civile du Clergé* (in *Revue du clergé,* June 1, 1908); *L'Eglise de Paris et la Révolution,* 1909; A. Mathiez, *Rome et le clergé sous la Constituante,* 1911; Champion, *Séparation de l'Eglise et de l'Etat en* 1791, 1903; Aulard, *La Révolution et les Congrégations,* 1903; *Annales revolutionnaires,* May-Aug., 1919.

13. Aulard, *Le Culte de la Raison et de l'Etre Suprême,* 1892.

14. A. Mathiez, *La théophilanthropie,* 1904; *Annales révolut.,* 1921, p. 441.

16. N. Hill, *The Story of the Scottish Church,* 1919.

17. J. C. Carlisle, *Story of the English Baptists,* 1906; art. *Bunyan* and *Menno* in Hauck; C. Henry Smith, *The Mennonites,* 1920; D. Saurat, *Milton,* 1928.

18-20. A. Workman, *Methodism,* 1912; W. T. Hutton, *John Wesley,* 1907; art. *Methodismus* and *Wesley* in Hauck; H. Bargy, *La Religion aux Etats-Unis,* 1902.

21-22. E. E. Miller, *History of Irvingism,* 2 vols., 1878; art. *Darby* and *Irving* in Hauck.

23. Hauck, *Encycl.,* vol. xiii, p. 69 (*Christian Scientists*).—M. Geiger, *Christian Science,* in the *Süddeutsche Monatshefte,* June 1909.

24. Art. *Anglo-Israelites,* in Hastings' *Encycl. of Religion,* vol. i (1908).

26. Art. *Testakte* in Hauck; Amherst, *History of Catholic Emancipation,* 2 vols., 1886.

27-34. Art. *Ritualismus, Traktarianismus, Newman, Pusey* in Hauck; P. Thureau-Dangin, *La Renaissance cathol. en Angleterre au XIXe siècle* (1865-1892), 1906; Ch. Sarolea, *Cardinal Newman,* 1906.—G. Planque, *Chez les Anglicans* (in *Revue du clergé,* March 1908, p. 542); F. de Pressensé, *Le cardinal Manning,* 1897; Shane Leslie, *same subject,* 1921; A. Galton, *The Message and Position of the Church of England,* 1899.

34. Art. *Channing* and *Unitarier* in Hauck; Renan, *Etudes,* p. 357.

35. Art. *Nordamerika* in Hauck.

36-37. Art. *Mormonismus* in Hauck; Burton, *The City of the Saints,* 1861 (with facsimiles of the tablets); Ed. Meyer, *Die Mormonen,* 1912.

38. K. Ritter, *Kaiser Joseph II.,* 1867; H. Franz, *Reformen Joseph II.,* 1909; Pirenne, *Hist. de Belgique,* vol. v, 1920.

39. Art. *Oesterreich* in Hauck.

40-41. K. Grass, *Die russischen Sekten,* 1907-1909; Pisani, *A travers l'Orient,* 1897; F. C. Conybeare, *Russian Dissenters,* 1921.

42. Art. *Krüdener* in Hauck.

43. Peyrat, *Le Directoire* (in *Hist. et Religion,* p. 153).

44-45. Matthieu, *Le Concordat,* 1903 (*cf.* Rambaud, *Journ. des Sav.,* 1904, p. 96); Boulay de le Meurthe, *Hist. de la négoc. du Concordat,* 1920; Welschinger, *Le pape et l'empereur,* 1905; D'Haussonville, *L'Eglise romaine et l'Empire,* 3rd ed., 5 vols., 1870; Debidour, *Hist. des Rapports de l'Eglise et de l'Etat* (1789-1870), 1898; Baunard, *Un siècle de l'Eglise de France* (1800-1900), 1901; Lanzac de Laborie, *Paris sous Napoléon, la religion,* 1907.

46. Brosch, *Geschichte des Kirchenstaats,* vol. ii, 1881; Ranke, *Die röm. Päpste,* vol. iii, 1874 (English transl.); Stillman, *The Union of Italy,* 1898.

47-48. Biographies of Pius VII., Leo XII., Pius VIII., Gregory XVI. and Pius IX. in Hauck.—Art. *Mortara Case* in the *Jewish Encycl.* (a similar case in 1840, *Rev. hist.,* cxxxvii, p. 49).—On the Syllabus: Ollivier, *L'Empire libéral,* vol. vii, 1902; Ch. Beck, *Le Syllabus, texte et commentaire* (Brussels), 1905; P. Viollet, *l'Infaillibilité et le Syllabus,* 1904.—Hauck, art. *Empfängniss* (Immaculate Conception) and *Vatikanisches Konzil.*—Prince Jérôme Napoléon, *Les alliances de l'Empire* (in *Revue des Deux Mondes,* April 1, 1878).

49. J. de Maistre (Ste.-Beuve, *Portr. litt.,* vol. ii, p. 379, and *Lundis,* vol. iv, p. 150).—Bonald (*Lundis,* vol. iv, p. 328).—Veuillot (*Nouveaux Lundis,* vol. i, p. 42).—On the *Action française* (condemned in 1927 by Rome) and the Catholic atheism of some of its leaders: D. Parodi, *Pages*

Libres, May 30 and June 6, 1908.—The verses by V. Hugo quoted are in *Les Châtiments.*

50. Ch. Boulard, *Lamennais,* 1905.—Lacordaire (Ste.-Beuve, *Lundis,* vol. i, p. 208, and *Nouv. Lundis,* vol. iv, p. 392).—Montalembert (*Lundis,* vol. i, p. 74; Peyrat, *Hist. et Religion,* 1858, p. 86); J. Weill, *Hist. du cathol. libéral en France,* 1909. There are full bibliographies in Hauck's articles.

51. Marc Sangnier, *Cléricalisme et démocratie,* 1907.—Condemnation of *Le Sillon* by the bishops: *Revue du clergé,* March 1909.—On the *Sillon,* see *Pages Libres,* April 24, 1909.—Italian social modernism: A. della Torre, appendix to the Italian translation of *Orpheus,* vol. ii, p. 1013.

52-53. E. Daudet, *La Terreur blanche,* 1887; G. de Grandmaison, *La Congrégation* (1801-1830), 1889; A. Bardoux, *Le comte de Montlosier et le gallicanisme,* 1891.

54. Thureau-Dangin, *L'Eglise et l'Etat sous la monarchie de Juillet,* 1880; Colani, *Le parti catholique sous la monarchie de Juillet* (in *Etudes de critique,* p. 137); H. Michel, *La loi Falloux,* 1905; F. Mouret, *Le mouvement cathol. en France* (1830-1850), 1917.

55. See the histories of the Second Empire by Taxile Delord and P. de la Gorce.—E. Bourgeois and E. Clermont, *Rome et Napoléon III.,* 1907.

56. A. Debidour, *L'Eglise catholique et l'Etat sous la troisième République,* 2 vols., 1906-1909.—P. Cloché, *Le seize mai* (in *Pages Libres,* October 10, 1908).

57-59. J. Reinach, *Histoire de l'affaire Dreyfus,* 7 vols., 1901-1908; T. R., art. *Dreyfus* in the *Jewish Encycl.*—L. Chaine, *Les cathol. français et leurs difficultés actuelles,* 1903 (confessions of a Lyonese Catholic on the ugly part played by the Church during the crisis); Anat. France, *Le parti noir* (Brussels), 1905; Fred. Conybeare, *Roman Catholicism,* 1901. —P. Sabatier, *Séparation des Eglises et de l'Etat,* 1905; Russacq, *Après la Séparation* (in *Pages Libres,* September 28, 1907); Eth. Taunton, *The Holy See and France* (in *Nineteenth Century,* March 1906, p. 495).—C. Coignet, *Le protestantisme français au XIXe siècle,* 1908; T. Bricout, *Les Eglises réformées de France* (in *Rev. du clergé,* 1908, pp. 156, 268); H. Kuss, *Constitution des Assoc. cultuelles des Eglises réformées en France,* 1907.

60. Wœste, *Histoire du Kulturkampf en Suisse,* 1887.

61-66. Art. *Jesuitenorden* in Hauck; M. Charny, *Cahiers des droits de l'Homme,* June 25, 1922.

67-70. Art. *Altcatholicismus, Döllinger* and *Ultramontanismus* in Hauck; J. F. Schulte, *Döllinger,* 3 vols., 1901.—On the *Kulturkampf:* G. Goyau, *L'Allem. religieuse, le catholicisme,* 4 vols., 1905-8; L. de Behaine, *Léon XIII. et Bismarck,* 1898.—A. Houtin, *La question biblique au XXe siècle,* 1906; *La crise du clergé,* 1907; *Le Pére Hyacinthe,* 1920-1922.

70-76. P. Parfait, *L'arsenal de la dévotion,* 9th ed., 1879; *Le dossier des pèlerinages,* 4th ed., 1879; *La foire aux reliques,* 1879; Colani, *Essais,* p. 123; G. Téry, *Les cordicoles,* 1902; art. *Herz Jesu* in Hauck.

77-80. Lea, *Inquis. of Spain,* vol. iv, p. 2 *et seq.;* R. P. Rolfi, *La magie moderne,* 1902; D. P. Abbott, *Behind the Scenes with the Mediums,* 1908; Thulié, *Phénomènes mystiques* (in *Rev. mensuelle d'anthrop.,* October 1908); L. Wintrebert, *L'occultisme* (in *Revue du clergé,* August 1, 1908, p. 327); *cf.* art. *Magie* in Hauck.—On Neo-Buddhism: Barth, *Rev. Hist. Relig.,* 1902, vol. xlv, p. 346; art. *Blavatsky* and *Theosophy* in *Brit. Encycl.*—E. Caro, *Saint Martin,* 1862.—E. Bersot, *Mesmer,* 1853.—O. Trobridge, *Swedenborg,* 1907.

81. Rob. Freke Gould, *Concise History of Freemasonry,* 1887.—Vau-

thier, *Rev. Univ. de Brux.*, November 1908, p. 134.—Art. *Freimaurer,* in Hauck.

83. Lea, *Léo Taxil, Diana Vaughan and the Roman Church,* 1901.

86. G. Weil, *L'Ecole Saint-Simonienne,* 1896; Lévy-Bruhl, *Philos. d'Auguste Comte,* 1899; G. Dumas, *Psychologie de Deux Messies positivestes* (Saint-Simon and Comte), 1905; Ch. de Rouvre, *Comte et le catholicisme,* 1927; *cf.* on the Mysticism of Comte, S. R., *Cultes,* vol. i, p. 456.—Positivist calendar: Morley, *Critical Miscellanies,* vol. iv, 1908. —H. Bourgin, *Fourier,* 1907.—On the anti-military ideas of the early Christians: Harnack, *Militia Christi,* 1905; P. Gerosa, *S. Agostino e la decadenza dell' Impero,* 1916.

88. Schleiermacher, *Reden über Religion,* 1800.—A. Otto, *Fr. Schleiermacher,* 1899; art. *Schleiermacher,* in Hauck; A. Neander, *General History of the Christian Religion and Church,* Engl. ed., 1853 (coll. Bohn); art. *Neander,* in Hauck; Hegel, *Vorlesungen über die Philosophie der Religion,* 1832.—See also art. *Tübinger Schule* (School of Tübingen) in Hauck.

89. Edm. Scherer, *Alex. Vinet,* 1853.

90. Houtin, *L'Américanisme,* 1903; Marcel Hébert, *Le Pragmatisme,* 1908; L. Stein, *Philosophische Strömungen,* 1908, p. 37 *et seq.; Edinburgh Review,* April 1909 (Pragmatism).

91. Guignebert, *Modernisme et tradition catholique,* 1907; A. Houtin, *La crise du clergé,* 1907; *La question biblique au XXe siècle,* 1906; *La q. bibl. au XIXe siècle,* 1902; *L'apostolicité des Eglises de France,* 3rd ed., 1903; *Hist. du modernisme,* 1913.—Evolution in theology: S. R., *Cultes,* vol. i, p. 410; Bricout, *Le développement du dogme* (in *Revue du clergé,* April 5, 1908, p. 150).—Works of the Abbé Loisy: *L'Evangile et l'Eglise,* 1902 (in answer to Harnack, *Das Wesen des Christentums,* 1900); *Autour d'un petit livre,* 1903; *Quelques lettres* and *Simples réflexions,* 1908.

On Strauss, Reuss and M. Nicolas, see the articles in Hauck's Encycl. —On Nicolas, see also E. Stapfer, in *Etudes de théologie,* 1901, p. 153.— On Renan: Séailles, *Ernest Renan,* 2nd ed., 1895; J. Boulanger, *Renan et ses critiques,* 1925.—On the syllabus *Lamentabili,* see *Pages Libres,* August 10, 1897.

92. Modernism in England and Germany: *Revue du clergé,* March 1909, p. 541, 678.—Miss Petre, *Life of G. Tyrrell,* 1912.

93. On Cardinal Billot: E. Perrin, *Rev. hist. litt. rel.,* 1921, p. 319.

95. M. Hébert, *L'Evolution de la foi catholique,* 1905, p. 132 *et seq.*

96. Converts: Huby, *Les Etudes,* May 20, 1918.

97. Art *Mission* in Hauck; J. B. Piolet, *Les missions catholiques,* 6 vols., 1902; Louvety, *Les miss. cathol. au XIXe siècle,* 1898; R. Allier, *Les troubles en Chine et les missions,* 1901; J. Feillet, *Maristes et Canaques* (Brussels), 1906.

99. M. Goyau, *L'Allemagne religieuse, le protestantisme,* 1898; *Le catholicisme* (1800-1870), 4 vols., 1905-1908.—Art. *Heilsarmee* (Salvation Army) in Hauck; *Les Etudes,* Aug. 20, 1920 (Booth).

100. Lea, *The Church and Slavery* (in *Studies in Church History,* p. 524).—Zadok Kahn, *L'Esclavage selon la Bible et le Talmud,* 1867.— Art. *Slavery* in *Encycl. Brit.;* art. *Sklaverei und Christentum* in Hauck.

102-3. See Colani's *Etudes,* which are full of judicious reflections on these questions, notably the essays on the Bible, and on the revival of the Catholic party in France among the middle classes in the reign of Louis Philippe.

104. See on "Scholastic Neutrality," G. Lanson, *Revue Bleue,* April-May 1905.

EPILOGUE

Small influence of the Churches in the World War.—Exalted patriotism as a substitute to sectarianism.—Spread of superstitions and spiritualism.—Impotency of Pius X.; clever policy of Benedict XV.; restoration of the Temporal Power.—The fear of Bolshevism fortifies Catholicism in the upper classes.—President Wilson and liberal Protestantism.—Schemes for the Union of Churches in English Protestantism.—Bolshevist Russia; signs of a religious revival; persecutions.—Young Turkey; Panislamism and Panturanism.—Successes and crimes of the nationalist government.—Anti-religious policy in Asia Minor.—Vain Armenian hopes; new massacres before, during and after the war.—Recoil of Christianity in Asia.—Betterment of the legal status of the Jews.—Agitation for the *numerus clausus;* the anti-Semitic wave in Germany.—Sufferings of Russian and Polish Jews during the war.—Emigration of Jews.—The Japanese Shinto.—Suppression of the official religion in China.—Survival of the peasant's religions.—Mystic nationalism in India.—Indian religions subordinated to the ambitions of free-thinkers.—Persistence under new disguises of Universalism.

1. Established Churches played a very small part in the great World War (1914-1918). No doubt, the chief offenders, Austrian and Prussian nobles, were Lutheran pietists or Roman Catholics; but their crime was a result of their greed, not of their creed. The various religions afforded solace for millions of broken hearts and broken limbs; they stimulated charitable work; but patriotism and love of humanity did just the same. Religions, as such, remained powerless. Vainly did the Khalif proclaim the sacred war: Arab Musulmans fought by the side of the British to conquer Jerusalem (December 1917). The Orthodox Church of Russia, enslaved and degraded by despotism, was no element of strength to be reckoned with when the war broke out, and collapsed miserably in the short struggle against miscreant Bolshevism. Even the Japanese *Shinto* was made subservient to a clever policy of "wait and see."

2. If established religions stood aloof, some sort of religion did not. Christianity is a universal religion, regardless of nations and frontiers; Rousseau even thought that it was

directly antagonistic to patriotism.[1] In the beginning of the twentieth century, decaying creeds had tried, like Paganism in the fourth century, to identify themselves with patriotism; it was generally said, though hardly believed, that a true Frenchman should be a Roman Catholic, a true Russian should be orthodox, etc. When the war began and shook the nerves of the nations, national feeling took over the emotional quality, energy and intolerance which once belonged to sectarianism.[2] National saints, like St. George and Joan of Arc, came to the fore; in Germany, the "German God" repeatedly appealed to by William II., was not the Christian God, but the Odin or Thor of Norse mythology. If Islam seemed to break down, Turkish nationalism took its place. The greater number of the Jews rallied around the flag of Zionism, not a form of religious Judaism, but a new religion founded on the misconception of race. In those days of strife and hatred between groups of nations, internationalism was looked upon with the same angry suspicion and ire as would have been free-thought in the time of the Crusades.

3. Superstitions of the grossest sort and childish legends —such as that of guardian angels protecting the British retreat from Mons—flourished both in the army and among distressed civilians. Soothsayers and mediums never had better opportunities; prophets found audiences; amulets and protective dolls sold by the million; the absurdities of occultism and spiritualism spread like prairie fire. Superstitions are older than religions; they are often disciplined and purified by these; they run wild when religions decline. Belief or disbelief in accepted creeds is a thousand times more attainable than reasoned rationalism, and therefore more frequent in our day.

4. One great spiritual power remained, which could have interposed to prevent the outbreak of the war. But Pius X. vainly bade his Nuncio admonish the Austrian Emperor; he failed even to get a hearing from that well-guarded old imbecile. The next Pope, Benedict XV., had to reckon with a

[1] J.-J. Rousseau, *Contrat Social,* chap. viii.
[2] *Times Lit. Supplement,* 1926, p. 630.

majority of pro-German cardinals, with the hatred of the monastic orders for "persecuting" France, with the aristocratic leaning towards *authority* which, in many Catholic countries, such as Spain, gained sympathy for the German cause. He strove to remain strictly neutral. He spoke words of solace to Belgium, but not one word of reproof to the invaders, murderers and burglars though they were; he protested against new and abominable methods of warfare, but did not condemn those who first resorted to them; he ordered prayers for peace, peace without victory, but disregarded the responsibilities incurred by the aggressors and the legitimate demands of the oppressed. The time came when truly Christian words about the infamy of the war and hopes for the advent of a better era were uttered only by the Protestant professor, President Wilson, whom Loisy, lecturing at the Collège de France, called "the Pope of humanity" (December 2, 1918).

But while Wilson's too personal policy soon came to grief, the Roman Pope managed to evade excessive disparagement and excessive enthusiasm. Perilous as it was to a degree, because over-cautious, his policy was not unsuccessful. He had deceived many expectations, but had wounded no susceptibility. His charity, if not his judgment, had been impartial. When the German star declined, Benedict found tender words for "his dear France"; the French national heroine, Joan of Arc, was canonised (1920); diplomatic relations were resumed between France and the Holy See (1921). More than that: the Italian government was no longer held in suspicion; Benedict's successor, the learned Pius XI., received official honours in Rome when he ascended the pontifical throne (February 1922), and seven years later (February 1929) a complete reconciliation ensued, the Pope becoming once more the sovereign of a small territory, including of course his palace of the Vatican.[1]

5. The prospects of Catholicism seem indeed brighter

[1] "The Roman question is buried. The successor of Victor-Emmanuel reigns over unified Italy from Rome, recognized as her sovereign by the successor of Pius IX., and the sovereign and independent Vatican City takes its unique place and rank among the States of the world" (*London Times,* June 8, 1929).

than they were in 1914. Two new independent States, Poland and Hungary, both Catholic, are in close contact with the schismatic Slavs, who may be induced to reunite. Syria and Palestine are under Christian rule, widely open to Catholic teaching and proselytism. Catholicism remains all-powerful in Austria and in western Germany. France, having recovered Alsace-Lorraine, where Catholic traditions prevail, and occupied for some years the left bank of the Rhine, has been obliged to modify her policy of ignoring the Church. Monks and nuns, once more in great numbers, have recovered their social influence; the government has even restored to them a part of their confiscated houses, in order that missionaries may be formed there to spread the French language and culture in distant lands. The only difficulty, which grows apace, is that of recruiting the secular clergy.

In the British Islands, Ireland has become practically independent (December 1921). In Great Britain, the Catholic orders and schools are very prosperous. Indeed, the feeling has been aroused that Catholicism is slowly, but surely, prevailing upon Anglicanism, and that may explain why a new prayer-book with Catholic tendencies, though approved by the bishops and the House of Lords, was rejected by the Commons (June 1928).

Catholicism rules French Canada and most of the Southern American republics, excepting Mexico, where an anticlerical war raged for over three years (1925-1929). In the United States, the Roman Church is more powerful than ever; a Catholic Union, that of the young men called *Knights of Columbus*, nearly outweighs the YMCA (Young Men's Christian Association), which is chiefly Protestant; both have made themselves equally conspicuous in peace and in war.

6. But that is not all. In our revolutionary days, a great and very ancient authority is an element of stability not to be depised. Russian Bolshevism has terrified the better classes all over the world. Even agnostics reverence a power which may avert sinister collapses of civilisation. This does not mean nor foreshadow a truly religious revival, though there are symptoms of such a revival in Russia; but

it does mean for all Churches, and especially for the well-organised Roman Church, a renewal of past influence on society. Empires and kingdoms have crumbled to dust; the "servant of God's servants" in the Vatican, having survived them all, and teaching a strictly conservative lesson, has at least a chance of being recognised once more as one of the firm pillars of this shaken world.[1]

.˙.

After these general considerations and the recognition of the now privileged situation of the Roman Church, I will pass more rapidly in review the other religious groups which have been affected by the political events of our time.

.˙.

7. Liberal Protestantism, with the old flame of prophetic spirit which persists therein, would have won a splendid victory if American opinion had followed President Wilson in his generous endeavour to marry morals and politics. Far from being followed, he was disavowed; in something like a fit of timidity, America renounced the idea of purifying the world in the name of justice and charity. Having fallen ill (September 1919), abandoned by the majority of the Senate, which refused to ratify the Versailles treaty, Wilson witnessed the crushing defeat of his party in the presidential election of 1920. His name will live, nevertheless, among the greatest in history, beside those of the most illustrious victims of fate.

8. Among British Protestants, the schemes for reuniting the Churches have preserved warm support. In expectation of that event, we have heard a Baptist and a Presbyterian minister preach in the Anglican Cathedrals of Canterbury and Durham. The Bishop of London, in 1919, put forward

[1] An encyclic (Dec. 25, 1925) created a new feast of "Christ King" to be held on the last Sunday of October. "The principality of Christ, said the Pope, involves three powers: legislative, judiciary and executive. The reign of Christ, though spiritual, extends to civil affairs. Men united by the ties of society are the subjects of Christ. Laicism is the pest of human society." Such words could have been spoken not only by Pius IX., but by Gregory VII. No wonder that, immediately after the signing of the Concordat with Italy, the Pope and Mussolini began to disagree on questions of public education.

a plan for reuniting with the Wesleyan Church. The Conference of Lambeth Palace (1920), attended by 252 Anglican bishops, gave much time to the question of unity, without neglecting the Orthodox Churches of the Near East which, denying any authority to the Pope, seem more apt, dogmatically, to coalesce with Anglicanism; but Roman Catholicism possesses a much stronger power of expansion and disposes alone of the matchless army of its friars.

9. The disinclination of millions of Russian recruits for warfare, the ardent thirst of the peasants for landed property, far excelled, in 1917, the religious scruples of the people and the devotion to the Tsar which religion tried to exalt. In consequence, when the Communist revolution occurred in November, the Orthodox clergy was of no avail. Since that time, the religious policy of Russia's new masters has gone through several phases. In the beginning, the Bolshevists were content to pillage the rich convents, to preach free thought in the schools and papers in their pay, but without attempting to dechristianise Russia by force. "We must," said one of the first manifestoes of the new power, "combat religion in enlightening the people; Churches have nothing in common with the State, and only concern the faithful; nevertheless, as children have a right to scientific truth, the clergy must be excluded from the schools." At Moscow, on one of the entries to the Kremlin, a poster was erected, with an inscription in huge letters: "Religion is opium for the people." Though outrages against clerics were numerous in 1917 and 1918, there was no regular persecution. Meanwhile, famine, epidemics and growing misery brought the people back to the altars; even among the soldiers and sailors of the Red Army, religious habits took again the upper hand. In many factories, the workmen put up the old icons; societies were founded to assure regular church services. That renewal of faith or, at least, of observances was officially deplored, at the end of 1919, in a report to the Congress of Commissaries. The Government answered with an explosion of intolerance. A body of anti-religious agitators was created "to unmask religion in the eyes of the masses." Confiscations, profanations of

churches, violences against the ministers of all creeds (the Musulmans excepted) multiplied to such an extent that the representatives of all creeds assembled to utter a collective protest (March 1923). The exception in favour of the Musulmans was a consequence of the policy of the Soviets who, in Central Asia and Northern India, courted the alliance of the Lamas, the Brahmans and especially the Mahometans against the power or influence of Great Britain.

In March 1929, the *Anti-God* society numbered 250,000 members, while orthodoxy still controlled 50,000 churches, 500 monasteries, 350,000 "white clergy" and 500,000 members of parish church councils. The unorthodox sects have some 6,000,000 members, making 25,000 communities. So it appears that Russian Christianity has not yet lost the support of the peasantry, which are nine-tenths of the total population.

10. The revolution which had given the power to the young Turks and their committee called *Union and Progress* (1908) pretended to be imbued with Western ideas; but the real object was Panislamism, a conception more political than religious, which appealed to the fanaticism of the lower classes against the Armenians, the Greeks and the non-Musulmans in general. Some exalted Young Turks even spoke of *Panturanism*, aiming at the rebuilding of a huge empire from Finland and Hungary in Europe to the shores of the Pacific: thus opposed to the Aryans, the Turanians invoked as national heroes not Musulmans, but Attila, Jengis Khan and Tamerlane. The triumph of Panislamism was to prepare the way to Panturanism, an ideal founded, in the minds of demi-scholars, on the conception of race and ethnography.

The war waged by Turkey against Russia, England and France excited no religious passion; the *djihad* or holy war proclaimed by the Khalif found little echo. The Arabs having allied themselves with England, the Arabic countries of the empire were detached from it (armistice of Mudros, October 1918); but, in August 1919, inspired by the clever general, Mustafa Kemal Pacha, a national government, independent of Constantinople, was founded in the tableland of Anatolia and refused to accept the Sèvres treaty, concluded by the victorious Powers with the Sultan (August 1920). As the Greeks, in possession of Smyrna, imprudently advanced into Asia Minor, the Turks defeated them completely and butchered Christians by the thousands; Smyrna was reduced to ashes. Europe, tired of war and disunited, did not interfere;[1] in what remained of the Turkish Empire in Asia and in Europe, the Greeks were compelled to leave the land, the Christians and the Jews excluded from office and subject to continual vexation. But Mustafa Kemal was the contrary of a religious fanatic. Master of an empire founded on religion, he destroyed religion as best he could. He made an end to the Caliphate (1924), drove out the dervishes and the mendicant orders (1928), shut many mosques and shrines, and sequestrated their possessions to the State. Even the Turkish writing, founded on the Arabic alphabet used for the Koran, was forbidden, and replaced by a Latin script. Turkey became a secular republic, and that almost without resistance, so that one is tempted to believe that the Turks never were religious, but a military, obedient people, desiring to be led and ruled.[2]

11. The accession to power of the Young Turks (1908) had been hailed by the Armenians as the dawn of salvation; but the massacres in Cilicia, which made more than 20,000 Armenian victims, soon convinced them of their mistake (April 1909). Fanaticism, masquerading as nationalism, was even more bloodthirsty. When Turkey joined Germany in the war (November 1914), her rulers thought it was a good opportunity to get rid of the Armenians. Horrible butcheries were ordered at Bitlis, Sivas, Trebizond (1915); tens of thousands of peaceful people were put to the sword, drowned or burned alive. What remained was driven like a flock of sheep towards Mesopotamia; most of those unfortunates died of starvation on the road. There were, it is reported, over 600,000 victims. The responsibility for these abominable crimes was shared by the German Staff, which

1 Peace of Lausanne (July 24, 1923), replacing the Sèvres treaty and revising it. Armenia fell once more under the Turkish yoke; Armenian exiles were not allowed to return; the Greeks were expelled from Constantinople, the Capitulations suppressed, etc.

2 *London Times,* March 26, 1929.

refused to utter a word to stop them, as proved by the record of the German missionary, J. Lepsius, published five years later. At the Peace Conference, the Armenian delegates pleaded for an independent Armenia, from the Caucasus to Cilicia; but if such a State was to endure some great Power should accept the *mandate* of protecting it. Unfortunately, the United States, on which European opinion placed confidence in those circumstances, flatly refused to render that service to humanity. Vainly did the Sèvres treaty stipulate the independence of a smaller Armenia, with some ports on the Black Sea; for lack of military power to support it, that scheme remained a dead letter. The Turkish Nationalists, solidly established at Angora, allied themselves with Bolshevist Russia; the Christian States, formed in the Caucasus since 1918, were crushed as in a vise. New hecatombs of Armenians marked the first months of 1920. At the beginning of that year, the Turks had followed their policy of extermination in Cilicia, where the French troops were too weak to resist them. The scheme of a small Southern Armenia, under French protectorate, had to be abandoned, as had been the scheme of the Northern one. Those disasters to the Græco-Latin and Christian civilization in Asia were still aggravated in 1923 by the massacre or the flight of the Asiatic Hellenes. As in 1453, at the end of the Hundred Years' War, the West was too exhausted to react. Many people even in England and in France admired the warlike energy displayed by the Turks and preferred them to their victims, Armenians and Greeks.

12. The legal condition of the oppressed Jews changed for the better since 1917; they received citizenship in Russia (1917), in Roumania (1918), in Poland (1920). The international treaties, in 1919 and 1920, recognized the rights of the ethnic and religious minorities, Jews included, under the ægis of the Society of Nations. But these reforms, in opening to the Jews the liberal professions and access to office, alarmed the middle class, which had almost the monopoly of those situations; a frantic agitation was started in order to reduce the number of Jews in the Universities (*numerus clausus*), or to make their lives impossible

there by ill-treatment. Hungary alone adopted the *numerus clausus* (1920); but continual upheavals of students occurred in Roumania and in Poland to impose the same drastic measure. That new kind of protectionism found many advocates in Austria and in Germany; even in the United States, a proposal in favour of the *numerus clausus* was submitted to the University of Harvard, but unanimously rejected by the professors (May 1923).

The fact that certain Jews played an important part in the revolutions since 1918—Trotsky in Russia, Bela Kun in Hungary, Kurt Eisner in Bavaria—gave credit to the silly idea that the Jews, as a whole, had hatched a plot against Christian civilisation, family and property. That untruth, which found supporters even in England and in America,[1] was propagated through hundreds of thousands of copies, translated into every language, of a ridiculous forgery, stolen from a satirical volume published in 1865, purporting to be the *Protocols of the Elders of Zion*, or the minutes of an imaginary conference held at Prague where the programme of the great conspiracy had been adopted. All the reactionary parties in Central Europe united to wage war against the Jews, under the emblem of the Indian *Svastika*, considered as the Aryan symbol *par excellence*. Violent disturbances occurred in Berlin, in Vienna and especially in Bavaria, now the most virulent hotbed of anti-Semitism, allied with German militarism (1922). There was nothing religious in all those excesses, which were condemned by several German cardinals. But, as in the days of the Black Plague, Jews were made responsible for public calamities; the pleasure of harming your neighbour and the fear of his concurrence found equal satisfaction in such outbursts.

13. With the exception of the Armenians, no religious minority has suffered as much as the Slavonic Jews. At the beginning of the war, they were driven back from Poland to Russia under the pretence that they could inform the enemy, while the real traitors were in the high ranks of the army or at Court. Mass plunder and hangings became a

1 The *Morning Post* and the *Dearborn Independent*.

daily occurrence. After the revolution of November, 1917, the Jews of Ukraine were abandoned to the ravenous gangs led by Petlioura and Makhno; 600 towns or villages were destroyed and more than 150,000 people killed (1919). On the other hand, the Russian reaction, in quest of a scapegoat to explain the misfortunes of the country, quite naturally turned on the Jews, many of whom, just like Tsarist officers obliged to earn their bread, had taken service with the Bolshevists; it was even reported and believed that Jews alone had murdered the imperial family! The so-called *White armies*, in their unsuccessful attempts to resume power, plundered and killed Jews all the way. The occupation of Galicia by the Polish army was disgraced by similar outrages. The number of Russian and Polish Jews who were murdered or died of starvation is estimated at more than a million. In Berlin, Belgrade and even in Paris, the Russian reactionaries have always associated their hopes towards a restored autocracy to that of gigantic *pogroms* (massacres of Jews).

Unable to earn their living in the towns, where the Bolshevist régime had annihilated commerce and crippled industry, thousands of Jews turned to agriculture; thus the immense *ghetto* of Western Russia began to empty itself towards the East of the country and Siberia, the more so as restrictive measures almost suppressed immigration to America. Palestine, a country with small resources, has not attracted a large number of Jews.

14. In Japan, where religious fanaticism is unknown, *Shinto*, the national religion, tainted with Buddhism, has long become an exalted form of patriotism and loyalism. In China, the substitution of a Republic for the old autocracy (1912) has well-nigh destroyed the official religion. Since 1916, not one public sacrifice has been offered to Heaven; a musical kiosk has been erected on the place where the emperor used to plough at spring-time. Free schools have been opened under the invocation of Auguste Comte. But if European agnosticism has so speedily gained ground among the cultivated classes, now dispensed of the examinations in which official religion was all important, nobody can

tell what ideas subsist and ferment in the dense masses of the peasant population. It would be contrary to all the lessons of history if they passed without a transition from ancestral worship to indifference.[1] Taoism, Buddhism and Islamism have not yet spoken their last word in China, of which, however, direct study has been made almost impossible by the duration of civil war.

15. If the decadence of Indian religions has not been stopped, the nationalist and anti-British movement, continually gaining in strength, has found an ally in the mysticism natural to the Hindu. One of the first apostles of the cause of *Svâraj* (self-government) was the English theosopher, Annie Besant (*b.* 1847), a pupil of the Russian Helena Blavatsky, who founded and presided over the *Indian Home Rule League.* Twenty years younger than that lady, the agitator Mohandas Karamchand Gandhi was an ascete to whom miracles were attributed by the natives; the teachings of the *Bâghavatgita* ("revelation of the Lord"), a mystic and moral poem inserted in Canto VI. of the *Mahābharata,* were associated in his mind with those of the Russian Tolstoy (1828-1910), whose "letter to a Hindu" (December 1908) stated the program of non-co-operation and passive resistance which, called *Satyagrana,* has been the essence of Gandhi's policy since 1918. In 1920 he demanded that Indians and Mahometans should co-operate against the British, and rejected, as Gautâma Buddha had done, the system of caste. The violent deeds of some of his followers, in contradiction with his own doctrine of wielding purely moral forces, compromised him without enfeebling his authority. The movement of which he is the leader found its chief upholders in the semi-literate students, but also a support in the superstition of the lower classes, six per cent of which only can read or write (1911), while the far too numerous Bengalese universities flood the country with freethinkers in quest of office. Politics are more interested than religion in the future of India, and that future depends on politics alone.

1 A religious movement, called *Universal union of ancestral doctrines,* began at Peking in 1920 and numbered, it is said, one million adherents in 1926. The chief authority acknowledged by it is Laotse.

16. We have seen that the ties of nationalities and languages are more powerful nowadays than those of religion; that means a certain recoil of universalism, of the ideas of human fraternity and solidarity. But as universalism and the exalted sentiments implied by it do not abdicate, they need develop on another plane, which is not that of established religions. The Society of Nations at Geneva, the liberal and scientific schools of Socialism, even the Third International at Moscow, answer such tendencies, though with quite different aims and methods.[1] "We cannot tolerate," wrote a Catholic thinker, "that the Socialists should erect, in front of the spiritual Church of Christ's disciples, another Church equally aspiring to Catholicity." Whether agreeable or not, that is just what we are witnessing now. After so many others, the very conception of the Church is being secularized, and new lay Churches without antiquated dogmas promise to afford a shelter of peace and justice for humanity.

BIBLIOGRAPHY

1. Germanic and pagan character of the war in Germany: *Rev. historique,* cxxvi, p. 130.

3. Bellucci, *Folklore di guerra,* 1920.

4. Loisy, *Guerre et religion,* 1920; Anonymous, *Revue de Paris,* Oct. 15, 1918; Ch. Loiseau, *Politique romaine et sentiment français,* 1923; E. Vercesi, *Il Vaticano e la guerra,* 1925; F. Girerd, *L'Espagne pendant le guerre* (*Rev. du clergé,* Feb. 1917).—Texts and documents on the Papal See during the war: S. R., *Cultes,* vol. v, p. 388.—H. Pernot, *Le S. Siège et la politique,* 1929; Amad. Giannini, *Concordati postbellici,* 1929.

7. R. S. Baker, *W. Wilson and the World Settlement,* 3 vols., 1923.

8. Art. *Church History,* in the supplement of *Encycl. Brit.,* 1923.

9. F. Haase, *Die religiöse Psyche des Russischen Volkes,* 1921; Sarolea, *Soviet Russia,* 1924; J. F. Hecker, *Le religion au pays des Soviets,* 1928.—Turkish alliance with the Soviets: *Correspondance d'Orient,* 1923, p. 114.

10. Bareilles, *Les Turcs,* 1919; L. Tschudi, *Das Chalifat,* 1926. The best source of information is the French periodical *Correspondance d'Orient.*

11. Article *Armenia* in the Supplement of *Encycl. Brit.,* 1923.

12-13. Marc Vichniac, *Le protection du droit des Minorités,* 1922; Th. Ruyssen, *La renaissance de l'antisémitisme,* 1923.—In Hungary: *Revue crit.,* 1923, p. 187.—Forged protocols: *Paix et Droit,* Sept. 1921.

[1] "Communism has all the ear-marks of a new cult, which, in its zeal to make converts, leaves no stone unturned to destroy its most serious rival, the established orthodox Church." (*Times Lit. Supplem.,* 1929, p. 72)

—The best source for contemporary Judaism in Russia, Poland, etc., is the London *Jewish Chronicle,* 1919 *et seq.*

14. M. Granet, *La religion des Chinois,* 1922. On the Taoist movement, called *Union of ancestral doctrines,* see *Mercure de France,* Oct. 15, 1926, p. 488.

15. Art. *Besant, Gandhi* and *India* in the supplement of *Encycl. Brit.,* 1923; G. West, *Annie Besant,* 1929.

16. Marc Sangnier, *Le Sillon,* March 25, 1909.

INDEX